Spirits

in Culture,

History,

and Mind

D1616872

Spirits

in Culture,
History,
and Mind

Edited by
Jeannette Marie Mageo
and Alan Howard

ROUTLEDGE
New York and London

Published in 1996 by

Routledge
29 West 35th Street
New York, NY 10001

Published in Great Britain in 1996 by

Routledge
11 New Fetter Lane
London EC4P 4EE

Copyright © 1996 by Routledge

Printed in the United States of America
Design: Jack Donner

Library of Congress Cataloging-in-Publication Data

Spirits in culture, history, and mind / edited by Jeannette Marie Mageo and Alan Howard.
     p.   cm.
  Includes bibliographical references and index.
  ISBN 0-415-91367-5. — ISBN 0-415-91368-3 (pbk.)
  1. Spirits—Comparative studies. 2. Spirit possession—Comparative studies. I. Mageo, Jeannette Marie, 1947– . II. Howard, Alan, 1934– .
BL477.S66   1996
299'.92—dc20   95-23713
                                                      CIP

Contents

Acknowledgments

This book is the product of a series of sessions at the annual meetings of the Association for Social Anthropology in Oceania (ASAO). We thank ASAO for the opportunities it provided and those participants who contributed to the discussions. Roy Rappaport and Dan Jorgensen read an earlier draft of the book and made many constructive suggestions for revision; we have incorporated them wherever possible. We gratefully acknowledge the efforts of Jan Rensel, who put in countless hours copyediting and proofing the final manuscript and compiling the index to this volume. Lastly, we wish to thank all the contributors to this volume for their patience in responding to our nagging requests for revisions and demands that they meet what seemed an endless succession of deadlines.

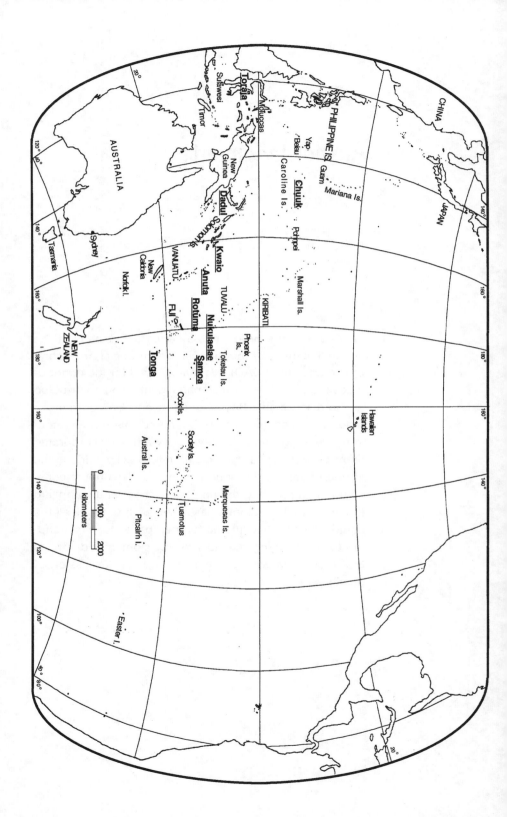

Introduction

Alan Howard
Jeannette Marie Mageo

In his introductory text *Anthropological Studies of Religion*,
Brian Morris laments a "seemingly sharp and unnecessary
line of demarcation" between folk and historical religions
(Morris 1987:3). By historical religions he means doctrines
that have at one time or another been associated with states
and that, like states, have recorded histories—what one might
call "high" religions. While acknowledging that literacy and
state systems have important implications for religion, Morris notes a bias in comparative studies: only high religions
"are treated as conceptual entities" while

> the religion of tribal cultures is dismembered and treated
> piecemeal. . . . [T]he general tendency has been to concentrate
> on one aspect of the ideological system. Symbolism, spirit
> possession, myth, and witchcraft, for example, are often
> treated as an autonomous set of beliefs and activities, almost
> independent of other aspects of the culture, and theoretical
> perspectives are directed specifically to one facet of religious
> life. (Morris 1987:3)

In this volume we argue for a more equitable approach to
high and folk religions, one that relies on an appreciation of
cultural as well as historical contexts. We see the gods of high
religions and the spirits of folklore as ends of a continuum,
the entirety of which has an important presence in every religious system. All religious phenomena—those institutionalized by states and those gossiped about by folk—are only

superficially understood when isolated from other aspects of culture, or when shorn of their historical dimension.

We address the theoretical disjunction that Morris identifies in several ways. First, like our intellectual ancestors—such Enlightenment thinkers as Spencer, Tylor, and Frazer—we seek, in chapter 1, to develop cross-culturally valid generalizations about the place of gods and spirits in systems of religion. These thinkers incorporated animism, totemism, belief in magic, polytheism, monotheism, and even science into a unified theoretical framework, albeit one now discredited because of its ethnocentric assumptions. Intellectualist and progressivist in orientation, they saw historical religions evolving from folk beliefs originating in the (mis)application of rationality to certain types of experience, such as dreams and death. Like nineteenth-century English missionaries who found "savages" in the slums and hovels of London (Comaroff & Comaroff 1992:265–296), evolutionary theorists of religion were surrounded by "superstitions" in their own land. They nonetheless anticipated that as people became more "civilized"—as they were exposed to the rigors of science—religion and spirits would fade away.

They were wrong, of course. As the ethnographic accounts in this volume bear witness, and as any observer of postmodern cosmopolitan society can attest, mystical folk beliefs have not only survived but have flourished alongside high religions and science. Rather than vanish, spirits have been assigned different roles in contemporary societies. Our aim in this volume is to examine the changing roles that gods and spirits have played in various cultures, relating them on the one hand to specific historical and cultural contexts, and on the other to cultural and psychological universals.

Unfortunately, the shortcomings of the early evolutionists' attempts at generalization have come to taint the validity of any comparative project in the anthropology of religion. The result is a mythic division in our intellectual genealogy reminiscent of the disjunction Lévi-Strauss (1963) assigns to totemic models of history: anthropology's lineage tends to be divided between a time of ancestors, when larger-than-life scholars held bold, encompassing views, and a present in which such pretensions are inherently suspect. Yet as the extent and quality of our data increase, anthropologists are in fact better placed to make comparisons. We therefore aspire in chapter 1 to transcend particularistic ethnographic accounts, informative as they are, and to seek again a comparative, universalist vision of religious experience.

Second, we endeavor to bring spirits back to their rightful place in theories of religion, beside the gods with whom they coexist. A corollary to Morris' observations—that state religions are treated as conceptual entities, and folk religions as collages of unrelated parts—is that discussion of spirits in the theoretical literature on religion has been marginalized. Although a number of outstanding ethnographic studies have focused on spirit-centered phenomena, such as spirit possession, the implications of these works have been more or less excluded from texts on comparative religion, whether anthropological, sociological, or philosophical in orientation. This exclusion may reflect, in large measure, the overwhelming influence of sociological theorists like Marx, Durkheim, and Weber, who focused more on gods than on spirits, and on the ways gods function in industrialized society. These theorists exiled spirits to the margins of human experience, rendering them more the results of psychological aberrations than culturally understandable constructs. But spirits as well as gods perform vital social, cultural, and psychological tasks for people occupying an uncertain world. The theoretical challenge, as we define it, is to determine what kinds of work each does when historical circumstances require, and the ways the work of gods and spirits articulate with one another in religious systems.

Taking shifting senses of self and the world that selves inhabit as our point of departure, we are committed in the ethnographic chapters to an analysis of culture at the intersection between psychological, social, and historical processes. We seek to overcome conceptual oppositions that have limited earlier anthropological thought about religion. Although the various chapters perform this task differently, we believe these differences represent the variety of theoretical approaches necessary to a cross-cultural understanding of contemporary religious practices, practices that controvert any set way of thinking about religion.

Some chapters address resistances and subversions (Mageo, chapter 2; Akin, chapter 7); others address silences and uncertainties (Howard, chapter 6; Feinberg, chapter 5) or cross-currents of sentiment and obligation (Gordon, chapter 3; Hezel and Dobbin, chapter 9); and still others consider the discursive and practical contradictions that spirits elicit from the living (Besnier, chapter 4; Whitehouse, chapter 8; Hollan, chapter 10). Through these diverse approaches, as well as various foci germane to spirits in culture (rites of reversal, dreams, illness beliefs, curing practices, and considerations of gender and cultural innovation), we seek to cast light on the relation of individual experience to cultural production.

Third, we consider spirits from the perspectives of colonialism and dawning modernity. Western colonists often assumed Christianity would simply displace its predecessors, monotheism being a logical development beyond the polytheistic religions of the colonized. Yet missionaries frequently oscillated between enthusiasm about their successes at conversion and despair at how quickly Christianity was reinvented, turned to local ends, and made to live beside older "superstitions." Local peoples blended Christianity with older beliefs and values and with the spiritual beings that represented them.

Christianity brought with it notions of the person and the state: the person as an autonomous subject with abstract, transportable, and putatively universal ethics, and the state as an overarching political unit, to which Christianity lent its imprimatur. Although Christianity acquired a central place in the culture and lives of Pacific islanders, in the context of missionization spirits came to represent what was local and "traditional" amid the often overwhelming encroachment of foreign ideas, including proselytizing, totalizing religions. Thus, throughout the Pacific spirit possession is named after the culture: in Samoa, possession and related events are "Samoan sickness"; in Tonga they are "Tongan sickness"; in Fiji, "Fijian sickness"; and so forth. Ailments that have no spirit associations are merely generic, subject to remedies of generic modernity; they do not speak of the enduring verities of local culture.

We have historicized spirit possession, conceiving it as a system of communication that responds to changing local needs and restraints. Whereas other studies have portrayed Christianity in opposition to possession beliefs and practices, the essays in this volume document ways in which contextually rich, local forms of missionization have led to the development of new types of spirit possession. The ethnographies demonstrate that spirit possession is intimately tied to relations of power, sometimes lending legitimacy to established authority, at other times presenting a means for resisting it.

Although spirits came to symbolize much of what was unique to cultural identity, they embodied their respective cultural traditions in imagined and transfigured forms. As Thomas (1992) has shown, parts of cultures often became metonyms for cultural continuity; in the process, specific segments of reconfigured historical experience came to stand for "tradition." We suggest that spirits—pagan and pre-Christian, irredeemable and recalcitrant—represent such emblems of cultural identity. For this reason, the cultural creativity associated with spirits is key to understanding contemporary feelings about, and definitions of, cultural identity.

In the cultures investigated in this volume, spirits became a crystal ball for the historical imagination: people not only reimagined themselves and their traditions within the ever-shifting contours of spirit discourse, but they used spirit discourse to think about the foreign and to dispute or integrate it selectively (see particularly Mageo, chapter 2; Besnier, chapter 4; Akin, chapter 7; and Whitehouse, chapter 8). In these imaginings, "natives" were not reaffirming a new version of the enlightenment distinction between prerational folk religion and more rational high religions. Quite the contrary: in the cultures we investigate, spirit discourses can be seen as commentaries on how change has been culturally accommodated. The literature on cultural reinvention often seems to imply that cultural borrowing is a naive process; many of the essays in this volume indicate that, on the contrary, cultural borrowing and subsequent cultural reinventions are often highly self-conscious and reflective. All cultures reimagine their identities and histories (Hobsbawm & Ranger 1983); where spirits survive, they are an important medium for this reimagining process. The process is, moreover, a means by which people effect historical readjustments of cultural values. In bringing fresh scholarly attention to spirits, we hope to shed light on these cultural-historical processes.

GEOGRAPHIC SCOPE: LIMITATIONS AND ADVANTAGES

The fact that the case studies in this volume are limited to the Pacific basin (see map) has certain advantages to offset the obvious disadvantage of limited geographical scope. To gain satisfactory worldwide coverage would require a series of volumes and would constitute a long-term, much more extensive project. A comprehensive, worldwide comparison would further be confounded by introducing massive differences in ecological and historical variables, potentially obscuring important commonalities. The Pacific basin offers, in contrast, sufficient similarities in ecology (islands) and history (European colonization, Christian proselytization, modernization) to allow a sharper focus on social and cultural factors. Differences between islands in ecology and history (volcanic islands versus atolls, missionization by various Christian denominations, degrees of urbanization, etc.) enable us to take advantage of the laboratory-like conditions, to which numerous scholars allude, that Pacific islands present. We therefore believe that the transformational processes illuminated in the ethnographic chapters, when refracted against the theoretical propositions articulated in chapter 1 and Lambek's concluding reflections, provide a template for developing a more comprehensive framework for understanding spirit phenomena as an important facet of religious experience.

OVERVIEW

Chapter 1 presents a theoretical framework that rests on a distinction between godlike and spiritlike attributes, with gods representing the moral order while spirits are encountered at its periphery. Our concern is less with defining gods and spirits as distinct conceptual entities than in setting out dimensions of a continuum along which notions of such beings, and spirits in particular, move. Levy, Mageo, and Howard argue that gods are associated with formal structures of society, whereas spirits are more personally experiential. When historical change radically alters a society's formal structures, traditional gods may disappear or take on spiritlike attributes, while spirits linger and reflect the changing qualities of personal experience. Hence an analysis of spirit-related beliefs, historically contextualized, can be revealing of moral and psychological change.

In the first ethnographic chapter, Jeannette Marie Mageo explores the ways in which Samoan spirits have changed from precontact times to the present, using cultural history to reflect on the concept of hegemony. In old Samoa, godlike beings embodied the salient values of social order, associated with a hegemonic discourse of respect and hierarchy; spiritlike beings represented a seemingly counter-hegemonic discourse that expressed resistance to these values. This discourse was expressed in entertainment routines, presided over by spirits. These routines, however, patterned refractory behavior in a manner that contributed to, rather than undermined, social stability and thus probably subverted resistance to cultural hegemony.

The most important of these spirit-affiliated entertainments was a night dance called *pōula*. Because of its obscene character and the leading role taken by young women, the *pōula* was banned by Christian missionaries. Through an in-depth analysis of the *pōula*, Mageo demonstrates that, rather than merely cease, the *pōula* splintered into parts. One part developed into a form of spirit possession resembling pre-Christian forms of spirit contact described in the early literature, but with telling differences. In pre-Christian Samoa, possession was intentionally entered into by mediums for the purpose of obtaining advice from ancestors and tutelary spirits and was mediated by either males or females; the new form of possession was involuntary and was experienced mainly by young women. In this novel form, young women's resistance to social morality could be played out—and subverted—in the guise of victimization by spirits. The new form of possession also became a medium for thinking about and mediating culture change. New theatrical and dance forms also descended from the splintering of the *pōula*. While the new dance form came to emblemize a Christianized version of tradition, the new theatrical forms, like possession, were identified with spirits and became mediums for mediating social change.

Tamar Gordon offers a cultural analysis of Tongan spirit possession, aiming to illuminate its place in the social body as an experiential bridge to tradition. As an overt contravention of dominant values and practices, spirit possession in Tonga is a radically marginalized event, one that constructs a bracket of "otherness" around individuals. Following Bourdieu, Gordon argues that practices like possession, which apparently fall outside the social ecology of control, belong to the same "habitus": dispositions that orient people's perceptions and practices in more or less patterned ways without strictly determining them. She sees the outcomes of particular practices like possession as a product of the relationship between habitus and contexts within which individuals exercise agency. The strategies employed by possessed Tongans, embedded and legitimated within the logical structures of possession, call attention to, and in some instances transform, the conditions that precipitated their episodes. By instigating a hegemonic discourse encompassing social, emotional, and historical contradictions, spirit possession in Tonga authorizes public dialogue about problematic structural relationships including social identities, divergent ideologies, gender, emotion and personhood.

In his chapter on Nukulaelae, an atoll in Tuvalu, Niko Besnier investigates ambiguities constitutive of spirit discourse. Since spirits do not readily reveal themselves, much of what is known about them on the atoll is from narratives of encounters that take place in foreign lands. While the spirit world is underdetermined in Nukulaelae experience, it is overdetermined in Nukulaelae discourse—spirits play a central role in everyday talk, in cultural models, in many social processes, and most generally, in the negotiation of truth. Besnier demonstrates that Nukulaelae discourse about spirits is heteroglossic, consisting of a multiplicity of competing and sometimes mutually incompatible voices, and he argues that coherence-seeking cultural explanations are not well equipped to deal with conflictual meanings in a people's accounts and actions. Rather than seeking a resolution to contradictions presented by talk about spirits, Besnier argues, one should seek an understanding of the contradictions themselves, and of how these contradictions reflect other aspects of society and culture.

Richard Feinberg's chapter begins with a discussion of spirit types distinguished and defined by the people of Anuta. These range from the generally spiritlike to the very godlike ghosts of deceased chiefs, and a variety of beings occupying intermediate positions. Yet, with the exception of the Christian God, all Anutan spiritual beings combine to some degree both spiritlike and godlike features. Anutan accounts of possession and spirit mediumship point to permeable boundaries between humans and spirits as well as self and other, and to an associative model of the person. Feinberg explores continuities and changes following the Anutans' conversion to Christianity: in discourse about spiritual beings, in the moral role assigned to spiritual beings, in the maintenance of social order and in newly invented numinals who combine elements of pre-Christian spirits and Christianity. He also explores the relativism that permeates Anutans' understanding of the spiritual realm, which helps explain their willingness to accept Christianity while maintaining a belief in the existence of pre-Christian entities.

The relationship between discourse and belief is the focus of Alan Howard's chapter concerning the island of Rotuma. He begins with the observation that talk about spirits has significantly diminished over the thirty years in which he has conducted research on the island, raising some interesting questions: What conditions have led to the change in discourse? What does the change imply about Rotuman beliefs? Are Rotuman spirits headed for cultural oblivion? Howard describes historical changes since his initial visit and suggests that they resulted in a disenchantment of the Rotuman worldview. Electrification, motor vehicles, formal education and exposure to cosmopolitan influences all may have contributed to a decline in the cultural salience of spirits. He then addresses the question of whether diminished talk about spirits signifies a shift from belief to disbelief, reflecting on the multiple dimensions of belief and the difficulty of assessing belief from the content of talk alone. At issue are the ways in which worldviews are constructed, how knowledge systems function in various cultural contexts, and the interrelationships between beliefs, emotions, thinking and social action. Howard assesses a number of possibilities that might account for diminished talk about spirits and what they suggest about the relationship between belief, discourse, and other forms of cultural representation.

David Akin's chapter focuses on Kwaio (Solomon Islands) beliefs about *buru*, foreign spirits who either are purchased abroad for their special powers or have emigrated to Kwaio on their own. *Buru* are contrasted with ancestral spirits who are at the core of Kwaio communities. For Kwaio, ancestral spirits personify a sense of place and associated virtues of stability, continuity, and permanence, all crucial to community strength and identity. *Buru*, in contrast, are foreign, roving and asocial, and thus lack the very qualities most valued in, and exemplified by, ancestral spirits. Correspondingly, Kwaio beliefs about *buru* are unsystematic, inconsistent and hazy compared to beliefs about ancestors. Akin argues that Kwaio beliefs about *buru* reveal a fundamental cultural relativism because imported spirits that wreak havoc in Kwaio are conceived as benevolent in their places of origin. More importantly, *buru* are a metaphor for dangerous outside ways, and the tragic results of their acquisition warn against the careless importation of foreign things. According to Akin this reflects a central theme permeating modern Kwaio religious, educational and political affairs—that the most serious threat to Kwaio culture comes not from foreign incursions, but from the adoption of alien ways by the Kwaio people themselves.

Writing about another Melanesian society, Harvey Whitehouse explores the ways spirits are experienced in Dadul, a village in East New Britain, Papua New Guinea. Since the early 1970s, almost everybody in Dadul has been a member of the Pomio Kivung, a large, centralized religious movement. Ideas about spirits in Dadul are profoundly affected by Pomio Kivung doctrine, which focuses extensively on relations with ancestors. The way these relations are conceptualized is steeped in Christian thinking, resulting from a long history of missionization in the region. The central thesis of this chapter is that in Dadul one can distinguish three basic types of spirits and spirit experience, each of which has a distinct set of psychological and political ramifications. First, Whitehouse examines experiences with spirits known as *sega*. Nowadays perceived as amoral spiritual agencies with no direct bearing on religious thought, *sega* are vaguely associated with forgotten initiation rituals, dances, and magic—cultural practices that were largely eliminated in the early phases of missionization. He shows that the cognitive experience of *sega* is impoverished, not merely by the loss of indigenous cosmology, but because the metaphors involved in ritualized interactions with *sega* lack the poignant and revelatory character of contemporary religious ritual in Dadul. Second, Whitehouse examines the experience of spirits (primarily ancestors) in the context of verbalized doctrine and routinized ritual in the Pomio Kivung. This experience is dominated by an elaborate, coherent, and logically integrated body of doctrine. In this context, ideas about spirits are codified in language, primarily the repetitive sermons of local orators. Third, Whitehouse describes the experience of spirits in a temporary splinter group that broke away from the mainstream Pomio Kivung movement in 1988. Splinter-group activities were concerned with the cultivation of sensually and emotionally arousing experiences of ancestors through collective rituals, some of which were markedly traumatic. Whitehouse argues that the experience of spirits is related to styles of codification, cultural transmission, and political association, and cannot therefore be reduced to a set of statements about local "beliefs."

The chapter jointly authored by Francis Hezel and Jay Dobbin focuses on the changed nature of spirit possession in Chuuk, Federated States of Micronesia. Following Mageo's analysis of Samoan possession, Hezel and Dobbin argue that while spirit possession occurring today in Chuuk is similar in form to possession described in the early literature, it shows some significant differences. As in

Samoa, possession incidents in Chuuk described in the early literature were intentional, aimed at obtaining important information from ancestors, and mediated by males or females; those recorded today are involuntary, occur largely at times of family stress, and involve mostly women as hosts. Chuukese today attribute many kinds of misfortune to the influence of spirits, ranging from injuries that Westerners see as the product of accidents to suicide attempts. People frequently speak of seeing ghosts and occasionally of being "bitten" by ghosts, and within the framework of Chuukese Christianity today, possession is associated with Satan and the forces of evil. Possession is considered dangerous because it represents an upheaval of the established social order. Possessed women defy the canons that govern social conduct in Chuuk: women flaunt their sexuality in the presence of male relatives; they voice publicly what ought to go unspoken; they flail, verbally and often physically, at those to whom they are expected to show respectful restraint. Hezel and Dobbin argue that in contemporary Chuuk, spirits do different kinds of work than they did previously. They make visitations in order to adjudicate family conflicts by allowing individuals to express themselves in ways that would normally be considered impolite and improper. They also provoke a temporary inversion of status relationships in Chuukese families. In contrast, God plays a more important role in the community at large, and may be called on to control spirit activities, or evoked to drive out possessing spirits.

In the final ethnographic chapter, Douglas Hollan surveys cultural and experiential aspects of spirit beliefs among the Toraja of South Sulawesi, Indonesia. The Toraja behavioral environment is densely populated with spiritual beings of traditional, Christian and Islamic origin. For most villagers, the question is not: Which of these spiritual beings actually exist and which do not? Rather it is Which of these beings—at any given moment—has the power to influence one's fate and fortune, and so should be acknowledged and perhaps propitiated? Hollan examines beliefs about, and experiences with, two of the most important and personally salient types of Toraja spirit beings—ancestral souls (*nene'*) and gods/spirits (*deata*). *Nene'* are clearly defined, personlike beings who are thought to take a direct interest in human affairs, while *deata* are amorphous beings whose actions and intentions are less predictable and less human-like. Hollan argues that the integration and complementarity between these two groups of spiritual beings, and the cultural and psychological work they perform, is consonant with a local social order that combines hierarchical and egalitarian characteristics, and with a broader pan-Indonesian culture that places a high value on balance in everyday life. In contrast to the declining significance of *deata*, Hollan concludes that *nene'* remain of central importance in the lives of Toraja individuals, Christian and non-Christian alike. This is in part because Church officials have accepted such beliefs as an aspect of traditional "custom" rather than as a remnant of traditional religion. But it is also because *nene'* beliefs and associated rituals continue to serve important social and psychological functions, including the maintenance of collective and personal conscience and the gratification of desires for continued parental support and advice. Also, unlike *deata* beliefs, which are experientially validated through the execution of costly and relatively infrequent rituals, *nene'* beliefs are reinforced each time a villager dreams about a deceased relative. Thus, while Christianity has tended to undermine the personal saliency of some traditional spirit beliefs, it has accommodated itself to, if not reinforced, that of others.

In the concluding chapter, Michael Lambek brings to bear his considerable experience studying spirit and possession phenomena. Reviewing the content of the ethnographic chapters, he draws attention to a number of key issues in the comparative study of religion: the inherent ambiguity of many types of religious experiences, the permeability of religious domains, the significance of hegemony and resistance in possession and related experience, the incommensurability of religious concepts, the heteroglossic nature of spirit communication, the relationship between forms of codification and the shape of religious experience. He concludes by pointing out that religion's fundamental nature cannot be grasped by structural synchronic analysis alone, that "the qualities and force of beliefs and discourses can only be revealed in their shifting employment."

If we were to summarize succinctly the central finding of our combined exploration, it is that religious experience cannot be reduced to simple, well-defined propositions regarding belief or faith. Nor can any theory of religion prove satisfactory if it ignores spirits in favor of gods. By supplying a vehicle for expression not offered by gods, spirits provide a necessary complement; they give to humankind mechanisms for coping with darker, unorganized thoughts, feelings and sensations. In doing so, they contribute to the realization of our humanness in ways that have not been fully appreciated.

Books on religion are inevitably controversial because most people, scholars included, hold strong views on the subject. In the contemporary world opinions are more varied than ever and paradigms are increasingly difficult to pin down. We make no pretense of presenting a paradigm; the various contributors were free to follow their own predilictions and to decide what approach best illuminated their case study. In our opinion, the diversity of theoretical perspectives enriches, rather than detracts from the volume. As editors we encouraged it, within the parameters discussed above. From prepublication critiques we anticipate that the theoretical chapter and Lambek's epilogue will prove most controversial. That is as it should be, for they both aim at generalization, although from quite different points of view. If the reader comes away provoked to criticize, to question and to rethink the role of spiritual beings in society and/or personal experience, we will have achieved our goal.

1 Gods, Spirits, and History

A Theoretical Perspective

Robert I. Levy
Jeannette Marie Mageo
Alan Howard

When one compares spirit-related phenomena, interesting similarities and variations—explainable in terms of social structure, local history, missionization, and so forth—are evident. We suggest that not only similarities and variations in the form and status of spirits, but even their latter-day attenuation or efflorescence, can be better understood by comparing the roles they play with those of gods. To facilitate analysis, we offer a set of propositions contrasting the implications of gods and spirits for social structure, personhood, personal experience and morality. Before exploring this comparative framework, however, a discussion of terminology is necessary to minimize confusion.

TERMS AND CONCEPTS

We find it useful to contrast "spirits" and "gods," while, at the same time, postulating a continuum of culturally defined spiritual entities ranging from well-defined, socially encompassing beings at one pole, to socially marginal, fleeting presences at the other. If we were to arrange spiritual beings along this continuum, the distribution would result in a clustering toward the former pole of entities to which we ordinarily apply the label "gods," while those we ordinarily label "spirits" would cluster toward the latter pole. This is not to say that every locally defined spiritual being can be neatly categorized as one or the other. Indeed, as several essays in this volume make clear, some beings defy categorization; on certain occasions what we take to be godlike qualities are attributed to them, and on other occasions their attributes are unmistakably spiritlike. Even the loftiest god can take on spiritlike qualities for some people on some occasions, while the most obscure of spirits can, on occasion, be idiosyncratically worshiped as a god. In some religions special classes of gods, such as the dangerous deities of Hinduism, display characteristics otherwise associated with spirits or demons (Levy 1990).

There are also many strange beings—giants, gnomes, fairies, phoenixes and the like—that fit uneasily into such a continuum because they have qualities we associate with neither gods nor spirits. They are on the fringes of the ordinary, at the edges of an uncanny zone, but unlike other strange creatures such as the orangutan cannot be captured, caged, and made, after a fashion, banal. As a general category, ghosts also present an attributional problem. The ghosts of powerful ancestors often attain the ritual potency of high gods, while the ghosts of disvalued people may roam only the darkest, most obscure corners of the social world.

In these domains, bounded solely by the limits of imagination, varieties of local terminology would seem wide open to cultural invention. Yet it is this relative freedom from contextual constraints (say, in comparison with fishing techniques and the universal reinvention of hooks, nets, and poisons) that makes the transcultural similarities that do come to our attention—the navigability of this realm to outsiders—particularly interesting.

In common parlance, the English terms "gods" and "spirits" are normally understood to distinguish different types of spiritual beings, with the term "spiritual" implying nonmateriality. The idea that gods and spirits are nonmaterial is supported by Cartesian dualism, but it is far from universally accepted. Robert Lowie's observation many years ago remains definitive:

> By common agreement spiritual represents the opposite of material existence. The difficulty is that if we insist on the notion of completely incorporeal being there are probably no examples to be found on primitive levels. . . . Nevertheless, some of these [examples given] belong to *a different order of existence* from that of men, beasts, and rocks. They are not, indeed, immaterial, but they are certainly less grossly material than the bodies of ordinary physical objects; and it is this subtler mode of corporeal existence that may be called "spiritual" in an ethnological sense. (Lowie 1970:99-100, emphasis added)

In most, perhaps all, communities, various categories of phenomena are distinguished from common sense reality and are associated with an extraordinary realm of uncanny mind-bearing beings. These beings' powers, logical status, and relation to space and time are different from those of humans in the ordinary social world. We assume, in contrast to the assertions of, for example, Levy-Bruhl (1931), that people everywhere distinguish the natural from the extra-natural, although the relations, boundaries, and ontological status of the two worlds may differ from place to place.

Returning to the problem of transcultural conceptualizations, the danger of ethnocentric bias in consideration of spiritual beings is by no means confined to the concept "spiritual." Anthropologists have also argued against the cross-cultural use of concepts such as "supernatural" (Hallowell 1960, Saler 1977), "witchcraft" and "sorcery" (Crick 1979, Fisiy and Geschiere 1991), and even "belief" (Needham 1972). Usually the argument attacks a particular term rather than the phenomenon it was meant to denote. Hallowell, for instance, suggested that "other-than-human" be substituted for "supernatural," while Van Baal (1985) offered the cumbersome phrase "referring to a non-empirical reality" as an alternative. Fisiy and Geschiere (1991) would replace "witch-craft" and "sorcery" with "occult powers." The concepts of "deity" and "god" have been less troublesome to anthropologists, in part, perhaps, because they are less pejorative—less pejorative because the West has contin-ued to retain a place, however distant, for its gods.

Given that none of the neologisms for supernatural seems appropriate, we adopt the term "numinous," following Rudolph Otto (1923), as an adjective to describe places and events that generate perceptions of potentially sacred, or at least spooky, beings, and to describe a realm more or less separated from the natural or ordinary. We further suggest the term "numinal" to refer to the vari-ous kinds of beings associated with numinous places and experiences[1]—the beings we have awkwardly been calling "spiritual beings." Numinous beings and human beings, however, do not generally exist in two absolute, discrete realms, but move between realms of experience: spirits enter the human world in possession; shamans enter the spirit world in trance and dream.

Within the general category of numinals we postulate a continuum anchored by ideal types in Weber's sense—that is, heuristic devices, never fully actualized empirically, but acting as points of reference and orienting guidelines against which observations can be compared. For convenience, one end of the contin-uum can be labeled "godlike" and the English term "god" used in reference to the corresponding ideal type; the other end can be labeled "spiritlike" and the English term "spirit" used to designate an opposing type.

To intermediate types are attributed more complex characters. They may roam free at times, perhaps at the margins of the domesticated world, but may also invade the human world in possession; they may be actively drawn into the moral order through rituals or other priestcraft in which they are temporarily bound and made use of when circumstances demand. The bound-aries between spirits and gods blur when beings initially conceived of as unbound are increasingly constrained by concrete representations (such as sculptures, masks, medicine bundles), and by ritual and prayer. Indeed, spirits can be transformed into "gods" in such instances.[2] Likewise, gods freed from social-moral constraints, as when a priesthood crumbles, can become very spiritlike in character. These ideal types thus not only call attention to salient features of the inhabitants of numinous realms and the phenomena clustered around them. They also provide an interpretive approach to deviations from the characteristics of those types.

DIFFERENCES BETWEEN GODS AND SPIRITS

We now present some propositions about the structural, psychological, experiential and moral aspects of numinous realms and their inhabitants in the hope of suggesting dimensions along which numinal beings tend to vary, of stimulating comparison, and of inviting productive disagreements.[3]

Structure. Gods are the foci of more elaborated social institutions than spirits. The attendants and mediators of gods, always necessary, are high-status "priests." The attendants and mediators of spirits, required only on special occasions, are people of low status, often socially suspect or ambivalently viewed.

Gods are related to and mark clear-cut divisions of space and time. They have territories, calendrical festivals, and often, fixed homes in shrines or temples. Spirits are more fluid, and are related to and mark emergent, contingent, unexpected occasions. Being more fixed in time, space and nature, gods can be bounded and conveniently contextualized. Their proper places and times can be clearly demarcated as belonging to the realm of the sacred. In contrast, spirits lack social boundedness, and are thus uncanny; they are difficult to bind and fix.

Although spirits in their free forms are dangerous to people and have the potential to enter, possess, and contaminate human beings, like the diseases with which they overlap conceptually, they can be bound through acts of power. They can be forced to enter into magic circles, shamans, material objects and masks. These bindings make it possible for humans to control spirits' power. While their power is often said to be used by those who control them for selfish and evil ends, it can also be put to community use. When spirits are successfully bound, new types of entities become possible; they can even be transformed into gods. A bound spirit, put to community use, therefore has to be distinguished from a free, or unbound, spirit.

The binding of a spirit is often done through the agency of a medium, shaman, or spirit doctor. This may be for the purpose of overcoming trouble caused by a spirit. Such control moves spirits closer to the clearly formulated and controlled arenas of cultural interpretation. Spirits may also be called upon to perform specific services for good or evil. They may drift into sharper sociocultural focus by providing omens or other socially relevant information. Where mediumship is institutionalized, spirits may be experienced in well-defined cultural frames, since mediums' roles may be central to a social system. Thus Tikopia mediums, differentiated from priests, were prominent figures "during certain religious rites of a public and very sacred kind" (Firth 1970: 263). They also performed on occasions such as the completion of major projects, the loss of a person at sea, and during grave illness or other crises (Firth 1967, 1970).

Personhood. Gods are conceived as being more like social persons, usually idealized ones. Their appearance is often canonically standardized, and they inhabit a humanlike world of social relations with humans and other gods. They are central to the cultural order and exist in times, spaces and causal chains closer to common sense reality. Gods can be manipulated through interpersonal moral techniques such as praise, supplication and gift giving—just as high-status humans can be. Spirits are vague forces; their appearances are difficult to discriminate. They are only minimally persons, closer to the kind of person exemplified in the dreamer or madman. They exist at the margins of the human order in a dreamlike world of shifting categories, vague motivations, and amorphous relations with other beings.[4] Spirits are either avoided or manipulated through devices of direct "magical" power. The relation between gods and spirits is representative of the relations between the center and the margins of the social order and has much to say about these relations.

We may note here that members of communities of gods making up pantheons often are thought to have humanlike familial relations and moral relations of friendship, competition and antagonism. Domains of spirits are often, perhaps usually, classified by features other than those of humanlike social relations—features having to do with appearance, power, and the ability to transform themselves into a number of forms.

Insofar as they operate in the realm of humans, gods act—usually in legendary time—in relation to heroes, seers, and saints.[5] Spirits are, in contrast, often experienced by people without much power or status, who are locally perceived as being weak; or they may be experienced by stronger people in marginal places or states (in the forest or bush, in the twilight or dark, entering or waking from sleep), and notably more often by women. They not only trouble, but at times assist, the "weak."

Experience. Gods and spirits have different ontological status and do different kinds of social, cognitive and psychodynamic work. Gods generally represent forces of social order but are characteristically more distant from sensual experience. Their acceptance is more likely to be grounded in doctrine or "faith." Spirits, while they can be made use of for social order, more often represent and give form to poorly socialized psychological and social processes. They are more directly experienced; people know they exist through the sensory warrant of their own experience or from accounts by people like themselves. Beliefs based on doctrinal authority and faith have different vulnerabilities than beliefs based on personal experience; hence gods and spirits are differentially affected by historical change. Local gods ordinarily disappear long before local spirits. Since Christianity does not provide a well-defined frame for experiencing spirits, it collapses them into a Christian demonic realm, which is much vaguer than spirits' traditional classification. So when old religions go (and with them former gods), spirits become even more unbounded, chaotic and shadowy.

Gods' distance from sensory experience, and their particularistic relation to specific communities or to segments of a community, means that they are known through the exercise of faith. In consequence, local gods, and the community-bounded forms of faith that create and sustain them, can be used to mark a particular population as a community of faith against outsiders who have different faiths. The way these commitments of faith are achieved in the course of education and ritual is an important part of socialization and social order. The social reconstruction of gods from generation to generation is therefore of a different kind than the social reconstruction of spirits.[6] In contrast, spirits are experienced in similar forms throughout wide areas, and do not serve to create or sustain the local social distinction of a community from other communities. Belief or involvement with particular spirits may, however, differentiate social and psychological cohorts within a community.

Morality. Gods and spirits have contrapuntal relations to the moral order. Being more personlike in conception and nature, gods are central to representing, responding to and sanctioning a community's moral order through socially adequate rewards and punishment. Spirits are vague and fleeting; they are often conceived as dangerous flesh-eaters or destructively seductive incubi or succubi. They represent the contents and logics of worlds of desire, dream, and fantasy—worlds in which morality is tangential at best—existing at the periphery of the work-a-day moral world of common sense. Spirits are related, typically, to people's bodies; gods, to people's consciences and to moral personhood.

Spirits are extra-moral, or, if they represent an antiworld in which community morality is irrelevant and thus negated, they are "evil." They function in relation to social control by representing the dangers of leaving the social domain, of passing beyond its boundaries.[7] Horrified by their encounters with "evil spirits," people retreat to the often tedious safety of the social and moral arena. Whatever it is that generates the cultural and personal presence of spirits, and whatever cognitive and expressive forces form them, they support social order in a quite different way than gods—by vividly representing the dangers of its absence.

In their free form spirits are threats to order and frequently must be purged so that order may be re-established; gods, in contrast, induce order and continually reaffirm it. Gods therefore can be used in various ways to protect against spirits. They can exorcise and control spirits, or at least aid in the struggle against them. They provide a cultural frame for dealing with spirits and make socially controllable some of the spirits' attributes.

In sum, spirits are different kinds of mental and social objects from gods. They are generated everywhere that people experience numinous phenomena at the boundaries of familiar structures in the social world. They persist until something happens to dissolve them. We will return to their dissolution after some reflections on possession.

Spirit Possession

The existence of a cultural domain of spirits allows dissociated psychological states to be recognized as possession. Possession, in turn, is one of the experiences that makes spirits experientially real.

We use the concept "full possession" to distinguish it from visionary experiences related to possession that do not do the work of possession in the communities we know. In the latter, people may encounter a spirit close up, see it, touch it, be touched by it. These experiences are much more common than the entrance of a spirit into the body as possession,[8] and are more likely than full possession to happen to men. Such visionary encounters are often experienced as assaults on the victim's body's surface, usually in states between waking and sleeping. Victims are unable to move. The spirit presses on their chest and makes breathing difficult; it may assault them sexually. Following a struggle, victims typically resume control of their muscles, often claiming afterward that if they had not done so they would have been destroyed. We might call this something like proto-possession; it supports doctrines and understandings of spirits and of full possession, but is not the same thing.

The free actions of spirits are frequently conceived as the ultimate cause of possession (see Gordon, Chapter 3), the spirits being the loci of power and will. But many cultures add a theory of witchcraft, whereby witches control the spirits (who sometimes possess the witch, but in cooperation with her will) and can induce them to harm and possess others. Unless they are primarily conceived as healers, possessed individuals who seek their own possession are most likely defined negatively—as dangerous, powerful persons, who parody divinity. Even successful healers are often viewed with suspicion and ambivalence.

We do not find the concept "altered state of consciousness," as used for example by Bourguignon (1973), adequate as a central idea for understanding possession. Certainly full possession seems to be associated with an "altered state of consciousness," which is necessary for shifting among internalized selves, but the concept applies to many phenomena other than possession (e.g., drug effects, out of body experiences, depersonalization). On the other hand the concept is not applicable to many forms of behavior that are generally considered closely related to possession, including signs of its potential onset such as involuntary motions and glossolalia. Furthermore, altered states of consciousness and dissolved boundaries of self are sought in many communities in meditation and quests for mystic experience, undertakings where entering into a possessed state would be considered a dangerous failure. "Altered states of consciousness" do not in themselves entail the personlike goal orientations and intentionality necessary for possession. The mobilization of such goal-directed states, which are necessarily ego-alien, seems to be a central feature of possession. Thus an "altered state of consciousness" is neither centrally defining nor distinctive.

Full possession behavior is highly skillful. It requires a mastery of role playing and of subtle, specialized kinds of communally significant communication. It is wrong to interpret it as "pathology," incompetence or breakdown in the same sense as schizophrenic psychosis or senility. Possessed individuals operate as competent persons in the moral realm in established webs of communication. They are essentially thought of and act as though they contain and exhibit a possessing person[9] who is radically different and discontinuous from the possessed person. Both persons are mind-bearing actors, with communicative competence, intentions, and all the characteristics of selfhood. (This kind of multiself behavior was called "dissociation" by psychiatrists at the turn of the twentieth century.) The idea of possession as a skillful communicative act implies an audience in a relatively integrated community for its full flourishing. It is a culturally crafted coping behavior that is useful because it is understood and responded to helpfully. It changes its function and eventually its form in disintegrating communities on the one hand, and complex modern ones on the other.

Full possession uses conventionalized frames—traditional communal forms that limit and provide interpretations—although it may play upon or reinvent these forms. Conventionalized frames are used to express realities that are rarely or never revealed in everyday life. The use of a mode of expression that is dramatic, bounded, extraordinary and based on a kind of role playing gives possession illuminating relations to theater and dramatic performances (see Mageo, Chapter 2; Hollan, Chapter 10). We may also note other resemblances: the need for an audience, the intelligibility of what is being expressed to that audience, and the special moral privileges of the actors while they are within their special, non-ordinary sphere, as well as the lack of any blame for what they have done on stage when they move off stage into the ordinary world.

When a body is taken over in full possession the inhabited self is transformed and the body becomes the identified place where two or more fully formed selves contend—selves with their own voices, intentions and different kinds of social skills. In such instances the socially suppressed can be expressed (as it is in different situations in other sociocultural forms such as art, women's poetry, rituals of reversal, carnival, and so on).

Nevertheless possession is not voluntary acting or pretending. It certainly must not be perceived as such by the audience, nor in all probability by the possessed person, if it is to do its psychosocial work. Although culturally formed, it is not the type of cultural act that most people can do willfully, nor the type of performance that some people can do at all. Only certain kinds of people, in special sociocultural and historical contexts, can do it, or alternatively put, allow it to happen to them. In all these respects possession is a different kind of social and psychological game than acting.

The person transformed by possession is a locus of power. This power is different from that of a witch. In the voice of her possessing spirit the possessed person has power to reveal socially suppressed material, and is a source of gnosis—revealed knowledge immediately recognizable to everyone as being intuitively true, but coming from beyond the overtly tolerable, discussible and, often, thinkable knowledge of family or culture. Possession therefore is a means by which new, and usually unwelcome, information threatens to enter cultural systems. Spirits in general are associated with hidden meanings because they represent suppressed modes of knowing.

Reports from throughout the world (Lewis 1971, Wilson 1967, Bourguignon 1973), and data from the communities discussed in this volume indicate that women are far more likely than men to be possessed. This raises questions not only about the possible reasons for gender differences, but also about the differentiating characteristics of those men who become possessed (where possession is primarily expressed by women), and about those communities in which the gender difference does not exist or is reversed. Some suggest that women's greater susceptibility to possession is related to their lack of access to other sources of power, including traditional activities central to the worship and manipulations of gods. Spirit possession provides women with a privileged and mystified opportunity (the "vulnerable" woman, only possessed by the strong spirit and not in control of it) to make potent, spirit-backed claims and demands (e.g., Lewis 1971, Wilson 1967), and to tell some uncomfortable truths.

Two conditions are necessary for full possession to flourish: people who are psychologically disposed to dissociation, and a cultural environment that makes conventional use of possession episodes. Change in either of these conditions alters the prevalence and meaning of possession. In late nineteenth century Western society, for example, coordination between these two conditions broke down as a result of changes in cultural interpretations; personal behavior that might once have been shaped into and defined as possession came to be redefined as moral weakness, malingering, or psychological or neurological disease (e.g., "Grand Hysteria"). The identification of possessed women as witches rather than as legitimate vehicles of suppressed messages (as in seventeenth century Europe and eighteenth century America) might be thought of as an intermediate move in the delegitimization of possession.

A change in social conditions also modifies what types of cultural messages are suppressed, and this in turn may alter the form and content of possession. In pre-Christian Samoa, for example, direct commerce with spirits usually occurred in the form of mediumship undertaken by high-status priests, chiefs, and chiefs' sisters. In Christian Samoa, spirits take over the bodies of low status persons, usually girls. Missionization also generated a repression of female sexual expressiveness, which was condoned in certain pre-Christian contexts. Consequently the content of possession episodes in Christian Samoa often concerns female sexual expressiveness (Mageo, Chapter 2).

SPIRITS IN HISTORICAL CONTEXT

Why do spirits flourish in certain spaces, times and populations and diminish or disappear in others? If it is true that spirits are particularly dependent on experience then it follows that they are much more sensitive than gods to changes in conditions that generate relevant experiences. It is not just changes in cultural doctrines that affect the presence or absence of spirits.

In various places (for example in Levy's studies in Tahiti, Nepal, and the Tuamotos [Levy 1984]), people say that spirits leave places that are brightly lighted during the night. The more experience that takes place in well-lighted settings and in the built-up areas that progressively replace nearby wilderness, the less room there is for spirits. The poorly-lighted night and the socially uncolonized spaces (bush, forest, wilderness) around communities are perfect settings for uncanny experiences (Levy 1973:151ff.). The sensations produced by these experiences are closely related to what Otto (1923) called "numinous feelings," feelings that are taken as a direct experiential warrant, a direct perception of the realm of the "holy." They seem to be generated in situations where it is difficult to make "those categorizations that help anchor us in 'commonsense' reality," where the familiar and dependable schemas of time, space, size, cause and logic hold. Situations where these schemas seem not to hold are intrinsically uncanny (Levy 1973:151ff.). Thus the transformation of numinous places into banal ones through lighting, and rebuilding—leading to the disappearance of "empty" or "alien" environments—may make a profound difference (see Howard, Chapter 6).

Modern naturalistic systems of explanation and control transform, cognitively and experientially, other phenomena that once seemed uncanny—for example the peculiar skin disease, the dream, the dissociated state. The classical evolutionists believed that "primitives'" use of mystic systems of explanation had something to do with a lack of differentiation of realms in the primitive mind, a problem that was presumably overcome with progress to civilization (e.g., Tylor 1871). But even in the West (and in communities affected by it) there has been an historical shift toward naturalistic explanation—what Max Weber termed "the disenchantment of the world."[10] When communities find themselves disenchanted, spirits depart. Possession changes its forms and may disappear altogether. In the normative "enlightened" modern situation, even in the rare corners where the uncanny may be encountered, its *validity* as a knowledge-yielding experience is now discounted. It becomes a fascinating illusion, or a cover story for supermarket check-out magazines. Experience, doctrine, and epistemology have all shifted. As we pass beyond the modern, all this may shift again.[11]

Spirits, gods and possession flourish within a certain range of social and psychological conditions. Many of their classical attributes occur in conditions of relative equilibrium within fairly stable communities. In times of change, particularly in highly stressful times, insofar as they are still useful, their characteristics and uses change. Multiple variables operate in preindustrial societies, some favoring the demise of spirits, others working to increase their salience. Processes of modernization, including higher levels of formal education, urbanization, mechanization and electrification have indeed led, as Weber said, to "driving the magic from things."

In some places (e.g., Rotuma, see Chapter 6) these processes have contributed to a noticeable decline in the social presence of spirits; at the very least there is less talk about them. In other places spirits not only remain viable, they flourish in the face of these same processes. We propose that spirit experiences ought to increase during times of social stress and disorder, and that spirits should thrive among the disenfranchised or marginalized as long as contextual, doctrinal and epistemological features that make spirits possible still hold. As for possession, it is not just the "shared repressed" generated by a particular community order that spirits talk about; they also bring into the public domain widely shared if poorly understood moral, social, personal and interpersonal problems that are generated by social change, and that threaten or overload traditional values and structures. Their voices may be cathartic and/or provide nuclei for new forms. Thus in contemporary Pacific societies new stresses seem to have given spirits new and altered life.

Spirits, however, having had an essential role in the ongoing life of traditional Pacific communities, having survived the attacks and redefinitions of Missionary Christianity, having changed their nature and flourished in conditions of anxiety-producing social change, are now beginning to disappear in some locations, due to modernization and integration into more cosmopolitan sociocultural systems.

GODS, SPIRITS, AND THE SOCIAL ORDER

We have argued that gods are clear models for social order, while spirits are vague expressions and representations of socially marginal states, although they can be put to useful social work. It may be that in centralized and hierarchically ordered groups gods have special prominence, or at least special characteristics, and that spirits may be more prominent where local autonomy and a more mobile and shifting order prevail. While this proposition receives considerable support from the ends of the spectrum (contemporary nation-states on the one hand, hunting and gathering groups on the other)—a fact made much of by the nineteenth century evolutionists—the data are more problematic, and more interesting, in "middle-range" societies such as those dealt with in this volume.

In the kinds of societies considered here, gods and spirits co-exist, though they may be given differential emphasis in different places and in different times. In early-contact Polynesia, for example, the stratified societies of Hawai'i, Tahiti and Tonga had well-defined categories of high gods who were sacrificed to, worshiped and propitiated. In these societies, the emphasis was on the power of the major deities.[12] In Polynesian societies without hierarchy and central authority—where local autonomy was pronounced—the role of gods was less central and spirits appear to have had a greater presence.

Yet size and complexity of polity are not definitive. As Durkheim showed, social cohesion is also important. Gods thrive within well-defined moral orders, where sentiment supports the moral authority of leaders. Spirits flourish where moral authority is tenuous—where subgroup allegiance overwhelms commitment to a higher order. The contrast between Samoa and Tikopia is instructive.

Despite its well-developed political system, old Samoan society was organized around autonomous villages rather than a central authority. Even within villages orators have long manipulated skillfully and subtly the relative ranking of titles, elevating the status of some titles and denigrating others. Every Samoan family is convinced vocally or discretely (depending on context) of the importance of its ancestry and claims to position. Competition for status precluded common acceptance of established hierarchy for any length of time, a condition inimical to the public worship of a limited pantheon of high gods and favoring the proliferation of spirits. When the missionary John Williams arrived on the scene, he was told by other Polynesians that the Samoans were "godless" (1842:142; see also G. Turner 1984:17); however, he reported more beliefs about spirits in Samoa "than in any other islands" (1842:143; see also Pritchard 1866:106; Wilkes 1845 II:76-77, 131, 133).

In contrast to Samoa, Tikopia was a far smaller polity, but it enjoyed a much greater degree of cohesion. The social hierarchy was well established and accepted at the time of European intrusion, and the moral authority of chiefs was unquestioned. As described in Raymond Firth's peerless accounts (1940, 1970), Tikopian concepts covered a wide range of spirit beings, many of whom "were the object of such specific worship that they may be appropriately termed gods" (Firth 1970:20). Firth characterized the religion of Tikopia as "polytheistic" insofar as it admitted the worship of many gods, all of them local. Only the members of the category he labeled common spirits (*atua vare*) were unbounded. Common spirits lacked "precise identification and incorporation in any coherent scheme of spirit worship," and "responsibility for a whole range of accidental and untoward occurrences affecting human beings" was attributed to them (Firth 1970:69–70). Ghosts, or "spirits of the dead," were regarded as leading a relatively ordered existence, and the spirits of former chiefs were ritually invoked on occasion (Firth 1970:74-75). Thus on Tikopia some spirits were regularly transformed into gods, while in Samoa they remained to a considerable degree unbounded.

THE IMPACT OF CHRISTIANITY

The coming of Christianity had dramatic effects on Pacific societies. It radically altered the cultural frameworks for numinals, selectively overthrowing or demoting the gods, replacing a rich diversity of conceptualization with an undifferentiated residual and negative category of "devils" or "demons" (Mageo, Chapter 2; Howard, Chapter 6). Whatever godlike qualities some numinals may have had were threatened, if not eliminated, by Christian prohibitions on worshiping or propitiating them. Yet as long as they were not considered gods—as long as their godlike qualities were minimized—Christianity allowed them a place in the company of spirits. Missionaries themselves often believed with considerable anxiety in local spirits, used them to explain the fallen state of the people, preached against them and exorcised them. They placed spirits under the hegemonic definition and control of Christianity, and in so doing gave them a powerful place within colonial (and postcolonial) religious domains. This has produced parallel belief systems in many Pacific cultures that exist in dialectical relationship to one another. In some instances the resultant heterodoxy has served to subvert Western cultural dominance.

SELFHOOD, MIND, AND THE NUMINOUS

Some ethnographers have argued that traditional Pacific societies, in contrast with modern Western ones, emphasize what has been called a situation-centered, rather than person-centered, selfhood (Shore 1982; Howard 1982; Watson-Gegeo and White 1990). It must be emphasized that these terms refer to comparative differences between any two particular societies rather than absolute differences. Thus Levy (1973, 1989, 1990) found Tahitian village discourse and action relating to self to be more person-centered than Nepalese Newar discourse and action. Perhaps these different cultural emphases on qualities of self correspond to differing emphases on a continuum ranging from a monotheistic god to an undifferentiated plenitude of spirits.

Restricted pantheons, and particularly monotheism, may be related to the ideology and structural realities of more unified, person-centered selves, especially insofar as deities are sources of identification and are the moral "others" against which one measures oneself. A diffusion of deities, and even more radically an emphasis on the diffusion of subself fragments represented by spirits, may be more closely associated with situation-centered selves and, perhaps, fragmented selves. The imagery of Bateson and Mead's Bali (1942)—where creaturelike disembodied body parts freely roam the cremation grounds—is, in conjunction with their discussion of Balinese selves, provocative here.

Other interesting aspects of self and mind may have some regular relation to local numinous worlds. We can ask which variables affect the intellectual acceptance of doctrines that take uncanny experience as direct evidence for the existence of numinals, and which variables affect the generation of numinous experiences, or in the case of gods, the emotional experiences on which deeply felt (as opposed to conventional) faith might be based.

The acceptance of numinous doctrine is, in part, a matter of local epistemologies—the general ways in which experience is held to be the warrant of true knowledge. The rejection of spirit doctrine and the radical thinning of meaning, if not quite rejection, of deities, seems related to a more general suspicion of experiences known now to be generated in the fear- and desire-driven parts of the mind. This is the internal component of the "disenchantment of the world," thought to be particularly characteristic of "modernity." One may speculate as to the conditions under which such an epistemological shift might be affecting the vicissitudes of spirits and gods in the new Pacific.

The *interpretation* of uncanny experience is one cultural variable, the prevalence of that *experience itself* is another. We have noted changes in community forms that have diminished the conditions for those experiences. But are there psychological variables that affect their likelihood? Levy (1973:151 ff; 225, n.6), noted village Tahitians' great susceptibility to frightening numinous sensations when alone in sensorially obscure places and the fact that the presence of another person, even a small child, was usually sufficient to protect against them. He speculated that a relative lack of isolation from others in childhood is instrumental in the formation of selves that were comparatively sensitive to feelings of uncanny strangeness when alone, and thus to the experience of spirits (see also Mageo 1989a:187–190). It may be that social and historical conditions that generate more person-centered selves encourage childhood experiences of separation, loneliness and individuation. Once childhood anxieties are mastered, these experiences make adult sensitivity to the uncanny less likely.

LOCAL MEANINGS AND COMPARATIVE PERSPECTIVES

We have treated numinals and possession as a complex family of human phenomena affected by and formed in fields of historical, communal, contextual, and personal forces. We have not tried to propose any core, essential explanations, but have probed for features of comparative interest. Documenting local uses, meanings and constructions has been left to the ethnographic chapters that follow.

Many contemporary scholars argue for confining the treatment of these phenomena to particular communities. They often dismiss the transcultural usefulness of terms like "spirits" and "possession," finding in them various dangers: the imposition of our own biased values and conceptions; the meaning-destroying intellectual game of searching for essentialistic and reductionist explanations; and the submerging of local cultural inventions into abstract schema. Michael Lambek provides us with a useful example of someone who argues for a focus on particularistic phenomena, but at the same time, accepting as he does possession as a category of analysis, avoids making particular local situations radically incomparable with others.

In a recent review of the literature on trance and possession, Lambek (1989) argues for an approach to possession that treats it as a culture-constructing performance, rather than reductively. He observes that most of the interpretations he reviewed suffer from a largely unexamined acceptance of the naturalist paradigm that, he writes, has dominated Western discourse. He advocates "recolonizing the terrain for culture." Possession can enter into virtually all areas of life: illness and therapy, interpersonal relations, private experience, marriage, the articulation of family boundaries and continuity between the generations, worldview, divination, social thought, morality, political process, conflict resolution, myth, fantasy, and fun. It cannot, therefore, he argues, be explained in simple terms. In fact, its very penetration into so many areas of life and the diversity of its functions and expressions suggest that students of these phenomena should turn away from causal, etiological explanations toward an examination of possession's structure, organization, reproduction, and meaning.

Possession, Lambek argues, is as social a phenomenon as marriage, and contemporary anthropologists would not think of explaining marriage institutions in terms of underlying motives or account for individual marriages in terms of physiological or psychological functions. "In many of its manifestations," he argues, "possession violates our own cultural distinctions and deeply held assumptions concerning the 'natural' difference between such pairs of opposites as self and other, seriousness and comedy, reality and illusion, and, perhaps most critically, art and life. Because possession transcends these oppositions, our models must, too." (Lambek 1989:52–3)

In an earlier work analyzing trance in Mayotte, an island in the Mozambique channel between Madagascar and Tanzania, Lambek (1981) viewed possession as "text." This led him to look for types of constraints, grammars of production and interpretation, modes of representation, and avenues of creativity. Reflecting on this approach in his review article he observed that:

> Possession occurs in the context of a tradition of possession. It is formed by specific genres, rhetorical devices, images, and metaphors, as well as by a confrontation with a specific historical and social experience. Like poetry, or the art of the diarist, possession is a means of symbolically articulating experience. Most of the time it makes use of an essentially public code. Like various forms of Western art, it can be self-reflexive; it is superbly suited to handle paradox. Like much mythology . . . possession accepts ambiguity . . . [T]here is a creative tension in Mayotte possession between the syntagmatic dimension (the emergence of order from chaos) and the paradigmatic dimension (the opposition between orderly human and chaotic spirit worlds). Frequently possession is a kind of serious parody of orthodox religion, social convention, or the accepted language of power relations. Possession may even be self-parodic.[13] (Lambek 1989:53–54)

Despite its advantages, Lambek notes, focusing on the product rather than the process of production makes the text model too static; it also tends to unduly limit and reify the subject of analysis. He therefore advocates using a discourse model because "it directs us to look beyond the immediacy of specific, highly formal events (performances) to broader, more pervasive processes and less discrete or formal occasions" (1989:56).

Commenting on the advantages of discourse analysis for understanding possession, he writes:

> As a particular kind of system of communication, possession establishes channels, senders, receivers, and information. It constructs new things to think and talk about and new ways to do so, new forms of experience. . . . Possession can "thicken," i.e., add new levels of meaning to, social relationships . . . and it allows for "privileged discourse" . . . providing a certain quality of social space in which therapy is implemented. Possession demands both reflexivity and the engagement of onlookers, but it is neither injurious nor therapeutic per se. Not intrinsically functional, possession is simply a discursive practice. Here we move beyond the dominance of the external, collective models for possession behavior in order to account for its open-endedness, the unexpected outcome, the continuing conversation. The discourse operates in the personal, interpersonal, and public domains, constructing a multiplicity of ongoing, overlapping, emergent "objects." More than an idiom for the articulation of personal experience . . . possession provides means and procedures that contribute to an ongoing, historically located process constituting the self and subjectivity. (Lambek 1989:56)

This emphasis on how possession (and other aspects of numinous phenomena) is constituted, reproduced and enacted, and the wide field of cultural events and forms into which it is interwoven in particular places, complement our comparative focus. Lambek accepts the cross-cultural usefulness (or even reality) of a phenomenon he calls possession and acknowledges that it has, across cultures, some interesting features, such as its tendency to transcend Western oppositions. Possession thus becomes a tool for probing the organization of life in a community (along with disease, sexuality, moral controls, exchange, ad infinitum). Insofar as possession (or spirits, gods, the numinous, etc.) is useful for understanding aspects of a particular community, then the problem flips over again, and we are led to ask why this should be so. We are then constrained to look beyond the particular culture, text, or practice in a never-ending dialectic between the particular and the universal.

NOTES

1   The Kantian "noumenal," a homophonic but quite different term which characterizes a world not perceivable through the senses (in contrast with the Kantian "phenomenological" world), has been proposed by Roger Keesing (1982:73) as a useful designator of the "spiritual" world. Since it is not the unperceivability of this world that is at issue, but the peculiarity of the phenomena that are perceived, we find this usage inappropriate.

2   The significance of formal representation was implicit in early scholarship on the origins of religion. Thus for Tylor (1871), who saw religious beginnings in primitive speculations leading to the notion of soul, animism was the source of religiosity. Spiritual agency was attributed to natural phenomena, but social

representations played a minimal role in this scenario. For Durkheim (1965), however, the origins of religion were social, expressed in totemic representations of the tribe. Tylor's approach led to a focus on spirits in "primitive" cultures, Durkheim's to a focus on gods.

3   These claims are based on the papers and discussions presented in the ASAO conference sessions on which this volume is based, on Levy's, Mageo's, and Howard's work in Polynesia, and on Levy's comparative studies in Nepal (1990). In Nepal the numinous realm of a Hindu city is elaborated in ways that are informatively different from those of small Oceanic communities.

4   Ghosts are uncanny persons in dissolution from their previous this-worldly social and logical categories, and their nature is generally closer to spirits than to gods. The presence of ghosts means that the spirit realm has two kinds of beings—those that were never alive, and those that were once alive.

5   When saints or gods themselves encounter spirits it is often as a "temptation," or a significant test, something to be overcome through strength.

6   Mageo (1991) suggests that spirits are often constructed from the disordered fragments of social life and thought that are left out of education, established ritual, and socialization—fragments that intrude upon experience in a peculiar way because of this neglect. As such they are often a pastiche of cultural elements and cultural codes rather than integrated entities.

7   Levy (1985) has developed this idea in relation to the idea of "horror" and the Dracula story.

8   The spirit can enter the body as illness, but this introduces the related question of local taxonomies of illness and raises issues that are peripheral to our interests.

9   The spirit typically becomes more personlike when it possesses someone, unless the behavior is simply inchoate ecstatic behavior.

10   According to Donald MacRae (1986:86), the phrase that Weber took from Schiller that is usually translated the "disenchantment of the world" is more accurately translated (in a way very relevant to this chapter) as "driving the magic from things."

11   The recent proliferation of marginal cults and "New Age" ideology suggests a renewed receptivity on the part of some contemporaries to a re-enchanted universe.

12   The tendency toward spiritual specialization "reached its high point in Hawaii, where a god existed as a counterpart for every form of social specialization. . . . In the Stratified [Polynesian] societies, a concept of deistic hierarchy corresponding quite closely to political hierarchy seems to have replaced the dualism ["good" deities versus "bad" ones] of [the other] . . . societies. The emphasis was on the power of the major deities and upon the theme of specialization. Malevolent spirits, while prominent, were simply a class among many" (Goldman 1970:560).

13   Perhaps this is why comedy is expressed through the metaphor of possession in many Pacific cultures (Hereniko 1991).

2 Continuity and Shape Shifting

Samoan Spirits in Culture History

Jeannette Marie Mageo

Samoa, located at the southeast corner of the Polynesian triangle, is not featured in eighteenth-century accounts of Pacific explorers. This is probably because when LaPerouse visited Samoa in 1787 several members of his crew were killed, and, through LaPerouse's report, Samoa acquired a reputation for savagery that protected it from foreign incursions until the late 1820s (Linnekin 1991). More or less immediately thereafter, however, Samoa became a favorite locale for missionaries, whalers, and South Seas adventurers alike. Unlike LaPerouse, they attributed a native gentility and great hospitality to Samoans. Some missionaries were so taken with their Samoan converts as to believe them to be the lost tribe of Israel. Colonial powers vied for possession of the tiny islands; several warships of the major Pacific powers were lost in a hurricane as they sat glowering at one another in Apia harbor. Despite this intensity of foreign attention, however, Samoa remained a bastion of flourishing Polynesian culture long after her Polynesian sisters, Hawai'i and Tahiti, found themselves awash in foreign customs and values. This chapter reflects on Samoan cultural tenacity in relation to religious practice and upon the cross-cultural implications of this tenacity.

Religion is a cultural domain where hegemony shows its figurative slip. Hegemony, an idea originating in the work of Gramsci, resembles the idea of worldview in earlier decades of anthropological thought. Like worldview, it denotes a cultural way of understanding experience, but unlike worldview, hegemony denotes a way of understanding that naturalizes a set of power relations such that these relations are taken as givens, passing beneath the level of notice or argument (Comaroff & Comaroff 1992). These under-standings are reflected in hegemonic discourses, in which certain power rela-tions are presumed to be self-evident; widespread participation in these discourses makes these power relations seem natural. In asserting this "order of nature" on the grandest scale, however, religion conjures beings that are no part of nature, at least for those outside the cultural system. But if culture's conjuring tricks seem implausible in their religious guise, they are often enduring: "superstitious" reactions may betray a backhanded loyalty on the part of people even when their cultural circumstances are in grip of thoroughgoing change.

I married a Samoan, Sanele, named after the first Polynesian saint, who now works at Bloomingdale's in New York City. He has long had more than a little critical distance on his culture, and yet I remember a warm, full-moon night in Samoa when, on impulse, we shed our clothes to bathe in a deep tidal pool on a small peninsula, gently washed by an occasional layer of white reflective foam. The tide was low, the water calm; out of nowhere a series of pounding waves arose, almost sweeping us out to sea. Sanele mumbled, "I don't believe in you Telesaˉ, I don't believe in you Telesaˉ."

Telesaˉ, also known as Letelesaˉ, is one of the class of Samoan spirits (*aitu*) that is the subject of this chapter.[1] Sanele had enlisted a standard maneuver: in Samoa, denying belief in spirits is a defense against them. Telesaˉ likes beautiful young men and had harassed Sanele's father, Toa, in his better days. Toa was a catechist who carefully schooled all his handsome sons not to be afraid of Telesaˉ. When she followed one of them, Niko, home from school one day, frightening him badly, Toa made Niko climb up on the roof of their house and shout insults at her. By climbing on the roof, Niko placed himself above Telesaˉ, and this was likewise an insult. To this day Niko is the most susceptible of Sanele's brothers to uncanny experiences, but in every culture child training often seems to have an opposite-to-intended effect.

Relative height—being above or below—is a fundamental metaphor for Samoan power relations. We will see that in old Samoa, chiefs, who embod-ied these power relations, were thought to resemble numinals. Numinals were a class, or set of classes, that ranked above living chiefs in the Samoan version of a cosmological chain of being that included humankind. By climb-ing on the roof, Niko was at once resisting and learning to replicate this set of power relations; the event probably served as a lasting template of these relations in his imagination.

The power relations naturalized by hegemonic discourses and enshrined in religious beliefs skew social reality in favor of some and not others, and one wonders why this skewing does not undermine the widespread support and hypnotic leadership that Gramsci assigns to hegemony (Bocock 1986). Further, the assumptions upon which hegemonic discourses rest are subject to historical tumult and foreign encroachment, as are all cultural assumptions. And yet, at least in Samoa, cultural hegemony has continually reasserted itself in face of these potent challenges. This chapter questions how religious aspects of Samoan hegemony achieve this tenacity, seeking an answer in the relation between spirits and popular entertainments.

People tend to resist inequitable power relations through counter-hegemonic discourses in which these relations are reversed. Popular entertainments involve counter-hegemonic discourses of reversal (Turner 1977; Babcock 1978). While ceremonies are the province of gods, whose sanction is often invoked in ceremonial talk, popular entertainments are one of the principle haunts of spirits. In popular entertainments a participant will often act as one possessed and this experience—having one's normal self swept away—may be taken as a gauge of enjoyment and thus as a measure of the entertainment's success. Spirits typically prescribe resistance to established power relations in popular entertainments, but this chapter argues that they do so in forms that support these relations, thereby actually subverting resistance in the guise of promoting it.

When I attribute agency to spirits it is, of course, a manner of speaking. What I mean to suggest is that, except under conditions of extreme oppression, people express their dissatisfaction with their cultural order in forms that work for, rather than against, this order and that spirits and spirit events are a means to this end. People cooperate in the subsumption of their own resistances because being at odds with their social order places them in an awkward and unprofitable position. This statement, however, applies best to a synchronic version of culture because in diachronic experience the impetus to resist often becomes amalgamated with heterodox foreign ideas and results in reinvented social forms. Hegemonies are expressed in master narratives, for example religious cosmologies, that are presented as immutable, like natural laws. In hegemonies that are historically tenacious, however, this fixity is a front for an energetic if inconspicuous reinvention of cultural beliefs and practices, for example, a reinvention of spirit beliefs and possession practices such as those considered in this chapter.

Lack of available data makes it more convenient to consider precontact Samoa in the synchronic mode and postcontact Samoa in the diachronic mode, although this is admittedly a heuristic device. In the guise of spirits, participants in the popular entertainments of precontact Samoa reversed normal power relations. These reversals, however, were purely discursive in nature and did not threaten Samoan hegemony; in fact, they perpetuated it.

After contact, spirits and popular entertainment changed their shape in tandem. In colonial Samoa, when certain entertainments were banned that had provided an arena for spirit reversals, these same reversals came to be expressed in new forms of possession, suggesting an open border between popular entertainments and possession experiences. In postcolonial Samoa, when possession became infrequent, the reversals that had been expressed in possession drifted back into the sphere of entertainment.

A question raised by this history is: To what extent was resistance to cultural hegemony merely subverted in new forms and to what extent was efficacious resistance reflected in reinvented forms? Taking a synchronic view, Gluckman (1956) observes that institutionalized reversals of normative behavior are most likely to occur where a set of norms is securely established. Reversal expresses resistance to hegemonic relations, and this potentially revolutionary content can prove volatile when norms are in dispute. In diachronic perspective, however, norms are always in dispute in the sense that they are in a continuous process of reformation.[2] In some respects we will see that in Samoa Christianity expanded upon pre-Christian power relations, but it also supplied heterodox foreign ideas that supported resistance to these relations. In turn, popular entertainments and possession episodes constituted arenas for thinking about foreign ideas and in this sense may have also contributed to creative adaptations and historical responsiveness in the Samoan cultural order.

In this chapter I rely on early students of the culture—missionaries, philosophical travelers, military and civilian government functionaries in the employ of European powers—for accounts of pre-Christian numinals. For more recent accounts, I rely on ethnographies, travelogues, interviews I conducted and entertainments I attended or watched on local broadcasting while residing in Samoa between 1981 and 1989, and my experiences as the wife of a Samoan and as a member of a Samoan extended family. I also utilize the data provided by my American Samoa Community College students, who conducted interviews in disparate villages of American and Western Samoa between 1986 and 1988.

PRE-CHRISTIAN NUMINALS

The nineteenth-century missionary Stair listed four classes of Samoan numinals: *atua,* the original gods who dwelt in a land called Pulotu; *tupua,* deified spirits of chiefs; *aitu,* descendants of the original gods or spirits whose aid was invoked; *sauali'i,* ghosts and mischievous sprites (1897:211; see also Mead 1969:152–155). All these numinals are grades of idealized chiefs, not morally idealized, but idealized in power or *mana.* (1) *Atua*: Tagaloa, the prototypical *atua,* was chief of the gods. (2) *Tupua*: When high-status chiefs died, they might become *tupua.* (3) *Aitu*: While they lived, chiefs were often said to be part *aitu.* (4) *Sau-ali'i*: This word for the lowest order of numinals is built on the word for high chief—*ali'i.*[3]

If numinals were all chiefly beings in old Samoa, *atua* and *tupua* had special dignity and authority and were in this sense godlike; *aitu* and *sauali'i* interacted directly with humans and tended to be mercurial and spiritlike. Yet these distinctions were not clear-cut, for some *aitu* ranked among the highest class of gods. Stair, for example, reported that the war goddess Nafauna was the only deity worshiped by all Samoans, but Nafauna was an *aitu* who was the daughter of an *aitu*, Savea Si'uleo, chief of the underworld (Stair 1897:220; see also Turner 1984:38–40; Stuebel 1976:37–44). In general, however, *atua* was an encompassing category for older or higher-status numinals. Thus while Stair distinguishes between *atua* and *tupua*, he sometimes refers to *tupua* as *atua* (1897:211). *Aitu* was an encompassing category for younger or lower-status numinals, although with missionization this category expanded to include all surviving pre-Christian numinals. This redefinition was appropriate, as numinals' status declined in Christian times, although they still outranked humankind.

In pre-Christian Samoa *atua* embodied respect; *aitu* reversed it. Tagaloa, for example, was a being of great dignity; he cut a boy in half because the boy marred the dignity of the first kava ceremony by joking. *Aitu* were born as "clots of blood." "A clot of blood" is the Samoan euphemism for a miscarried fetus; a miscarried fetus is the putative consequence of incest, and many *aitu* trace descent from an incestuous union (Cain 1971). Nafanua, for example, the female *aitu* who was a tutelary spirit in war, descended from an incestuous union. Pili, the *aitu* who was the Samoan approximation of a culture hero, began his adventures by incest with his sister. In Samoa, incest is seen as the absolute failure of respect (Shore 1981).

SPIRITS AND SAMOAN HEGEMONY

The age-status break between *atua* and *aitu* in Samoan numinal categories replicates the structure of Samoan power relations. The fundamental Samoan model of society is the extended family, in which those lower in age tender respect to elders. The Samoan concept of respect, however, also refers to avoiding words or deeds with sexual or scatological connotations in the presence of categorical brothers and sisters. One might call the former hierarchical respect and the latter sexual respect. When being polite one addresses everyone with deference and is circumspect around all opposite-sex persons: one acts as if others are older relatives and as if opposite-sex persons are categorical siblings, evoking the extended-family model.

If hierarchical and sexual respect are distinct in the social personages that emblematize them, they are conflated in the words and gestures through which they are expressed. Both are denoted by one term—*fa'aaloalo*. The same conflation is characteristic of terms for disrespect. In childhood, for example, failure to show hierarchical respect is most often characterized as *tautalaitiiti*, "to talk above one's age," a word that denotes disrespect for authority. Yet a boy who exposes himself to a girl is also called *tautalaitiiti*. Conversely, flaunting one's sexual or scatological side is used by Samoans as a trope for hierarchical disrespect (Mageo 1989b:396–397; 1992:445–446). Mooning, called *sigo*, is the most extreme insult to another's status and dignity.

Hierarchical respect is emblematized by the chief; sexual respect is emblematized by the sister and by the village *taupou*. The *taupou* is a virgin who prepares kava for chiefs in ceremonies and who is also an idealized sister figure (Mageo 1991b:355). The tableau of the *taupou* preparing kava in ceremonies portrays the relation between hierarchical and sexual respect. Samoan ceremonies celebrate hierarchical respect through an exchange of honorifics and prestations in which parties symbolically demonstrate deference to one another (Churchward 1887:99–101; Wilkes 1845:149; Mageo 1995). By giving the *taupou* a key role in ceremonies and by treating her as a titled dignitary, ceremonies also express sexual respect. Nonetheless, we will soon see that this tableau rightly implies that sexual respect serves hierarchical respect in Samoa, having an auxiliary usefulness to overarching power relations, just as *taupou* serve chiefs.

In Samoa hierarchical respect is hegemonic, predicating a host of power relations. While the model for these relations is that of extended family relations between elders and youngsters, this model is used to naturalize a much broader set of relations: relations between chiefs and commoners in the village, between powerful families and families that are less so, and formerly between villages and districts that won wars and those that lost. In each case, those lower in the status hierarchy are to show a circumspect deference to their superiors. Certainly in old Samoa this expectation was taken for granted, but it must have inspired resistance in those who had to defer.

In their incestuous nativity and conduct, *aitu* embodied a failure of sexual respect; however, in this guise they permitted discursive forays against hierarchical respect. Perhaps the most important of these was the carnivalesque night dance of ancient Samoa, the *poʻula,* which in its structure resembled a possession induction. At *poʻula* Samoans expressed resistance to respectful relations through the fictive persona of *aitu*; however, this spirited acting out was also a means of ensuring the continuing viability of existing power relations. Let us turn, then, to *poʻula* and to the part spirits played within them. I begin with a description of the event itself, going on to discuss its spirit entailments. This portrait of the *poʻula* is synthesized from a number of early sources and is, therefore, interpretive.

PŌULA

Poʻula were hosted by the *aualuma,* the association of sisters and daughters of the village (Shore 1977:318). Members of the *aualuma* began the evening by summoning all to the *aualuma* house through "singing a spirit song" (Williams 1984:246). The hosting party occupied one side of the house, the visitors occupied the other side, and performances were exchanged between the sides (Pritchard 1866:78). The exchange had two distinct parts, each having three aspects or phases, diagrammed below.[4]

Part I: Synchronized Dances
Leader: *Taupou* [Village Virgin]
  and High Chief
1. Sitting Dances
2. Standing Dances
3. *Taualuga*

Part II: Comic Dances
Leader: *Fa'aaluma* [Clown]
1. Mimetic Dances
2. Exhibitionistic Dances (*Sa⁻e⁻*)
3. *'Ale'aleaitu*

Part I featured an exchange of synchronized dances. In the first phase of Part I, a *taupou* led sitting dances in which movement was in unison (Kraemer 1978 V. II:389–391).[5] The second phase of Part I consisted of standing dances. The third was an elegant dance, usually led by a high chief, in which the dancer's movements were controlled and abbreviated and those who danced accompaniment moved in a stately manner (Pritchard 1866:78; Kraemer 1978 V. II:391–394; Stair 1897:133–134; Moyle 1988:209). This concluding dance is unnamed in early accounts, but resembles a dance today called the *taualuga* (Moyle 1988:209).

Part II of the evening featured *ula*, "joking." *Po⁻ula* means "*ula night.*" Inasmuch as the evening as a whole was called *po⁻ula*, it would seem that *ula* was its signature activity, the stately dances of Part I being only a preface to the heart of the event. *Ula* is specific kind of joking, most often sexual or scatological in nature, delivered either in a verbal or a gestural idiom. Thus when someone makes a sexual quip, it is *ula*, and when giggling girls grab at one another's breasts and genitals, this is also *ula*. Inasmuch as *ula* is often explicitly carnal, it reverses sexual respect. We saw, however, that showing off the private parts of the body is a Samoan trope for hierarchical disrespect and that baring the buttocks, *sigo*, is the ultimate Samoan gesture of contempt. Inasmuch as *ula* entails joking about corporal things, it plays upon an established Samoan strategy for denigrating the dignity and prestige of the other and thereby also reverses hierarchical respect.

In Part II of the evening each group was probably led by a *fa'aaluma*, "a conductor-clown," usually male. The first phase of Part II was devoted to mimicry, which was often comic in nature (Kraemer 1978 V. II:391–394; cf. Moyle 1988:213–219). Animals were a frequent subject. Kraemer, for example, describes a chorus of dancers who imitated dogs, some "crawling in four footed fashion ... while the rest ... jerk their heels to the beat inwards and outwards, at the same time howling like a miserable dog, their mouths distorted" (1978 V. II:391–392). There were other sorts of imitations as well, sometimes involving extensive solo performances and whole comedic skits (Turner 1984:132; Kraemer 1978 V. II:393; Sloan 1940:100–107; Kneubuhl 1987).

In the second phase of Part II movements grew more improvisational and hilarious. Probably because of their *aualuma* role as village hostesses, girls were responsible for breaking the figurative ice (Williams 1984:247–248; Wilkes 1845:130,134,140; Colvocoresses 1852:87; Stair 1897:134; Shore 1977:314). Churchward, a nineteenth-century British consul, describes the girls who danced as losing "all command of their actions, distorting their countenances in the most hideous manner, and performing such undesirable antics, that ... they appear ... like a lot of demons let loose from below" (1887:230; cf. Williams 1984:246–247).

These "antics ... let loose from below" led to increasing abandon (Williams 1984:247–248; Pritchard 1866:78; Stair 1897:134; Turner 1984:125). Abandon mounted toward a dance called the *sa⁻'e⁻*. In the *sa⁻'e⁻* the old women began dancing naked and singing a chorus of sexually explicit songs (Kraemer 1978 V. II:394). As the *sa⁻'e⁻* progressed, everyone but the young people departed, banter became obscene, and then began the final phase—the "spirit frenzy" (*'ale'aleaitu*)—in which all dancers tore off their own and one another's clothes, after which "many bonds of love, more or less transitory" were forged (Williams 1984:247–248; Kraemer 1978 V. II:398). Recalling his youth, one of my middle-age informants says, "The *'ale'aleaitu* means whoever you are dancing with at that time, you will take off the lavalava, and you can run off, elope" (cf. Kneubuhl 1993).

PŌULA MEANINGS AND DISMEMBERING AITU

While the *po⁻ula's* opening invocation focused on spirits, and the dance concluded with a "spirit frenzy," it is not immediately obvious what the body of the dance had to do with spirits; this connection lies in the dance's semiology. The sitting dances, the standing dances, and the final *taualuga* of Part I focused on the *taupou* and the high chief. We saw that chiefs were often looked upon as part *aitu*; likewise sisters were regarded as having spiritlike qualities, amplified in the *taupou* (Cain 1971). The chief and the *taupou* together, therefore, might be regarded as stand-ins for those spirits who were initially invoked in the spirit song sung by the *aualuma*.

If spirits were invoked in Part I of the *po⁻ula,* they were impersonated in Part II. This impersonation began in the mimetic dances. A pervasive cross-cultural understanding of spirits is that they are shape-shifters. Thus Halloween—the night when European and American spirits are free to walk about—is a night when one plays at being a spirit by changing one's shape or persona through costumes. In Samoa, too, spirits were and are understood as shape-shifters. *Aitu* commonly take on animal forms, and may take the form of the opposite sex or of persons of varying ages (Williams 1984:265; Stair 1897:216; Keesing 1934:399; Holmes 1974:64; Shore 1977:308; Schoeffel 1979a:405, 407; Kneubuhl 1987:173). The male spirit, Tuiatua, for example, is said to become a female to seduce handsome young men. So when *po'ula* dancers began to shift their shapes through mimesis, they were not simply imitating things in the world: on a meta-level they imitated—or impersonated—the shape-shifters, *aitu*, themselves. Indeed the house in which the *po'ula* took place was called a *faleaitu*, a "spirit house" (Shore 1977:318; Kneubuhl 1993).

The impersonation of *aitu* in the mimetic dances progressed toward a symbolic identification with *aitu* in the exhibitionistic dances (*sa"e"*). Samoans associate nudity and wildness—such as that of the old women dancing the *sa"e"*—with the behavior of Samoan spirits. One English-speaking informant, describing how in his youth boys would sometimes walk nude through a deserted forest, says "and the farther you are into the woods, your lavalava may end up on your neck, and you walk.... You behave like a ghost, you behave like an *aitu*." Part II of the *po'ula* climaxed with the *'ale'aleaitu*, in which the remaining dancers shed their clothes. When clothes were torn off at the height of the *'ale'aleaitu* it was called "Tearing off the eye of the *aitu*," (*Sasae le mata ole aitu*). Even today "Tearing off the eye of the *aitu*" is a euphemism for having a good time.

This progressive symbolic identification with *aitu* might be regarded as a playing at possession that I call "ludic possession." Through ludic possession participants at *po'ula* reversed respect relations. The stately dances of Part I—which focused on the *taupou* and the chief—made a statement about the specific forms of respect that Part II was meant to reverse. Part II was comprised of the mimetic and exhibitionistic dances. The mimetic dancing often involved poking fun at others (Kraemer 1978 V. II:391; Moyle 1988:218), reversing hierarchical respect. The exhibitionistic dances reversed sexual respect. The reader will recall, however, that exhibitionism (as in mooning) was also a Samoan metaphor for hierarchical disrespect. It follows that the exhibitionistic dances signified shedding respect in the general sense. In normal life *aitu* were the guarantors of respect: those who disobeyed chiefs hazarded spirit sickness; so did brothers who failed in sexual respect toward their sisters (Mead 1961:44; Cain 1971). The shedding of respect that characterized the final *'ale'aleaitu* was, therefore, equivalent to a ritual dismemberment or "tearing" of the *aitu*.[6]

We have seen that sexual respect derived from incest-avoidance rules between categorical brothers and sisters; however, these rules were generalized as a model for polite conduct in the presence of opposite-sex relatives. Within old Samoan villages opposite-sex persons were likely to be at least distantly related. Sexual respect, therefore, could be looked on as a set of incest–avoidance rules expanded to encourage village exogamy. The later stages of *po'ula* took place between the boys of one village and the girls of another, so incest was not a likely danger. By encouraging young people to dramatize a reversal of incest avoidance in this context, *po'ula* put resistance to Samoan hegemony in the service of finding spouses, elopement being the primary Samoan form of marriage (Schultz 1911:22–30; Keesing 1934:412; Schoeffel 1979a:210). As an informant says of po῾ula, "That's how ... the traveling party from the other village will intermarry, that's the time they find spouses.... That's how many couples are able to find each other." Marriage between young people of different villages initiated ritual exchanges and friendly relations, which served as a basis for the shifting military and political alliances upon which hierarchical forms of governance relied in old Samoa. Thus sexual respect served Samoan hierarchy even in its reversal, just as the *taupou* served chiefs in ceremony. Further, because of the lexical and symbolic conflation of hierarchical and sexual respect, culture members could express resistance to sexual respect in entertainment contexts—and thereby indirectly express resistance to hierarchical respect—without remotely infringing upon hierarchical relations.

CHANGING SPIRITS AND SPIRIT EVENTS IN CHRISTIAN SAMOA

With missionization, *atua* (the upper class of Samoan numinals, like Tagaloa) were soon replaced by the Christian deity. *Aitu* (the lower class of Samoan numinals) survived and subsumed *sauali῾i*, "ghosts," and *tupua*, "deified chiefs," who once were second in rank only to Tagaloa. Even missionaries showed a vulnerability to belief in this welter of lower spirits. The missionary Stair tells tales of *aitu* bowling with oranges all night in the hallways of his Samoan house (1897:261–268). His guests, none of whom he ever forewarned about these hauntings, would complain about the cease-less noise made at night by his "servants." Stair patiently explained that his servants returned to the village every evening. The poor reverend finally gave up his house because the *aitu* were overtaxing the nerves of his wife!

If the continuing vitality of *aitu* was a fact to which even missionaries could attest, the province with which *aitu* were associated—popular enter-tainment—did not fare well under missionary influence. Missionaries heartily disapproved of po῾ula and particularly of girls' roles within them (Moyle 1988:205–206, 210). Samoans had taken to Christianity with a vengeance soon after the first missionaries arrived around 1830. By the 1860s the majority of the population was Christian, the majority of Samoan children were attending mission schools, many were literate and read the only text available in Samoan, the Bible (Turner 1986:18–19, 27, 61–78; Willis 1889:52; Mead 1961:270; Gilson 1970:102; Holmes 1974:61; Schoeffel 1979a:446–447, 1979b:3, 1983; Garrett 1982:125; Freeman 1983:183; Huebner 1986:339, 401). Missionaries, therefore, soon had a degree of veto power on Samoan cultural practices such as the po῾ula. In response, Christian Samoans invented new practices, composed of transfig-ured pieces of the po῾ula to which, for one reason or another, missionaries did not object.

Part I of the po῾ula consisted of synchronized dances that, while energetic, were not explicitly sexual and ended with the *taualuga*, in which a high chief danced in a stately manner, accompanied by other dancers who synchronized their movements with those of the central dancer. This segment of the *po̅ula* has become synonymous with the dance in Christian Samoa and is called *siva*. In contemporary Samoa one sees many sitting dances as well as male slap dances. Both are synchronized dances and are concluded by the performance of a *taualuga*. Part II of the *po̅ula* has been dropped. This truncation seems an obvious form of censorship; however, the present-day *taualuga* is a product of condensation, including elements from both the respectful and less than respectful *po̅ula* segments of yesteryear.

Today the participants who encircle the *taualuga* dancer may still move in a stately manner, but they are just as likely to *'ai'aiuli* this dancer. To *'ai'aiuli* is to engage in gestural *ula*, performing in a wild, uncontrolled and ridiculous manner that provokes laughter and may be sexual in character. Samoans characterize this *'ai'aiuli* accompaniment as a method of paying "respect" to the central dancer (Shore 1977:317). Even the name of this dance (*'ai'aiuli*) means to humble oneself so as to draw attention to another (Milner 1979:10). Yet this definition is cultural camouflage for an inclusion of *po̅ula* antics in what was once an entirely dignified dance. Through mockery and sometimes flagrant sexuality the *'ai'aiuli* permits a surreptitious (if diminished) inversion of respect as an accompaniment to its celebration.

A scholar of Samoan dance comments that "it seems odd" no written mention was made of the *'ai'aiuli* in the nineteenth century, given its "sheer visual impact ... which has attracted and excited twentieth century visitors" (Moyle 1988:231). In fact great mention is made of the *'ai'aiuli* in the nineteenth century, but this dance style went under another name: it is simply a transformation and a stand-in for the *sa̅'e̅*, which had to be sacrificed to missionary sensibilities. It is noteworthy, however, that young women no longer lead the way in choreographic antics. Often as *taupou*, or playing the role of *taupou* for the purpose of an entertainment, they dance the *taualuga*. In any case they dance only in a stately style, while antics are danced by boys, men, or older women.

Part II of the *po̅ula* consisted in mimetic dances, exhibitionistic dances (*sa̅'e̅*), and the "spirit frenzy" (*'ale'aleaitu*). I suggest that these phases were isolated from their former choreographic frame and synthesized with other existent institutions to elaborate new institutions, still identified with *aitu*. The mimetic dancing was combined with other Samoan theatrical practices, developing into an all-male comic theater called *faleaitu*, "spirit house." The ludic possession of the *sa̅'e̅* and the *'ale'aleaitu* was conflated with pre-Christian forms of mediumship and ideas of illness as spirit induced, developing into a new form of actual possession. These new institutions are the descendants of the *po̅ula* and represent the colonial domain of spirits, a narrower domain than spirits enjoyed prior to the advent of Christianity, but a significant place in the Samoan symbol system nonetheless. In this narrower territory, spirits continued to provide culture members with a means for expressing their resistance to Samoan power relations through temporary and circumscribed inversions. In Christian Samoa, however, the nature of power relations changed, and spirits had new work to do.

Sinavaiana observes that in colonial Samoa hierarchical respect expanded, coming to include not only traditional authority figures but also colonial authority (1992a); I argue that sexual respect also expanded. Further, the burden of sexual respect once shared between brother and sister shifted to the sister. Prior to Christianity, upper-class girls were cloistered, but for commoners the limiting sexual principle was incest, which applied to both sexes (Pritchard 1866:125; Kraemer 1978 V. I:67–68; Cain 1971:177). While lower-status girls had to exercise more judgment in mating than their male counterparts, this was a difference in degree, not in kind. With mission-ization, however, the idea that all girls should be virginal until marriage gathered force, and the nuances of sexual respect changed. Sexual respect became a quality that girls sustained through their virginity, although it was also given them by their brothers. Yet the brother who discovered his sister was not a virgin might beat her—which in Samoan semiology is the opposite of respect.

The particulars, the timing, and the reasons for this ingress of foreign values—for it stemmed not only from colonialism but from internal cultural dynamics—is a lengthy subject that I have considered elsewhere (Mageo 1992, 1994b, n.d.). For present purposes it is sufficient to note that girls resisted this new morality (Williams 1984:117; Hutton 1874:149); newly invented versions of possession by novel spirit personages became a means of dramatizing their resistance.

INVENTED AITU AND POSSESSION IN CHRISTIAN SAMOA

Today English-speaking Samoans consistently gloss *aitu* as "ghost," but in fact two surviving subdivisions of *aitu* survive: there are souls (*aga̅ga*) who return from the dead to bother their living relatives and who are, therefore, ghosts in the Western sense of the term, and notorious spirits. These notorious spirits are no longer referred to as descendants of the original gods, since pre-Christian gods have come to be looked upon as mythological. Shore rightly calls them liminal beings, neither living nor quite dead (1978). As already mentioned, they may originate as miscarriages; alternatively they may be humans "taken alive" by spirits (Kraemer 1949:29; Stuebel 1976:37,42,94; Cain 1971, 1979; Good-man 1971:470; Clement 1974:83; Shore 1977, 1978; Schoeffel 1979a:405; Henry 1983:64, 1980:76,93–93; Hovdhaugen 1987).

Dead souls are classified as *aitu*, but the reverse does not hold; notorious *aitu* are not classified as *aga̅ga*. Indeed the term *aitu*—despite its neutral significance in the case of the dead—connotes pre-Christian spirits. Thus one appropriately says *Aga⁻ga Pa'ia* for the Catholic Holy Ghost; however, to say *Aitu Pa'ia* would be a sacrilege. Under Christian influence the notorious *aitu* have come to be regarded as *tevolo*, a Samoanized version of "devils." Notorious *aitu* differ from ghosts in other important respects. While dead ancestors are local, notorious spirits are widely known. Eminent spirit personages are said to travel in motorcars and on the airlines around the Samoan islands, and even to Hawai'i to call upon the goddess Pele (Schoeffel 1979a:406–407; Mageo 1991b:361). Although this penchant for traveling sounds modern, it is not: *fo⁻lauga aitu,* "voyaging spirits," have been reported since the nineteenth century (Stair 1897:235; Holmes 1974:64).

Within the category of notorious *aitu* are two major subdivisions: a male type consisting of idealized chiefs (the *tupua* of pre-Christian times), and a female type consisting of idealized sisters. While *taupou* are idealized sister figures, female *aitu* are idealized *taupou*. In ceremonies *taupou* wear a special headdress decorated with human hair bleached to a reddish brown. Female *aitu* are most frequently described as having hair of this color. They are often said to have been extraordinarily beautiful *taupou* in high-status families prior to being "taken alive" by spirits (Cain 1971:174; Goodman 1971:470; Schoeffel 1979a:404–405,421). If *taupou* are idealized sisters, and female *aitu* are idealized *taupou,* it follows that female *aitu* are doubly idealized sisters.

To say female *aitu* represent idealized sisters is not to imply they are moral idealizations. Stories about the origins of female *aitu* emphasize their status as offspring of incestuous unions (Cain 1971:178). Female *aitu* seduce young men, who in old Samoa might die as a consequence (Kraemer 1949:16–17; Mead 1929:269; Stuebel 1976:94–95; Schoeffel 1979a:401). Schoeffel argues that the fantasy of seduction by a female *aitu* expresses incest anxiety (1979a:412). If this fantasy is about incest, it suggests a symbolic equivalency between the figure of the female *aitu* and the figure of the sister; the death of young men from union with *aitu* represents the frightening moral and social consequences of incest. Thus female *aitu* are not merely sister figures; they are sister figures that symbolize the reversal of sexual respect. As such they embody what was once expressed in the *po⁻ula,* having migrated to the domain of possession.

The most famous male *aitu* is Tuiatua, a deified chief from the district of Atua in Western Samoa; also widely known is Tuifiti, a deified chief of Fiji (Turner 1984:62–63; Stuebel 1976:14–20,54; Cain 1979:204–205,209; Shore 1977:350–365; Meleisea 1987:42). The most famous female *aitu* are Letelesa⁻ and Sauma'iafe. While contemporary male *aitu* appear to be the deified chiefs (*tupua*) of pre–Christian times, most contemporary female *aitu* appear to be post-contact beings, not corresponding to any category of numinal described in Stair's early report. Stair's account was written from field notes collected during a seven-year residence in the 1830s and 1840s, the first two decades after contact (1897:12–13). The first record I found of these beings is Stuebel's, a German consul to Samoa in the 1880s. The discrepancy between Stair's and Stuebel's reports suggests that *taupou*-like *aitu* may not have become culturally salient until relatively late in the nineteenth century. This surmise is supported by the long hair ascribed to them; long hair for women was a missionary importation. Elsewhere I argue that these female spirits represented a reaction against Samoan-Christian norms for young women (Mageo 1991c). In this regard it is interesting that they should have made a cultural debut just as the missionaries were effectively censoring *po̅ula* and girls' roles within them.

SAMOAN POSSESSION IN HISTORICAL PERSPECTIVE

Most typically in pre-Christian Samoa, priests, chiefs, and their sisters practiced mediumship, deliberately entering into trance states to become spirit intermediaries (Williams 1842, quoted in Freeman 1983:176–177, 339; Stair 1897:222; Shore 1977:308; Meleisea 1987:37). Illness was also thought of as spirit induced (Turner 1986:130; Macpherson & Macpherson 1985:1–16, 1990:38–41,61,151). Today one no longer finds mediumship in Samoa. One finds passive possession that is looked upon as an illness induced by spirits (*ma'i aitu*), in contrast to ailments that are physical in origin. The onset of this "illness" is marked by the victim's dissociated manner and by physical symptoms that do not respond to ordinary treatment and that have either no apparent physical cause or a cause that is disproportionately minor. Relatives then seek the aid of a healer specializing in the treatment of spirit ailments (Macpherson & Macpherson 1990:118, 199–201). Treatments aim at inducing the possessing spirit to speak and can involve massaging the sufferer with leaves, covering them with dirty sacks from an earth oven, or a number of other practices. When the spirit speaks, it accuses either the victim or her relatives of behaving badly. Some negotiation is made to propitiate the spirit, who then leaves the victim's body.

In old Samoa, professional spirit mediums were called *taula̅'itu*, "spirit anchors." In modern spirit possession, healers are called *taula̅'itu* and are not entered themselves. Neither is the possessed person a source of desired information, although the possessing spirit may be prescient. Rather, the "advice" given by the spirit is a reproach for reprehensible actions, especially for failing to show hierarchical or sexual respect. Like *po̅ula* dancers, possessed women have a penchant for shedding their clothes, an inclination not characteristic of mediumship in missionary reports.

Another remarkable change in the cultural orchestration of possession concerns the gender and age of those possessed. In accounts from old Samoa, the gender distribution of those who had commerce with spirits was equitable. Mediums were largely older and were commonly chiefs or chief's sisters, or priests or others with special oracular abilities; all were highly honored (Freeman 1983:177–178). In accounts of possession from the second half of the twentieth century, the victims of possession are largely young women of no particular importance (Goodman 1971:471; Schoeffel 1979a:394–395; Mageo 1991a). It is unlikely the new demography of possession is longstanding. Missionaries and early ethnologists discuss spirits at length (Turner 1984, 1986; Stair 1897; Kraemer 1978; Stuebel 1976) but do not lead one to believe possession is the special affliction of young women. In early travelogues, too, I have found no reports of the possession of young women (Grimshaw 1907; Sloan 1940). Freeman, who worked in Samoa from 1940 to 1943, documents a possession episode suffered by a boy (1983:224–225). He does not mention female possession, even though a high incidence of female possession could easily have been used to support his case for the sexual repression of young Samoan women.[7]

In what follows I consider forms of possession common among Samoan girls. Girls are not the only victims of possession in Samoa today. As noted in Chapter 1, when forms of possession exist to satisfy the needs of a particular group, others may borrow these forms for more idiosyncratic purposes. I suggest that contemporary forms of possession express the resistance of girls to the Christian version of respect, and particularly sexual respect, just as po‾ula expressed everyone's resistance in pre-Christian times.

Girls' Possession

In Christian Samoa, just as two subdivisions of *aitu* exist—dead relatives and notorious spirits—so also there are two basic forms of spirit possession that I call "elder relative possession" and "notorious spirit possession." Sometimes girls may also be possessed by an animal, but "animal possession" can be considered a subcase of notorious spirit possession, as notorious spirits often take the form of animals (Stair 1897:216; Holmes 1974:64; Shore 1977:308; Meleisea 1987:36–37). The motifs that compose animal possession, however, show intermediate properties, bridging elder relative possession and notorious spirit possession proper. I, therefore, treat it as a third type of possession intercalated between the other two.

1. Elder Relative Possession

When a healer induces the spirit to speak in "elder relative possession," a deceased grandparent or other venerable ancestor reproaches a parent for abusive behavior toward their possessed descendant. During a period in which one of my Samoan sisters-in-law felt particularly ill-treated by her mother, she was possessed by her grandmother. The grandmother scolded her mother for maltreating the girl. This form of possession offers the young person a legitimate vehicle for reversing hierarchical respect. The ethic of obedience to elders is, however, also reiterated by a spirit's insistence that the guilty parents obey their own dead elders, so the episode ultimately validates the power relations it temporarily preempts.

2. Animal Possession

When the healer induces the spirit to speak in "animal possession," the spirit announces that the girl abused some animal and that it had taken the form of this animal. Youngsters are sometimes told, if they see a cat, dog, pig, or any animal strolling on the road, particularly later in the day or early evening, they should respect the animal and say "*Tulou*" (because it may be an *aitu*). *Tulou* means something like "excuse me" and is the simplest example of respectful address. In a society like Samoa, where young people are consistently forced to show deference to a multitude of superiors, they may be tempted to show disrespect where they can get away with it, by kicking or otherwise abusing animals.

Through a spirit accusation, animal possession retrospectively highlights a girl's inversion of hierarchical respect—that is, her abusive treatment of an animal, who turns out to be an *aitu,* who is by definition high ranking. In the persona of a spirit, the girl declares, "I did it!" without actually offending any people to whom she owes respect. Yet animal possession also ratifies the principle that one should be constantly vigilant in demonstrating hierarchical respect, for it is orchestrated as an attack on a girl who has acted disrespectfully.

The theme of sexual respect is often implicit in cases of animal possession as well, as the following incident illustrates. During the early 1970s my husband had a cousin of about 17 years of age who lived in Pago Pago. One day she was possessed by Tuiatua, who haunts Pago Pago and several other areas of American Samoa. She was in the habit of walking to choir practice at dusk through a park. When Tuiatua spoke through her, he said, "I was the toad that you kicked," "You came on the park with your hair down," and "You came over and picked a hibiscus [for your hair]."

In Samoan iconography, wearing one's hair down symbolically displays one's sex (Mageo 1991b, 1994b). Adorning one's hair with a flower is thought to be highly attractive and also self-exhibiting. Hair itself is a Samoan trope for sexuality and fecundity; self-display and self-decoration that involve hair are Samoan tropes for sexual expressiveness (Mageo 1994b). Thus Tuiatua's reproach highlights a reversal of sexual respect. Tuiatua is notorious for seducing lovely girls. Inasmuch as the fantasy underlying this possession episode entails behaving seductively toward Tuiatua, and as Tuiatua appears in the guise of a toad, the episode evokes the motif of the animal-bride, a motif associated with adolescent sexuality (Bettelheim 1975).

3. Notorious Spirit Possession

In "notorious spirit possession," the girl is possessed by a spirit known throughout the Samoan islands. Which one usually depends on the locale, although the correlation is not exact, for these spirits love to travel. Possessions on the island of Tutuila, American Samoa, are most commonly attributed to Tuiatua; possessions by notorious spirits on 'Upolu, Western Samoa, are likely to be attributed to Letelesa‾ and Sauma'iafe; in Savai'i possession is often ascribed to Tuifiti; in Manu'a, Holmes reports Sauma'iafe and Tuiatua possess people and that, in Manu'an legend, Sauma'iafe comes from Manu'a (1974:63).[8] In notorious spirit possession, the spirit acts as if it has been disrespectfully treated, insinuating hierarchical issues are at stake; however, the issue of sexual respect is also rife. Whether possessed by a male or female spirit, the girl is often said to provoke possession by various forms of self display, like those described in the possession by Tuiatua narrated above. Possession is particularly likely if these behaviors occur in the haunt of a spirit.

When possessed, a girl's face and carriage is said to become like that of a female *aitu*. The appearance of female spirits is characterized by those symbols for sexual expressiveness that are associated with possession in girls: female *aitu* wear their long hair down and are likely to have reddish hair, decorated with a red hibiscus (Mageo 1991b:359–362); they may even be said to glow red, as may those whom they possess (Kraemer 1949:16A). Red coloration is another Samoan trope for sexual expressiveness (Mageo 1994b). Female *aitu* also actively pursue young men. It follows that to be possessed is to become like a female spirit, which is to become sexually expressive. This train of implications is generally submerged in Samoan discourse about spirits, but is confirmed during possession: the girl's behavior is often explicitly exhibitionistic. She is apt to wander about half-clad or wholly naked, and her language may become obscene (Schoeffel 1979a:413; Mageo 1991b:364, 367–369).

In the course of possession the spirit is likely to reproach the girl for some sexually tinged deed or desire, although not erotic behavior enacted during the course of the possession episode; while possessed it is not she who acts but a spirit. In general, possession is looked upon as the spirit punishing the person (Goodman 1971:469). The girl may also lose her long hair in negotiations with the *aitu* to leave her body (Goodman 1971:469; Schoeffel 1979a:399; Mageo 1991b:365–366, 369–371). Cutting off a girl's hair is a standard parental punishment for sexually indiscreet behavior. Thus, while the discursive content of notorious spirit possession expresses resistance to sexual respect, its consequences validate this ethic.

In his work on Samoan spirits and their associated institutions, Shore argues that spirits serve as a "homeostatic" control for particular individuals disposed by temperament, personal history, or current circumstances to violations of respect (1977: 307, 1978; cf. Schoeffel 1979a:414). This argument is persuasive in notorious possession, where inversions of respect often precipitate an assertion of social control, namely cutting off a girl's hair. In this sense *aitu* appear to have a regulatory effect. It is also possible, however, that notorious spirit possession simply carried on the discourse of sexual flaunting that once characterized *po̅ula*. The behavior of possessed girls in notorious spirit possession is reminiscent of the exhibitionistic phase of Part II of the *po̅ula* and of the *'ale'aleaitu*, the spirit frenzy, in which clothes were stripped away and language became obscene. As in Freud's accounts of dreams, obsessive acts and ceremonials, in notorious spirit possession desire—expressed tropically or in the form of an accusation—is disguised as a punishment (1942, 1953). However, here desire is conflated with resistance that is coded in impertinent/exhibitionistic behavior; the punishment is losing one's hair or simply the fact of being possessed. This cloaking of desire-resistance in the guise of punishment displaces the focus of judgment: possessed girls are objects of sympathy rather than objects of reproach even though, unconsciously, their performance is creative and may, therefore, preserve a sense of agency.

The new trappings of counter-hegemonic discourse, however, also reflected new limitations in the social world: unlike *po̅ula*, possession episodes did not end in elopements but in a loss of the girl's hair. Hair is pivotal to the constitution of attractiveness in Samoa and is symbolic of sexual potency (Mageo 1991b; 1994b). By "sexual potency" I mean a capacity on the part of either sex to enter into fruitful sexual relations. In demanding that a girl's hair be cut, notorious *aitu* are likely to impair her capacity to enter into sexual relations by making her less attractive in Samoan terms; they also decrease her symbolic sexual potency by depriving her of the ability to display the prime Samoan symbol of her capacity for fruitful sexual relations, her hair. Lambek argues that possession is often a "serious parody" of "orthodox religion, social convention" and "the accepted language of power relations" (1989:53–54); the same can be said of the ludic possession of the *po̅ula*. In the new forms of possession found in Christian Samoa, however, gestures that had once been parody remained, but festive comedy "evolved" into a drama of judgment and punishment.

Inasmuch as possession continued *po̅ula* traditions, for girls institutionalized reversals of respect came to consist in an "unconscious practice," by which I mean a practice the historicity and meaning of which was obfuscated. If possession among young girls existed in pre-Christian Samoa, it is unlikely that it resembled the type of possession described above. Wearing one's hair down could not have been a catalyst for possession in old Samoa because the girl's head was mostly shaved at puberty (Stair 1897:121; Williams 1984:117; Turner 1984:122; Willis 1889:17; Schoeffel 1979a:433); wandering in a state of undress would have had little psychological purchase for girls who attended *po̅ula*.

If notorious spirit possession is the *'ale'aleaitu* in reinvented form, it also tends to include novel historical features. In one case of possession, for example, Telesā reproached her victim for being interested in a traveler on a tour boat, a young man whom she herself admired (Mageo 1991c). In another, Saumaʻiafe saved a girl from another female *aitu* who was jealous of the attentions the girl received from a male *aitu*; the *aitu* had been an American Marine, crashed in Savaiʻi in World War II (Mageo 1991d). In both cases the sexuality that is expressed and censured includes elements of the foreign. Here "foreign" may stand for a newly personalized relation to sexuality.

In pre-Christian Samoa the matings of lower-status girls was a route to the ascent of family status (Mageo 1992, 1994b, n.d.). Missionaries, however, encouraged marriages based on personal feeling (Mead 1961:101). This orientation toward mating and marriage was probably reinforced by the avalanche of foreign men who descended on Samoa in World War II (Stanner 1953:327–328; Franco 1989:386). During World War II, there was a good deal of sexual contact between American soldiers and Samoan girls (Stanner 1953:327–328). Although the wartime visitors had status in Samoa, sexual relations with them were generally associated with a loss of status (Mageo 1994b:418–419). Here girls exercised sexual agency not in the service of family status but for reasons of personal preference. Foreign men probably became a metonym for this personalized relation to sexuality and thus for a species of individualism. Inasmuch as foreign men are recurrent characters in notorious spirit possession, possession may have become an arena to register and remember more individual forms of social relation and social action, forms that posed an enduring threat to the communally oriented hierarchies of Samoan society. Indeed these new forms, first articulated by missionaries and later by servicemen, may be embedded in the reinvented forms of possession itself.

Unlike *poʻula,* the new form of possession took place within the context of the family. By embedding a rite of reversal in family relations, the new possession provided a medium to express resistance of a more personal nature and, in some measure, to adjudicate power relations as they bore upon people individually. As a result of possession an oppressed child might get her way. An adolescent girl who wanted to exhibit herself got attention, not just as a member of a dance troupe but as a special person, special at any rate in her affliction. Thus the personal dimension of resistance found greater scope and acknowledgment, despite the fact that this acknowledgment was received in a form that validated communal-hierarchical relations.

ON THE ORIGINS OF SAMOAN SPIRIT THEATER

While the missionaries strenuously objected to the naked, salacious dancing that concluded Part II of the *poʻula,* the theatrical mimicry that opened it was much less objectionable and so became the focus of festive evenings. Earlier we saw that *poʻula* took place in what was called, for the purpose of the evening's entertainment, a *faleaitu*, "house of spirits." Aptly this became the name of the theatrical form that took the place of *po'ula* in public entertainment. Actors in *faleaitu* are referred to as "*aitu*." This name implies that Samoan comic theater is a form of ludic possession: the actors impersonate spirits, as dancers in the mimetic phase of the *po'ula* once did. In this sense *faleaitu*, like the *siva*, is a colonial descendant of the *po'ula*: it is an identifiable piece of the *po'ula* that survived the collision between public entertainment forms and missionary ethics. *Faleaitu* did so by employing male as opposed to female comedians and by leaving out the dancing that once accompanied and followed *po'ula* skits. After all, it was the salacious dancing and girls' lewd humor to which the missionaries most objected.

Except for the lack of choreography and fact that theatricals never progressed to the bawdy dancing and "frenzy" of the *'ale'aleaitu*, early comedies may not have differed greatly from *po'ula* themselves, being relegated to those occasions on which a *po'ula* would have taken place and employing those antics characteristic of *po'ula* girls. Comedies took place at night, often in the context of entertainments for traveling parties (*malaga*), and employed "extensive verbal play ... especially ... of a sexual nature ... with occasional lewd gestures or postures used as a kind of comic punctuation ... scantily clad actors and ... use of obscenity" (Sinavaiana 1992b:196–197). Initially *faleaitu* may have even included both boys and girls (Tuiteleleapaga 1980:50). It was probably only gradually, as the Samoan-Christian notion that girls should be models of sexual respect gathered force, that they lost their place in *faleaitu*.

FALEAITU AND REVERSING RESPECT

Inasmuch as *faleaitu* derives from the *po'ula* antics, one might say that the boys who clowned in comedy skits entered a traditionally feminine province and inherited girls' roles as leaders of jest. But there is ancient precedent for male clowning in Samoa. Churchward, who was British consul to Samoa from 1881 to 1885, describes the clowning of *fa'aaluma*, "clowns," who performed on occasions of state, as "untranslatable, being of a nature that, if printed, would ensure the suppression of the medium for their circulation" (1887:98; cf. Turner 1984:125–126). The most important of these were probably the *salelesi*, who "roamed about attaching themselves to various chiefs" (Stair 1897:123; see also Turner 1984:125–126; Churchward 1887:312–13, 324; Moyle 1975:232–233; Tuiteleleapaga 1980:48–49). While the unprintable nature of these clowns' witticisms makes it clear that they reversed sexual respect, *salelesi* were most renown for their farcical attacks on the dignity and privileges of chiefs (Tuiteleleapaga 1980:49).

Faleaitu combined a female tradition characterized by *aualuma* girls at *po'ula* (which most emphatically expressed a reversal of sexual respect) with a male comic tradition characterized by the *salelesi* (which most emphatically expressed a reversal of hierarchical respect). These two elements—the reversal of hierarchical respect and of sexual respect—in fact conspire in Samoan comedy: the characteristic style of *faleaitu* actors reverses sexual respect, while *faleaitu* plots reverse hierarchical respect. The characteristic style of the *faleaitu* actor is that of the male transvestite (Shore 1977:318–333, 1978:178; Mageo 1992:454; Sinavaiana 1992b:196). In Samoa, the transvestite's style is a caricature of the sister and of the *taupou*. The sister is supposed to be dignified. The transvestite affects an exaggeratedly dignified manner and speaks in a elocutionary style associated with dignified behavior (Shore 1982:273; Ochs 1988:57). The sister is politely assumed to be virginal and is referred to as a *teine*, "girl." The transvestite is also referred to as a "girl"; however, the word for transvestite is *fa'afafine*, which literally means "the way" (*fa'a*) of "women" (*fafine*). The term *fafine* has connotations of active sexuality. These connotations are justified by the bawdy manner and jesting of the *fa'afafine*. By marking "herself" as like the dignified sister—and then behaving scandalously—the transvestite makes a caricature and a joke about the sister and about sexual respect.

Because actors tend to effect a transvestite style and because the Samoan transvestite's style is bawdy, one's initial assumption is that the *faleaitu* actor portrays a girl who wants to express illicit sexual impulses, or secondarily, that the actor portrays a boy who wants to behave effeminately. Yet in this multi-leveled disguise of indiscretion and effeminacy, actors may "ridicule the highest chief" (Kneubuhl 1987:171). In fact, ridiculing the hierarchical power relations that chiefs emblematize is the point of *faleaitu* plots.

In *faleaitu* plots risible superiors exercise their authority without sense or conscience: Samoan fathers use their daughter's marriage to elevate their personal status, addled Samoan pastors exploit their parishioners, English princes are imbeciles, and so forth. On the other hand, ludicrous inferiors mercilessly abuse those whom they are supposed to serve: Samoan sons exploit their foolish fathers, Samoan schoolchildren poison their naive Caucasian teacher, and so forth (Shore 1977:318–331; Sinavaiana 1992b:201–209; Mageo 1994a). As Sinavaiana points out (1992a, 1992b), many *faleaitu* plots burlesque colonial authority. However, they also burlesque the unsettling of pre-Christian power relations, for example, relations between men and women—women who acquired new earning power in the colonial regime. One of Sinavaiana's *faleaitu* wives, for example, works night shifts; her economically dependent and self-pitying husband stays home to look after the children (Sinavaiana 1992a:116–117).

In husband/wife skits, the wife's incorporation of Christian-colonial values often changes the balance of husband/wife roles. In the skit "Jealousy II," for example, the wife and the husband argue, and the wife scores against him by speaking in English—a language associated with education and status in colonial Samoa—while the husband insists that all would be fine (and presumably he would win the argument) if they would just speak Samoan (Sinavaiana 1992a:104–106). Sinavaiana points out that here speaking Samoan is a metaphor for acting in accord with older Samoan values. Thus *faleaitu*, like modern possession, has been a medium to register and to ponder historically shifting balances in hegemonic power relations.

Shore argues that possessing spirits (who are "malicious and dangerous") regulate sexual relations and that the spirits of Samoan comic theater (who are "benign and merely funny") regulate relations of authority (1978:196). It is true that emphases differ in modern Samoan possession and *faleaitu* but, contra Shore, possession and *faleaitu* are actually dimorphic, each including issues of hierarchical and of sexual respect; it is just that these issues are frightening in possession and "merely funny" in *faleaitu*. Elder relative possession is a particularly obvious example of a type of possession in which authority is an issue. We also saw that hierarchical respect is an important theme in animal possession. Even in notorious spirit possession, however, the possessed girl may insult others or order her elders about (Mageo 1991b:369–373), so here too hierarchical respect is implicated. While *faleaitu* is a discourse on authority, it also expresses sexual issues through the device of transvestism.

A more fundamental, although not strict, distinction between the dangerous and the benign displays of *aitu* is a gender distinction. It is necessary in Christian Samoa that girls be regarded as passive and victimized in any scene in which a lack of respect is dramatized because they have become full time models of respect; therefore, when girls take center stage (as in possession), *aitu* show their dangerous side. When *po'ula* were banned, however, boys maintained the right to *ula* and could, therefore, carry on the comic traditions of *aitu*.

ON THE DEATH OF SPIRITS

At this chapter's opening, I cited a passage from the nineteenth-century missionary Stair (1897:211), who lists four classes of Samoan numinals: (1) the high gods, *atua*; (2) the deified spirits of chiefs, *tupua*; (3) those spirits who communed with humankind, *aitu*; (4) those "apparitions ... ever ready for mischief and frolic," *sauali'i*. It is tempting to suggest that, while *aitu* became a general category for numinals and *tupua* survived in possession episodes, *sauali'i* came to be impersonated in *faleaitu*, such that all of the apparently lost Samoan pantheon found a place in colonial Samoa, save the highest gods. In post-colonial Samoa, however, *faleaitu* and possession are less in evidence than once they were.

Although modern forms of possession and *faleaitu* were, I think, produced by the impact of colonial values on earlier religious and quasi-religious practices, they have become representatives of tradition. Both *faleaitu* and possession now occur primarily in remote rural contexts that serve as preserves of older versions of Samoan culture (Sinavaiana 1992b:197; Mageo 1994b).

Faleaitu is also performed during annual national celebrations that valorize "traditional" culture: Independence Day in Western Samoa and, to a lesser extent, during Flag Day in American Samoa. The story does not end here, however, for if possession and *faleaitu* are the colonial descendants of the *po'ula*, they also have a post-colonial descendant, Samoan transvestism.

Not that transvestism is new to Samoa; it is a trans-Polynesian form of long duration (Levy 1971:12–13, 1973:130–131; Williams 1986:255–256, 313; Besnier 1994). Nonetheless, transvestism was not culturally salient in Samoa until recent decades, when full-time transvestites began to take over the arena of public comedy from the thespian transvestites of *faleaitu* (Mageo 1992:443–444). When *fa'afafine* take center stage, their performances tend to be exhibitionistic, as girls' performances originally were at *po'ula*, and later were in states of possession. Today *faleaitu* has migrated to rural villages, while transvestites migrate to urban centers; transvestite comedy can be seen as a modern and urban counterpart to *faleaitu*. In urban contexts, transvestite impresarios express resistance to hierarchical and sexual respect vicariously for girls who are gradually losing their belief in *aitu* and who, consequently, cannot be possessed (Mageo 1991b, 1992).

Personalized sexual sentiment—what we call "romance"—is an important element in *fa'afafine* performances: they are apt to sing popular American songs about sex, romance, and love. I suggested earlier that personalized sexual sentiment is a vehicle for the idea of individualism, an idea potentially disruptive to the communally oriented Samoan hierarchy. A favorite song of contemporary *fa'afafine* is "My Way," a song that probably alludes to their sexual difference but that also tags a new individualism. Threaded through the performances of the contemporary *fa'afafine*, as through girls' performances in possession, is a resistance to sexual respect newly conflated with foreign ideas that may have larger transgressive connotations.

If *fa'afafine* now do what *aitu* once did, they might be seen as *aitu*-substitutes, and symbolically, this is a role they play. Girls' cricket games are the one surviving domain in which they make bawdy choreographic jokes, resembling in diminished form their ancestresses at *po'ula*. In Samoan cricket games a clown (*fa'aaluma*) holds the whistle and makes a choreographic joke when her team scores, a joke which is then imitated by her team members. Thus girls' cricket games resemble the constellation of *po'ula*—in which there was a jocular exchange between two sides, each led by a *fa'aaluma*—although today girls perform vis-a-vis other girls rather than boys. Probably in having two opposing sides, each led by a clown, night dances reflected more general entertainment structures in pre-contact Samoa, to which cricket games still show a family resemblance.

Moyle points out that Samoan cricket is more like a pre-contact game (*ta'ga'ti'a*) than it is like its English counterpart (1988:99; cf. Kraemer 1978 V. II:406). In *ta'ga'ti'a* one member of each team was a choreographic clown who "would leap about in joy" when the team scored (Moyle 1988:99). This *fa'aaluma* was called an *aitu*. In modern-day girls' cricket, if there is a transvestite on the team (they are included in female activities), "she" will be made *fa'aaluma*. In historical perspective, when girls choose a transvestite to be a *fa'aaluma* in cricket, they are selecting "her" to play a role that is analogous to that of the *fa'aaluma* in *tāgātiʻa*, the historical prototype of modern Samoan cricket. If cricket is the modern-day analog of *tāgātiʻa*, then the cricket *fa'aaluma* is a modern substitute for the *tāgātiʻa aitu*.

These connections, however, are esoteric and are not a conscious part of local knowledge. Rather, like *aitu* themselves, the symbolism that links the reversal of respect relations to spirits has become an arcane backdrop to experience. Perhaps for this reason, when modern Samoan transvestites clown—when they carnally and choreographically invert hierarchical and sexual respect by the same gestures that *poʻula* girls once did—they do so without the invocation or the blessing of *aitu*. The only spirit element that remains is that of the shape-shifter, for transvestites, like *aitu*, are subjects who have changed their shape and do so for the purposes of presiding at rites of reversal.

Rites of reversal are prototypical occasions for counter-hegemonic discourse. The licentious and disrespectful discourses of *poʻula*, of possessed Samoan girls, of *faleaitu*, and of contemporary *fa'afafine* are counter-hegemonic: they are all wonderfully transgressive and expressive of resistance to the power relations intrinsic to Samoan culture. But these events also show us that, unlike ideologies and the dictatorships that perpetuate them (cf. Comaroff & Comaroff 1992:28–29), lasting hegemonies do not exist in any rigid opposition to counter-hegemonic discourses.

At the opening to this chapter I suggested that spirits uphold hegemonies by offering the synchronic possibility of reversal and the diachronic possibility of social change. In synchronic perspective, the mesmerism that Gramsci assigns to hegemonic discourses comes from a conspiracy with those on margins of worldview, as Samoan chiefs had *salelesi* always in their retinue and sponsored *poʻula* alongside every important ceremony. In diachronic perspective hegemonies remain viable by a subtle provisioning of the socially muted voices of the disenfranchised because, like the proverbial prophet crying in the wilderness, those that gainsay the status quo offer their societies the capacity to forge necessary adaptations in ways of life, as possessed girls, *faleaitu* actors, and transvestites provided their culture with an arena to think about and integrate foreign ideas within a Samoan matrix. Williams (1977:109) asserts that hegemony is never total. I would go further: the viability of a hegemonic discourse is contingent upon its incompleteness, where incompleteness consists in a tacit openness to heterodox ideas that can be usefully articulated with existent and taken-for-granted cultural attitudes and practices. Spirits, vague and blurry in their contours, shifting even when one can fleetingly delineate them, are the very image of this secret openness within a cultural system.

NOTES

Acknowledgments. I thank Alan Howard for his unremitting support, generosity and advice throughout this project. I also thank the National Endowment for the Humanities and University College London for research fellowships that made the writing up of the material possible, Tamar Gordon and Michael Meeker for their comments, and Sanele Mageo for his invaluable help and support.

1   Prior ethnographic accounts that treat the subject of *aitu* focus on cataloging spirit lore or on those who heal spirit sickness (Turner 1984:23–77; Stair 1897:210–241; Kraemer 1978; Mead 1969:152–155; Cain 1971, 1979; Goodman 1971; Stuebel 1976; Schoeffel 1979a). Shore attempts to explain the place of *aitu* in social structure (1977, 1978), seeing *aitu* as having a "homeostatic" function in relation to this structure.

2   Some view popular entertainment as supporting the social order, for example Bateson in his work on the Naven (1958); others, as subverting that order (Davis 1978:154–155). My perspective reconciles these positions.

3   On these grades of numinals, see further Kraemer (1978:61), Stuebel (1976:78), Schultz (1985:90), Meleisea (1987:37).

4   Alternatively, Moyle suggests *poula* had a tripartite structure (1988:205–220), and Shore breaks the *poula* into five stages (1977:315–316).

5   Sometimes a *manaia*, the male counterpart to the *taupou,* might lead one side of this dance, as when a party of males visited a village and were entertained by the women's association (Moyle 1988:210–212).

6   Shore sees the concluding dance of the *poula,* the *'ale'aleaitu,* as a form of group possession that caused *poula* dancers to temper their passions. When participants began to lose sexual control, *aitu* appeared, frightened everyone out of the dancing house, and thereby restored order (1977:313–315, 1978:179). However, I know of no nineteenth-century reports to indicate that *poula* dancers were actually possessed. If there was a period in the twentieth century in which *poula* provoked actual, as opposed to ludic, possession, it seems likely that this was a reaction to missionization.

7   During the period that I associate with a high incidence of possession among Samoan girls, suicide was epidemic among Samoan boys (Bowles 1985; Macpherson and Macpherson 1985, 1987). Freeman discusses suicide among both men and young women (1983:220–221). Higher rates of suicide were found in villages with higher ratios of chiefs to untitled men (Bowles 1985); so hierarchical respect appears to have been a salient issue. Suicide also appears to be correlated with a decline in copra prices. As a result of this decline, untitled men must do significantly more labor to "respect" elders and chiefs who have become accustomed to Western commodities (Macpherson and Macpherson 1987; O'Meara 1990). Girls also commit suicide; however, their motives commonly have to do with illicit passion rather than with inordinate demands for service. In a 1986 BBC documentary on Samoa ("Prisoners of Paradise"), for example, a young man explained that his sister had committed suicide because she wanted to marry her cousin. Freeman reports several such cases (1983:221).

8   Holmes also reports the Nifoloa and Nafanua possess people in Manu'a. The Nifoloa is a notorious male *aitu* usually said to reside on Savai'i (Turner

1984:41–42; Stuebel 1976:90; Schoeffel 1979a:403). According to my informants, while female *aitu* and the *tupua*, Tuiatua and Tuifiti, regularly speak through possessed humans, the Nifoloa only causes physical symptoms. Nifoloa sickness takes the form of a splinter in the flesh that is believed to be the tooth of the Nifoloa. Samoans, however, refer to physical symptoms with a spirit provenance and possession by the same term, *ma'i aitu*, "spirit sickness." For girls even the kind of *ma'i aitu* caused by Nifoloa can have sexual themes. One of my Samoan sisters-in-law, for example, was possessed by the Nifoloa because she was wearing perfume when she crossed a bridge he haunted. My sister-in-law felt she had gotten a splinter on the bridge, which hurt when she returned home. None of her siblings could find the splinter. That night her foot and lower leg became swollen. A *faivai* was summoned but did not come because in the darkness he could not find the leaves he needed to treat her. In the morning he sent the girl's siblings to two places where he had seen the requisite leaves. The leaves could not be found at the first location—according to the *faivai* because the Nifoloa had hidden the leaves, as *aitu* are wont to do. The siblings found the leaves at the second location. The *faivai* made an herbal smoke that he blew on the girl's foot, resulting in a loud popping sound. One of the girl's sisters said the sound was the splinter exploding. In Western Samoa, Nafanua was reported to have possessed chief Le'iataua Tamafaiga⁻ in a historic war as a reward for the courtesy he showed her daughters (Stuebel 1976:44, 76; Meleisea 1987:37). I have not heard recent reports of her possessing people, however. If Nafanua does regularly possess Manu'ans, she is something of an anomaly, being of a more ancient vintage than most spirit girls.

3 They Loved Her Too Much

Interpreting Spirit Possession in Tonga

Tamar Gordon

The Tongan archipelago consists of some 150 islands, thirty-six of which are permanently inhabited by about 96,000 racially and linguistically homogenous people. A constitutional monarchy, the Kingdom of Tonga is the most conservative and highly stratified of the contemporary Polynesian nations, with three hereditary social classes: the king, a chiefly nobility of thirty-three families, and commoners. Tonga is still primarily agricultural, and inherited lands—nominally administered by chiefs and owned and farmed by commoners—are inalienable. However, rapid economic development generated in the capital, Nuku'alofa, and fed by emigration has given rise to a substantial, educated middle class rooted in civil service and small business. Given these developments, Tonga has recently seen public challenges by commoner members of Parliament to the traditional system of privilege. Urbanites and villagers alike participate in a redistributive economy consisting of ceremonial exchanges, feasting and resource-sharing among extended family groups called ka͞inga. Tonga has never been colonized by a European power. Rather, sovereign statehood was indigenously orchestrated in the nineteenth century by King Taufa'ahau Tupou I, who strategically allied himself with Wesleyan missionaries to reconstruct Tongan polity and society. While the official state religion is Wesleyan Methodism, eight other denominations (three of them homegrown) have long been players on the Tongan Christian scene. Village life is multidenominational and organized around the different churches and their activities.

Possession by spirits is a commonplace reality among modern-day Tongans, many of whom can expect, at one or more times in their lives, to be catapulted into this "other" state. This chapter offers a cultural analysis of Tongan spirit possession, known traditionally as *'aʻvanga*, and colloquially as *puke fakateʻvolo*.[1] The Tonga literature contains rich descriptions of *'aʻvanga* as a medical and social phenomenon in the writings of Claire Parsons (1981, 1983, 1984, 1985); Wendy Cowling (1987); and psychiatrist Wolfgang Jilek (1988). Rather than duplicate their work, my aim is to build on their insights about the cultural etiology of *'aʻvanga* and, drawing upon my own research, to further elucidate its historical and contemporary role in the social body.

During my two years' stay in Tonga it was impossible to avoid the fact of *'aʻvanga*. Everyone knew people or had relatives who had experienced possession at least once, including those who had emigrated overseas. References to *puke fakateʻvolo* cropped up in every conceivable conversation and setting. I heard snippets about possession in kava circles, at funerals, feasts, rugby games and fund-raising dances. *'Aʻvanga* surfaced during gossip sessions, embedded in longer narratives about the proclivities of different families and individuals. *'Aʻvanga* is a markedly special condition for Tongans. Despite its "specialness" as an experiential state, however, *'aʻvanga* can be situated within the "normal" or normalizing spectrum of Tongan cultural discourse as essentially continuous with the various means that Tongans draw on to control, discipline and morally comment on people and events.

Tongans believe that spirits are attracted to people who find themselves (often unwittingly) as protagonists in an unbalanced social environment that has been the scene of moral transgressions (particularly in familial behavior), breaches in *tapu*, powerful emotional distress, or extreme behavior. In the seeming absence of these, an *'aʻvanga* attack can precipitate a breach of normality that may throw submerged and forgotten conflicts once more into relief; the victim need not be at fault, but may simply have stepped into the line of fire, so to speak. As a discourse of morality and cultural critique, *'aʻvanga* exposes cultural paradoxes and untenable social situations.

Tongans say that the dead are even more morally outraged than the living by social transgressions. The spirits' desire to exert moral restraint over a person intensifies when specific *tapu* are violated. For example, one young woman whom I knew officially died of heart failure; the explanation going around at her funeral was that the spirit of her recently deceased father had entered her body and had *'aʻveaʻi ia*, "taken her away." This girl had been extremely close to her father and had lovingly nursed him in the final months of his fatal illness. Her mother, aunts and sisters said that she died because she had broken the *tapu* on handling her father's bodily wastes.

People are often possessed by spirits who "love them too much," as with the brokenhearted daughter described above. The early researcher E. E. V. Collocott noted this ethos of loneliness and lost love: "The poor ghost longs for companionship that it has lost.... It enters, or approaches, the body of a living friend, usually by the way of a hysterical woman, and she may become so violent and excited that several people are required to hold her" (1923:138).

Another young woman of my acquaintance was stricken with recurrent *'a vanga* shortly after both of her parents died. At age twenty-two she developed what doctors at a Honolulu hospital termed a "hysterical pregnancy," but she and her maternal aunts claimed it was a spirit pregnancy caused by the entry of her dead parents into her body. Treatments by several *fefine faito'o,* "women healers," in Hawai'i and Tonga caused the pregnancy symptoms to disappear, but her dead parents troubled her with other signs of *'a vanga* for years afterward. As Collocott observed, victims can also exhibit preternatural strength: during an *'a vanga* attack in Tonga, this young woman was said to have thrown five restraining policemen off the Queen Salote wharf in Nuku'alofa.

Polynesian cultures thematize morality as ideal structures, stances, demeanors, and behaviors, and as bringing the inner self into line with the conventional obligations, rights, and duties of social situations. Studies on Polynesian language and socialization practices note that the qualities that are reinforced are respect for status, conformity, personal constraint, and social relatedness (Ochs 1988; Ritchie and Ritchie 1989). As a radically marginalized event, one that constructs a bracket of "otherness" around individuals, spirit possession appears to counter dramatically these ideal values, demeanors, and practices. An individual possessed seems subversive and uncontrollable; yet *'a vanga* is far from counterhegemonic. I would argue that practices such as possession, which apparently fall outside of the social ecology of control, all belong to the same "habitus," that is, the totality of dispositions that orient people's perceptions and practices in more or less patterned ways without strictly determining them (Bourdieu 1991).

Bourdieu's related notion of "bodily hexis" is salient for understanding Tongan spirit possession, especially in light of its historical durability and its persistence as cultural practice in overseas Tongan communities. The possessed body—one variety of the socially constructed Tongan body—is a site through which structures and meanings of Tongan history and culture reproduce themselves. It is the "embodiment" of specific practices of social discipline and censorship. Bourdieu's model of the organizing effects of culture and history upon individuals does not, however, preclude agency—the capacity to interpret and to act upon situations in such a way as to generate outcomes that are not strictly in line with cultural rules or ideals. The outcomes of particular practices like *'a vanga* can be seen as products of the relationship between habitus and context-dependent "fields of action" within which individuals exercise agency. For example, several Tongans whose possession accounts appear in this chapter were able to manage their *'a vanga* episodes as a form of cultural praxis. Their strategies, which were embedded and legitimated within the logical structures of possession, at the very least called attention to, and at best transformed the conditions that precipitated their possessions.

An *'avanga* episode typically gathers a variety of players—victim, practitioner/healer, significant relatives, friends and onlookers—and the event accumulates meaning through their gossip, their pronouncements, their furtive and open questioning. So, many voices ensure that there is variation in the narratives that Tongans construct from their explanations for the motives (or lack of motives) of the spirits involved. But regardless of how a given *'avanga* episode is interpreted, narratives about possession tend to establish an unimpeachable framework that provides motives and invites specific kinds of action. *'Avanga* narratives contain stereotypic elements that thematically link a variety of cultural realms to other morally laden issues and implicate a panoply of cultural tensions. An *'avanga* attack often locates individuals—usually, but not always women—within the crux of a social conflict and, in doing so, reveals momentarily a whole social fabric with all its tensions and contradictions: 1) a dual descent system in which matrilaterality is structurally less powerful than patrilaterality, 2) the competition of unequally ranked kin in securing the loyalties and resources of an individual, 3) the pressure on individuals for dividing loves and loyalties among competing interests, and 4) the mutual framing of anger (*'ita*) and love (*'ofa*) within a context of loss and filial punishment.

Stricken individuals become emblematic of the apparent contradictions inherent in these tensions. The cultural narrative that explains their condition dramatizes not only the social roots of their specific distress, but aspects of the system that do not bear directly on the victims' particular needs or desires. Seen in this light, *'avanga* is actually a hegemonic discourse that encompasses social and emotional contradictions and supplies a niche for their enactment and resolution. My analysis draws upon a variety of sources: the ethnohistorical record of William Mariner and the work of early anthropologists, the extensive existing literature on *'avanga*, and my own field work in 1982–84 on Tongan religious identities. Because *'avanga* is such a ubiquitous aspect of life in Tonga, I had numerous opportunities to observe healings and to elicit possession narratives from people who had been possessed or had been involved in possession scenarios.

THE TRADITIONAL REPERTOIRE: DEATH, LIFE, AND SPIRITS

Spirit possession, along with its myriad political entailments, has ancient roots in Tonga. This can be glimpsed in the unique ethnohistorical account—one of the richest in the Pacific literature—of William Mariner's sojourn in Tonga.

William Mariner was captured by Tongans in 1806 at age fourteen and spent four years living as an adopted son of chief Finau 'Ulukalala. Shortly after he was returned to England, Mariner related his story to physician John Martin, who chose to inscribe and organize the material as a sophisticated ethnography rather than as a conventional captivity narrative (Martin [Mariner] 1981 [1871]). An invaluable glimpse into pre-Christian Tongan society, Mariner's account contains a wealth of data on traditional religion and its articulation within culture and society. Tongans believed in a shadow island called Pulotu that lay to the northwest of the Tongan archipelago. Pulotu housed the hierarchy of gods (*'otua*); the paramount chief, or Tu'i Tonga; the spirit essences of dead chiefs (*hou'eiki*); and their ceremonial attendants (*ma͞ta͞pule*)—all of whom could return to speak through the mouths of priests. Commoners (*tu'a*) possessed an essence that would die with them and be buried together with the body under the earth. Mariner noted that commoners were buried in cemeteries called *fa'itoka*, while chiefs were interred in *langi*, or raised graves. (These can be seen in Tonga today.) Unlike the shades of dead chiefs, commoner spirits did not sail away to Pulotu at the moment of physical death. Their business remained unfinished; they normally could not reappear to meddle in worldly affairs.

'*Avanga* was a diverse phenomenon, falling on both sides of the formal/informal, elicited/spontaneous, control/chaos, high-status/low-status divides. Mariner's descriptions of possession comprise two broad categories: ritual/formal and personal/spontaneous. Ritual *'a͞vanga* worked officially through a caste of priests—mainly men, but including some women—who were routinely possessed by the gods and dead chiefs to whose living households they were attached. These greater and lesser deities were elicited as players (or pawns) in a constantly shifting and flexible political system; the warnings, prophesies and injunctions that issued forth from them through the mediumship of the priests played a significant role in the status rivalries of living chiefs. Mariner tells of a variety of issues and events upon which priests were consulted: warfare, political intrigue, decision-making, natural disasters and the annual *'inasi*, or first-fruits ritual. Priest mediums also had the power to heal, and people who were physically ill, injured, dying, and possessed were brought to their homes to receive interpretation and prognosis of their maladies.[2]

Priestly possession was a formal affair, embedded in political praxis. When a priest was called upon to mediate between gods and people, a kava circle of chiefs and commoners formed before him. A ritual frame thus established, the priest was considered "inspired" (Mariner's word) from the moment he sat down in the circle. His message delivered and the kava and food consumed, the priest finished by striking a club on the ground, thereby releasing the spirit and its *mana* from his body. Mariner describes his symptoms in this way:

> When he speaks he generally begins in a low and very altered tone of voice, which gradually rises to nearly its natural pitch ... all that he says is supposed to be the declaration of the god, and he accordingly speaks in the first person as though he were the god. All this is done generally without any apparent inward emotion or outward agitation; but on some occasions his countenance becomes fierce, and as it were, inflamed and his whole frame agitated with inward feeling. He is seized with universal trembling, the perspiration breaks out on his forehead and his lips, turning black, are convulsed; at length, tears start in floods from his eyes, his breast heaves with great emotion, and his

utterance is choked. These symptoms gradually subside. Before this paroxysm comes on, and after it is over, he often eats as much as four hungry men, under other circumstances, could devour. (Martin 1981:84)

Spirits spoke to other high-ranking people outside of the ritual containment of the kava circle. Mariner writes that the spirit of Chief Finau appeared to his grieving widow as she lay sleeping on his grave (an extreme practice even by the elaborate standards of Tongan mourning). Assuming a "disappointed" mien, Finau pointed out a conspiracy launched against his son by political rivals in Vava'u. Mariner notes that the spirits of chiefs often appeared in dreams and visions to their relatives and descendants, who in turn publicized their messages. Finau's son, for example, was regularly possessed by dead Tu'i Tonga who advised him on political and personal matters.

The second type of *'a̅vanga* was widespread, spontaneous and not marked by ceremony:

It happens in the Tonga Islands, that persons, who are not priests, are often visited by the gods, particularly females, but who are never affected in the manner above described. They are generally low spirited and thoughtful as if some heavy misfortune had befallen them. As the symptom increases, they generally shed a profusion of tears and sometimes swoon away for a few minutes. The height of the paroxysm generally lasts from a quarter to half an hour. These are also called fits of inspiration, and are firmly believed to be visitations from some god who accuses the party of neglect of religious duty, not by an apparent audible warning, but by an inward compunction of conscience. (Martin 1981:85)

Mariner describes an informal possession of a young chief by a lovesick spirit. His account has some of the stereotypic elements of a modern-day *'a̅vanga* narrative.

On one occasion a certain chief, a very handsome man, became inspired, but did not yet know by whom. On a sudden he felt himself exceedingly low spirited and shortly afterwards swooned away. When recovered from this, still finding himself very ill, he was taken to the house of a priest, who told the sick chief that it was a woman, mentioning her name, who had died two years before and was now in Bolotoo [Pulotu], that had inspired him; that she was deeply in love with him, and wished him to die (which event was to happen in a few days), that she might have him near her. The chief replied, that he had seen the figure of a female two or three successive nights in his sleep, and had begun to suspect he was inspired by her, though he could not tell who she was. He died two days afterwards. (1981:86)

Unofficial possession was diffusely linked with a broad repertoire of cultural imperatives, much as it is today. Spirits who possessed common people and whose messages were then interpreted by priests pointed both directly and indirectly to broken *tapu*s and to inappropriate behavior, for example, inordinate attachment to a deceased spouse or lover, too-fierce mourning, transgressions of respect protocol, and breaches in what Mariner termed "religious observance."

Sixteen years after Mariner returned to England, the first Methodist missionaries arrived in Tonga. In the twenty years following the introduction of Christianity, the entire traditional religico-political apparatus was officially dismantled by its most powerful convert, King Taufa'ahau Tupou I. The rest of the nineteenth century saw the indigenization of Wesleyan Methodism and the arrival of other churches seeking to reconstitute the vestiges of traditional beliefs as Tongan Christian discourse.

Gifford wrote that in the new Christian order, folk-healers of both sexes replaced the fallen priestly specialists, and the spirits of dead ancestors supplanted the gods (1929). The afterlife likewise was "democratized" with the understanding that even commoners possessed *lauma'lie* (in chiefly language "life," denoting the chiefly essence that persisted after death), which now glossed as the Christian soul.

'ĀVANGA IN MODERN TONGA

'Āvanga persists in late twentieth century Tonga largely as a parallel (though not contradictory) belief system to conventional Tongan Christianity. Tongans can keep the frames of reference and practices separate or, on occasion, syncretically combine prayers and church contributions with the exorcism process. They assert that neither conventional *lotu*, "prayer," nor Western medicine alone address the true ontological status of a spirit attack. Although contemporary *'a'vanga* lacks the hegemonic power to interpret and control events that it had in the traditional order, it nonetheless signifies and problematizes the same themes—status, rank, kinship, gender and emotion—and enlists the body as the conduit through which these themes are socially encoded and resolved.

Possession in modern Tonga is not (nor was it ever) a neat phenomenon. While young unmarried women are most often affected, people of both sexes and of all ages, ranks and statuses are susceptible to the intrusion of spirits.[3] Some ghosts remain nameless and strike hapless passers-by with no apparent motive. More often, however, people are struck by identifiable spirits of close and distant kin. Tongans also recognize that certain people are prone to *'a'vanga* through a particular temperament; they are sad, angry, or violent by nature. Tragedy and trauma likewise are said to predispose people to recurrent *'a'vanga*, especially if they are unable to relinquish ties with recently deceased loved ones. Spirits often strike people who are embroiled in domestic struggles. In many cases, the onus of resolution clearly falls on certain kin of the victim. Claire Parsons stresses this function of *'a'vanga* when she characterizes it as an "idiom of distress" embedded in a system of kinship-sickness. She notes that once an *'a'vanga* episode is made public, it implicitly requires certain parties to take action and make interpersonal changes, including confessing wrongdoing and requesting forgiveness (1984). Breaches of kinship ideology are indeed major elements in Tongans' constructions of the meaning of an *'aʻvanga* attack, as my cases show.

MODERN IDEAS ABOUT DEATH, MOURNING, AND SPIRITS

While Tongans no longer conceive of an afterlife in terms other than heaven, echoes of Pulotu appear in the euphemistic phrase for death, *folau he vaka,* "sail away by boat." During my research on Tongan Christianity I heard older people utter this phrase in *malanga,* "sermons," *lotu,* "prayer," *talaloto,* "an emotional, extended prayer of confession and supplication," and in ordinary conversation. When I pressed one woman to tell me, *"Pe ʻoku folau ki fe ʻae vaka?"* "But where does the boat sail off to?" she replied, *"Oku folau peˉki he feituʻu ʻoku te ʻalu ki ai heʻete mate,"* "It just sails to the place where one goes when one dies."[4]

The Tongan cemetery is a parallel world charged with power, where the concerns and activities of the dead mirror those of the living. The sandy mounds and fluttering grave decorations are resting places of beloved relatives who have reached the ultimate, orderly unification of social personhood with kindred and place of origin. But the cemetery is also an unpredictable, frightening domain in which the dead strike (*taˉʻi*) the living, scrutinize them carefully, and bring them closer to the underworld. The threatened dissolution of order and social control into the dramatic chaos of other-worldly encounters necessitates adherence to *tapu*s that provide protective hedges. It is very important to comport oneself respectfully and discreetly in or near a *faʻitoka* so as not to risk disapproval and leave oneself vulnerable to attack by the dead: "Don't point with your finger," "Don't shout," "Take that *sei,* 'flower,' out of your hair," "Don't sing *hiva kakala* 'love songs' or 'rock songs,'" "Don't enter the cemetery at night," "Announce your arrival (to a buried relative) so you don't surprise her." The dead must lie undisturbed under the ground as well. Sometimes an *'aˉvanga* attack requires that relatives of the victim perform a *tangaki* or exhumation of a particular corpse whose bones are suspected to have been crushed, pushed out of the coffin or invaded by tree roots. Once the grave is cleared of debris and the body realigned, the victim's symptoms may cease. When these and other taboos are violated in the neighborhood of the spirits, illness, either in the form of possession or in the medical sense, is the likely outcome.

ʻĀVANGA AND MEDICINE

The Tongan etiology of disease attributes most illnesses (if not all) to the entry of spirits into the living body (Jilek 1988; Parsons 1985; Helu, personal communication). Before Christianization, priests served as healing specialists. Today, the extensive pharmacopia of plants that comprises Tongan ethnomedicine is widely known and available to all people, some of whom train to become healers. *Faitoʻo,* "medicine," is mainly, but not exclusively, practiced by women. Every village has its practitioners, often specialists in one ailment or another. Individuals gain reputations as particularly adept in both the supernatural and pragmatic components of healing, and Tongans often travel between villages and islands to consult them. (See Parsons 1983 for a full description of Tongan medical practice.)

During my stay in a Vavaʻu village, I needed to consult a local *fefine faitoʻo* who specialized in "breast boils." While applying poultices of alkaloid and antiseptic leaves to the boil she manipulated its underlying *akaaka,* or "root system," and murmured for the spirit to "leave the girl alone." The boil disappeared over several sessions. On the last visit she filled a tub with warm water and leaves, took me to her bathhouse and splashed the water on me, saying to the spirit "'*Alu ai pe* ̄'!"—"Go away forever!" This was the *kaukau,* "bath," a finale that was integral to the structure of the treatment.

ʻAvanga also occurs by itself, without the presence of what Westerners would identify as a distinct physical malady. Common Tongan terms for spirit possession reflect the perspective that the condition is not healthy. For example, *puke fakateʻvolo* is "spirit sickness," while *fakamahaki* literally means "make sick," with the spirit as the agent. Tongans also use the term *mahamahaki,* "continually or recurrently sick," to refer to chronically or intermittently possessed individuals such as the young woman with the spirit pregnancy. The term *teʻia* refers to "a blow struck by the spirit": a sign *(fakaʻilonga)* that may or may not appear with a spectrum of other symptoms such as bruises and bites, swollen limbs, temporary rolling or narrowing of the eyes, and heart attack.

The Treatment

At the first full-blown manifestations of *ʻaʻvanga* —"any combination of moaning, writhing, nonstop crying, blank facial expression, extreme listlessness, wild shouting and swearing, striking out"—the afflicted person is brought to the practitioner who sends people to gather the appropriate leaves. The most radical treatment consists of sieving particular varieties of crushed leaves, vines and bark with water and pouring the thick green liquid into all the orifices of the head. Although *ʻaʻvanga* may later recur, the *tuluʻi,* as the application of the liquid is called, has the effect of immediately dissipating the energies of the victim, leaving her or him passive and open to recounting the experience. Other treatments, such as rubbing the body with a mixture of orally macerated leaves and coconut oil *(vali, fotofota),* inhaling steam, and drinking teas of those materials may have the same effect (see Parsons 1981; Jilek 1988; Cowling 1987; and Singh et al. 1984 for more complete presentation of techniques and pharmacological properties).

Immediately following the *tuluʻi,* the practitioner holds a conversation with the patient, indirectly addressing the causes of *ʻaʻvanga* by asking the patient what she remembers of the experience: where was she and what was she doing when the spirit appeared to her, what did the spirit look like, did the spirit have a name, did the spirit offer her any food or other objects, did they speak to one another. Victims typically remember having worn a flower in their hair, having shouted too loudly near a cemetery, or running to the bush or beach.

When the medicinal leaves are being gathered, some patients are said to manifest a supernatural sharpening of the senses, not only to see the spirits, but to smell the medicinal leaves and to hear the practitioner and her helpers approaching from a great distance. I witnessed a demonstration of such powers at the start of a treatment. The patient, a schoolgirl of fourteen named Manu, was writhing slowly under a sheet on the veranda of the practitioner's house. Her movements suddenly quickened and she grew wilder; the relatives who had brought her simply nodded knowingly and continued their card-playing. A minute or so later the dogs started to bark, announcing the return of people bringing the medicinal leaves. We had not heard their approach; the patient apparently had.

Once the *tulu'i* liquid had run out of her nose and mouth, Manu was calm and ready to respond to the practitioner's repeated questions. We bent expectantly over her to catch her story. She answered in a low, faint voice that she had seen "angry faces" all around her. She said that she gave in to the urge to run into the bush and was met there by a woman who offered her *te͞volo* food. Like Persephone, who was doomed to spend half the year in Hades for eating six pomegranate seeds, Manu was pulled into the dead world by ingesting its shadow foods. Visions of spirits are not limited to the victim. Two well-known practitioners, both of whom were treating the young woman with the spirit pregnancy, told me they are capable of seeing and hearing the offending *te͞volo* in the course of a treatment. Cowling (1987) and others report that practitioners sometimes encounter the spirit in dreams. Apart from their medical efficacy, practitioners potentially have moral authority in the context of healing. Their interpretive skills and intuitive rendering of social situations that might have encouraged the interference of spirits (with the discretion to appear noninterfering and indirect that is valued by Tongans) are given special weight. Manu's *te͞volo* was identified by the *fefine faito'o* as "a woman named Mele" whose spirit apparently frequented fringe areas around her village. This spirit had no known connection to Manu and her family. Manu stayed with the *fefine faito'o* for two weeks, as some patients do, drinking various follow-up *vai*, "medicinal drinks," and sleeping on the veranda. Her recovery was gradual, and her circle of contacts and activities expanded a little every day. I was a frequent visitor to this house because the *fefine faito'o* was the wife of the chief of my home village. The household was always bustling with people, activity and news, and lately with visitors casually inquiring about Manu's progress. The first week, Manu's gaze was alternately intense and blank, her eyes squinting through narrow slits. When I greeted her, she acted as if she didn't see or hear me. Soon she was quietly helping out with the cooking, and finally she started to speak again. When her stewards felt she was ready to return to school, she went home.

In many other cases, the practitioner's identification of the *te͞volo* and her rendering of the event are merely the start of an interpretive process that involves many individuals in the network of the victim, and sometimes lead to solutions that complement and enhance the staying power of mechanistic treatments. I will demonstrate this below where I present three cases and their analyses. First, we turn to additional relevant cultural features that inform Tongans' interpretations of an *'a͞vanga* event, and the conditions under which individuals fall stricken.

TONGAN KINSHIP AND DOMESTIC ARRANGEMENTS

Victor Turner (1968) attributed the ritual possession of Ndembu women by the spirits of their mothers to the chronic structural conflict between matrilineality and patrilocality. His model holds explanatory power for the tensions inherent in the Tongan kinship system, and its articulation with ideas about sickness, healing and social balance. Like Claire Parsons, who casts ruptures in familial relations as a prime symbolic determinant in *'a͞vanga* events, I also look to problems of Tongan social structure for key moral referents and value-laden tasks to be managed and resolved. I want to add, however, that *'a͞vanga* episodes need not presuppose obvious or dramatic abuses in kinship practice. Kinship themes occur frequently as a mode of explanation but not always as causal agents. Sometimes they simply provide the possession narrative with an underlying ethos of poignancy and loss. As the cases show, by historicizing stricken people's possession experience in terms of lineage conflicts—conflicts that need not bear directly on a victims' present life—individuals involved in the victims' lives strategically invoke kinship-related motives to account for episodes.

In contemporary Tongan kinship, roles and statuses on both mother's and father's sides engage an individual in obligatory relations of respect and reciprocity. Various segments of people's *ka͞inga*, or extended family network, compete from birth to beyond death for their loyalties and resources. This competition is particularly marked for married people, each of whom brings two sets of structurally relevant kin to their union. Father's and mother's sides, however, are unequally ranked; patrilateral relatives have chiefly status in relation to ego, while matrilateral kin are metaphorical commoners (Kaeppler 1971).[5] Within this unequally ranked system, the father's sister (ego's *mehekitanga*) still has considerable influence over the resources and destiny of her nieces and nephews. She and her children "please themselves" (*fa'ite͞liha*) with her brother and his children; this is called a *fahu* relationship. It follows that mother's brother (*fa'e tangata*: literally, "male mother") has a reciprocal relationship with ego. He, and other classificatory matrilateral relatives are indebted to, and continually helping ego. As a result of patrilaterality and an ideal rule of patrilocal residence following marriage, authority in this system is weighted in favor of paternal kin. *Mehekitanga*, an extension of the father's family's authority, commands respect, formality and distance, while *fa'e tangata* and his family represent unconditional, voluntary warmth, nurturing and sharing (see Rogers 1977 for a full account of the traditional powers of the *mehekitanga*).

Ideally, people want to live equally close to relatives on both sides, balancing formal and informal relations and the flow of resources. This occurs only in relatively rare situations when a husband and wife were born in the same village or general area, however. In a culture where commoners regard even the most remote genealogical connection between lovers as incest, young men and women often must go outside their village to find marriageable partners. Patrilocal residence is the norm (though exceptions are widespread), and wives who live in their husband's villages are removed from their natal families on a day-to-day basis. When a woman moves to her husband's village, her children come under the control of their father's family, overriding her rank.

Tongan men and women nurture ties to their natal *ka͞inga*s. They do this in a variety of ways: by borrowing and lending money, labor and other resources, by adopting children of relatives, and by offering their own children for adoption. Tongans travel considerable distances to visit relatives and to participate in the various events that mobilize groups of people, such as weddings, funerals, sporting competitions, church events, school graduations and fund-raisers. In this way, relations of *maheni*, "warm familiarity," have an opportunity to develop between geographically distant kin.

Women can preserve consciousness of their descent by keeping their own family names among the various names they go by, thereby publicly marking that particular side or "part" (*konga*). The identification of place (village and island) with *fa͞mili*, *ka͞inga* and *ha'a* (a traditional system of overarching lineages, the significance of which is still recognized in many villages) is often the idiom through which kinship identity and relations are expressed. People are quick to say who comes from where. The answer to the question: *"Ko hai 'oku ne mali ai?"* "To whom is she married?" may be, *"Oku ne mali ki Tu'anuku"* (literally, "She is married to [the village of] Tu'anuku"). This answer is also appropriate for a man who, for economic, personal, and political reasons settles in the village of his wife.

Life-crisis events require the presence of representatives from both maternal and paternal sides to fulfill special ceremonial statuses and roles. Rituals activate the competition between families for the stronger identification of a person with one side over another. They bring together people from near and far and excite strong feelings of jealousy and displays of corporate solidarity. The politics of marriage—which side contributes what to a wedding and to a new household, how ceremonial presentations and exchanges between families are handled, who the couple will live with, and which side will garner the greatest commitment of the couple's resources—causes gossip and tension. Funerals continue this competition beyond the death of the individual. Questions pertaining to the village in which the deceased is buried, and who contributes or fails to contribute to a funeral, highlight the status and degree of corporate solidarity of kindreds that coalesce in these situations from less well-defined *ka‾inga* networks.

'ITA AND 'OFA: ANGER AND LOVE/EMPATHY

An *'a‾vanga* victim typically expresses a great deal of affect, but not randomly. *'A‾vanga* is a patterned emotional and cathartic experience, drawing upon a culturally legitimated wellspring of appropriate feelings—most saliently *'ita,* "anger," and *'ofa,* "love/empathy." These signifiers occur frequently in narratives of possession, both in my own material and in cases presented by other scholars in this area (Parsons 1984 calls attention to these stereotypic signifiers by bold-facing recurring emotional terminology in her narratives).

What follows is a brief discussion of the culturally constructed relationship between *'ita* and *'ofa,* and in particular, the articulation of these emotions with socialization and familial relations. In addition to their significance as emotions shaped by socialization, *'ita* and *'ofa* are also cultural ideologies that mediate social and political relationships. When they are invoked within the interpretive frame of an *'a‾vanga* attack, in the context of accounts that Tongans offer to make sense of the motives of spirits and the feelings of victims, the narrative can acquire strong explanatory power.

It has been widely noted that in Polynesia, anger (*'ita*) is a problematic and difficult emotion, ideally avoided (i.e., Shore 1982; Mageo 1989a; also see White and Kirkpatrick 1985). In Tonga, spontaneous, reactive anger indicates loss of control, and shame (*ma‾*) ordinarily follows. *'Ita* is semantically linked with the *loto,* the seat of drives, appetites and the unknowable essence of a person. The outward show of *loto'ita,* "the state of anger," is generally suppressed in favor of an exterior demeanor, or *anga,* whose ideal form is placid, humorous and pleasant (typically *angalelei,* "nice") (see also Mageo 1989a, 1991a for Samoa).

On the other hand, there *is* cultural license, even an imperative, to express anger. Controlled anger and punishment are the prerogatives of situationally higher-ranked people. From childhood on, Tongans experience the effects of others' *'ita* as natural concommitants to low status. Punishment (*tautea*) of children in the form of *ta‾'i,* "beating," is a common style of discipline in the home, in school and in other settings where children are subjected to authority. In addition to serious disciplinary measures, threats of "Do that or I'll hit you, slap your ear, etc." are routinely uttered in a nonthreatening tone of voice, and children exhibit little fear at hearing these statements so prosaically expressed in the course of the day.

Tongan informants say they physically discipline their children for two reasons. First, the parent does it to prevent behavior that in the future will embarrass their children outside the household. Second, parents (especially mothers) are concerned about acquiring a bad reputation for not properly training their children in normative behavior and attitudes. The unchecked consequences of disobedience reflect badly on the entire family and will affect a child's future options (see also Gerber 1985 on the relationship of anger to punishment in the Samoan context). A Tongan-American woman who works as a guidance counselor in northern California told me her views on parental discipline and the dilemma inherent in her work, saying, "We believe that if our children grow up too *faikehe* [different; distinctive], they won't fit in. We have different ideas about discipline. So it's a big problem when *palangi*s [whites] come in and try to impose their ideas about child abuse on the Polynesian community. I don't personally hit my kids, but it's hard for me to tell other people to stop doing it. That's the way they show their love for their children."

'Ofa, "love/empathy," is ideologically complex, with multiple referents; it overlaps only partially with the American referent of "love" (Niko Besnier, personal communication). Like its cognates throughout the Pacific, the Tongan concept of *'ofa* constitutes the core moral value that binds together other core values, such as *faka'apa'apa*, "respect," and *fuakavenga/faifatongia*, "fulfilling obligation." In addition to its emotional referents, it is also contextually invoked as an economic ideology underlying the moral economy of reciprocity and resource sharing. *'Ofa* is commonly equated with gifts, hospitality and service; on ceremonial occasions, guests end by saying, "Thank you for your love." Hosts will likewise thank contributing kin for their love. The term *fe'ofo'ofani*, "loving one another," frequently mentioned in religious and political discourse, designates the ideal state of community. Tongan parents might remark that a son or daughter who supports them with remittances from abroad "has much *'ofa* for us." Someone who is stingy, selfish and unwilling to reciprocate properly is *ta'e'ofa*, literally "without love."

People who find themselves in pitiable states and situations, without emotional or material support, are *faka'ofa*, "a state that instigates a causation of *'ofa*; someone who moves others to love/pity." I found that *faka'ofa* was frequently used to refer to different aspects of the *'a¯vanga* victim's experience and its effect on others. She is *faka'ofa* if caught in an untenable domestic situation, or if she has been longing for a lost loved one, or if she has been spurned in love. The spirit can be *faka'ofa* too, lonely and trapped in death. A family suffering along with a victim is *faka'ofa*. A public *'a¯vanga* attack can precipitate a flood of emotions in people because it causes them to remember, and to identify with, the intimate relationship the victim enjoyed with a close relative before death.

In the discourse of family relations, *'ofa* and *'ita* are linked. When a parent angrily beats a child in order to protect him or her from impulses that will ultimately result in ostracism, the action gains the larger dimension of a gift that symbolizes the bond between parent and child. The expectation is that this gift will be reciprocated later in the child's adult life when he or she takes responsibility for caring for aging parents. In the most extreme cases of *'a¯vanga* involving parental spirits, the victim may repay the *te'ia*, "[angry/loving] blow," with her or his own life. If the victim dies in the grips of *'a̅vanga*, from a heart attack or lingering illness, then the dead have succeeded in repairing their painful separation from the living. If love and anger are a unified phenomenon within both the familial and *'a̅vanga* contexts, then it makes sense that Tongans explain the violent actions of a spirit parent as loving.

POSSESSION NARRATIVES AND THEIR INTERPRETATION

The remainder of this chapter will be devoted to an analysis of three possession narratives. The first was told to me from memory by a twenty-two-year-old woman, whom I'll call Sisifa, as we rested in the cookhouse during her sister's funeral, exhausted from lack of sleep and days of preparation. The circumstances of her sister's death, and events of the funeral caused her to remember her own brush with the spirit world. Another victim's father told me the second narrative; his six-year-old son became possessed when he visited his grandparents' village for the first time. The third *'a̅vanga* victim told me her story and in doing so involved me in her circle of supporters.

Sisifa

When she was thirteen years old, Sisifa visited Tofoa, her mother's natal village for the first time. She stayed with her *fa'e tangata,* "maternal uncle," who still lives there. She didn't know (*'ilo*) the place, and its inhabitants didn't yet know her. Sisifa went to the *fa'itoka,* "cemetery," with some of her maternal cousins to *vakai pe̅ pe ko hai 'oku 'i ai,* "just take a look at who was [buried] there." A boy told her to take her *sei,* "flower," out of her hair as a sign of respect in the *fa'itoka,* but she didn't heed the warning. Sisifa was punched in the head, and her *sei* was ripped out by a force she couldn't see; everyone who was with her witnessed the actions of the *te̅volo.* She felt and acted very strange (*faikehe*). She told me, "I didn't know a thing. I was almost crazy." Her cousins took her in this state to the house of a practitioner, where she again felt the *te̅volo* pull her hair and push her around. This time she saw the *te̅volo,* and it was definitely a person, though she couldn't identify it. The practitioner crushed leaves and rubbed them on her. The *te̅volo* "hated the smell" and left. The practitioner offered no explanation, but relatives who surrounded her during the treatment suggested the *te̅volo* was a relative of her mother's who no longer knew her.

The theme of maternal kin striking long-lost relatives in their natal village—usually in the *fa'itoka*—is a stereotypic element in *'a̅vanga* narratives. The competition and pull of such kin as they are felt across generations is a pervasive element of Tongan social consciousness. People are chastised for not "knowing" place or family if they fall out of kinship networks and don't make the effort to establish *maheni,* "warm familiarity." The mutual aid networks formed by extended kindreds called *ka̅inga* grow or contract depending on such visits.

Cemeteries are critical social domains in Tonga because they provide a definitive snapshot of an individual's incorporation into one *ka̅inga* over another, and the ultimate identification of *ka̅inga* with *feituʻu*, or place. Incorporation is particularly problematic for women, who ideally move to their husbands' villages, but who seemingly subvert the loyalty to their in-laws and their kindreds by maintaining strong, loving ties with their natal families and villages. These strong natal ties are complementary to the obligatory relations a woman has with her husband's kin. They provide her children with the maternal kindred who will be obligated to *them*. Maternal ties serve overall to maintain and diversify resource networks, and to preserve kindreds that extend status links to high-ranking relatives.

If Sisifa had died of her *ʻa̅vanga* episode in Tofoa (despite the fact that her burial would almost certainly have been in her father's village), the wish of her maternal ancestors and living relatives for reincorporation would have been fulfilled at that moment. The interpretation offered by Sisifa's maternal cousins of the *te̅volo*'s actions is a commentary on the need for recruiting her into their *ka̅inga* network. I found Tongans to be acutely aware of the desirability, not to mention the pleasure, of forming strong, new kin ties that they can call upon for various favors. New ties also give them an opportunity to visit new places and to present a united front in key situations.

Following this incident, Sisifa said she visited Tofoa more often and became close to her maternal cousins. Subsequent visits to the cemetery afforded her no trouble. When Sisifa's sister died in 1983 (the forementioned girl who had nursed her father and was struck dead by his spirit), a number of her maternal relatives—even distant relations whom she had not met—came to the funeral in their role as *liongi*, metaphorical commoners in relation to the more chiefly deceased, who was their classificatory father's sister's daughter. Above and beyond their obligatory presence at this funeral, I observed that they were extraordinarily supportive of Sisifa. When she dramatically threw herself onto her sister's coffin, one of these cousins helped to pull her off and attempted to provide comfort by feeding her. The events and relationships set into motion by Sisifa's possession episode nine years earlier had come full circle.

Corey

The next possession narrative was told to me by the father of the victim, a six-year-old boy named Corey. Sione is a young Tongan man, married to a *palangi*, "Westerner." They are Mormons, and Sione has a prestigious managerial position with the Mormon Church in Tonga. They live in the exclusive Liahona compound which was built by the church for its employees, many of whom have intermarried with Americans and New Zealanders. Sione's family enjoys the acculturated lifestyle of overseas Mormons, with a material standard of living comparable to that of middle-class Mormons living in the United States (see Gordon 1990).

Sione's parents died when he was a child, and he was raised in a village not far from Liahona by his older sister, who had ten children of her own. They were devout Wesleyans, and Sione's conversion to Mormonism as a teenager and his education and resulting career in the Mormon Church constituted a major break from his family and culture. He has very little interest in maintaining his Tongan identity or in maintaining relations with his kin, finding instead that his nuclear family and the Mormon Church community provide for all his needs. When his wife returned to the United States to have their second child, Sione took their son, Corey, to the natal village of both his parents for a rare visit. There, unseen forces "bit" Corey, leaving bruises and sores all over his legs, and slapped him around. He screamed for the *tevolo* to leave him alone. Sione insisted that many others witnessed this. The practitioner who treated Corey told Sione that the *tevolo* were the ghosts of Sione's parents and other relatives who didn't "know" him, and found his "half-caste complexion" very "strange." She said it was the spirits' way of "welcoming Corey to his place." Sione accepted this explanation.

The spectacle of Corey's *'avanga* was readily understood by Sione and his attending relatives as renewing ties with parts of family that had fallen out of his *kainga* network. Beyond that, the episode generated a moral discourse that called attention to the loss of Tongan identity and abdication of family loyalty. Corey and his mother speak no Tongan, and thus had no meaningful relationship with any of Sione's family. Corey had maintained close ties only with his mother's family. The vigorous agreement of Sione's relatives who attended the healing was an expression of corporate solidarity, with the different but overlapping *kainga* networks of both his parents' sides strategically concurring.

Nevertheless, Sione remains committed to raising his children within the most assimilated portion of the Tongan Mormon community. Corey's encounter with the spirits did not alter his path.

Sina

Sina met us at the San Francisco airport when my husband and I returned from Tonga in 1984. Since she was my husband's first cousin, we grew quite close and saw and helped each other frequently. Sina was an unmarried woman of twenty-four who had lived in the San Francisco Bay Area with her paternal aunt, or *mehekitanga*, for five years. Her mother had died in Tonga several years before, leaving Sina heartsick and distraught. Mother's Day and her mother's birthday were the most difficult days for her, she told me. Her father lived in Tonga with his second wife, who doesn't get along with Sina. Sina was very unhappy living with her aunt, who had earned a reputation as a gossip and an aggressive status-seeker. The aunt placed many onerous responsibilities on Sina, including paying the entire household's monthly $500 phone bill to Tonga. Because of her aunt's rank, Sina was powerless to directly refuse any requests. Sina threatened to move out—a common strategy among disaffected Tongans who move more or less easily among different households. She didn't, however, because she was loathe to become the subject of gossip by other Tongan-Americans in her neighborhood. She was also afraid of reprisals by her aunt, whom she thought capable of reporting Sina's lapsed visa to the immigration authorities.

One day Sina called to tell me that the spirit of her dead mother had appeared to her on two consecutive nights as she lay in bed. Her mother wore a scowl on her face, and by this Sina understood that her mother was somehow very angry at her. The second time her mother appeared, she stood on Sina's leg and caused her knee to swell up painfully. On account of this *te'ia*, Sina missed two days of work and wore an Ace bandage for two weeks. She was treated by a *fefine faito'o* in San Bruno who maintained a pharmacology of medicinal plants from Hawai'i. Not knowing Sina, the practitioner did not speak to her much either during or after the treatment, but heard and accepted her story. Sina subsequently presented the case to various Tongan relatives and friends, but without voicing her speculations on the motives of her mother's action. In a conversation with a sympathetic cousin—my husband—she asked, "I wonder why my mother was so angry with me?" He replied, "It was because your household treats you so badly."

Why would the spirit of Sina's mother seek to hurt *her* if she was having a rough time with her aunt's family? Sina told me that while her mother was still alive, she was not happy to see Sina living with her father's relatives, especially because this particular *mehekitanga* was known to abuse her authority. Before she died, her mother had expressed the wish for Sina to live, not with her *mehekitanga* in America, but with Sina's older sister in New Zealand—the least onerous situation. Sina's mother was clearly attempting to countermand the desire of her husband's sister to control her daughter's welfare and resources. As is often the case in struggles for control played out between between in-laws—who are unequally ranked but constrained from confrontation by *faka'apa'apa*, "respect for status"—Sina's mother had to preserve the illusion of good relations, or *va⁻ lelei*. This tightrope act is expressed proverbially as *vaha'a ngatae*, "between two *ngatae* trees." Her cousin's remark, implying that the spirit mother's motive was to get back at the aunt for mistreating Sina, is consistent with the practice of making confrontational statements while pre-serving *vaha'a ngatae*: a parent will conspicuously beat the child who is the focal point of the conflict regardless of her or his role in causing it. When played out properly, the *tautea*, "punishment," scenario publicizes the grievance and jogs a sense of guilt in the offending household. The expectation is that fear of gos-sip will cause them to modify their behavior and even to make amends.

An *'a⁻vanga* episode can be a powerful tool toward ameliorating those con-ditions if the dissemination of information is managed correctly. The efficacy of Sina's strategy depended on implicit, interpretive collaboration with sympa-thetic maternal relatives who were already aware of her plight, such as my hus-band, who interpreted her oblique question as a plea for help as well as clarification. Several of her maternal relatives invited Sina to move in with them, and five months after her *te'ia*, Sina accepted an offer. Since we could not accommodate her in our graduate student apartment, my husband and I were relieved that Sina had found a comfortable solution.

CONCLUSION

'Āvanga was central to the politico-religious order in pre-Christian Tonga. The priestly possessed body is no more, yet *'aʿvanga* persists wherever there are Tongans, reconfigured of many of the same cultural themes.

Tongan educator Futa Helu used a positivistic framework in analyzing *'aʿvanga*, labeling it a "temporary psychosis" produced by the conflict between sexual desires and the extreme social constraints on Western Polynesian women and men (1985). The cases he presents involve young female virgins with thwarted love interests, and their possessions occurred in liminal spaces of bush and beach. The individuals I describe here were stricken in the thick of social relations and controls—inside houses and in a cemetery surrounded by people. Sina's encounter with her dead mother happened in her shared bedroom in California, and neither Sina nor Sisifa reported a love interest in their possession narratives. Corey is a little boy who is not culturally Tongan. *'Āvanga*, moreover, is much more than a mechanistic response or social strategy to ameliorate blocked desires. As a public discourse that implicates social structure, gender, emotion, and personhood, *'aʿvanga* serves to articulate individual consciousness with social consciousness, and the individual body with the historical "bodily hexis." *'Āvanga's* potent marginality provides a tool for social critique on a potentially wide scale, and in doing so, stimulates discourse on culture itself. In communities outside of Tonga, possession episodes have the effect of reproducing culture and identity, albeit through the idiom of conflict. Seemingly subversive and anti-cultural in its manifestations, *'aʿvanga* is nonetheless of a piece with the conflictual and shifting practices of the Tongan habitus, and with Tongans' enduring historical experience of social life.

NOTES

Acknowledgments. Fieldwork in the Kingdom of Tonga from 1982 to 1984 and subsequent work in the California Tongan community was funded by a Regents' Traveling Fellowship from the University of California, Berkeley, and Lowie Scholarships from the Department of Anthropology, U-C Berkeley. I wish to thank Niko Besnier, Scott Christianson, Futa Helu, David Hess, Alan Howard, Jeannette Mageo, Barbara McGrath, Charlie Stevens and Heather Young-Leslie for their comments on this and earlier drafts. I am indebted to my Tongan consultants for their insights and hospitality, and especially to Tevita Toli Halaʿapiʿapi for our fruitful discussions of this material.

1   The term *'aʿvanga*, denoting a state of possession, is absent from Mariner's 1817 glossary. Churchward's dictionary, compiled in 1959, provides two, linked definitions: possession by spirits (the root word being *'avea*, or "carried away"), and a state of intense longing for a particular lover (p. 555). Futa Helu and Tavi

assured me of its antiquity. Modern Tongans invariably use the term *puke fakatevolo*, "spirit sickness." *Tevolo*, "devil," obviously originated with mission Christianity.

2   Gifford (1929) tells us that priests were known as *fa'ahikehe*, "different side" or "different kind," and were generally feared, though Mariner describes them as taciturn men leading ordinary lives. Priests appear in Mariner's glossary as "*fahegehe*." In modern Tonga, *fa'ahikehe* can refer metonymically to the state of possession and also denotes spirits as a class.

3   It appears that in modern times, women are possessed far more frequently than men; there are also more women healers. Why the profound shift to women? *'Avanga* is no longer implicated in macropolitical intrigues, leaving it perhaps doubly marginal and doubly liminal: a female domain characterized by *noa*, or absence of order. Another clue could lie in the emotional ethos surrounding *'avanga*. Both men and women express a controlled version of grief in a variety of ceremonial contexts. However, Tongans of both sexes claim that women are considered emotionally weaker and more volatile than men. In addition to certain qualities for which Tongan women are culturally marked—sexual control, ceremonial respect and beautification (see Ortner 1981)—they have historically carried the responsibility of expressing *uncontrolled* grief. The paradox of the forementioned constraints connected with ceremonially high status, and the imperative to loudly mourn perhaps combine to make women psychologically susceptible to possession states in death contexts. I find Cowling's suggestion persuasive (though not exhaustive) that adverse effects of modernity fall heavily on Tongan women—with ever-diminishing status, modern patriarchy, and the familial stresses caused by out-migration and mobility—rendering them more vulnerable than ever to "culture-reactive" disorders (Cowling 1987; see also Gailey 1987). This problem surely needs to be explored.

4   Our conversation about the death boat, which was pointedly *not* going to heaven, did not index Christianity in this context. However, I heard the *vaka* mentioned in two Church of Tonga sermons in euphemistic reference to death. There is clearly a heteroglossic discourse of death in Tonga, one which warrants more research.

5   Hierarchy is *the* hegemonic principle in Tongan kinship, superceding other symbolic distinctions and relations (see James 1987). Like all hegemonies, however, hierarchy simultaneously invites resistance (how radically resistant is another question) in many forms, such as *'avanga*, which can markedly remind people of the conflicts and contradictions created by hierarchical structures, and in some cases redress such asymmetries.

4 Heteroglossic Discourses on Nukulaelae Spirits

Niko Besnier

Nukulaelae is a very small atoll (449 acres) in the southern region of a chain of nine islands called Tuvalu, today a nation-state of 9,000 inhabitants on the boundary of Polynesia and Micronesia. Nukulaelae islanders speak a dialect of Tuvaluan, a Polynesian language, and make a subsistence living, mostly in swamp-taro cultivation, reef and ocean fishing, pig husbandry, and coconut-sap tapping. The local economy has long been partially monetized, although the importance of money has increased dramatically in the last two decades. In the absence of local cash-generating resources, islanders seek employment elsewhere: in the government bureaucracy in the national capital, Funafuti; on phosphate-rich Nauru Island in Micronesia; and on merchant ships owned by Hong Kong and German companies who find in Tuvalu a source of very cheap nonunion labor. Even though the atoll is visited by a ship only about ten times a year, Nukulaelae islanders travel widely. The most popular destination is Funafuti, where the largest expatriate Nukulaelae community resides. Almost all Nukulaelae islanders adhere to a nominally Congregationalist brand of Christianity, initially introduced by a London Missionary Society teacher from Samoa in the 1860s. A chiefly system is in place in which the chief presides over a Council of Elders, but these institutions are alleged to be recent reconstructions of an ancient political system and coexist, often uneasily, with a fierce spirit of egalitarianism (Besnier In Press).

Nukulaelae was first sighted by Westerners in 1821, but significant contacts were rare until the latter part of the eighteenth century. Very little is known about Nukulaelae society before that time. Traumatic transformations between the

1860s and 1890s account for much of this dearth of knowledge. Peruvian slave traders raided the atoll in 1863 and made off with 70 to 80 percent of the population (see Besnier In Press). All victims of the raid perished abroad within a few years, taking with them most of Nukulaelae's historical memory.

Nukulaelae's precontact cosmology and religious practices are especially obscure. What can be gleaned on the subjects from journals of missionaries (who rarely visited the islands for more than a few hours a year and can hardly be considered unbiased observers) suggests that Nukulaelae people may have practiced an ancestor cult involving the skulls of forebears. Supernatural beings apparently were manifested in events like lightning and shooting stars and were iconicized in the shape of unworked stones. Spirit mediums, called *vaka atua* (literally, "vessel of god[s]," sometimes referred to as *taulaaitu,* a post-missionization borrowing from Samoan), are said to have functioned as religious practitioners, engaging in prescience, divination, and communication with the spirits of dead individuals, probably paralleling the patterns found in pagan and early Christian Tikopia (Firth 1967, 1970).

Cultural categories such as spirits frequently present complex analytic problems for anthropological description. In most cultural contexts, spirits are liminal entities, whose ambiguous social status poses problems for cultural accounts of self and personhood. In many Pacific societies, spirits dwell in the outer regions of culture, making them particularly inaccessible to the inquisitive probing of outsiders. Not only are they encountered in geographical and temporal margins, such as the bush, the beach, and nighttime, but they are linked with areas of social life that are least controlled and systematized. When anthropologists finally get a grip on the spirit world of their hosts, they often find that their informants talk about spirits only with embarrassment and reluctance, and lack a collective cover story on the topic.

In short, the world of spirits and the cultural processes with which it is associated (e.g., mediumship, possession, sorcery) are fraught with ambiguity, contradiction, and shiftiness of a kind for which traditional models of cultural anthropology, with their emphasis on structure and coherence, are ill-prepared. Based on this case study in a Polynesian atoll society, I demonstrate that spirits and their world cannot be understood through a search for a *resolution* of such ambiguities and contradictions; rather, these qualities must be perceived as constitutive of the very nature of spirits.

The 350 inhabitants of Nukulaelae take great interest in spirits. Few performances captivate the attention of Nukulaelae audiences more than the dramatic, suspense-ridden account of an encounter with a strange creature in the bush in the dead of night. No rumor can damage a person's reputation as effectively as an allegation of conniving with spirits through sorcery. In appropriate contexts, episodes of spirit mediumship and possession are discussed with great gusto. Yet, while they are talked about a great deal, spirits manifest themselves only rarely to Nukulaelae islanders. Much of what people on the atoll know about spirits comes from narratives of encounters that take place in foreign lands. The spirit world is underdetermined in Nukulaelae *experience*, insofar as Nukulaelae people interact with the world of spirits only under very special circumstances. At the same time, the world of spirits is overdetermined in Nukulaelae *discourse*, where spirits play an important role in everyday talk, in cultural models, in many social processes, and, most generally, in the institutionalization of the notion of truth on the atoll. In this chapter, I describe and attempt to explain the disjunction between the experiential underdetermination and the discursive elaboration of Nukulaelae spirits. I argue that both the lack of firsthand experience with spirits and the fluorescence of discourse about spirits are symptomatic and definitional of the nature of Nukulaelae spirits.

My argument rests principally on an examination of how Nukulaelae people talk about spirits, and on a search for what verbal representations say about local models of their nature: what they are made of, what they do, how they manifest themselves, and how their presence and actions articulate with other symbolic categories and social processes. This choice of focus is in large part determined by what Nukulaelae has to offer; indeed, there is very little to know about Nukulaelae spirits independently of what Nukulaelae discourse can reveal. In such a situation, representation is largely coterminous with the object of scrutiny. I am less concerned here with actual social practices surrounding the presence and actions of spirits than with how these are represented in narratives. In particular I draw attention to details foregrounded in spirit discourse recurrently and across contexts.

One does not find on Nukulaelae a well-articulated, institutionalized set of beliefs and expectations on the nature and role of spirits like that described for many cultures of Melanesia (e.g., Knauft 1985b) and Africa (e.g., Lambek 1981), among others. Rather, Nukulaelae discourse about spirits and the processes and contexts with which they are associated are *heteroglossic*, namely, consisting of a multiplicity of competing and sometimes mutually incompatible voices. Heteroglossia manifests itself in various ways. The qualities that discourse attributes to spirit actions are themselves heteroglossic; for example, spirits usually speak foreign languages, and their manifestations in settings like mediumship sessions feature several voices (e.g., the medium's and the spirit's voices) competing for the floor. In addition, Nukulaelae talk about spirits is framed so as to allow speakers to weave subtly in and out of "believing." Thus heteroglossia operates on several levels at once. I argue that heteroglossia is particularly important in understanding the social roles that spirits play in the community, and further, that the heteroglossic nature of Nukulaelae spirits requires a theoretical approach that recognizes culture as a battleground between conflicting voices.

CATEGORIES OF SPIRITS

The generic term for "spirit" in the Nukulaelae dialect of Tuvaluan is *agaaga*.[1] The same term is also used to refer to the soul of a living or dead person, in a

Christian sense. Nukulaelae people are wont to elaborate on the relationship between spirits that are said to roam the bush and the souls of dead persons, and they do see the two as associated with different epistemologies. From early childhood, they are told in no uncertain terms that there is no room for the former type of spirits in the dominant Christian epistemology of the atoll community. The Christian religion has the potential to cancel the effectiveness and relevance of spirits (although not necessarily their existence, as will be discussed below).

The relevance of spirits to the lives of Nukulaelae islanders is not a simple question. The most simplistic form that this question can take is whether Nukulaelae people believe in spirits, ignoring for the moment the complexities that the notion of "belief" entails (see Howard, chapter 6). "Belief" translates roughly as *talitonu*, a borrowing from Samoan with strong Christian connotations, like other borrowings from Samoan.[2] A belief system (e.g., a set of religious doctrines and, by extension, a religion) is referred to as a *talitonuga*, the nominalized form of *talitonu*. The word is conspicuous in metatalk about spirits, as the following typical excerpt from an ethnographic interview illustrates:[3]

> A te tokoukega i te fenua teenei, toko uke eeloo e talittonu eeloo paa ki agaaga, me e isi eeloo ne agaaga. Kae isi ne tino, see fakatalitonu nee laatou, paa, me e isi ne agaaga.
>
> [L&S 1991:2:A:024-028]

The majority [of people] on this atoll, many people very much *believe* in spirits, [believe] that there are indeed such things as spirits. But there are people who don't *believe*, like, that there are such things as spirits.

Thus one is not dealing with a consensual belief system, but rather with a model whose validity is open to disagreements and conflicting interpretations in the community. Indeed, the above quote is both an indication of lack of consensus and an example of how talk about spirits is permeated by conflictual oppositions of various types. In this particular example, the implied opposition between "they" and "we" is striking, although conflicts in spirit discourse are not limited to disagreements between various members of the community over whether or not spirits exist; rather, they pervade many levels of Nukulaelae spirit discourse.

When the existence and relevance of spirits are recognized to have some validity, a loose distinction is made between more "permanent" spirits and those associated with a recently dead person, which may or may not be a manifestation of the dead person's Christian soul. Unlike the spirits of dead people, more permanent spirits may have names of their own and are often referred to generically as *Te Lasi*, literally, "The Big One," or *Saumaiafi* (sometimes *Saumaiafe*), a Tuvaluanized form of its Samoan name, *Sauma'iafe*. Permanent spirits manifest themselves periodically over much longer periods of time and are suspected to have much more power and more malevolent intentions than the second category of spirits. They are also much more mobile and volitional than spirits of the second type, and may manifest themselves under many different guises, whereas spirits of the dead typically have the same physiognomy as the dead person with whom they are connected. Spirits associated with the dead typically manifest themselves *right after* death around the fresh grave or at places frequented by the person while alive.

In contrast, permanent spirits frequently appear *prior* to a death. Nukulaelae people interpret the sudden appearance of a spirit as a warning that someone is about to find him- or herself in a life-threatening situation. Yet the spirit and the human victim are often not connected. This behavioral difference reflects an implicit distinction between permanent and circumstantial categories of spirits, albeit one not reflected in Nukulaelae terminology, and neither strongly elaborated nor consistently clear in discourse.

Spirits may manifest themselves as tangible entities, or in dreams, although the latter experiences are received with more skepticism than sightings of "real" spirits. Spirits also may manifest themselves through unexplainable events, such as loud noises, shuffling in the vegetation, or unusual and localized weather patterns such as dark whirlwinds. Spirit presences are associated with a feeling of intense fear (*mataku*); as I illustrate below, spirits have a stake in inducing fear in humans. As tangible entities, spirits can take a variety of forms. Descriptions of the physical appearance of spirits commonly are replete with superlatives (e.g., *maattugaa* "enormous," *kkii* "very," *silia* "to surpass"); spirits are frequently enormous, or, less often, minuscule (*tamaa* "tiny"):

> Maattugaa *tino, e lasi* kkii, *kae* silia *mo te faamalama.*
>
> [L 1991:1:A:231–232]
>
> An *enormous* person, it was *very* big, *surpassing* [in height] the window [through which I saw it].

> Naa laa, i a- au e puke atu paa ki ei, [. . .] ana tamaa vae ne tamaa mea! E paakkaa fua! Teenaa, kaa poi ei au, kae fai au me se mea- paa me se mea fakaaattea.
>
> [L 1991:1:A:179–181]
>
> Then I- I grabbed it like this, [. . .] his *tiny* legs were just *tiny* things! So thin! And I was about to get startled, thinking that it was something- like something out of the ordinary.

The complexion of spirits is often extremely dark (hence ugly and scary) or, less commonly, noticeably pale. Spirits are usually adults, often frighteningly old, and more likely to be women than men. They sometimes also manifest themselves as babies, as land animals (pigs, dogs, and cats, which just about exhausts all Nukulaelae faunal possibilities), or as one of the more ferocious creatures of the sea (e.g., large sharks and moray eels). They have an uncanny ability to change appearance quickly, sometimes during the same apparition. Recurrent themes in spirit narratives are the invisibility of parts of the spirit's body, and witnesses' difficulties in making out the spirit's features. For example, in several narratives, spirits face away from human witnesses, even when they are talking to them.

Spirits are powerful; they can kill people, usually by strangling, smothering, suffocating, or "eating" them. They often appear as attractive women to young men, whom they seduce and ultimately smother in an isolated place (e.g., on a fishing canoe at sea). Spirits are also capable of human feelings. They are often angry (*kaitaua*) and prone to being offended and retaliating (compare Gordon, chapter 4). They get particularly angry when they perceive that someone is not afraid (*mataku*) of their authority. However, spirits are also capable of feeling *alofa*, "empathy," toward humans, and this emotion sometimes restrains their destructiveness.

It is difficult to talk about spirits on Nukulaelae without bringing up the topic of sorcery. What I call sorcery here is a complex category termed *vai laakau*, literally, "liquid [or water or juice] of vegetable substance."[4] This term straddles several related areas of meaning on Nukulaelae, as on neighboring Nanumea (Chambers and Chambers 1985). In its least morally marked sense, *vai laakau* refers to Western medicines like aspirin and antibiotics. It may refer to local pharmacopoeia and practices designed to improve the health of its recipients (e.g., oils for rubbing, infusions to be taken internally). In its most morally marked sense, *vai laakau* refers to substances, and practices using substances, that have the power to change the normal course of events so as to benefit the designs of the practitioner at the expense of the community at large (euphemistically, *taafao ki mea maassei*, literally, "to play with bad things"). These substances are usually liquid infusions of herbs, barks, and juices (and thus are commonly referred to with the euphemism *fagu*, "bottle") used for a whole panoply of purposes: killing enemies; increasing one's success in fishing and erotic pursuits, prescience and divination; and ensuring victory for soccer teams from one's home island in Tuvalu's national tournaments.[5] The boundary between morally marked and unmarked *vai laakau* is blurred: people suspect that individuals who know how to concoct morally unmarked *vai laakau* also know how to make the bad stuff. Furthermore, morally unmarked ends, e.g., the curing of a disease, can sometimes be arrived at through recourse to "bad" *vai laakau*; for example, arthritis, a common ailment on the atoll, can be cured with exorcism, magical potions, and secret formulas.

Spirits come into play in *vai laakau* in at least two major ways. First, spirits often talk about *vai laakau*. For example, spirits typically visit mediums to make bold accusations of *vai laakau*. Second, *vai laakau* cannot be potent without the intervention of spirits. In order to "play" with *vai laakau*, a sorcerer must first call (*kalaga*) a spirit, without whose power *vai laakau* is ineffectual. Conversely, in their most prescriptive moments, Nukulaelae islanders state that spirits only manifest themselves to owners of "bottles." However, the very same people who make such prescriptive statements also admit to spirit encounters, while denying categorically any involvement in *vai laakau*.

Spirits always demand a *taui*, "price, retribution, compensation" (a Samoan borrowing), for their assistance. Typically, this takes the form of a misfortune: childlessness, crippling disease, or a handicapped offspring. Certain misfortunes are associated with particular types of *vai laakau*; for example, one of the dangers of using *vai laakau* for erotic purposes is that it can unwittingly affect a close relative, thus leading one to commit incest, one of the worst transgressions in this society. Such compensations are most immediate when a person dabbles in *vai laakau* that does not belong to his or her family. (Like most knowledge, knowledge of *vai laakau* is the property of particular descent groups.)

Spirits manifest themselves in two other important contexts, namely spirit mediumship (*fakalleo*, literally, "to give [someone] a voice") and possession (*pukea* or *ulufia*, a Samoan borrowing).[6] Briefly, a spirit enters (*ulu*) the body and mind of the medium or possessed person and takes over its "normal" human functions, particularly its voice, leaving the medium or possessed person in a trancelike state. As Firth (1964:247–8, 1967:296) found in Tikopia, Nukulaelae islanders characterize possession as an essentially involuntary event, and hence a kind of sickness (*masaki*) that can be cured with *vai laakau*; in contrast, mediumship is a voluntarily induced state during which the spirit is called (*kalaga*) to enter the body of the medium. Yet agency in mediumship does not rest with the medium; the spirit's caller is always someone other than the medium, usually a relative of higher status than the medium (e.g., an older man), who hence has some degree of control over the medium's actions.[7] Crucially, the words and actions of mediums are intelligible and interpretable, while those of possessed persons are not; in mediumship, "the accent is on communication" (Firth 1964:248). While the two events are not always distinguishable—mediums are prone to possession—together they comprise the quintessential contexts in which spirits and humans interact and are the most compelling evidence of the existence and power of spirits.

Mediumship and possession activities are seen as antithetical to Christian teachings, and because Christianity is the overarching reference scheme for morality, communicating with spirits is regarded as profoundly immoral. Semiotic tokens of Christianity, such as the simple presence of a Bible, can exorcise spirits from mediums and possessed persons. Spirit-related altered states of consciousness on Nukulaelae thus are associated with radically different moral evaluations from those described for many African contexts. For example, here we have none of the playfulness, social legitimacy, and institutionalization that characterize spirit possession among Mayotte Comorans (Lambek 1981).

In contrast to other islands of Tuvalu, Nukulaelae itself has very few incidents of mediumship or possession; these events most commonly are witnessed off the atoll, giving them a foreign flavor.[8] Because of the strong negative sanctions associated with voluntary dabbling in spirit mediumship on Nukulaelae, possession is more frequent than mediumship. In the last two decades, mediumship or possession episodes were reported for only about a half-dozen people, including a man in his early twenties, a young child, an older woman, and a highly marginalized young woman who died in 1986. During my three-odd years of field work on the atoll, spread over more than a decade, I witnessed only one case of possession, which took place at a dance performance. The possessed person was the marginalized young woman to whom I refer above, who was at the time the only person in recent memory to have been subject to possession repeatedly and chronically; her episodes drew little attention, other than annoyance. Yet mediumship and possession episodes that take place on other islands, particularly the most accessible, the capital Funafuti, are discussed with enormous interest. Indeed, mediumship episodes that take place on Funafuti are made relevant to Nukulaelae life; while in temporary residence there, many Nukulaelae people attend mediumship sessions to elicit from spirits explanations of events on Nukulaelae. Thus suspicions of *vai laakau* activities are confirmed, new accusations arise, unexplained deaths are explained, and the future or secret deeds of particular Nukulaelae islanders are revealed. These accounts are quickly reported when witnesses return to the atoll, and can become the central focus of gossip and rumor for quite some time.

HETEROGLOSSIA IN SPIRIT DISCOURSE

Such was the case in 1990 and 1991, when a young Funafuti woman named Suunema, recently abandoned by her husband, embarked on a major series of mediumship episodes, from which most of my data on mediumship are drawn. Suunema's mediumship had a significant impact on Nukulaelae social relations, which became a major focus of my 1990 field work. The details are very involved, and a complete account is beyond the scope of this discussion. Suffice it to say that Suunema was the host of Saumaiafi (sometimes Saumaiafe), a powerful female spirit from Samoa who also appears in Samoan spirit discourse (see Mageo, chapter 2). According to Nukulaelae narrators, Saumaiafi, through the medium of Suunema, was able to tell who had killed whom, who had performed love magic on whom, and where lost keys and watches could be found. Nukulaelae narrators invariably talked about the last item as particularly powerful evidence that the medium was not faking her episodes.

A characteristic of Saumaiafi mediumship that Nukulaelae narratives consistently emphasize is the foreign quality of everything that concerns the spirit and her manifestations. This foreignness is highlighted in several ways. First, the mediumship sessions take place on a different atoll, among the bright lights and accompanying moral depravity of Funafuti. Saumaiafi claims to have gone to and been able to land at all atolls and islands of Tuvalu, with the exception of Nukulaelae:

A: *Ana pati a ia heki vau eiloa kkonei, te fenua nei, vvela, vvela! Ana pati,*
    "Taapaa! Te fenua teelaa, peelaa eiloa me he afi!" A ia kaa vau, a ia palele
    eiloa te lalolagi. Ana pati, "Au palele te lalolagi!" Vau ia ki Tuuvalu nei, kaa-
    mata mai ia i Soofaea, oko ki Nanumea, a ia e fano saale aka eiloa ki uta i
    fenua katoa, me e isi sena taugaasoa. Kae i Nukulaelae, heeai heana tau-
    gaasoa i ei. Teelaa laa, a ia kaa hanaka, hee ana mauaga (ia) ki uta i te- te
    vvela. Teelaa laa, taku fakattau kaati hee- heki tuu eiloa kkonei. Kae hee
    iloo, hee iloo atu laa maafai ne vau, kae hee iloa atu!

[Saumaiafi 1990:1:A:229–239]

A: She said that she has not been here, [because] this atoll is very, very hot! She
    said, "Wow! That atoll, it's just like a fire!" When she wanted to come, she
    had [already] been everywhere in the world. She said, "I've been everywhere
    in the world!" When she came to Tuvalu, she started with Sophia Island [i.e.,
    Niulakita], all the way up to Nanumea, on every other island she was able
    to land, because she had friends [on each island]. But on Nukulaelae, she
    had no friends. So when she [tried to] land, she couldn't stand the- the heat.
    So I think that she hasn't- hasn't been here. But who knows, who knows if
    she's been here, but nobody knows about it!

The convenient geographical distancing of the mediumship sessions and the
spirit herself places them well outside the tight moral control of tradition and
church on Nukulaelae, but of course does not prevent Nukulaelae people from
making full use of the medium's services while visiting Funafuti and from report-
ing in great detail what the spirit said upon their return home. In fact, the
extraterritorial locus of mediumship sessions legitimizes their use by Nukulaelae people: narratives of mediumship sessions can confirm, among other things,
the outlandishly immoral nature of life on Funafuti, where such "heathenish"
(*pouliuli*, literally, "dark"; a Samoan borrowing) practices as spirit mediumship
are allowed to take place.

Second, Saumaiafi, as mentioned above, is from Samoa. Nukulaelae people,
like all other Tuvaluans, are familiar with many features of Samoan culture,
including the Samoan language, which for many decades was the language of
church and government. But their acquaintance with Samoans themselves is generally secondhand, and many Samoan things stand out as highly marked in
Tuvaluan contexts, despite massive borrowings since missionization. So when
Suunema, the medium inhabited by Saumaiafi, begins her mediumship session
by performing a dance Samoan style, which Tuvaluans find particularly graceful,
this event becomes highly centralized in every narrative:

Paa eeloo me ne vau i Saamoa! Te poto i te saka!

[L 1991:1:A:277–278]

It's just as if she had [just] come from Samoa! That's how good her dancing was!

Third, Suunema-Saumaiafi never speaks in Tuvaluan during mediumship episodes. Although she sometimes employs other languages, her favorite language is

Samoan, and when she speaks Samoan, *Se tinaa Saamoa eeloo!*, "She's a quintessential Samoan!" (L 1991:1:A:353–354). For some, the fact that she speaks
Samoan as well as a handful of other languages is strong evidence that the mediumship episode is legitimate:

> *A ko ttalitonuga ki agaaga, e isi eeloo ne agaaga. Te mea e fakatalitonu foki nee
> au a tino fakalleo, taatou peenei mo Lina nei, nee?, e ana iloaga o faipati faka-
> Saamoa. Kaafai e faipati mai, e isi se llave. A ko ttino fakalleo, kaa faipati mai,
> see iloa nee koe, paa me se tino-. [...] A ttino teelaa fakalleo faka-Saamoa kaa
> faipati mai, se Saamoa eeloo. Teenaa ssuaa mea e fakatalitonu ei nee au a tino
> fakalleo, nee?*
>   [L&S 1991:2:B:311–320]

As far as believing in spirits, spirits do exist. The thing that makes me believe spirit mediums, is, like us here, like Lina [for instance], see?, she knows how to speak
Samoan. [But] when she speaks it, she stumbles. But the spirit medium, when she
speaks, you don't know [she is not a native speaker], she sounds just like a [for-
eign] person. The medium, when she speaks Samoan, she's a real Samoan. That's
another thing that makes me believe spirit mediums, see?

For others, the same evidence can be turned on its head: Saumaiafi's careful
choice of those languages in which Tuvaluans have some competence is a dead
giveaway:

> *A tino foki Nukulaelae ne maafua mai eiloo, me laatou e ppoto i te faitauuga o
> ttusi paia Saamoa, nee? Seei loo laa se kkese o te faipati mo te tusi paia, teelaa e
> iloa nee koe o faipati a pati Saamoa i loto, nee? Seei loo se kkese. Koe e iloa foki
> nee koe o faipati, e iloa nee koe, iaa koe e faitau oki i pati kolaa, ttusi paia ne pati
> Saamoa, seei ne pati-.*
>   [L&S 1991:2:A:138–144]

Nukulaelae people, from the very beginning, they knew how to read the Samoan
Bible, see? There is absolutely no difference between speaking and [reading] the
Bible, inside of which you know how to pronounce the Samoan words, see?
Absolutely no difference. You just know how to speak, you just know, because
you've read those words, the Bible is in Samoan, not in [some other language].

A comparable foreign flavor also permeates many other aspects of Nukulaelae
discourse about spirits, spirit-related altered states of consciousness, and *vai
laakau*. For example, a wide variety of people over the years consistently told
me that Nukulaelae islanders know little about *vai laakau*, compared to, say,
what is known about it on the northern islands of the group, particularly Nanumea and Niutao. What Nukulaelae people do know about *vai laakau* and the
role of spirits in it consists primarily of bits and pieces that they have gleaned
from Northern Tuvaluans. In Nukulaelae eyes, it is on those islands that knowledge of the world of spirits and their power is most elaborated, and where the
practice of *vai laakau* is given most prominence.

Nukulaelae people who return from extended visits to these islands are often suspected to have acquired competence in *vai laakau* or at least a *fagu*, "bottle [of potent concoction]." Knowledge of *vai laakau* can also trickle south to Nukulaelae through kinship or adoption ties with other islands of the group, particularly Niutao. These ties are not uncommon, as the 1863 raid by Peruvian slave traders made necessary a pattern of aggressive exogamy to ensure the survival of the atoll's population (Besnier In Press). Because most survivors of the Peruvian raid were women, many men from other islands of Tuvalu (and other parts of the Pacific) came to settle on Nukulaelae, bringing with them their various secret *logo*, "knowledge," which are still transmitted from generation to generation. The *logo* of contemporary Nukulaelae islanders are reputed to be mere fragments of what is known and practiced on other islands of Tuvalu, but their foreign origin is a significant aspect of their socio-cultural value for contemporary Nukulaelae.

The attribution of sorcery to outside sources is not peculiar to this situation; among many groups, positing sorcery as external to the community can reinforce a sense of internal cohesion and a belief in moral superiority over the outside world (Rivière 1970, Forge 1970). Both these explanations are probably valid for Nukulaelae. However, the foreign nature of Nukulaelae spirits, their associated categories and processes, is part of a broader picture in which spirits are embedded in a fundamentally heteroglossic conceptual domain. Heteroglossia, a term I am borrowing from Bakhtin (1981, 1986), refers to the proliferation of voices, a voice being the relationship between utterances and ideology. More often than not, voice proliferation is characterized by conflicts and contradictions between voices. To paraphrase Bakhtin loosely, a voice is never monologic, but is always embedded in a cacophony of other voices.

Heteroglossia manifests itself on many levels in Nukulaelae discourse about spirits. In the most orthodox sense, it characterizes the very definition of mediumship. Mediumship is a competition between the voice of a spirit and the voice of a medium, since the two have only one mouth to speak through. Also involved is the voice of the person in control of the session (the spirit's "caller"), the voices of audience members who interrogate the spirit, the voices of narrators who subsequently broadcast what the spirit said, and, potentially, the voices of individuals whom the spirit accuses of being sorcerers. In addition, spirits themselves take on multiple voices depending on what they have to say:

Niisi taimi, koo ffuli mai faka- o vau fakamaatua, nee?, peelaa mo ko te maatua. [. . .] (Kae) kaafai e faipati fakamaatua, tena leo e (t)tagi mai eiloa peelaa me he maatua, nee?, paa, faka-fafine-matua. Faipati fakatamaliki, peelaa i ttamaliki, ttinaa tamaliki!
[Saumaiafi 1990:2:A:114–126]

Sometimes, [Saumaiafi's voice] changes to that of- it comes out like that of a mother, see?, as if she were a mother. [. . .] When she speaks like a mother, her voice sounds just like a mother's, see?, like an aging woman. She [also] speaks like a child, like when children- she sounds like a real child!

Heteroglossia is thus a central aspect of the dramaturgic ventriloquism that takes place during mediumship. Finally, heteroglossia is manifested in the extraterritorial identity of spirits, their polyglot skills, and their apparition during mediumship sessions. Otherness involves heteroglossia by default, because voices from the outside are always potentially in opposition to native voices. Its most straightforward manifestation is the choice of a foreign language and code switching, a central concern in the case of Saumaiafi.

Heteroglossia is not just a characteristic of spirits and mediumship, but also a major component of discourse *about* spirits and associated categories and processes. Otherness plays a striking role in discourse about spirits, who are commonly represented as relevant only to the lives of "others" (see also Favret-Saada 1980 for comparable statements from rural Normandy). Several illustrations have already been presented here; for example, spirits are frequently said to appear only to owners of sorcery bottles. In other words, encounters with spirits only affect "others."

Spirit encounters are also incriminating events, in that they provide evidence that those involved are responsible for bringing about these events and, by the same token, harbor evil intentions. The contrast between self and other drawn in this discourse establishes a moral order in which the speaker emerges with a clear advantage over "others." In addition, the multiple and contradictory affective stances that Nukulaelae islanders take in spirit narratives are further manifestations of heteroglossia. A Nukulaelae narrator can relate a spirit story with much conviction, drama, and gusto (and audiences of spirit narratives generally display as much fascination for these stories as the narrators themselves) and, at the same time, frame these narratives with expressions of doubt, disbelief, and cynicism. For example, one of my respondents, after narrating story after story of encounters with spirits, concluded with the following remark:

> See iloa laa nee au, me see iloa laa nee au me e isi ne agaaga me ikkaai.
> [L 1991:1:A:258-259]

> [In answering my question, "Do you think it was a spirit that came to visit you that night?"] I don't know, because I don't know whether or not there are such things as spirits.

The resulting effect can be contrasted fruitfully with Butler's analysis of narrative practices in L'Anse-à-Canards, Newfoundland, where "the narrative raises the expectations of the audience, rises to a climax, and then reveals the rational explanation of what initially seemed to be a supernatural encounter" (1990:102). Although Nukulaelae spirit narratives with antithetical codas share some formal features with L'Anse-à-Canards narratives, the latter are strategically geared to discredit other people's beliefs in spirits, and thus are not heteroglossic performances in the way that Nukulaelae narratives are. No comparable intentional ploy underlies the uncertainty and contradictions of Nukulaelae narrative performances.

Vagueness and uncertainty suffuse Nukulaelae spirit discourse across many contexts: interviews with my respondents, casual conversations I overheard, and formal meetings that, for one reason or another, touched on the supernatural. The vagueness and uncertainty are most prominent in interviews, for the obvious reason that the topic is morally charged, and my respondents are reluctant to commit themselves in front of an outsider, however familiar. However, I had the opportunity to interview individuals from other islands of Tuvalu about spirits and sorcery. Even though these topics have roughly the same moral associations on other islands, these individuals (with whom I was considerably less intimate) talked about spirits and *vai laakau* in no uncertain terms and did not mitigate their accounts with conflicting signals, in sharp contrast with my Nukulaelae respondents. Witness, for example, the certainty with which an elderly man from Nanumea, whom I interviewed while he was visiting Nukulaelae, asserts his belief in the existence of both spirits and *vai laakau*:

> *Me i vai laakau nei laa, fai mai nei laa peelaa me seeai, peelaa, e see faka-maaonigina, nee? A ko toku fakama- toku iloa laa, e tonu eiloa mea kolaa. E isi eiloa ne vai laakau. [. . .] Kae nei laa, i ttou maaloo laa i te maaloo seki faka-maaonigina peelaa, nee? [. . .] A ko taku iloa laa, se mea tonu kkii. E isi loa ne agaaga.*
>
> [T 1991:1:A:420–429]

> Because as far as sorcery is concerned, it is said that it doesn't exist, that it's never been proved, right? But I know that *these things* [i.e., sorcery] *are true. There is such a thing as sorcery.* [. . .] But then our government, the government has not accepted it, right? [. . .] But I know that *it* [i.e., sorcery] *is a true thing. Spirits very much exist.*

Even though the Nanumea man addresses me here, a complete stranger and a non-Tuvaluan, his assertions display none of the contradictions and ambivalences of Nukulaelae spirit discourse. Hence the conflicting messages that characterize Nukulaelae spirit discourse cannot be explained simply as resulting from a concern to appear detached from the topic in the eyes of an outsider. Rather, these characteristics are indicative of the multivocal texture of spirit discourse, a multivocality that sometimes results in several seemingly conflicting voices being heard at once, or in rapid succession to one another within the same speech event.

Conflicting voices are present in an even more striking manner in talk about belief in spirits (compare Favret-Saada 1980). Below are two excerpts from the same ethnographic interview that illustrate patterns of contradiction extant in such discourse. In the first, the respondent first asserts unequivocally that she does not believe in spirits:

> *Au laa see talitonu lele loo ki mea naa! See taaitai eeloo o talitonu! Konei taatou nei, e olo saale, e olo saale, kaiaa see vau ei te agaaga ki taatou nei?*
>
> [L&S 1991:2:A:413–414]

I absolutely do not believe at all in those things [i.e., spirits]! I am not about to believe [in them]! [Look at] us here, [we] run around, [we] run around, why doesn't a spirit come to us here?

According to this testimony, people who claim to have encountered spirits are not telling the truth. Yet, a few minutes later, she affirms that spirits are selective in their manifestations:

Au e talitonu ki- i agaaga e mafai eeloo o olo ki tino kolaa e kaallaga saale ki agaaga. Kae see mafai o soo naa vau ua kia maatou kolaa see fiaffia atu kiaa ia, kae fano eeloo ki tino kolaa e fiafia a ia ki ei o fakataugaasoa ki ei, me ne kalaga atu kiaa ia kee vau.

[L&S 1991:2:B:193–198]

I believe in- that spirits can go to people that are in the habit of calling out to spirits. But it [i.e., the spirit] can't come any old way to those of us who are not friendly with it, but it always comes to people who are happy to make friends with it, because they called out for it to come.

Semanticists have long argued that all utterances rest on presuppositions, i.e., unspoken assumptions upon which depend the truth value and felicity of spoken utterances. Presupposition is a complex and heterogeneous semantic category, and its exact nature has been the subject of much debate since Bertrand Russell argued at the turn of the twentieth century that the utterance "The king of France is bald" presupposes that there is a king of France (see Lyons 1977:592-606 for details). Suffice it to say that the last conversational excerpt presupposes, in the most straightforward way, the speaker's belief that spirits do exist. Thus the presupposition of the last quote contradicts the statement that the same speaker made a few minutes before.

Such contradictions cannot be attributed simply to the vagaries and inconsistencies of casual conversation. Indeed, they are associated conspicuously with certain specific topics. An even more striking example is found in the text of a dramatic meeting of the Nukulaelae Council of Elders in June 1991 (for a more detailed account, see Besnier 1993a). This extraordinary meeting was called by a middle-age Nukulaelae man, Pito, who had been accused by Saumaiafi of conniving with spirits to kill potential contenders for his prestigious post of head (*toeaina*, literally, "elder") of the Nukulaelae community on Nauru. The sudden death of one of his relatives against whom he was alleged to bear a grudge had already "proved," for many people, that Pito was engaged in *vai laakau*; he had also been seen on a deserted beach on Nauru calling out to a spirit, which manifested itself in a dark cloud. Shortly before the meeting, Nukulaelae's Council of Elders had ordered him to resign from his lucrative job on Nauru and to return to Nukulaelae. During the meeting, held a few days after his arrival, Pito made a series of emotionally charged speeches arguing that he knew nothing about *vai laakau*. (Since his social demise was already a *fait accompli*, he was defending what little there was left, namely his own face and prestige.) Halfway through the meeting, a prominent member of the council, a recently retired pastor with strong political ambitions, stood up and extemporaneously engaged both the Council of Elders and Pito in the following dramatic exchange:

Silo: {falsetto} *Koutou e talittonu ki vai laakau?* {very fast} *Pito, koe e fai vai laakau?*

Pito: *Ikaai!*

Silo: {very fast} *E tii taaua, maafai e tonu koe e fai vai laakau?*

Pito: *See iloa nee au!*

                                     [Fono Taupulega 1991:2:A:301–304]

Silo: {addressing the council, falsetto} You believe in sorcery? {addressing Pito, very fast} Pito, are you a sorcerer?

Pito: No!

Silo: Will you cast a die with me to see if you are a sorcerer?

Pito: I know no such thing!

Silo went on to shame the council, not for believing in *vai laakau*, but rather for admitting, in a thoroughly public context, that such a thing exists:

> *Ttuuvalu e nnofo, kae aumai e tasi eiloa te pati, "A Pito ne aumai, e fai vai laakau!"*
>   [Fono Taupulega 1991:2:A:305–306]

> [All of] Tuvalu is here [listening], and [you] only say one thing, "Pito was recalled, [because] he's a sorcerer!"

He then made the following statement:

> *Kae kaafai laa, Pito, e isi eiloa seau mea peelaa, seau lito e iloa nee koe, kae tavili koe i loto nei me e faipati mai koe, "E seeai," aa!, a koe e tai faaeteete maalie i te Atua.*
>   [Fono Taupulega 1991:2:A:334–336]

> But if ever you did do, Pito, such a thing, [if] you know even a tiny bit [literally, a bud] [of sorcery], but you speak in this house, and you say, "No," ah! you had better be a bit careful with God.

Underlying Silo's threat of immanent justice here is the presupposition that *vai laakau* exists, which contradicts his just uttered ridicule of the council for having implied the very same thing. While this case focuses on *vai laakau* rather than spirits, we must remember that accepting the validity and relevance of *vai laakau* presupposes an acceptance of spirits as real, since *vai laakau* cannot work without the mediation of a spirit.

    These contradictions permeate discourse about beliefs in spirits, and are yet another way in which spirit discourse is multivocal: the voice of belief coexists with, but contradicts, the voice of disbelief. Manifestations of heteroglossia in this type of discourse belong to an area of analysis beyond the most immediate features of linguistic representation. When one finds contradictions across utterances and their presuppositions, one is dealing not simply with the literal, referential meaning of linguistic signs but with issues of ideology. I propose that the heteroglossia I have described here is an instance of what Tambiah (1990:92–3) calls "multiple orderings of reality," i.e., the coexistence of diverse "mentalities" (e.g., mystical belief and logico-empirical rationality) in all individuals and cultures.

A possible explanation of these patterns of heteroglossia would attribute them to a contrast between Christianity and a "local" tradition in Nukulaelae culture. The local tradition, the presumed heir of pre-Christian modes of thought, would animate the voice of belief, while Christian doctrine would refute it. Some support exists for this interpretation: dealing with spirits is certainly branded as *pouliuli*, "heathenish," and thus antithetical to Christian thinking. However, while this account might make some sense in other cultures, its simplicity here is suspect. On Nukulaelae, Christianity *is* "tradition" (Goldsmith 1989), and the two cannot be separated. Furthermore, this model fails to account for other forms of heteroglossia in spirit discourse, such as Saumaiafi's choice of the Samoan language (which incidentally was the language of the church until recently). Clearly, the heteroglossic situation I have described cannot be reduced to some separation of spheres in Nukulaelae society and culture. I will return to the question of explanations later in this chapter.

THE SOCIAL DIMENSIONS OF HETEROGLOSSIA

One of the major events of 1990 on Nukulaelae was Saumaiafi's sensational confirmation that Lina, a twice-widowed, attractive woman in her early forties, practiced *vai laakau*, something that everyone suspected. This revelation, which Saumaiafi spoke through her usual Funafuti medium, Suunema, explained why this woman's two husbands died under mysterious circumstances, why she was constantly followed by a court of suitors half her age, why she was seen gathering flower buds at dawn in the bush, and a number of other things. (Lina is childless, a condition widely attributed to her involvement in *vai laakau*.) Also implicated was her adoptive sister, who, although much more subdued than Lina, was also twice widowed and attracted much attention from the atoll's men, married and unmarried. Depending on the narrator, the spirit is reported to have said that the latter was either an apprentice to or a victim of her sister's *vai laakau*. The accusation spread like wildfire the instant that the Nukulaelae islanders who had participated in the session with the medium returned to Nukulaelae. (Wasting no time, they began circulating the rumor while they were still wading to shore from the ship that brought them.) This gossip resulted in the two women being severely ostracized for several months. Lina, educated in the school of hard knocks, seemed to fare reasonably well under the circumstances; I would venture that she even drew some personal enjoyment from being in the limelight of these accusations. Her sister, whose sense of identity depends on a much more traditional role in life, found them extremely distressing; she confided in me at the time that she felt *loto mmae*, literally, "painful heart."

Gossip plays a major role in day-to-day negotiations of prestige and power on the atoll. But this role is far from straightforward because, overtly, Nuku-laelae islanders strongly disapprove of gossip (Besnier 1989, 1990a, 1993b, In Press). The predicament they face is how to gossip without appearing to do so. This problem is becoming more serious as Nukulaelae people grow increasing-ly aware of the possibility of recourse to Western-style legal institutions. (Until recently, Nukulaelae people saw formal law as a compliance-enforcing mecha-nism, which is indeed what British colonial authorities designed it to be, but this image is rapidly changing to a means of seeking retribution for wrongdoings.) In the late 1980s, the first civil case concerning slander reached the court, setting a dreaded precedent for Nukulaelae islanders, who until then had rarely hesi-tated to degrade one another by concocting outlandish stories. Already attuned to questions of responsibility, evidence, and attribution, Nukulaelae gossips are becoming painfully aware that their favorite pastime can backlash both sym-bolically *and* materially.

Against this background, Saumaiafi's words and deeds were a godsend. Indeed, Nukulaelae participants in the sessions on Funafuti elicited from the spirit slanderous accusations of all kinds, which then could safely be circulated as narratives of what the spirit had said. I do not have recordings of the gossip that Saumaiafi's pronouncements generated on Nukulaelae, but I obtained many retellings. Witness the following narrative by one of the leading rumor-mongers:

> *Ka ne fai foki loo taku pati peenaa, nee?, taku faipatiiga i konei, au ne faipati foki loo peelaa, "Mea naa ko pati a te agaaga, kae hee hai atu paa kee olo koutou, peelaa, o fakamaasei nee koutou io me aa, a ko pati hua ne llogo ei maatou i pati a te agaaga, nee?" Kae hee hai peelaa ne pati e- e- (paa) iloa atu loo nee taatou ne pati e ttonu, peelaa, ne mmai maatou o fakamatala i konei me ne pati e ttonu. Peelaa, nee? A ko te mea ne faippati eiloa maatou i pati ne llogo i ei, pati katoa loo, mea valevale, nee?, kolaa ne faipatiga nee te agaaga. Peelaa! Peelaa ne mmai maatou o faippati nee maatou i konei, nee?, kae hee hai peelaa ne faippati peelaa me ne mea eiloo koo iloa tonu nee maatou ne mea e ttonu, nee? Peelaa.*
>
> [Saumaiafi 1990:2:A:239–247]

But this is also what I said [to people on Nukulaelae], see?, what I said here, I also said this, "This is what the spirit said, but I'm not telling you so that you can go, like, for you to go and denigrate or whatever, but this is just what we heard the spirit had said, see?" And these words are not as if we- we-, like, we knew that these words are true. Like that, see? And all we did was to repeat what we had heard, everything we'd heard, all sorts of things, see?, that the spirit had said. Like that! Like what we said here when we came here, right?, it's not as if we pre-sented these words as words that we know are true, right? Like that.

The narrator exploits heteroglossia in at least four ways. First, by simply quoting what the spirit says, he divulges the *vai laakau* accusations while standing on firm ground. The accusation is attributed to the spirit, not to him as narrator. Second, by engaging in shifting dialogue about belief and nonbelief, he shifts responsibility for giving credence to the accusation onto his interlocutor. Third, he attributes beliefs in spirits to "others." Witness the following striking excerpt from the same conversation:

> *Ttou fenua oki laa kaati hee lotou iloaga a uiga o te olooga o pati, nee?*
> [Saumaiafi 1990:2:A:226–227]

This island of ours, they just don't pay attention to what they say, you see? [Literally: "This island of ours, they just don't know the meaning of the way in which words go, see?"][9]

The real culprit is thus a generic, third-person plural entity, i.e., unspecified members of the island community ("You *know* how they can be!"), who spread rumors about spirit mediumship, thereby tacitly endorsing the validity of spirits and admitting their belief in them. Ultimately, if the victims of Saumaiafi's accusations and subsequent rumors become angry, which indeed happened in this case, their anger can be construed as an indication that *they* believe in spirits. In turn, this can be belittled as an indication of lack of *maafaufau*, "maturity of mind, thoughtfulness," and as giving legitimacy to something that should not be legitimized. Following is a superb example of this reasoning (the fact that the entire narrative is in reported dialogue form further complicates the heteroglossic tangle):

> *Fanatu a Eesau. "Fitu! Koe laa naa kai logo?" Aku pati, "Kae aa?" "Ae- a- isi ne tino koo iita!" Iita ki maatou konei ne mmai, nee? Aku pati, "A tino konaa kaafai e iita, kaati see iloa nee laatou o maafaufau." Aku pati kia Eesau, nee? Muna a- aku pati kia Eesau, mo Faavae eeloo, laaua toko lua, aku pati, "Kiloko! Ttino poto i tena maafaufau, taatou hee talittonu ki mea konei! Mea konei e faipati fua nee taatou, me ne pati ne fai i ttaimi ne tupu i ei te mea, nee? Teelaa, ne laumaiga nee te mea teelaa, teelaa laa, mmai mo taatou, faipati fua nee taatou i konei. Kae see fai peelaa ne mmai eiloo mo taatou, fai nee taatou, peelaa, ee?"*
> [Saumaiafi 1990:2:A:372–381]

Eesau came to me [and said,] "Fitu! Have you heard?" I said, "What now?" [She said,] "Some people have gotten angry!" Angry at those of us who came back [from Funafuti], see? I said, "If those people get angry, it's probably because they don't know how to *think properly*." That's what I told Eesau, see? I said- I said to Eesau, and to Filemoni, both of them, I said [to them], "Look now! Those of us who've got *an intelligent mind* don't believe in these things! These things we've told because these are what was said while [spirit-mediumship] was taking place, right? Like, that's what [that spirit] said, so that's what we said when we got here. So it's not as if we had brought these words here, as if we stood behind those words, like that, right?"

These masterfully subtle shifts in what Goffman (1979) calls "footing," which rob the victims of any due process, hinge crucially on the multiplicity of voices associated with spirit discourse. Narrators capitalize on this multivocality to disparage others while safeguarding their entitlement to narrate a good story.

Heteroglossia has consequences not just for the social uses of discourse about spirits, but also for the social relationship between the medium, the spirit, and the many people about whom the spirit makes allegations. Over the course of time, Saumaiafi talked about a great many people from Nukulaelae and elsewhere. But the attribution of responsibility for her allegations is tricky business. When Pito, the Nukulaelae man accused of having performed *vai laakau* on Nauru, went to confront the medium (clutching in his hand a letter threatening to take her to court if she did not retract the accusation), this is what he encountered:

> *Taa, fakamolemole atu kiaa ia, iaa ia see iloa nee ia. Mea konaa ko ana pati e fai maafai a ia e ulufia nee te agaaga. A kaafai ia e nofo peenei, see masaua nee ia.*
> [L 1991:1:A:365–366]

So she apologized to him, [saying] that she did not know [anything]. These were words she uttered while she was possessed by the spirit. But when she's just sitting there, she doesn't remember [anything].

Even more dramatic is the case of a Funafuti man, Manu. During another mediumship session, Saumaiafi had accused him of engaging in *vai laakau*, attributing a foot ailment he was suffering to his having hurt himself when, out of exasperation (*ffiu*) with his constant calls (*kalaga*) to her, she had pushed him off his bed. A furious Manu came to confront the medium. Unfortunately for him, he found her in the middle of a mediumship session. Consequently, he got to speak to the spirit but not to the medium:

> *Manu vau, tuu mai tua, mo koo pati maasei nee ia te agaaga, mo koo ( )-. Kae muna a te agaaga taa, "Koe- koe see mataku i au?" Kae fai mai paa, "E aa?, koo llei tou kaaiga? Ka koo ita mai koe- kaa ita mai koe kia au?" Teelaa, mo koo fai paa Manu, "Ne aa igoa o aku mea ne fai atu kiaa koe?" Kae fai mai te agaaga paa, "Au koo ffiu iaa koe i te kalaga ssoko atu kee vau au, i- kee fai te aavaga a tau tama, kee fai- kee fai te tiimu a Funaafuti."*
> [L 1991:1:A:434–439]

Manu came along, stood outside, and started insulting the spirit, because ( )-. And the spirit said, "You, aren't you afraid of me?" And she said, "So, [rhetorically] your kin group is fine? And you are angry, you are angry at me?" So Manu said, "What did I do to you [to deserve this]?" And the spirit said, "I've had it with your calling out to me for me to come and get your daughter married, to make- make Funafuti's [football] team [win]."

In this encounter, Manu is interested in talking to the medium, to whom the question, "What did I do to you [to deserve this]?" is most likely to be addressed. But he is forced to converse with the spirit inhabiting the medium at the time. The ensuing tragi-comedy of errors is a direct result of the multivocal nature of mediumship. Later on, when Manu returned to see Suunema, threatening her, like Pito, with a lawsuit, the medium gave him the same answer as his predecessor: "Hey! I have no idea that I said these things! [. . .] When I get to that point, I don't know what I am saying" (L 1991:1:A:441-442). Nukulaelae islanders know that court authorities in Tuvalu do not allow (talia) arguments involving spirits and sorcery, but this fact does not lead people to conclude that the medium can be sued for libel; rather, they assume that she is immune from the legal process. The premises implicit in their reasoning rest on the shiftiness of responsibility inherent in mediumship.

Spirits and associated categories and processes provide attractive resources for the manipulation of social relationships, an attractiveness largely attributable to the multivocality of these resources. I propose that areas of culture most suffused with ambiguity and contradiction are privileged as a font of such manipulative resources.

CONCLUSION

Spirits play a very serious role in Nukulaelae social life, even though they rarely appear on the atoll, and despite Nukulaelae islanders' intermittent insistence that they do not exist. They can indeed affect one's personal reputation, social status, and prestige. Ironically, the roles that spirits play crucially depend on the indeterminacy that multiple voices generate.

The arguments I have presented here rest heavily on the analysis of narratives collected in a broad variety of contexts. The nature of my ethnographic data necessitates this orientation. My understanding of Saumaiafi mediumship, to focus on a particularly pertinent example, is limited by the fact that, since I was on Nukulaelae while mediumship sessions were being conducted on Funafuti, I never witnessed one.[10] However, my situation is no different from that of most Nukulaelae islanders, who nevertheless revel in narratives of mediumship sessions and squeeze from them serious consequences for social relations. An approach privileging a view of culture as discourse is particularly relevant to a characterization of Nukulaelae spirits. In addition, while Nukulaelae may appear at first glance an internally homogeneous cultural microcosm isolated from the rest of the world, an image that the islanders themselves like to project, spirit discourse highlights the degree to which Nukulaelae society and culture are involved in a complex network of social relations and cultural processes that extend beyond the confines of the atoll. Indeed, the spirits that affect Nukulaelae, and their various manifestations, have an interesting way of interweaving social action on Nukulaelae with what takes place in other parts of the group, particularly Funafuti.

As many social theorists have argued, human beings constantly engage in making sense of their symbolic world, and this process informs and shapes their social action and their interpretations of other's actions. This process of making sense is what we hear when we direct why-questions to our respondents and when we overhear them passing judgment on one another's actions. I have adopted a stance here presupposing that the process of making sense is not separate from the symbolic world in which people live, but rather is constitutive of it (i.e., it both shapes and reflects); the process is an integral component of this world of symbols. More often than not, cultural models that members of a particular group present are theoretical distillations of cultural processes. The process of distillation, the results of which I have termed discourse, is precisely what is of interest, particularly when the picture it yields is as complex, shifting, and conflictual as in the case I have investigated here. (Perhaps anthropologists should be more worried about simplicity than complexity in what they are told and overhear.) Of course, heteroglossia is not always easy to spot and understand, particularly if one holds a view of culture as an internally coherent and consistent system. For example, I have shown that heteroglossia may reside not in the literal meaning of people's self-explanations, but in tensions between literal meaning (itself a complex category [Besnier 1990b], particularly across cultural boundaries) and what Tyler (1978) has broadly termed the "unsaid" of discourse, e.g., unstated presuppositions. An understanding of these tensions opens the door to comprehending cultural categories and processes.

In the presence of a cultural model whose various aspects contradict one another, and whose nature is context-bound in such a complex manner as to make the description of context very difficult, one is faced with a theoretical problem. As Abu-Lughod (1990, 1991) and others before her (e.g., Clifford 1988) have argued, anthropological explanations in terms of "culture" have all too often suffered from an inherent tendency to find coherence where it doesn't exist. Coherence-seeking cultural explanations are not well equipped to deal with seemingly conflictual meanings in a people's accounts and actions. Instead, an approach centralizing discourse as the organizing key of people's lives and understandings yields more fruitful results in situations where explanations are multiple, mutually contradictory, and shifting (Abu-Lughod 1990). Rather than seeking a resolution in the contradictions presented by these materials, one should seek an understanding of the contradictions themselves, and of how these contradictions articulate with other aspects of society and culture.

NOTES

Acknowledgments. Field work on Nukulaelae was conducted in 1980-82, 1985, 1990, and 1991. The last two field sojourns, during which the data relevant to this discussion were gathered, were funded by the National Science Foundation, the Harry Frank Guggenheim Foundation, and the Wenner Gren Foundation. I thank the government of Tuvalu and Nukulaelae's Council of Elders for permission to conduct field research; my field assistants, Avanoa Luuni and Tuufue Niuioka, for their invaluable labor; the many individuals on Nukulaelae who shared their insights with me; and

Mike Goldsmith, Tamar Gordon, Vili Hereniko, Alan Howard, Jeannette Mageo, and Jan Rensel for insights and advice. This paper was presented in colloquia at the universities of Auckland, New England, and Western Australia, where audiences offered useful comments.

1   Reflexes of other common Polynesian terms for supernatural entities are also found in this language. The Samoan borrowing *aitu* is sometimes used to mean "spirit" in its non-Christian sense. *Atua* refers to the Christian God or to pagan gods in the Biblical sense (e.g., "false gods").

2   In Samoan, the word can be etymologized as *tali*, "to accept, to receive" and *tonu*, "true, correct." The question of whether this etymology has any psychological reality for Nukulaelae people is very difficult to answer. Even if it does, it would simply shift the problem from understanding Nukulaelae notions of "belief" to understanding Nukulaelae notions of "truth."

3   Transcript excerpts quoted in this paper follow a phonemic orthography, in which double graphemes indicate geminated segments; geminated oral stops are heavily aspirated, and other geminated phonemes are articulated for a longer period of time than their ungeminated equivalents. The letter *g* represents a velar nasal stop, *l* is a central flap, and all other letters have their approximate IPA value. The transcripts represent an unedited rendition of what is audible on tapes, including false starts, repairs, etc.; however, volume, tempo, and voice quality are not indicated here. Parentheses indicate conjectured or inaudible strings, [...] indicates that a string of words has been left out of the transcript, and material provided in square brackets in a translation represent additions, for the sake of intelligibility, that are not present in the original text. Recording references (e.g., [L&S 1991:2:A:024–028]) appear between the original text and its translation.

4   I am not claiming that this etymology is relevant to everyday talk about the category. In this discussion, I use the term *vai laakau* in its original form to avoid the straightjacket of an English translation. However, in the translation of cited excerpts, I gloss *vai laakau* as "sorcery" to alleviate the difficulty inherent in following these texts.

5   This use of *vai laakau* is the reason why the Samoan spirit Saumaiafi, which I discuss at greater length further on, became involved in the daily affairs of Nukulaelae and Funafuti in 1990. The cultural extension of sorcery to new realms of social interaction is certainly not unique to this society, and militates against the common view that sorcery and social change are in opposition to one another (cf. Fisiy and Geschiere 1991).

6   The term *fakalleo* is a complex one. It can take as a grammatical subject a reference to the medium, the spirit speaking through the medium, or the audience, which is "making" the spirit speak through the medium. This grammatical versatility indicates that we should not take its etymology as a causative verb too literally; when Nukulaelae people talk about mediumship, they do not necessarily envisage a situation is which someone is causing someone else to have a voice.

7   As Karp (1989:89) demonstrates, both possession and mediumship involve a complex combination of the involuntary and the desired, thus suggesting that one should not bank too much on agency in drawing an analytic distinction between the two.

8   I am drawing this contrast both as a description of an ideological stance and as an empirical observation. Nukulaelae people frequently insist that their community is much less prone to deal with spirits than other islands, and their statements

to this effect fit very nicely with the arguments about the foreign nature of spirits that I develop in the next section. In my experience, Tuvaluans from other islands of the group have a different attitude toward spirits than Nukulaelae people; for example, they are generally more willing to acknowledge the presence and relevance of spirits to me, even though I am even more a stranger to them than to Nukulaelae people.

9   This framing statement is thick with shifting indexicality, from pronoun use to hedges to syntax.

10 At the end of my sojourn in the field in 1991, I could have tried to attend a mediumship session while in transit on Funafuti. However, I decided against it, as Saumaiafi had implicated me as the purported victim of sorcery, and I had made known on Nukulaelae my displeasure with this accusation. (This affair is involved enough to be the topic of an entirely different paper.) I feared that an encounter with the medium might have placed her in a very awkward position.

5 Spirit Encounters on a Polynesian Outlier

Anuta, Solomon Islands

Richard Feinberg

Anuta, the easternmost island in the Solomon Islands, is a half-mile in diameter and has about 250 residents. Its nearest neighbor, Tikopia, which it resembles closely in language and culture, lies just over seventy miles to the southwest. Still farther west are the Melanesian islands of the Santa Cruz group.

Anutans trace their ancestry to immigrants who came from the Polynesian islands of Tonga and Uvea approximately fifteen generations ago. Later arrivals from Samoa and Rotuma augmented the community. The contemporary social structure was formed about nine generations ago when a chief named Tearakura, assisted by his two younger brothers and his brother-in-law, slaughtered the remainder of the island's male population. These four men became the founders of Anuta's four major descent groups known as *kainanga*, "clans."

The earliest recorded European sighting of Anuta was by the *HMS Pandora* in 1791. Missionary activity did not begin, however, until a century and a quarter later when the Anglican Bishop of Melanesia left two Tikopian teachers on the island. The first systematic anthropological studies of Anuta occurred during the 1970s, making reconstruction of pre-Christian activities problematic. Fortunately, the memories of older Anutans as well as those who have worked to keep alive the island's oral traditions are affirmed by comparative material from Raymond Firth's detailed investigations of Tikopia beginning in 1928-1929 (see particularly Firth 1936, 1939, 1967, 1970), when half the population still actively practiced the traditional religion.

I have been engaged in study of Anuta since the early 1970s. From the start, as I have gratefully acknowledged elsewhere (e.g., Feinberg 1981), my hosts seemed happy to share information on most topics. The one exception was traditional religion.

Anutans had adopted Christianity more than fifty years before, and I thought pre-Christian numinals were long forgotten. Granted, there were some discrepancies. Traditions were recited making reference to former chiefs' becoming major deities upon their death (see Feinberg 1979, 1981). Reference was sometimes made to kava ceremonies. Chiefs were said to have extraordinary *mana*, "supernaturally derived potency," derived from their position as descendants of the premier gods. Ideas of honor and taboo remained intact, and failure to respect persons of higher rank was thought to bring on illness, accident, or death (see Feinberg 1979, 1986). Still, I tended to perceive these scattered bits of information as relics of a distant past.

My first clear indication that non-Christian spirits retain much of their importance in Anutan life occurred on New Year's morning 1973. While walking through the jungle in the predawn darkness, a boy at my side noticed a phosphorescent glow just off the path. He grabbed my hand, shouted out, "A spirit!" and instructed me to shine my flashlight on it. When I did so, the glow disappeared, but when I turned the flashlight off again, it reappeared. After I had done this several times, my companion started to pull frantically at me exclaiming, "Let's go! Let's get out of here!"

Throughout that day, people kept inquiring whether I had seen the spirit. This gave me an opportunity to ask about their own spirit encounters, and soon a new world was opened to me. Over the next twenty years, I learned that people of Anuta recognize a plethora of numinals, ranging from a few that might well be described as "godlike" to a number that could be termed "spirits." In general, however, they emphasize categories that shade into one another, avoiding terms or concepts that imply absolutes.[1]

Anutan numinals may be arranged along a number of continua involving: degrees of power; whether the entity was collectively worshiped or individually experienced; the number of people participating in worship practices; the clarity with which the entity was defined, distinguished, and endowed with a unique name, personality, and other characteristics; the degree of moral virtue attributed to it; and the degree to which it is perceived, today as in the past, to play a positive social role. Anuta has neither entirely free spirits whose personae are wholly unbound and whose wills cannot be influenced by human actions, nor beings that are always fully bound. God and spirit—or even spirit and human—are not rigidly distinct and separate categories.

The merging of numinal and human beings suggests issues of possession and spirit mediumship, the existence of permeable boundaries between self and other, and an associative model of the person. Key elements in contemporary Anutan discourse about numinals are Christianity and the conversion process, continuities and contrasts between the old and new religions, and the role of numinals—both godlike and spiritlike—in moral discourse and in the maintenance of social order. Finally, a theme that runs throughout this chapter involves a form of relativism that permeates Anutans' understanding of the spiritual realm and helps explain their willingness to accept Christianity while maintaining a belief in the existence and importance of pre-Christian gods and spirits.

TYPES OF SPIRITUAL BEINGS

Anutans recognize two levels of existence, which they term *i a tangata* and *i a nga atua*. These may be roughly translated as "pertaining to the world of human beings" and "pertaining to the world of numinals."[2] In addition, they perceive a realm between these two great worlds. This is the realm in which numinals inhabit (*pakatino,* "become embodied in") natural objects. Sometimes they inhabit plants, cliffs, caves, or stones, thereby making themselves visible and tangible to human beings. They may be seen as otherwise unexplained lights on the sea or in the bush; as animals that act in a manner out of character for their species; or as abnormally large, powerful people who are able to appear and disappear at will and perform superhuman feats. Under certain circumstances, numinals can enter people's bodies, control their behavior, and speak through their mouths. This ability to possess ordinary mortals is seen in spirit mediumship, a common Polynesian phenomenon in olden times and, in modified form, perhaps even today (e.g., see Firth 1967, 1970; Feinberg 1979; Besnier, chapter 4).

Undistinguished Spirits and Ghosts of Ordinary People

Anutans have two basic terms for numinous beings: *atua* and *tupua*. Of these, *atua* is the more common, and it applies generically. The most frequently encountered are *atua vare,* "common spirits" or "undistinguished spirits."

Atua vare are the most spiritlike of Anutan numinals. They haunt the bush, primarily at night, lurking in dimly lighted places rarely frequented by humans. It is difficult to see their faces, although their bodies often are quite visible. They may cause accidents or minor misfortunes, but tend to be more frightening than truly dangerous; thus, it is possible, albeit difficult, to face them down (cf. Mageo, Chapter 2). Occasionally, Anutans attribute distinct names and personalities to such spirits, but they usually do not.

Some *atua* are believed to be the incorporeal remains of deceased people, but most are viewed as never having taken human form. Some people, when they die, are said to become *atua* and return to haunt the living; others do not. *Atua vare* have inhabited the world since time immemorial and continue to be a major feature of Anuta's cultural landscape. Yet, despite their generally spiritlike character, such *atua* also manifest some godlike features. They are sometimes differentiated, occasionally named, may be bound to particular places, objects, or circumstances, and quite readily appear to persons occupying any status in the social hierarchy, including chiefs.

Identifiable ghosts of the recently deceased often behave much like *atua vare*. Both types of spirit make brief appearances, then quickly disappear. They typically are witnessed by one or two people who have been temporarily isolated from their companions. The witnesses seek out support from other people, describe their experience, and if possible return in force to the scene of the events; but by the time they get back to the site of their encounter, the spirit has always disappeared.

Such spirits are most likely to appear in times of stress, either to the individual or the community. The period surrounding the funeral of a close relative is a time when spirits are particularly apt to display themselves. Their appearance usually induces overwhelming fear, perhaps reflecting a reluctance to let go of friends and relatives, combined with fear of death and a reminder of one's own mortality.

When spirits are seen, they often look like people, only larger and more powerful. Observers feel they have a relatively clear view, yet they can rarely see the spirit's face. Thus, his or her identity must be inferred from context or judged from body contours, and is often subject to interpretation and debate. If someone has recently died, the spirit is likely to be identified as that person's ghost. Otherwise, there may be no particular identification, and the intruder then is said to be an "undistinguished spirit." Such encounters may be illustrated by the following accounts recorded in my 1972–73 field notebooks.

Several informants told me of how a man named Pu Penuakimoana and a girl known as Corrine had seen Corrine's father, Pu Raroipi, shortly after his death. On the day of the funeral, Pu Penuakimoana saw Pu Raroipi while on his way to the spring. Later the same day, Corrine observed him on the hilltop and ran to a man named Pu Atapu who was nearby but apparently did not notice anything peculiar. Neither of these people saw the spirit's face, but the events took place in broad daylight, so the principals got a good look at his body. Corrine's brother, Pu Nukuriaki, interpreted his father's appearance as an indication of the strength of his love (*aropa*) for his daughter. He noted that he had no wish to be loved as much as his sister. . . . *"Kau mataku pe,"* "I am fearful."

One night Pu Maravai and Pu Nukumanaia were in a tree, hunting birds. Pu Nukumanaia had gone first and was higher in the tree. An *atua* started climbing up the tree toward Pu Maravai, who became frightened and suggested that they urinate on the spirit to cause him to leave. However, Pu Nukumanaia's fright was less than his revulsion at the idea of climbing down a tree trunk saturated with urine. So he handed his net to Pu Maravai and climbed down the tree to do combat. He went to step on the *atua*'s hand, but the latter pulled it away and fled before Pu Nukumanaia could touch him. Pu Nukumanaia gave chase, but no *atua* was found.

Ghosts of Deceased Chiefs and Ancestral Shades

At the opposite extreme from *atua vare* in the traditional religion are deceased chiefs. They were powerful, systematically worshiped, and bound in material representations as well as prayers, songs, oral traditions, and ordinary discourse. The most important of such beings is Tearakura.

Tearakura was a culture hero, a man of great *manuu*, "mana; supernaturally derived potency," and a prominent ancestor in the present chiefly line. After his death, he became the island's premier deity. Kava ceremonies (*pai kava*) were performed on his behalf, during which the senior chief invoked his assistance to ensure the land's productivity and the community's prosperity.

In such ceremonies, the chief was represented by one of his ritual assistants, known as *mataapure* (see Feinberg In Press a). *Mataapure* recited prayers, threw out bits of food, and poured water on the ground. The kava plant (*Piper methysticum*) is absent from Anuta and, therefore, not used despite the ceremony's name.

According to Pu Nukumarere, who had witnessed kava ceremonies as a child, the ritual was characterized by elaborate organization. The rites were led by specialists but involved the whole community in such activities as fish drives and collective feasting. In the rites that he observed, special attention was given to Tearakura and to a stone that served both as his resting place and material representation. Tearakura, like other gods, had power of autonomous movement; yet even he was bound in some degree to the ceremonial ground, Tapu Ariki, and to his special stone located therein. The stones were elaborately decorated, similar to the way Anutans decorate themselves for dances or for major rites of passage.

Other deceased chiefs also achieved divinity and were regularly worshiped. Of special note in this regard were Toroaki, Pu Tepuko, and Pu Tauraro. Toroaki was Tearakura's great-grandfather and the first of the current line to hold chiefly office. Pu Tepuko was Tearakura's younger brother and became Anuta's first junior chief. Pu Tauraro was Tearakura's great-grandson, a later holder of the Tui Anuta title. Like Tearakura, he was born with his face "colored like a rainbow" (*pani marara*), which marked him as an *ariki pakatomo* or *ariki manuu*—a chief of exceptional mana.

Other chiefs entered the spirit world as well after their deaths, and they were sometimes worshiped. However, they were less important than the *ariki manuu*, and less is remembered about them.

After death, non-chiefs also survived in spirit form. People who had been extraordinarily imposing in life tended to become major presences in the suprahuman world and were at times invoked by their direct descendants. But they exercised less power than former chiefs, were not worshiped through formal kava ceremonies, and were invoked by their particular descent lines rather than on behalf of the community at large.

One major exception to this rule was Nau Ariki, Tearakura's older sister. As her name implies, she is regarded as an *ariki papine*, "female chief"; indeed, she is the only one recorded in Anutan oral history. Little information exists about her, but she appears not to have had much of a political role, and her recognition as *ariki* was primarily honorific. Still, she is said to have possessed tremendous *manuu*; commanded worship in the form of kava rites; assisted those who worshiped and respected her; and taken awful retribution against those who failed to give her proper recognition.

The power of deified ancestors had its limits. They had many of the character defects one might expect to find among living people and could be deceived, coerced, and bluffed. Normally they communicated with "priests" (*ariki* and *mataapure*), but occasionally they appeared to ordinary people. While these were Anuta's most important pre-Christian numinals, deified ancestors were not rigidly distinguished, conceptually or terminologically, from spirits of other kinds.

Totemic and Land Spirits
Between gods (*tupua tapu*) and undistinguished spirits (*atua vare*) are beings known as *tupua penua*, "land spirits," and entities that might be termed "totemic spirits," which have no distinct class label in Anutan.

The names of great pan-Polynesian gods—Rongo, Tu, and Taane—evoke from Anutans little hint of recognition. Tangaroa figures in some narratives recited for the benefit of children, mostly as bedtime stories. The name applies to a group of spirits associated with the ocean.

According to local tradition, Anuta was initially pulled from the ocean floor by the demigod Motikitiki—a character with analogues on many Polynesian islands. Other stories refer to Te Ao Rere, "Large Magellanic Cloud," and Te Ao Toka, "Small Magellanic Cloud," as female spirits (see below). Manu, "Bird," is a male spirit seen in a constellation consisting of Sirius (his "body"), Canopus (his "east wing"), and Procyon (his "north wing"). Manu's north wing is shorter than his east wing, having been broken in a fight with Motikitiki over the female spirit Taro (Antares). Since the establishment of Christianity, adults no longer take these stories seriously, referring questions of creation to the Book of Genesis.

Totemic spirits date to Anuta's settlement from Tonga and Uvea about fifteen generations ago. The immigrants brought tutelary spirits from their homelands: the Tongans' god was named Putiuraua and was embodied (*pakatino*) in the eel (*te toke*); the Uveans' god, Tokitaaitekere, inhabited the body of the lizard (*te moko*). After the creation of Anuta's four-"clan" system in the time of Tearakura, each *kainanga* had a special relationship with particular *atua*, residing in certain types of fish or other sea creatures. The Kainanga i Mua, Kainanga i Tepuko, and Kainanga i Rotomua all had the shark (*te mangoo*) as their *atua*. Spirit sharks could be identified by their unusual behavior, such as a propensity to come onto the reef to "lie" or "sleep" (*moe*) in front of Tapu Ariki near

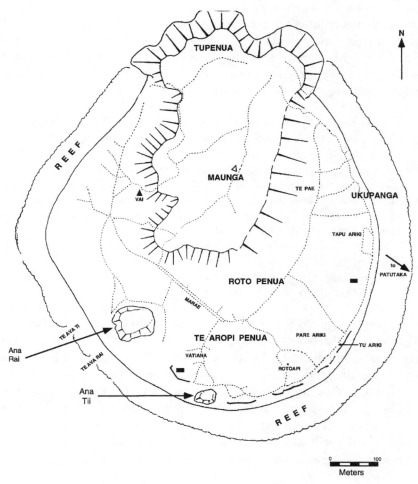

Figure 5.1 Map of Anuta Island

Rotoapi village (see map, figure 5.1). The shark was *te atua taa tangata,* "a man-killing spirit" or "war god." Another *atua* associated with the Kainanga i Mua was *te peke,* "the octopus," a female spirit connected with voyaging.

The Kainanga i Pangatau was associated with *te ponu,* "sea turtle" and *te ririko,* "manta ray." In contrast with the shark, which anyone might eat, turtles and rays were *tapu* for Pangatau "clan" members in pre-Christian times. The *ririko* seems to have been Pangatau's voyaging spirit. In addition to the ray and turtle, Piita or Piitia i te Rangi was cited as a major god of Pangatau. This deity was male and not associated with any particular animal. He was both a voyaging spirit and a war god.

Little detail seems to be remembered about totemic spirits. By contrast,

Anutans have a good deal to say about *tupua penua*. These were native to Anuta, perhaps from the time of its creation (*pakatupu*). Some informants claimed they were *atua tapu,* sacred spirits that helped people who respected (*pakaepa*) them and brought misfortune to the rest. They were numerous and of both sexes. Most preferred to live in caves, and some stories tell of battles for dwelling sites among *tupua penua*. Spirits of this type are discussed in greater detail in Feinberg (In Press b). Among the more prominent are:

> *Uuperuu*, a female spirit with one very long, folded breast (*na uu e peruperu*), which she used to lasso men and force them to have sex with her.
>
> *Uunapine*, a female spirit who lived in a cave known as Te Ana Rai "The Large Cave" (see figure 5.1) near the main passage to the ocean.
>
> *Rua Taka*, meaning "Two Spinsters" (*rua*, "two"; *taka*, "unmarried"), denotes a pair of sisters whom Tearakura banished from Anuta after a series of confrontations. Eventually, these spirits ascended to the heavens and became embodied in the two Magellanic clouds.
>
> *Paaira*, who was sometimes male and sometimes female, is said to have had white skin "like a European."
>
> *Uuarenga*, *Matarua*, and *Pu Roa* were male spirits inhabiting a number of caves in different sections of Anuta's beach.

Tupua penua are godlike in that they are named, individuated, powerful, bound to natural phenomena (rocks, trees, caves, etc.) that served as their material representations, and may have been invoked through prayer. Their exploits and personalities are captured in story and song. But they are spiritlike in that they are amoral, egoistic, and dangerous. They have little positive role and, even in pre-Christian times, were usually avoided or placated rather than worshiped. Totemic spirits were somewhat more free-flowing in their representations, being bound in animals of various species, but they were godlike in that they were positive forces representing moral order and often called on for assistance.

Christian Spirits: God and Satan

In the modern era, Satan has been vested with many characteristics of *tupua penua*. Unlike his predecessors, he is a relatively recent arrival on Anuta and is not bound to a particular locale. However, he is powerful, evil, not worshiped, and best avoided, although he may be involuntarily encountered. Such encounters are described as very frightening. One was related to me in the following terms:

> Shortly after the death of Pu Ororiki, two young men who were looking in a mirror that had been set up near the grave site[3] saw Satan approach the grave. Before he got there, the grave opened up and a column of smoke descended from the sky. The Devil had come to bear off Pu Ororiki's soul to hell, but God rescued it

and carried it to heaven before Satan could fulfill his plan. The two men ran back in a panic to St. John village at the opposite end of the island.

Finally, the Christian God is designated by a variety of descriptive terms. These include: *Te Tupua i te Vaerangi*, "The Tupua in the Heavens"; *Te Tupua Tapu*, "The Sacred Tupua"; and *Te Tupua Rai*, "The Great Tupua." The (Anglican) Melanesian Mission introduced Christianity during the second decade of this century, and conversion was swift and complete. This, however, did not mean denial of the older gods and spirits. Rather, the community was introduced to a more powerful God who demanded precedence in its system of worship but shared major characteristics of the more familiar numinals. Although Anutans have abandoned formal worship of pre-Christian gods, they occasionally invoke their assistance (see below and Feinberg In Press b), and the bush continues to be haunted by spirits of the *atua vare* and *tupua penua* varieties.

A MATTER OF BELIEF
This leads to the question of belief. Howard (Chapter 6), addressing a precipitous decline in spirit encounters over the past three decades, questions whether belief is a meaningful category in terms of which to discuss Rotuman thinking about spirits. By contrast, I can speak with little hesitation of Anutan spirit beliefs.

The word *pakatonu*, literally "make straight," is used in almost precisely the manner of the English "to believe." Anutans are very much concerned with truth and falsity. After relating a story or an incident, they ask each other whether they "believe" (*pakatonu*) the narrative's assertions. They debate the evidence and attempt to evaluate, as systematically as possible, the likelihood of the story's truth.

Their approach to spirits is similar. They regularly ask each other about spirit encounters, attempt to determine whether strange experiences are best explained in terms of spirits or a mundane cause, and propose alternative explanations and evaluate their plausibility. They have asked me many times about my possible encounters with Anutan spirits and whether I "believe" in them. They have observed that Europeans generally do not experience spirits when visiting Anuta, a fact which they explain by noting that most European visitors do not "believe" in local spirits.

Anutans have emphasized to me repeatedly their certainty that gods of old played an important role in the community's affairs. They display equal certainty of the activity of "undistinguished spirits" (*atua vare*) and commonly are fearful about walking through the bush alone at night. Catechists and other leaders of the island's church are as convinced as anyone of the existence and activities of local spirits. Nor are such convictions questioned by the one Anutan who has an advanced degree from Kohimarama Theological College on Guadalcanal.

Possession and Spirit Mediumship

Anutans explain their belief in the existence and activity of spiritual beings in terms of a variety of observations and experiences (see Feinberg 1979, In Press b). Prominent among these are possession and spirit mediumship.

By possession I mean the phenomenon of a spirit entering one's body and taking it over, so that the person's words and actions are interpreted to be those of the spirit. When this is done under relatively controlled circumstances for the express purpose of having spirits communicate messages of concern to the community, it is spirit mediumship (Firth 1967:296), and the session is a seance. Those spirits that possess and communicate through a particular medium are that medium's spirit familiars. Mediumship in this sense requires possession, but possession does not necessarily entail mediumship. This distinction has a number of implications.

Mediumship involves reciprocal communication between the spirit and the human community, whereas other forms of possession are taken to involve one-way communication emanating from the spirit. Since spiritlike beings are less bound than their godlike counterparts, it is relatively easy to conceive of them entering and possessing human beings. On the other hand, two-way communication is most apt to occur with beings concerned with the community's welfare who have important information and are inclined to share it if properly approached. A medium's spirit familiars, therefore, tend to be godlike while ordinary possession most often is attributed to spiritlike beings.

The context for mediumship is likely to be a formal seance in which the spirit familiar speaks through the medium to an interested audience. The messages are, therefore, relatively explicit, albeit open to a degree of interpretation. Other forms of possession are likely to occur in private; persons other than the victim learn about the episodes secondhand, and the messages tend to be implicit, somewhat cryptic, and subject to speculation.

Mediumship, unlike other forms of possession, involves a degree of voluntarism, and in that respect is similar to witchcraft (Chapter 1). But unlike the witch, the medium uses possession for positive social purposes. Finally, a medium's unusual behavior is attributed to the spirit inhabiting his or her body and is expected to abate after the seance. Nonmediumship possession, by contrast, tends to be associated with psychological derangement or an illness of significant duration, requiring human action to alleviate.

The common Anutan term for "spirit medium" is *vakaatua*, "spirit vessel" or "spirit vehicle." Little detail is remembered about *vakaatua*. Pu Nukumarere, my one informant in 1972 to have witnessed seances during his childhood, described them follows:

> When spirit mediums (*vakaatua*) existed, an *atua* rushed hither to enter the medium. The spirit announced that he wished a betel chew. The medium chewed his betel. Then his body shook violently.

When he was done chewing his betel, the spirit fell from the medium and fled. Then another entered. He would also come and chew. This was another spirit. Then his body shook again. Thus, he also chewed. When his chew was finished, he would also exit and depart. These were the spirits.

The spirits who entered mediums were our grandparents and ancestors. One's deceased father might also enter the medium. Even a child who predeceased his father might return and enter his father's body.

According to Moses Purianga, Anuta's acknowledged expert in oral tradition and ancient custom,[4] the major gods were more selective than their lesser counterparts in choosing mediums. In particular, Tearakura and Pu Tauraro, the *ariki pakatomo*, approached only certain individuals. The great gods *kairo e rere vare*, "do not run about aimlessly." Mediums entered by the leading deities were not termed *vakaatua* but *tauraatua*, "spirit anchors." Two men are especially remembered as *tauraatua*. One was Pu Maatopa, the son of Pu Pangatau, founding ancestor of the Kainanga i Pangatau; the other was Pu Taneanu, an important figure in the Kainanga i Mua.

Possession, whether involving mediumship or not, seems commonly to have been a positive phenomenon before the church. Although mediumship is no longer positively valued, spirits are still thought capable of entering a person and radically altering his/her personality and behavior. I heard reference to several such events during my field research.

One case occurred in the Russell Islands of the Central Solomons. Pu Nukuoika (Misak Taukoroa) became involved in a dispute with a man from Malaita. One day, as he was on his way to work, he found himself surrounded by a group of Malaitans, all armed with bush knives. Frightened, he called on the spirit of his uncle and former chief, Pu Teukumarae, for assistance. Suddenly, he felt Pu Teuku enter his body. All fear vanished. He grasped his knife and proclaimed that he was leaving and would kill anyone who tried to stop him. The circle parted, and he walked away without a fight.

The case about which I have the most information occurred during my first visit to Anuta in 1972–73. It is described at length in earlier publications (Feinberg 1979, 1980). Here I summarize the highlights.

The story involves a woman I have called Nau Tetupua (Feinberg 1979) who suffered from considerable psychosocial stress. She was from the leading "clan," the Kainanga i Mua, and married into the lower-ranking Kainanga i Pangatau. Her husband separated from the extended-family domestic unit (*patongia*) that he had shared with his two brothers. Shortly after that, he died. Her eldest son had already left Anuta to attend school overseas.

The elder of the two remaining sons was responsible and energetic in helping his mother; within a few years, he was appointed assistant catechist in recognition of his industry and good nature. From his mother's point of view, however, this meant that he spent more time away from home and less discharging his domestic duties. During this period, she had a dream in which a man instructed her to have her son step down from his position in the church. The boy, supported by public opinion, resisted this advice.

Shortly thereafter, Nau Tetupua's eldest son visited Anuta and left the following day, thus inadvertently reminding her of her isolation. Almost immediately, she experienced a severe change of personality. She became withdrawn and refused to attend church. She ceased all social intercourse and spent her time alone inside her house. The catechist paid her a visit and suggested that they pray together, but Nau Tetupua refused. She proclaimed that she had been possessed by God, to whom others pray but who does not pray Himself. In a later conversation, the catechist affirmed that she was very likely possessed, but by Satan rather than Jehovah.

These two cases make implicit statements about the social, moral, and religious order. Neither case involved spirit mediumship, since neither involved purposeful reciprocal communication between the community and a spiritual being. Pu Nukuoika's experience, however, was positively evaluated both by him and by the general community. Far from a parody of orthodox religion (Lambek 1989:53–54), it was an affirmation of and appeal to (an earlier) orthodox religion in the interest of personal and social preservation.

Nau Tetupua, by contrast, was universally condemned. Her possession could perhaps be characterized as a parody of orthodox religion and a protest against the established order. She was described as having "lost her mind" (*na atamai ku reku*) and was asserted to have been possessed by *te tupua kovi*, "an evil spirit," probably as punishment for some misdeed.

As in many cases of possession, Nau Tetupua's body was seen as the site of contention between two fully formed, autonomous selves, and this provided a context in which socially suppressed feelings could be given voice, at least indirectly. However, while it might be viewed as "culturally crafted . . . coping behavior," it is difficult to see Nau Tetupua's behavior as "highly skillful" and avoid interpreting it as "'pathology,' incompetence or breakdown" (Chapter 1). Indeed, because of its clear pathological dimensions, Anutans were able to dismiss her claims as groundless and attribute her behavior to her own misdeeds or self-inflicted contact with the Devil.

ANUTAN POSSESSION IN COMPARATIVE PERSPECTIVE

Who is likely to become possessed? What do patterns of possession indicate about Anutan personality and culture? Why have possession and mediumship on Anuta declined so precipitously since the introduction of Christianity when they have, in other communities, persisted largely intact? If possession served important functions on pre-Christian Anuta, have such functions become unimportant in recent decades? Or are they performed by some other mechanism? In this section, I explore these comparative questions.

In many communities (e.g., Samoa, Chapter 2; Tonga, Chapter 3; Chuuk,

Chapter 9; Toraja, Chapter 10), possession is a tool through which the power-less and downtrodden are able to become centers of attention, bring their concerns to the awareness of their relatives and neighbors, and exercise some influence over those around them. Victims are largely women, adolescents, young adults, and others occupying low positions in the social hierarchy.

Anutans distinguish mediumship (*vakaatua* and *tauraatua*) from other types of spirit encounter. *Tauraatua*, mediums for the high gods, included only men of special prominence. *Vakaatua* apparently included men and women representing a variety of social statuses. Nonmediumship possession includes both positively and negatively evaluated forms. Positive instances often involve men under conditions of physical threat. The negative case described above—that of Nau Tetupua—conforms more closely to the common pattern, involving the disadvantaged and socially isolated, or those under unusual stress. It appears, however, that such possession no longer occurs with any frequency. This raises the question: what does possession do, and as it diminishes in prominence, is it supplanted by other phenomena?

Spirit mediumship and possession may serve several purposes. In addition to empowering the disenfranchised, it can provide explanations for otherwise apparently inexplicable events (e.g., Malinowski 1954; Spiro 1952); yield information not accessible through ordinary sense experience; and achieve consensus on controversial issues facing the community (Firth 1967). The medium is in some sense a locus of power (Chapter 1; Glick 1967), particularly power to acquire esoteric knowledge. As Hanson (1987:425) observes, "Gods had knowledge superior to that of humans—knowledge of what was happening far away, or would happen in the future." And people, when controlled by gods, acquire some of that power. Hanson also notes, however, that intercourse with gods can have negative consequences, and it is these negative consequences that Anutans presently associate most often with possession.

In discussions leading to this volume, some suggested that possession, under conditions of cultural stress and social change, might cease to serve a communicative purpose and so disappear, replaced by more clearly pathological phenomena. On Anuta, mediumship and possession appear to no longer serve the communicative purpose they once did, and they have been largely discontinued. Fortunately for Anutans, nonpathological alternatives exist.

Information not readily available to the senses can be obtained through dreams or visions in which spirits "speak" (*karanga*) to the recipient, "revealing" (*pakaari*) what is hidden from the view of others (Feinberg In Press a, In Press b). Furthermore, there may be fewer imponderables of the type that mediums used to address. With better transportation and communication, the fortunes of distant travelers can more readily be monitored. And the availability of Western medicine makes many illnesses less problematic than they were a century ago. Consensus about the proper course of social action sometimes is achieved through proclamations by the chiefs and their advisers, or by the catechist. In other instances, however, it is not achieved and conflicts fester, perhaps creating a kind of social pathology. This is a point to which I return below.

Nor is possession essential to empowering disenfranchised individuals. Those who feel denied the opportunity to realize their aspirations often can emigrate to urban centers and advance their goals through education or wage employment. Even on Anuta, those lacking the genealogical qualifications for prominent status in the political and ritual systems can gain respect by demonstrating strength, wisdom, competence at crafts, or skill in storytelling, sailing, fishing, gardening, and navigation. To these traditional avenues to social mobility one now can add the church, which carries no genealogical requirements for assumption of leadership positions. This is not to say that opportunities for gaining prominence are adequate to preempt all conflict. Occasionally, fights, suicide attempts, and psychological disturbances occur. Still, many outlets are available to relieve frustration even in the absence of possession.

Levy et al. (Chapter 1) cite two conditions necessary for the occurrence of spirit possession. These are: inclusion in a community of people predisposed to dissociation; and a cultural environment that attributes special meaning and utility to possession episodes. Anuta offers the first of these conditions, as the following section will show. The second has drastically diminished. With a few exceptions, possession is no longer positively valued. The Christian God is most unlikely to possess an ordinary mortal. Local spirits are still present and sometimes possess Anutans, but in the modern era they are defined predominantly in negative terms.[5]

SPIRIT AND SELF

Anutans have a strong sense of themselves as historically situated. Their view of personal identity grows out of a past that is marked by the island's ancient customs (*nga tukutukunga mai mua*) and their personal genealogies. They are intimately concerned with questions of where they came from and what places their forebears visited in the course of their travels. Identification of the self with grandparents and ancestors is observable in the Anutan naming system (see Feinberg 1982b, 1983) and in Anutan spirit beliefs.

The presumed existence of ancestral spirits serves as affirmation that the past has been incorporated into the present. Parents, grandparents, and prominent ancestors may be long dead, but they are still present as spirits. Their personalities remain, and they continue to take interest in the world of mortal human beings. They are concerned about the welfare of their children and descendants and use their powers to ensure their progeny's prosperity and health. Moreover, human beings, by having spirits enter and possess them, are in some sense merged with spirits, who are at the same time historical personages.

Hanson makes much of the Polynesian continuity between gods and people. As he puts the matter:

Humans, arriving at birth from the supernatural realm, apparently were thought to have a spiritual existence before birth, and they definitely were thought to return to the spiritual realm as ghosts and ancestral gods after death. (Hanson 1987:431; see also Kaeppler 1987:432).

Similarly, on Anuta the ability of people to experience possession blurs the notion of the individual. The same person is at once a spirit and the human being whom others know in ordinary life. Thus, the Western notion of the person as a clearly bounded, mutually exclusive self (Geertz 1976:225) is compromised in the Anutan scheme.

Transcendence of the separation between human and spirit also may be seen in the process of adding new gods to the pantheon and is well illustrated by the case of Dr. C. E. Fox, an Anglican missionary from New Zealand who lived for decades in the Solomons. Over several generations, Fox influenced thousands of Solomon Islanders, shaping their perceptions of and relations to the church; by the time he left in 1973, he was revered throughout the archipelago.

Fox (1985) says that he visited Anuta once. Anutans claim, however, that he secretly appeared among them several times after crossing the ocean on foot. In addition, he had occasional contacts with Anutans who had emigrated to the central Solomons. He corresponded with Anutans (as with other Solomon Islanders), answering questions and giving advice. More importantly, perhaps, his reputation as a wise and powerful church leader preceded him throughout the islands and was well established in Anutan minds. When I asked if Dr. Fox was a man or a spirit, I was told that he was clearly not an *ordinary* man. Very likely, he was an *atua*—someone perhaps like John the Baptist. Anutans rejected my suggestion that he was the second coming of Jesus but acknowledged that he had performed many Christ-like miracles (see Feinberg In Press b).

Anutans are apparently more god-oriented than some other Oceanic peoples (cf. Shore 1982; White and Kirkpatrick 1985), but they seem to have a similarly situational view of the person. Thus, the senior chief could tell me in the most deprecating terms about a major disagreement he had with his junior colleague, the Ariki Tepuko, yet a few days later, in a different context, extol the latter's chiefly virtue with comparable eloquence.

Elsewhere, I have argued that a kind of relativism permeates Anutan culture (see particularly Feinberg 1988a:92-100, 1988b). What is good in one situation is bad in another. What is appropriate for a person of high rank may be wholly inappropriate for a commoner (Feinberg In Press a). Someone may be chiefly (*ariki*) in comparison with one person and "commoner" (*pakaaropa*) in relation to another. Something may be *tea*, "white," in comparison with a dark object and *uri*, "black," when compared with a lighter one. Directions tend to be characterized in terms of *ngaatai*, "seaward," and *ngaauta*, "toward the center of the nearest island," so that the same location may be *ngaatai* in relation to one object and *ngaauta* in relation to another. Anutans tend to speak of "upward" (*runga*) and "downward" (*raro*) rather than top and bottom. And wind compass directions are defined in relation to each other rather than in terms of absolute positions.

Similarly, Anutans seem to find untenable a rigid opposition between self and other or of "man" (*tangata*) and "spirit" (*atua*). Rather, they blend into one another, so that the same entity can be human in one context (e.g., before death, or a medium while not under the control of a spirit familiar) and spirit in another (e.g., after death or while possessed by a spirit familiar). A few individuals, like Dr. Fox, are spoken of as simultaneously man and spirit (*ko te tangata pe ko te atua*). Nor do Anutans draw a clear line between gods and spirits. This form of relativism, I further suggest, is common in Polynesia and present in associative views of the self.

DISCOURSE AND BELIEF: HISTORICAL PERSPECTIVES

Historical documentation for Anuta is sparse, and prior to this century was almost non-existent. Therefore, it is difficult to reconstruct historical events, beliefs, and practices with any certainty. However, several strands of evidence are, at the very least, suggestive. These include: oral traditions; the memories of most elderly informants; statements by Anutans on Tikopia to Sir Raymond Firth during his periods of field work, especially in 1928–29 and 1952; and comparative material from Tikopia, which Firth has richly documented. Over the past century, the apparent constancy of Anutan discourse and belief regarding spirits is impressive, particularly considering that this period includes the introduction of Christianity and conversion of the entire community. Despite such consistency, however, noteworthy shifts occurred in perspective and emphasis.

Changing Modes of Discourse

Although Anutans now evince few misgivings about their pre-Christian past, this was not the case in 1972. At that time they often spoke disparagingly of their traditional religion. The island *ne nopo poouri,* "dwelt in darkness," until the church brought them *te maarama,* "the light." They spoke of the morally questionable behavior of their ancestors, who often failed to show *aropa,* "love" or "compassion," and killed uninvited visitors. Nonetheless, embarrassment was tinged with ambivalence. Anutans value strength and fighting prowess, and they like the image of themselves as strong and aggressive. They take pride in stories of their ancestors repelling invasions from much larger islands. More than once I heard such comments as: "Before the arrival of the church, we killed anyone who came to this island. We were *bad* then, weren't we!" But this was always followed by a chuckle, suggesting a degree of pleasure in the image of their "badness."

Perhaps more importantly, most Europeans whom Anutans had encountered were Christians who neither believed in nor respected non-Western religions.

Therefore, Anutans' claims to have accepted Christianity almost immediately when it was introduced can be understood at least in part as a strategy for projecting what they imagined would be a positive image to a Western audience.

As on Tikopia, structural parallels between the old and new religions made Christianity a less radical departure from tradition than might seem obvious (Firth 1970:313–15). Still, some changes are inevitable in perceptions of, approaches to, and discourse about gods and spirits. If nothing else, the old gods were demoted in importance. Less attention is paid to them, and significant resources no longer are put into winning their assistance.

This is apparent in abandonment of separate sets of names by which the old gods used to be addressed in contexts secular and sacred. To invoke a god's assistance in pre-Christian times, one called him by his sacred name (*ingoa pakaepa* or *ingoa pakataputapu*). If one should speak a sacred name in profane contexts, the god would hear that he was being called upon for trivial concerns, grow annoyed, and offer punishment (see Feinberg In Press b). Today, Anutans often call gods by their sacred names regardless of context, and in many instances secular names have long been forgotten.

As Anutans spend less time discussing local gods, the relative attention paid to the more spiritlike of numinals increases. And as Anutans look toward the Christian God for positive intervention in their lives, other numinals take on an increasingly negative aspect. There have, however, been marked oscillations in discourse about local gods and spirits.

Missionization was followed by a period of uncertainty, during which many people went back to reliance on spirit mediums, local deities, and abbreviated kava ceremonies in times of stress or sickness. The period seems to have been characterized by some polarization, where advocates of the new religion actively disparaged the old gods as malignant and their supporters as reactionary or worse. Yet even during the time between missionization and my first field research, people felt indebted to the ancient deities for helping their forbears survive a precarious existence. Moreover, Anutans' historical consciousness led them to maintain an interest in older spiritual beings' activities, identities, and personalities. They were grateful to the ancient deities for their creation of, and support for, major features of Anuta's social structure, including their chiefly system. The most important gods were valued ancestors and former chiefs. Through oral traditions, Anutans preserved some memory of the old gods and their most basic attributes. Still, many details were forever lost, and those who did have information hesitated to divulge it to whomever they believed might view the old religion critically. They were reluctant to discuss with Europeans their pre-Christian past, and in 1972–73, I was on Anuta for almost a year before people would confide in me about spirit encounters (see Feinberg In Press b).

Since my 1972 field study, Anutans have been more open with me about their experience with gods and spirits. To some degree, this may reflect a change in my relationship with them and their increasing confidence in me. At the same time, Anutans' views of their religious history, and the way they speak of it among themselves, have also likely changed. With time, insecurities about commitment to the new religion have undoubtedly diminished. Thus, Anutans now feel more at liberty to acknowledge their emotional connections with deceased relatives and ancestors. Indeed, some people even voice regret that their parents and grandparents allowed so many details of the old religion to be lost.

Today, Anutans have still further reason to be interested in their traditional religion. As they spend longer periods away from their home island, attending school, working for wages, or visiting relatives, they come into more intensive contact with representatives of other cultures. Consequently, they have grown self-conscious about symbols of local identity. In this respect, their old religion is now emblematic. Even *atua vare* and *tupua penua*, although in some ways threatening, represent a common place and common experience. The major gods were, in addition, positively valued in their own right. Thus, pre-Christian gods and spirits have become shared symbols of identity, to be nurtured and protected—held and guarded against further loss or diminution.

Spirits, Moral Discourse, and Social Order

Levy et al. (Chapter 1) suggest an association of gods with control and spirits with situations in which control is in abeyance. If correct, then gods are likely to be most conspicuous in hierarchical societies with centralized authority, while spirits predominate in societies that emphasize local autonomy.

All Anutan numinals occupy positions between the extremes marked by these ideal types, so even the most spiritlike of them have godlike properties and vice versa. Anutans are about equally concerned with the more spiritlike and the more godlike beings. As the model would suggest, Anutans occupy a middle ground between commitment to hierarchy and centralization on the one hand and local autonomy on the other. They have, in theory, a rigid hierarchical system, based on genealogical seniority, and are led by a paramount chief who exercises both political authority and spiritual leadership. Yet because of the community's small size and isolation, the formality of sociopolitical relations breaks down and local autonomy becomes compatible with centralized authority. Furthermore, in accordance with the model, Anutan spirits tend to be most prominent when chiefly authority is challenged.

As in their social structure and concern with gods and spirits, Anutans take a middle ground in discourse about order and disorder. Their conversation reflects concern with social breakdown, and they speak a great deal about rules or laws, phrased in terms of "custom" (*nga tukutukunga*). This, in turn, leads to a major point of continuity between the old ways and the new: the role of religion as a forum for moral discourse.

The behavior of pre-Christian supernaturals was not always morally commendable. Tearakura, who eventually became the premier deity, led the slaughter of most of the island's population, intimidated his fellow islanders, arranged for his younger brother's death in order to marry his widow, drove his daughter to suicide, and then hanged himself in a fit of shame for what he had done. Later, as a spiritual being, he assisted his descendants in slaying visitors from other islands. Still, he and his fellow deities were a moral force in the Durkheimian sense of providing collective representations that encouraged members of the community to identify with one another and with the community at large (cf. Durkheim 1965; Parsons 1968). They rewarded those who remained faithful to societal rules and who expressed allegiance through collective worship and respect for the existing hierarchy. They looked after the material well-being of their descendants so long as the living paid respect to their authority and power. And they enforced adherence to social norms by punishing all those who flouted the established social order.

I have never heard Anutans criticize the Christian God or suggest that He might be, in any way, morally deficient. They cite biblical passages referring to Him as a loving God, thereby reinforcing their cultural preoccupation with *aropa* (see Feinberg 1981, In Press a, and elsewhere). The church provides a center of social activity and moral guidance, and most of Anuta's ceremonial calendar is controlled by the church. Perhaps God's most frequently discussed attribute, however, is His wrath. Anyone who fails to attend church or follow religious dictates, who challenges the social order, or fails to respect and obey chiefs and others at the upper reaches of the social hierarchy is bound to suffer serious misfortune. Should people violate tradition or fail to care for their relatives, God, like the deities before Him, is thought to be offended and to punish the community with cyclones, drought, famine, or epidemic.

When social discord strikes the island, each side looks to heaven to visit misfortune on the other, thereby vindicating its own position. And when disaster hits, Anutans invest a great deal of energy trying to identify the culprit and misdeed responsible for bringing it about.

This inclination is illustrated by a series of conflicts that occurred among Anutans during the late 1970s and early 1980s.[6] One faction was led by the senior chief. The other opposed the chief on a variety of issues centering around sale of locally-grown crops and organization of the church. At their height, the conflicts threatened to turn violent.

Before long, the island was plunged into famine, epidemic, and a series of misfortunes, and the chief's opponents seemed to fare far worse than his supporters. One man came around to the *ariki*'s side after his wife died in the epidemic. Another's wife and child became severely ill until he joined the chief's faction, at which point they recovered. Throughout this period, spirits roamed the island, causing havoc. People huddled in their houses, fearing to go out, especially at night. Occasionally, spirits were said, uncharacteristically, to have entered people's homes.

My informants were uncertain as to the immediate efficient cause of the misfortunes. Some attributed them to curses uttered by the chief. The chief himself suggested that the misfortunes were the automatic consequence of disobedience to him and failure to respect the island's ancient customs. Still others held spirits responsible. But the final cause, in everyone's opinion, was God—creator of the universe and the laws by which it is governed.

All of my informants evaluated this period of unusual spirit activity in negative terms and took it as a sign of the community's moral defects. People disagreed as to who was to blame, but everyone agreed that local spirits and the Christian God alike objected to the conflicts that were tearing the society apart. Victor Turner, in a well-known essay, suggests that the Ndembu of Zambia interpret illness and misfortune as an indication from the spirit world that "something is rotten" in the body politic (Turner 1967:225). As among the Ndembu, the trauma of misfortune convinced Anutans that they had better mend their ways—at least for the time being. Thus, although "undistinguished spirits" and similar beings may be negatively valued and are most frequently encountered during times of social stress and moral breakdown, in another sense they are no less a force promoting order and control than Tearakura or Jehovah.

CONCLUSION

Anutans recognize a wide variety of superhuman beings, forming a continuum from "undistinguished spirits" to the island's premier gods. These beings are a major feature of Anutan life despite three-quarters of a century of Christianity; the shift toward naturalistic explanation, found in many communities, has not occurred on Anuta. Thus, the observation that "it is not just changes in cultural doctrines that affect the presence or absence of spirits" (Levy et al. Chapter 1) is borne out. Reasons for maintenance of spirit beliefs in their present form include the following:

The Anglican Church has not attempted to eradicate belief in local spirits so long as Anutans do not actively worship them. Anglican doctrine itself recognizes a variety of numinals; part of the dedication ceremony for a new church house constructed in 1972 involved the Bishop of Melanesia exorcising evil spirits from the premises.

Parallels exist between the structure of the old religious system and the new, making it possible for the Christian God to be incorporated as a new deity, greater in power but not fundamentally different in kind from those to whom Anutans once dedicated kava ceremonies. Anutan Christianity may have, in some ways, redefined and recontextualized local spirits and the old religion, but it has not *de*contextualized them.

Still, spirit encounters on Anuta, as in many other communities, ebb and flow with the course of events. Howard (Chapter 6) accounts for the decline in spirit activity on Rotuma partly in terms of changes in the island's physical environment that have removed much of the mystery of daily (or nightly) life. As Levy et al. note, "The more experience that takes place in well-illuminated settings, the less room there is for spirits" (Chapter 1).

For Anuta, what determines the frequency of spirit encounters seems to be social relations and the community's overall well-being rather than the physical environment *per se*. When life is proceeding smoothly, Anutans are reasonably cavalier in their meanderings even on the darkest nights. By contrast, when the community is torn asunder by social conflict and natural disaster, spirits are encountered even inside people's homes and in broad daylight. As Levy et al. suggest, "Numinals who touch upon personal experience tend to proliferate during periods of intense upheaval" (Chapter 1). External pressures generating social discord on Anuta have increased, creating a situation in which one might expect to encounter spirits, and nothing fundamental has changed to cast doubt on spirit presence and activity. Anutan spirits thus promote social and cultural stability, although not primarily through possession. The advent of flashlights and kerosene lanterns has not, any more than Christianity, meant the demise of Anutan spirits.

In addition to appearing at times of social discord, spirits tend to be encountered at times of personal stress. Many of the episodes related to me involved ghosts of recently deceased relatives, close friends, or other prominent community members. This is illustrated by Corrine's encounter with the spirit of her father, and by Satan's attempt to steal Pu Ororiki's soul.

Anutans, like other peoples discussed in this volume, draw a connection between spirit activity and dissociated states. The dissociation, however, often is within the social order rather than the individual. On the other hand, Anutans generally account for the uncanny, the unexplained, the peculiar disease, or unmerited accident, in terms of taboo violation rather than spirits. Spirits tend to explain sensory peculiarities rather than answer great metaphysical questions.

Interestingly, Anutans say that they encounter spirits less overseas than at home. Perhaps urban dwellers have fewer unlighted areas with which to contend, but I was told that children in school in the Central Solomons did not hesitate to hunt for birds or crabs alone on moonless nights—something they would not do on their home island. Possibly, Anutans staying overseas to attend school or work for wages live in a more rigidly controlled institutional setting than they do at home, and it is the relative certainty about social relations that keeps spirits at a distance.

Finally, the Anutans' spiritual world, like other features of their cultural universe, resists classification in terms of rigid, mutually exclusive categories. Thus, as for other peoples discussed in this volume, there is no hard and fast distinction between God, gods, spirits, ghosts, and mortals.[7] This aversion to rigid categories facilitates belief in possession, as it once did in spirit mediumship. Further, it allows spiritual beings to be a focus of moral discourse while leaving sufficient ambiguity to permit an ongoing debate as to who is wrong or right and who is responsible for spirit intercession in the world of human beings.

NOTES

Acknowledgments. This chapter grows out of a series of sessions at annual meetings of the Association for Social Anthropology in Oceania. I am indebted to other participants and particularly the organizers, Jeannette Mageo and Alan Howard, for their encouragement and constructive criticism. I would also like to thank Jill McEldery-Maxwell for her careful reading and assistance in preparation of this manuscript.

1   They do dichotomize, as I have argued elsewhere (Feinberg 1980, 1982a, 1988b). However, they define their categories contextually, in relational rather than absolute terms. Indeed, a binary system implies conceptualization in terms of contrasts and comparisons. This issue is addressed further below.

2   *Tangata* has the same ambiguity as "man" in English. It may apply to all human beings, male human beings, or only adult males, the meaning in any utterance being inferred from context. For purposes of clarity, and in an attempt to avoid theoretical and political loading, in this chapter I gloss *tangata* as "people" or "human beings" when used in its generic sense.

3   This is the only reference I have heard to use of a mirror in such a context, and I was given no indication of why it was there. To my knowledge, Anutans do not normally use mirrors or other reflective devices for ritual purposes.

4   Moses has been, by consensus, Anuta's leading expert on such matters since Pu Nukumarere's death in the mid-1970s.

5   This, however, is changing. Particularly parents, grandparents, and ancestors are now thought by some Anutans to continue to be interested in their offspring's (or descendants') well-being, and they may be mobilized through proper invocation. Thus in a case described above, when Misak Taukoroa thought himself at risk of physical attack, he appealed to Pu Teukumarae for assistance. He staunchly resisted my suggestion that God or the church might object to such a request for support.

6   For a detailed account of these conflicts, see Feinberg (1986, In Press a).

7   As Hanson (1987:432) puts the matter:

> In Polynesia gods and people are aspects of the same reality and form a continuum of the sacred and the profane. Even as, in relative terms, the gods are sacred and the people profane, so also are the chiefs sacred and the commoners profane. . . . High gods, demigods, ancestral gods, culture heroes, spirits, elves, and people were intertwined in different ways.

6 Speak of the Devils

Discourse and Belief in Spirits on Rotuma

Alan Howard

Rotuma is a small volcanic island located 465 km north of Fiji, on the western fringe of Polynesia. Physically, linguistically, and culturally, Rotumans reflect influences from Melanesia, Micronesia, and particularly the Polynesian islands to the east: Tonga, Samoa, Futuna, and Uvea.

Following first European contact in 1791, Rotuma was intensively intruded upon by whalers, renegade sailors, traders and missionaries. The first missionaries arrived in 1839, and reflecting a prior political cleavage, approximately two-thirds of the people converted to Wesleyanism, the remainder to Catholicism. Exacerbated by national rivalries between English ministers and French priests, a series of skirmishes between the sides led the chiefs to petition Great Britain for cession in 1879.

From 1881 to 1970 Rotuma was governed as part of the Colony of Fiji with a resident commissioner (later a district officer) acting as governor, magistrate, and, usually, medical officer. The chiefs of Rotuma's seven semi-autonomous districts met in council but were relegated to an advisory role. When Fiji gained independence in 1970, the Rotuman chiefs opted to remain part of the new nation and, not without controversy, affirmed their decision after the military coups of 1987. While the position of district officer has been retained, the powers of governance have been reallocated to the Rotuma Council, composed of district chiefs and elected district representatives.

The Rotuman population reached a low of around 2,000 following a devastating measles epidemic in 1911. From then on it steadily increased and presently numbers around 11,000. Only about 2,600 individuals now live on the 43-square-kilometer island, however, down from a peak of 3,235 in 1966. The bulk of Rotumans have settled in Fiji's urban centers, although substantial enclaves have formed in Australia and New Zealand as well.

Rotumans place a high value on formal education and have done extremely well in occupational pursuits, being vastly overrepresented in the professions, managerial positions and high government office. English is spoken by all but a few elderly individuals and is the language of instruction from the third grade on. Although copra remains Rotuma's only significant export, remittances and a free flow of goods onto the island have resulted in an uncommonly high standard of living for such an isolated Pacific island.

Over the past thirty years I have noticed that talk about spirits on Rotuma has diminished significantly. During my initial period of field work on the island, in 1960, people spontaneously brought up the topic on innumerable occasions, whereas on my recent field trips (1987–91, 1994), mention of spiritual agency was conspicuously absent, even on occasions that would seem to call for it. This raises some interesting questions: What conditions have led to this change in discourse? What does the change imply about Rotuman beliefs? Are Rotuman spirits headed for cultural oblivion? Before confronting these issues directly, I summarize accounts of spirits, mostly provided by European visitors who obtained their information by talking with Rotumans.

CATEGORIES AND CONCEPTS

'Atua

The most general Rotuman word for spirits is *'atua*, which Churchward defines as "dead person, corpse, ghost." He adds, "The last is its commonest meaning, ghosts being very material beings ... to the Rotuman mind" (Churchward 1940:352). But such a simple, concise definition fails to do justice to the complexity of usage in Rotuman discourse. European visitors to Rotuma have, from the beginning, had difficulty coming to grips with such concepts, in part, it seems, because they have been more concerned with logical consistency and systemization of beliefs into religious theologies than with the contexts in which the concepts were used. That early European visitors to the island were disconcerted by the lack of systemization in Rotuman discourse about spirits is evident in their accounts (see, for example, Lesson 1838-9:437; Bennett 1831:478).

The conclusions of early commentators were likely a consequence of responses to a discourse format Rotumans found unfamiliar. Instead of discussing spirits in the abstract, Rotumans talked about spirits in rather specific contexts—when telling stories, expressing apprehension or a sense of foreboding, attempting to explain anomalous occurrences, coping with uncanny feelings and unnatural sensations, etc.

Not surprisingly, early European accounts of Rotuman "religious beliefs" or, as they were frequently designated, "superstitions" (which suggests irrationality as well as inconsistency and incoherence), fall back on anecdotal information. But Rotumans learned, rather early on, I suspect, to provide coherent accounts that were more satisfactory to European interrogators. Thus Churchward obtained a verbatim account (in Rotuman) from Mesulama Titifanua in response to queries concerning the meaning of various terms. With regard to the word 'atua, Titifanua replied:

> As soon as a human being dies he becomes an 'atua. It was held by [our] forefathers that it was the spirit ('ata) of the person that was the 'atua, and that he was able to go about. In their time, moreover, they were in the habit of summoning their dead to come to them that they might converse. This they did, at times, [just] because they loved their dead friends so much. They also had great confidence in them when they wanted to know various things, asking their 'atuas to tell them. Especially did they trust in [the 'atuas of] their prematurely born children. They said that the 'atua that had more power to deliver than any other was [that of] a child prematurely born. (Titifanua 1995:123–124; translation by Churchward)

Some aspects of the meaning of 'atua proved confusing to Europeans. For example, as Churchward's definition indicates, 'atua refers to a corpse as well as a ghost. This usage suggests a being devoid of "spirit." Hocart wrote that "any Rotuman will tell you that atua is a dead man (famör ala). It is actually used of the dead body, and once children playing with human bones told me that they were "the bones of atua" (sui ne atua)" (Hocart 1915:129). To make matters even more complicated, 'atua, modified by possessive markers used with edible items, is used in reference to a person killed in war or defeated in a wrestling match.[1]

Rotuman attitudes toward 'atua, and their efforts to control spirits' powers, were an endless source of fascination to European visitors. Here, too, outsiders encountered a range of propositions that failed to meet their criteria for a reasoned (and reasonable) religion. Gardiner reflects typical European perceptions in his discussion of relations between 'atua and human beings:

> Long before the advent of the missionaries to Rotuma, the religion of its people seems to have degenerated into the grossest superstition and a mere belief in atua, a generic name for all devils, spirits, and ghosts. It is also used for the soul, as we understand it. These atua were ever ready to punish and prey on any one who did not propitiate them with plentiful gifts of food and kava. Each hoag ["section of a district or village under the authority of a sub-chief"] had its own atua, but several hoag might acknowledge a big atua over all, while they each had their own atua. At the same time, so long as they propitiated their own atua, no great harm could happen to them, unless a greater atua laid a curse on them, causing sickness, etc.; the atua, though, could only affect them personally, and had little or no power over their crops. This atua might be termed "the god of the hoag," but there was also an inferior class of atua, who might be called "devil spirits," whose sole delight it was to go about causing sickness and death . . . Their dwelling-places were in trees, stones, and rocks . . . but some were said to enter into men . . . The still inferior class of atua, but a class with little or no power of itself alone, would best be termed "the ghosts of men." They could be to some extent called up at will by the relations to

assist them against their enemies and to cure them of sicknesses of a certain class, supposed to be due to the influence of soul on soul. (Gardiner 1898:466)

The compound form *sur'atua* is used in reference to possession [*sur* = "to enter"]. According to Churchward, the term signifies a person into whom the spirit of a deceased person has entered. It can also be used adjectivally to designate a person who has such visitations periodically, i.e., a spiritual medium, and in noun form to refer to a "seance." When a person was possessed by an *'atua* they were said to take on the appearance, mannerism and voice of the deceased person who entered them (Churchward 1940:317). In contrast, the phrase *to'ák 'atua*, meaning "to utter messages alleged to come from the spirit of a deceased person," does not imply possession, only the use of a living individual as a medium by the spirit (Churchward 1940:334).

The phrase *rē 'atua* [*rē* = "to do"] is used in reference to actions designed to harness the powers of *'atua* through ritual transactions. Various forms of cursing, attempts to gain advantage in conflicts or disputes by appealing to dead ancestors, and invoking the healing powers of *'atua* were so labeled.

'Aitu

'Aitu is a second term used in reference to spirits. Churchward defines *'aitu* in its noun form as "god, object of worship; shark, stingray, or other creature regarded as the habitat of a god"; as a verb "to regard as divine, to worship" (Churchward 1940:348). The distinction between *'aitu* and *'atua* was unclear to many European commentators, some of whom treated them as synonymous (Russell 1942:249). This may have been a response to the fact that certain kinds of *'atua* are considered to be *'aitu*, as in the case of a group of wandering spirits known collectively as *sa'aitu* (alternatively as *la' ti'ta*, "the big traveling company"). Titifanua described *sa'aitu* to Churchward as the souls of uncircumcised men who, in times of war, helped one side or the other to victory (Titifanua 1995:123–124). Other informants described companies of *sa'aitu* as composed of the spirits (*'atua*) of dead chiefs, or persons who died suddenly (MacGregor 1932, box 1).

A key to understanding the distinction between the two concepts for spirits lies in the fact that *'ait[u]* is often used as a verb in such compounds as *'ait'aki* [*'aki* = instrumental suffix], "to deify, to treat as divine," and *rō'aitu*, "to pray"[2] (Churchward 1940:349, 301), while *'atua* is never used as a verb. This suggests that although *'atua* is used as a generic term for spirits, including free-roaming malicious ones beyond human control, *'aitu* is reserved for spirits who have been brought into the human moral order through various forms of binding, a point made by Vilsoni Hereniko (1991, 1995). Whereas Churchward glosses the *sa'* in *sa'aitu* as cognate with the Tongan *ha'a* and Samoan *sa*, meaning tribe, family or class (1939:469), Hereniko argues that it derives from *sa'a*, "to weave." He thus glosses the term *sa'aitu* as "woven gods."

Hereniko derives his inspiration from a Rotuman myth titled " 'Äeatos," in which malicious *'atua* are neutralized by being caught in woven nets. He points out that *sa'aitu* served human interests, albeit at their own discretion. Pushing his case further, he convincingly argues that *apei*, "fine white mats," which are central items of ritual exchange at weddings, funerals, and other life-crisis events, are themselves given a godlike status in Rotuman culture. They can be thought of as containing (and constraining) spirits in their own right, a view supported by the fact that *apei* are consecrated through the ritual sacrifice of a pig.

Hereniko's analysis helps explain why the god of the *sau* and *mua*, Tagroa *sir'ia*, was an *'aitu*.[3] The *sau* was described as the "king" of Rotuma by European visitors, while the *mua* was considered to be a "high priest"; their main roles were to perform cyclical rituals designed to ensure the prosperity of the island (see Howard 1985). *Tagroa sir'ia* was prayed to for food, for rain, and for success in islandwide enterprises. He could be called on to avert hurricanes or other calamities. Significantly, Gardiner was told that Tagroa "does not concern himself with the doings of the *'atua*" (Gardiner 1898:467).

Whereas the phrase *to'äk'atua* refers to circumstances in which the spirit of a deceased person speaks through the mouth of a medium, *to'äk 'aitu* refers to a condition in which an *'aitu* speaks, unheard by others, to an entranced recipient who then relates the messages to a waiting audience (Elisapeti Inia, personal communication).

In an ironic twist of fate, the English Methodist missionaries and French Catholic priests who translated the Bible selected alternate terms for God and devil(s). Methodists chose *'aitu* for God and relegated the concept of *'atua* to "devils," while Catholics chose the reverse. Whether this exacerbated already existing tensions between the two groups is unclear, but it did provide a basis for adherents of the conflicting faiths to heap verbal scorn on one another. It also may have contributed to the confusion of the two concepts.

Tu'ura, Ape'aitu, and Tupu'a

The term *tu'ura* was used to designate a being that hosted an *'atua*. According to Titifanua, *tu'ura*

> really means what they [the ancestors] referred to when they said, "Such and such a woman has become a *tu'ura* living in an owl" [lit. "The woman, she has *tu'urad* to an owl"; note that *tu'ura*, though fundamentally a noun, is used also as a verb]; "while such and such a man has become a *tu'ura* living in a cat." [Thus] we sometimes use the expression "an *'atua* cat," the reason being that, when we say this, we think of an *'atua* as having entered into the cat. . . . [Our] forefathers said that animals into which *'atuas* had entered as *tu'uras* had a different shape from other animals, and they were able to distinguish an animal into which an *'atua* had entered as a *tu'ura*. (Titifanua 1995:125; translation by Churchward)

Several of MacGregor's informants considered human beings who hosted an *'atua* (or an *'aitu*) to be *tu'ura* as well. In fact some were unable to distinguish between *tu'ura* and *ape'aitu*, a term Churchward defines simply as "priests" (1940:174). MacGregor speculates that *ape'aitu* may have been prophets,[4] while *tu'ura* were mediums engaged by families to communicate with their deity. He comments that the terms were used synonymously when he visited Rotuma in 1932.[5]

Regarding the role of *tu'ura*, MacGregor cites an informant by the name of Varamua:

> When the tu'ura has been asked to prophesy or tell of [the reason/outcome of someone's] sickness, he goes to his house . . . and beats his drum to call the god. Then when he feels "very strong" or possessed with the god he eats uncooked taro and pig, even the head which is tabu to the chief, and takes kava, all of which is presented by the person who wished to consult the god. When he has eaten and had kava which are for the god (not the tu'ura) he becomes the mouthpiece of the god and answers questions as to sickness, prospects of a coming war. (MacGregor 1932, box 1)

Like Churchward, Gardiner equated *ape'aitu* with priests (and priestesses) insofar as they officiated at invocations and acted as mediums for local gods.

Another term associated with spirits is *tupu'a*, which Churchward translates as "immortal man; rock or stone reputed to be such a person petrified" (Churchward 1940:337). Certain rocks were thought to be *tupu'a*, and their spirits could be called upon by persons acting as mediums.

Spirit Abodes

Rotuman spirits were thought to occupy a wide variety of niches, according to type. *Tagroa sir'ia* lived in the sky, ancestral ghosts took up their abode in various offshore locations under the sea, while other *'atua* were said to dwell in trees, rocks, cemeteries, and isolated places on the island. Some spirits were free-roaming and could appear anywhere in the form of animals or apparitions.[6]

The most general term for the abode of spirits is *'oroi*, which means "to be hidden from view" or "hidden from knowledge, mysterious, unknown, unknowable" (Churchward 1940:360). In contrast, the material world is referred to as *rån te'isi,* "this world."

Every district but one had a named location offshore to which the souls of the dead migrated (see map, figure 6.1). The best known of these, or more accurately, the most talked about, was *Li'marä'e* [*li'u* = "deep sea" + *marä'e* = "open space within a village where gatherings are held"], off the west end of the island. The route to the *'oroi* regions went westward, through the village of Losa (Russell 1942:249). Gardiner states that *Li'marä'e* was "full of cocoanuts, pigs, and all that man could wish for . . . [and that] Any things buried with the body would be taken by its ghost" (Gardiner 1898:469).

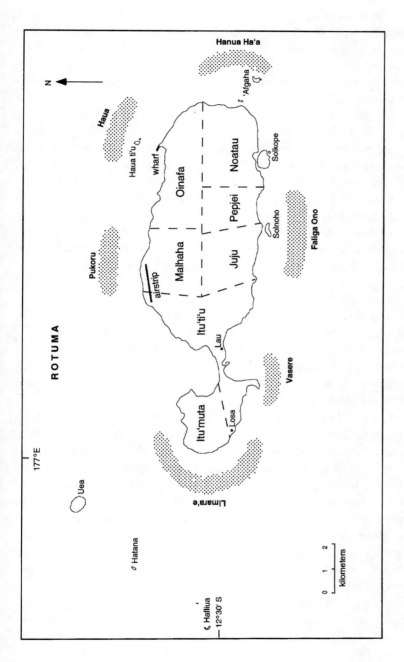

Figure 6.1 Map of Rotuma Showing Locations of Named Underworlds
Shaded areas show 'Oroi regions (after Russell 1942:231)
(Adapted from a map drawn by Joan Lawrence)

Bush areas were considered likely habitats for spirits, as were wells and certain kinds of trees (see Eagleston 1832:401–402 for an interesting example). One particular spirit, a legendary figure by the name of *hạnit e mạ'us*, "wild woman of the bush," sometimes appeared in the form of a succubus, a beautiful temptress who lured men into sexual liaisons in order to capture their souls. In general, it seems, the further removed one was from human habitats—from places under cultural control—the more likely one was to encounter spirits.

During my 1960 field trip a number of people reported having seen *'atua*. They told me that the road to Losa, which passes through the bush, is especially plagued by spirits, and that the night of a quarter moon is worst. A large *hefau* tree on the way was supposedly inhabited by a whole family of *'atua*. Individuals also reported having seen the figure of a woman standing facing a mango tree along the same road. She was described as nude, with long black hair down to her waist, and white skin. Those I interviewed claimed to be very much afraid of her. Another story concerned a large bird that flies through the air and, upon landing, assumes a human form. Some people claimed that the figure resembled someone they knew who had died (Howard 1960).

THE ACTIONS OF THE SPIRITS

Numinals were conceived as performing a wide range of activities, from malicious mischief to overseeing the prosperity of the island in *Tagroa Sir'ia's* case. Left to their own devices, most *'atua* were considered to be wanton destroyers of human beings. They engaged in a constant effort to steal the souls of humans and to feast on their bodies. These were the beings to which the English term "devils" was readily attached.

'Atua were said to lure human beings by presenting themselves as attractive paramours, particularly in dreams. Women were especially vulnerable to malicious spirits who sought to enter their vaginas when they were urinating, sometimes causing miscarriages. When outside, women were instructed never to urinate in an open space; instead they should relieve themselves near a rock or tree. If a woman is impregnated by an *'atua*, she will give birth to something resembling fish instead of normal children and will likely die soon afterward. Women who suspect they have been impregnated by an *'atua* can go to a native healer in order to drive away malignant spirits. Pregnant women must be especially wary of female *'atua* who try to capture the souls of unborn children.

Not all free-roaming spirits were evil, according to a recent account by Ieli Irava, a respected Rotuman educator. He contrasts *'atua* in the form of dogs, cats and owls, all of which were associated with malignant spirits, with stingrays, sharks and turtles, which were benevolent toward humans. He states that all good spirits were sea creatures, and speculates that being seafarers, Rotumans "put great emphasis on the good sea spirits in the hope of receiving good weather during their sea journeying or fishing expeditions" (Irava 1991:10).

The souls of recently deceased individuals were said to make their presence known through the cries of birds, an owl's flying by, or other unusual events. In other instances they appeared in dreams. This indicated the spirit was restless, and it was common for relatives to go to the cemetery to implore it to rest (Howard 1960; see also Russell 1942:251). The spirits of the newly dead were considered to linger in the vicinity for five days, after which a ceremony was held to end the death taboos.

IMMANENT JUSTICE

Ancestral spirits presumably remain sensitive to the actions of their descendants, and use their powers to punish bad behavior, especially disobedience to chiefs (Russell 1942:251). They also rectify wrongs and invoke justice. Almost every Rotuman can tell a story about someone who committed an egregious act and received his just deserts soon thereafter. Land disputes between relatives are prototypical, the underlying assumption being that spirits who are common ancestors of the disputants will punish the party in the wrong, or perhaps both parties if they share the blame. Justice is distributed in the form of luck, with those in the right prospering, those in the wrong suffering ill fortune. The consequences of wrongdoing may follow directly from the transgressions, or they may be called for by an aggrieved party in such forms as "the land has eyes," or "we shall see who is right."

The most feared curses are from the lips of chiefs, since they have channels to more powerful spirits. Chiefs usually call for immanent justice *(pū'ạki)* when serious offenses have been committed within their domains and no one accepts responsibility. A number of cases have become classics and are told with relish, though often without explicit reference to intervention by spirits (see Howard 1990:270 for an example).

INTERACTIONS WITH SPIRITS

Unbound Spirits

The most common way of dealing with unbound spirits is to avoid them. In 1960 Rotumans were reluctant to go out at night. If out after dark, they walked quickly past cemeteries, and stayed away from places spirits were said to inhabit. Despite the tropical heat, windows were often closed at night to keep out marauding *'atua*.

If avoiding malevolent spirits is impossible, making loud noises will frighten them off. At other times spirits have to be mollified by ritual. For example, any incident in which blood is shed should be followed by a ceremony called *hapag-sū*. The ceremony involves consumption of ritual foods, including a sacrificial pig prepared in an earthen oven. The goal is to placate the spirit or spirits who caused the event, so as to avoid a recurrence. *Hapagsū* are performed following surgical operations, as well as after accidents; in addition, they are held for prisoners returning from jail (Howard 1960).

Bound Spirits

Early commentators noted that each locality in Rotuma had spirits who were propitiated and were supposed to look after the interests of the local group. Such spirits generally took the form of animals and were treated with totemic respect. According to Gardiner:

> The *"hoag gods"* were usually incarnated in the form of some animal, as the *tanifa* (the hammer-headed shark), *juli* (sandpiper), *olusi* (lizard), *mafrop* (gecko), etc. Should a man by any chance have happened to kill one of the particular animal which was his *atua*, he would have had to make a big feast, cut all his hair off and bury it, just in the same way as a man would be buried. (Gardiner 1898:467–468)

Gardiner states that in warfare each *ho'aga* would propitiate its own *'atua*, rather than invoking *Tagroa sir'ia*, since "such small matters did not concern him and, as he was the god of both sides, it was quite unnecessary" (Gardiner 1898:471).

The most critical propitiations of spirits were rites performed in association with the *sau* and *mua*, for it was upon them that the welfare of the entire island depended. Such rites included a good deal of ceremonial feasting, kava drinking and dancing. Dancing was an especially important means of communicating with the spirits, and of exercising a degree of control over their activity (see, for example, the myth of *Kirkirsasa* in Titifanua 1995:86–91, and Hereniko's [1991, 1995] interpretation of the myth).

CHANGING CONTEXTS OF DISCOURSE ABOUT SPIRITS

Post-Contact Changes

Missionization, followed by the establishment of a British colonial administration in 1881, resulted in the elimination of nearly all public contexts in which traditional spirits were propitiated. By 1874 the institution of the *sau* and *mua* had disappeared, and along with it ritual observances to *Tagroa sir'ia* and the spirits of dead chiefs. The missionaries, depending on their denomination, labeled *'atua* or *'aitu* "devils," and used the other term as synonymous with the Christian God. This did not, however, result in the suppression of talk about spirits. Even devout Christians continued to speak about *'atua* as if their presence on the island were unquestioned, and Rotumans continued to perform rituals, such as kava ceremonies, pig sacrifices, and healing routines that presupposed the potency of spirits, in some instances invoking them directly through chants and prayers. Rotuman legends continued to be told, and were a source of knowledge about the antics of spirits. Furthermore, adults used children's fear of the spirits as a control mechanism (Irava 1991:10).

Rotuma 1960
In 1960, talk of spirits was still relatively common. The topic came up regularly as people spoke about their experiences in remote parts of the island, about their dreams, and about the cultural past. I was told numerous personal accounts involving possession, and legendary stories liberally sprinkled with reference to the antics of 'atua. I was warned of the danger of tempting 'atua by certain actions, such as wearing red at sunset, particularly in the village of Losa, and was instructed to stay away from cemeteries at night. Spirits had, in other words, a strong social presence, and were talked about openly and frequently.

Rotuma 1987–1991
I returned to Rotuma in 1987 for a brief visit, then for longer stays over the next three years,[7] and was struck by the fact that talk about spirits was much rarer. Only occasionally were the antics of 'atua used to explain events, and I learned of only one recent instance of possession. When I suggested the possibility that some anomalous creature might be an 'atua, people laughed, not in the nervous manner that signifies a defense against possible ridicule, but in the hearty manner of a good joke. People no longer close their windows at night, youngsters are regularly seen congregating in cemeteries, leisurely sitting on gravestones, and my wife and I were given absolutely no warnings or proscriptions for avoiding harmful 'atua. They had, in effect, lost much of their social presence.

SOCIOECONOMIC CHANGES 1960–1990
In many respects Rotuma has changed considerably in the past thirty years. What struck me most on revisiting the island were the physical changes, like the airport, which opened in 1981, and a wharf built in the 1970s. Another significant change was in housing. Hurricane Bebe destroyed almost all native-style, thatched houses in 1972. For the most part they have been replaced by concrete houses with corrugated iron roofs (Rensel 1991).

Far more of the island is electrified now. On my first visit only the government station and the Catholic church compounds at Sumi and Upu had generators. Now most villages provide electricity for a few hours per day, and many individual households have their own generators. Perhaps the biggest change in daily life, however, has been brought about by the presence of motor vehicles. In 1990, the district officer estimated around 300 motorbikes on the island, and the number has increased since. In addition, some thirty to forty privately owned cars and trucks are in use, along with vehicles regularly operated by the government and local business organizations. This means that everyone has ready access to some form of motor transport.

Another major improvement has been the construction of bush roads out of what were previously footpaths. This permits people easier access to their remote gardens by motor vehicles. In my recent visits it was rare to see men carrying baskets on a shoulder pole, or on horseback.

Educational levels have increased. In 1960, only a small number of adults on Rotuma were educated beyond standard eight (U.S. eighth grade). Today, most younger adults have at least completed Form III (U.S. ninth grade). This educational advancement, along with increased opportunities for travel, lends a greater air of worldly sophistication to Rotuman social life. People read more, are better informed, and less prone to accept authority in an unquestioning fashion.

WHY THE SILENCE, AND WHAT DOES IT MEAN?

Taken at face value, my experience on Rotuma suggests a dramatic change in spirit discourse. Talk, or at least public talk, about numinals has substantially diminished, raising several significant questions. Has the Rotuman worldview demystified in the interim? Has some social threshold been passed, making talk about spirits unacceptable? To what extent do changes in talk reflect changes in belief?

Let us begin by considering the possibility that Christianity has contributed to a demystification of the Rotuman worldview in recent years. Christianity has been a persistent foe of Rotuman spirits since the early nineteenth century. The missionaries actively undermined and eventually brought about the demise of the religion of the *sau* and *mua*, which incorporated a wide range of spiritual beings. They sought to focus discourse on God and Biblical heroes, leaving ghosts and local spirits on the social periphery. But the missionaries did less to deny the existence of Rotuman spirits than to relabel them as "devils." These changes were well-entrenched by the early twentieth century, and certainly by 1960. They cannot, therefore, account for alterations that occurred between 1960 and 1990. In both periods Rotumans spent a great deal of time engaged in church-related activities: saying prayers, singing hymns, and discussing the Bible. In 1960, however, Rotuman spirits retained a place in the islanders' discourse they have since lost.

What then of the physical, social and economic changes described above? Have they served to demystify the Rotuman worldview? I suspect they have but can only guess at the reasons. Increased levels of education and exposure to "scientific" discourse may well have resulted in a progressive substitution of naturalistic for supernatural explanation. Furthermore, as Rotumans have come into more intense contact with others, they may have found naturalistic forms of discourse to result in more acceptance, and so resort to them more often. Education and exposure to heterogeneous cultural contexts may have nurtured a more cosmopolitan form of talk, if not personal viewpoint.

One could also make a case for a change in the nature of experience brought about by different material and socioeconomic conditions. It was striking to me, for example, that many of the places on Rotuma that used to be remote, and associated with uncanny experiences, are now within easy reach by motor vehicle. As a result, men spend less time going through the bush to their gardens, and can go in daylight instead of predawn hours to reach their remote plantations in time to work during cool mornings. Vehicles also allow them to go in groups more easily. They therefore spend less time alone in contexts associated with spiritual encounters. Malicious 'atua, the kind one had to worry about and guard against, formerly were regarded as much more dangerous when one was away from one's home village—away from one's territory. This was perhaps a corollary of few opportunities for travel; most people visited other villages or districts only rarely. Now transportation is accessible to everyone, and many people travel to other localities on a daily basis. Perhaps it is easier to entertain a mystified view of other places when one rarely sees them than when they become familiar.

Physical changes may have also affected worldview by shifting the focus of experience from the natural to the manufactured world. In the past, building a home or making a canoe required individuals to spend time outdoors collecting materials. Now the cement, lumber, nails, and paint are delivered by truck. Appliances of all types command attention, including radios, tape players and videos, providing new contexts for entertainment. Machines and spirits are uneasy companions at best. Motorbikes, trucks, chain saws, and radios make loud noises, and noise, it will be recalled, is one way of warding off malevolent spirits. The main point, however, is that Rotumans appear to pay much less attention than before to natural phenomena, to the anomalies and sounds of nature that provided the raw material for talk about spiritual encounters. Paying close attention to nature is much less compelling when one (thinks one) has the means to control it, or at least to mitigate its more serious threats.

A drop in death rates may have had a similar effect. Illness and death are two contexts in which spiritual explanations are likely to be invoked, especially when people feel a lack of control over healing processes. As I have written elsewhere (Howard 1979), Rotumans always seem to have entertained alternate explanatory models for illness and death, one naturalistic, the other based on the actions of spirits. The balance between these two shifted noticeably toward the former with the introduction of wonder drugs in the 1950s, although supernatural explanations maintained a definite presence up to at least 1960. A radical decrease in infant and child mortality, and unanticipated deaths in general, may have also lessened the need to resort to supernatural explanations. In addition, I suspect that an expanded medical facility, with several Rotuman nurses trained in Western medicine, has shifted the balance even further in the direction of naturalistic discourse. As access to the clinic has increased because of improved transportation, and people come there more frequently to have illnesses treated, they talk about such matters in a context that discourages supernatural explanation. In the clinic setting, talk about spirits is distinctly devalued.

Finally, the changing role of chiefs may well have had a demystifying effect.

Chiefs were previously seen as the embodiment of community authority, and in earlier times, as important conduits to the world of spirits. Their authority, in large measure, was perceived as based on divine activity. To the extent that chiefs were so viewed, spiritual sanctions were at their disposal, and a chief's subjects had reason to fear his wrath. But in today's society chiefs are seen more as politicians than as divinely inspired incarnations of the community. They are no longer awe-inspiring, and are talked about in quite different terms, even ridiculed on occasion. In my recent visits, people expressed little fear of chiefly anger or curses.

Along with the politicalization of chieftainship has gone a diminished sense of community, of which some spirits, at least, were representations. Increased household and individual autonomy, facilitated by greater access to money through remittances and wages, has allowed individuals to refuse participation in community activities with much less penalty. Indeed, one of the topics Rotumans often talk about today, when contrasting the present with the past, is the absence of community spirit. To take Durkheim's point, a diminished sense of community may be related to a diminished set of collective representations in a spiritual mode.

Additionally, politicalization, not only of chieftainship but of the entire Rotuman community (Howard 1989), has diminished people's attention to their ancestral culture (in contrast to many other Pacific Island societies where "kastom" is of focal concern). They are now more engaged in thinking and talking about current economic and political issues than about past glories; correspondingly they pay less attention to their ancestors, who were known in the form of 'atua. From what I can ascertain, grandparents tell their grandchildren far fewer stories about the past, far fewer myths and legends than before. These were primary contexts in which the exploits of spirits were recounted. Contemporary children may be growing up hearing less about the spirits, and having less to tell about them.

In sum, good reason exists to believe that the Rotuman worldview *has* been demystified, and that a threshold has indeed been passed. Put differently, social contexts in which spirits are relevant may have changed so radically that spirits only rarely enter the realm of human conversation. Perhaps it is not so much that they have disappeared from the scene as that they now find far fewer contexts of existential relevance in which to emanate. As the contexts for talking about spirits have narrowed, and people have less information to share, evaluations of talk about spirits may have also changed. What was once clearly acceptable talk within a community-based discourse may now be relegated to the idiosyncratic, seen as indicative of an individual's views rather than a culturally preferred form of expression.

I am not arguing that spirit beliefs are incompatible with modernization. Spirit beliefs thrive in many cultures far more developed than Rotuma. Even in urban Bangkok, for example, Thais maintain spirit houses. But Thailand has a well-established great tradition in which spirits play an integral part. They are woven into literature, dance and art in a way that gives them a visibility absent on Rotuma. As a result, spirits play an important role in nearly every Thai's socialization, and reminders of their immanence are recurrent in daily experience. I suggest that spirits on Rotuma may have been particularly vulnerable to modernizing influences precisely because they lacked such objectification in artistic productions and performances. Instead, they were relegated to the margins of public experience following conversion to Christianity and relied primarily on talk to maintain their presence in the cultural milieu. Thus any factors reducing talk about spirits significantly diminishes their relevance.

TALK AND BELIEF

What does this apparent change in talk suggest about Rotuman beliefs? Have they changed accordingly? I find these questions much more difficult to assess, since I view the relationship between talk and belief as highly problematic. There was no word for belief in the Rotuman language prior to European intrusion, so the missionaries introduced a Rotumanization of the term, *pilifi*. The closest Rotuman equivalent is *aire*, "true, correct." The antonym of *aire* is *siko*, "false, untrue or incorrect." However, *aire* and *siko* are used primarily as terms of affirmation or denial of a speaker's claims (whether about events, rights and obligations, or other phenomena). They are not ordinarily used in reference to an individual's personal convictions about what is metaphysically true or real. Thus *aire* is used to signify agreement, and *siko* to signify disagreement, with a speaker's statements. This usage is similar in form to that described by David Gegeo and Karen Watson-Gegeo for the Kwara'ae in the Solomon Islands, and as they point out, it reflects a distinctive theory of truth (Gegeo and Watson-Gegeo In Press). As among the Kwara'ae, Rotuman discourse suggests an implicit link between potency and truth, such that to say something will occur puts one's *mana* to test. If events unfold in the way stated, the speaker's potency as a social being is affirmed and his credibility enhanced; if they do not, his potency is rendered dubious and his credibility diminished. Whether the speaker has control over the outcome is not at issue; the statement itself puts his *mana* at risk. As the Gegeos point out, since *mana* derives from spirits, such notions of truth reflect an assumed linkage between the world of humans and the spirit world (Gegeo and Watson-Gegeo In Press).

My skepticism concerning the relationship between talk and belief has been fueled by two types of experience on Rotuma, one of them personal. When I was on the island in 1960, I distinctly remember walking down a path on a dark night with some Rotuman friends. As we passed certain places they expressed apprehension and stepped up their pace. They may or may not have spoken of *'atua*, but it was clearly *'atua* they feared.[8] And I, too, experienced fear, perhaps by emotional contagion. This presented me with a dilemma. Did *I* believe in ghosts? If by "belief" one understands a commitment to a proposition about the existence of numinous beings, I would have to say that I was very skeptical, and hence a nonbeliever. But if an observer were to use as evidence my actions and expressions of fear then they might indeed conclude that I believed.

Nor am I the first European to have such experiences on Rotuma. Hugh Romilly, who was the British crown's deputy commissioner to Rotuma in 1880, just prior to Cession, claims to have seen the ghost of a Rotuman man who had been murdered. He wrote a book about his experience, titled *A True Story of the Western Pacific in 1879–80*. After describing in vivid detail his encounter, Romilly concluded, "I am not a believer in ghosts. I believe a natural explanation of the story to exist, but the reader . . . must find it for himself, as I am unable to supply one" (Romilly 1882:82).

The question such reports raises is: can we assume that when Rotumans express apprehension in the face of uncanny experiences, or when they report seeing apparitions, that this constitutes *prima facie* evidence of a commitment to the proposition that spirits exist?

The second type of experience that raised questions about the relationship between talk and belief is an inversion of the above. Although talk about spirits is now greatly diminished, people still tell stories about the "power" of certain objects, about immanent justice and about occult happenings that imply supernatural activity, but they leave out explicit reference to any presumed agency. They commonly attribute ill fortune to failures to perform customary ceremonies, but reference to the mechanism involved is conspicuously absent. For example, several people reported that when the maternity hospital was opened some years ago, a proper ceremony was not performed, and that subsequently four women, each young and attractive, died in childbirth.[9] When the new radio-telephone installation failed on initial attempt, my wife and I were told something similar—the ceremony, which we attended, had not been conducted properly. In other words, the logic of causality remains consistent with supernatural explanation, but spiritual agency is omitted from accounts.

RECONSIDERING THE NATURE OF SPIRIT BELIEF

With a few notable exceptions (e.g., Hahn 1973; Leach 1954, 1967; Needham 1972; Saler 1967, 1977) anthropologists have treated the relationship between belief, ritual practices, emotional expression, and talk about spirits as unproblematic, each regarded as a reliable indicator of the other. Perhaps this is consequence of focusing on intracultural regularities and neglecting intragroup variation. We have tended to treat belief as an undifferentiated category, as if any two statements about the actions of spirits can be given equivalent weight. But as a number of social scientists have pointed out with considerable vigor, belief has multiple dimensions that need to be taken into consideration if we are to comprehend relationships between thought, knowledge, and social action (for a summary of viewpoints see Bar-Tal 1989:16–20).

I use the concept of belief in reference to meaningful propositions (statements) that can be considered either true or false. To believe is to accept the truth of a proposition; to disbelieve is to reject it (Goodenough 1963:155, Saler 1967:30). Belief is ultimately a mental phenomenon, located in individual minds, and is subject to verification only through inference from talk or action. Nevertheless, beliefs may be shared, and groups may commit to certain propositions collectively, justifying the notion of group beliefs. Beliefs may be considered the building blocks of individual and cultural knowledge insofar as knowledge encompasses all the beliefs accumulated through personal experience, thinking, and social interaction (Bar-Tal 1989:5, Black 1973, Goodenough 1963). Underlying beliefs are presuppositions, or axiomatic assumptions about the nature of reality.

Perhaps anthropologists have so often skirted issues associated with belief because of the thorny methodological problems posed by the concept. How can one identify a belief with assuredness? In Western culture we take for granted that people articulate their beliefs, in both internal and external dialogues. Belief is a distinct category in Western discourse. Yet we often question statements professing beliefs, regarding them as insincere, self-serving, or inconsistent with an individual's behavior. We note that people frequently express contradictory propositions, and that affective expressions often are in opposition to what an individual avows. Furthermore, we often take actions and talk as indicative of beliefs even when people do not, and perhaps cannot, articulate the propositions directing them. When our concerns are with *changing* beliefs, these difficulties are compounded.

The problems of identifying beliefs are even more complex when dealing with non-Western cultures (Needham 1972).[10] What do we do in cases, such as in pre-missionary Rotuma, where no *emic* category approximates our notion of belief? One solution is to rely exclusively on answers to explicit questions. The presumption is that beliefs are consciously reasoned and can be articulated with a little thought. When employed with caution this approach has served some ethnographers quite well, but its pitfalls are many. Not the least is the possibility of forcing informants to engage in an unnatural form of discourse, resulting in their clumsily articulating propositions they may never have acted upon, nor talked or thought about—propositions that are artifacts of a unique, atypical situation.

Another possibility is to ignore talk entirely and to rely exclusively on behavioral manifestations of belief. The notion behind such an approach is that acceptance of a proposition is equivalent to a bet on its effectiveness in the world of action (Price 1969:254–7). If an individual takes vitamin pills with meals, we infer a belief in the effectiveness of vitamins. This approach has the advantage of allowing a researcher to identify unconscious or unarticulated adherence to propositions. It also eliminates ambiguities posed by individuals' saying one thing and doing another. While an "acting-as-if" strategy sidesteps the issue of inconsistencies between talk and action, it has the disadvantage of placing in limbo large areas of knowledge and understandings that are central to world-view, though only indirectly reflected in behavior, if at all. For the study of spirit beliefs, such an approach is too limiting.

A third approach is to analyze discourse in its various guises, both verbal and nonverbal. At the core of this perspective is the notion that beliefs impose form on, and shape the content of, communication structures. Talk in normal (socially recurring) contexts is privileged, although responses to an ethnographer's queries are not excluded. Rituals, artistic performances, visual representations, literary texts and other forms of communication are also examined for what they reveal about propositions, both explicitly and implicitly. Contexts for communications are taken into account and are made integral to resulting descriptions.

In approaching the question of spirit beliefs, the first approach, based on explicit interrogation, generates descriptions such as those obtained by Hocart, MacGregor and Churchward, reliant on lexical discriminations made by informants. Words for spirit types are defined in terms of appearances, motives, and activities (usually with the implicit assumption that the views of a "knowledgeable" informant are representative). Additional questions may be asked about how concerned humans deal with each spirit type, generating descriptions of rituals, prayers, avoidances and so on. Monitoring changes in beliefs so constructed relies on recognizing changes in vocabulary (expanded, reduced, or altered semantic content), as well as transformations of activities explicitly related to spirits. The resulting emphasis is on alterations in *content and form* rather than on strength of beliefs (or changes in other dimensions of belief; see below).

The "acting-as-if" strategy leads naturally to an assessment of the *degree* to which spirit beliefs play a role in shaping social action. Time spent engaged in spirit-related activities provides a ready measure of commitment to spirit beliefs, and of changes in belief. Choices of where to build one's house or plant one's garden, of when to travel the road or go on a fishing expedition— if based on the prospective actions of spirit beings—are indicative of belief intensity. From this perspective, spirit beliefs compete with other considerations for primacy in directing action. As they get stronger they play a more significant role in accounting for behavior. Talk is important only insofar as it helps to identify the extent to which spirits enter into someone's deliberations or otherwise influence actions.

From the discursive perspective, talk is far more central, although still only one of many ways in which spirit beliefs can be comprehended and monitored. Whereas the "acting-as-if" view focuses on the *effects* of belief in action, discourse analysis places its emphasis on the *reinforcement* of beliefs through modes of communication. As a general proposition (which I believe), the more explicitly spirits are represented in communication structures (including speech, art forms, ritual performances, etc.), the stronger the case for inferring belief. My assumption is that strongly redundant cultural messages make certain propositions so central to discourse that meaningful communication generally depends on their acceptance. Individuals who are exposed to an intense social-ization in which spirits are multiply represented and dramatized are particular-ly likely to take for granted the truth of propositions about spirit phenomena.

I find the discursive approach especially appealing for understanding the Rotuman case because the island did not develop representations of spirits in visual forms. This means that aside from certain rituals and dances, communi-cation concerning spirits relied heavily on talk. Although a case can be made that spirits inhabit fine white mats (giving them a special place in Rotuman cere-monies; Hereniko 1991, 1995), the association is not explicit. The paucity of alternative forms for representing spirits thus renders talk especially important to the perpetuation of belief. For this reason I regard a reduction in talk about spirits on Rotuma as of profound significance. Without talk about them, the spirits have no other means to ensure a place in Rotuman culture.

CULTURAL CHANGE AND DIMENSIONS OF BELIEF

My purpose in this section is to explore dimensions of belief that might be rele-vant to understanding the changes I observed on Rotuma between periods of field work. I do not intend to be exhaustive, nor to present a specific theory of belief change. Rather, I wish to illustrate the multiple possible ways to account for such change once we unpack the complexity that lies behind the common-sense notion of belief.

We can begin by distinguishing types of belief, based on what may be con-sidered their underlying presuppositions. From this standpoint existential beliefs can be differentiated from those whose presuppositions are evaluative or pre/pro-scriptive. *Existential beliefs* address the question of existence, as in "Do you believe in (the existence of) ghosts?" Existential assumptions have been fundamental to Western discourse about spirits. That such is not everywhere the case is nicely illustrated by an incident related by Torben Monberg con-cerning a discussion he had with people on the Polynesian outlier of Bellona. He had great difficulty getting the Bellonese to understand his question: "Do you believe that the gods propitiated by the residents on the nearby island of Rennell really exist?" The reply was straightforward enough: Of course they exist; who would be stupid enough to propitiate gods that do not exist (Monberg, personal communication)!

Evaluative beliefs concern problems of good and evil and their variants (e.g., moral/immoral, ethical/unethical, holy/unholy). Beliefs concerning the disposi-tion of categories of spirits are of this type. Some types of spirits are seen as basi-cally benevolent and trustworthy, others as malevolent and untrustworthy. Such judgments influence which spirits ought to be propitiated and which guarded against. The distinction between existential and evaluative beliefs was central to comprehending statements made by Rotumans, in response to questions during my 1960 visit, as to whether or not they believed in 'atua. They invariably answered negatively, although it was very clear that they behaved (and in other contexts spoke) as if *'atua* were present on the island. It became clear after a while that what they were talking about was *propitiation*. The most common statement after denial was, "I believe in [the Christian] God." In other words, propitiation, rather than existential reality, was at issue. This use of "belief" (the question was asked in English) corresponds to statements such as, "I believe in my doctor" or "I believe in capitalism"; it signifies trust versus mistrust rather than existence versus nonexistence (see Price 1969:76–77).

Prescriptive and proscriptive beliefs relate to a presumed causal connection between certain kinds of actions and their likely consequences. The belief that performing a specific ritual will bring blessings from the gods is prescriptive; the belief that stealing will bring misfortune is proscriptive.

Sources of belief can also be distinguished. Here we are concerned with what kinds of information are considered to be evidence for or against particular propositions. Information obtained from direct sensory experience can be contrasted with information obtained from interpersonal interactions and from impersonal media (books, motion pictures, radio, television). That we do not always believe our own sensory impressions is affirmed by the fact that many people believe the world to be round, despite the fact that our senses tell us otherwise. Sources of knowing may have quite different weightings in different cultural settings. Whereas in modern cosmopolitan contexts beliefs are largely structured by formal education and mass media (it is on the basis of the authority of scientists that most of us *do* believe the world is round), in many other cultural contexts interpersonal transactions are key to the formulation of beliefs. One can make a subdistinction here between relationships based on hierarchy and those that are not. Where relationships are structured hierarchically, the pronouncements of those in authority are given great weight; in more egalitarian contexts evaluations are based on a variety of considerations having to do with the credibility of a speaker. As pointed out above, Rotumans, like the Kwara'ae, relate truthfulness to the *mana* of a speaker (which is based on perceptions of his or her efficacy in making things happen). A Rotuman who conveys information that proves to be false, even though it clearly originated elsewhere, quickly loses credibility and is labeled unreliable. In other words, the overall credibility of a speaker is far more important in evaluating evidence than the intrinsic merits of the information conveyed. So whereas one person's report of an encounter with a spirit may be regarded as *prima facie* evidence, someone else's account may be dismissed out of hand.

Another set of dimensions can be applied to the characteristics of an individual's beliefs. Beliefs differ, for example, in degree of *precision*, or the clarity of their formulation. Some can be stated precisely (e.g., if X then Y; the meek shall inherit the earth), while others are only vaguely held, and cannot be easily articulated. In large measure precision results from discourse that places a premium on such considerations as logical consistency. Early European visitors to Rotuma were dismayed by an apparent lack of precision in answers to their questions about "religious" beliefs (but this may well have been the result of both language difficulties and inappropriate framing of questions).

Centrality is another dimension that a number of social scientists have identified (Rokeach 1960, 1968; Bem 1970; Bar-Tal 1989), although there is no agreed-upon definition. I use the term in reference to the degree that a given belief is basic to an individual's worldview, as indicated by the extent to which it shapes perceptions and other beliefs. A change in a core belief is likely to necessitate a change in one's whole perspective, whereas a change in a peripheral belief may have little effect on one's outlook. Assessing the centrality of spiritual beliefs would seem to be critical for determining how readily they might be altered or dropped when conditions change.

Conviction refers to the degree of confidence with which one holds a belief. Some beliefs are held quite tenuously, as indicated by expressions of doubt or a willingness to entertain alternative propositions. Others are held with great assurance, as if firmly anchored in unassailable evidence. Closely related to conviction, but distinguishable from it, is *commitment*, which indicates tenacity in the face of no or contrary evidence (a word frequently used in English to express commitment as I have defined it is "faith"). Commitment is especially relevant when a belief is regarded as indicative of something of great importance to an individual, like membership in a group. Indeed, the less evidence there is to support a belief, the more powerful it becomes as an indicator of commitment to a group that professes it. *Potency*, which I use to denote the degree to which a belief motivates action, is an additional dimension. People may hold certain beliefs with great conviction, even though they may have little motivating potency (e.g., Venus rotates around the sun). Other, less vigorously held beliefs, may be strongly motivating, at least in certain contexts (e.g., God helps those who help themselves).

Integration of beliefs into coherent structures has also been widely discussed (Rips 1990). An array of propositions held by an individual may logically cohere, forming a structure or schemata, or they may have minimal interdependence, with specific propositions supported more by external considerations than their relationship with one another. At a lesser level of integration, certain beliefs may be coupled such that one is perceived as implicating the other.[11] For example, on Rotuma, belief in immanent justice and belief in the power of *'atua* were coupled in the past insofar as spirits were said to be agents of justice.[12] The question this poses is: under what conditions can beliefs become uncoupled?

When dealing with beliefs at a group level, some additional dimensions need to be considered. What *forms of expression* are beliefs given, for instance? Are they articulated in speech, in ritual, in artistic productions? How explicit are the renderings of specific propositions in various media? *Degree of redundancy* for specific beliefs must also be considered. How frequently are various beliefs given expression, and how many channels are employed in representing them? A belief that is voiced through limited channels (e.g., a single ritual) may be jeopardized if those channels are blocked, whereas one given expression in multiple channels is likely to be less vulnerable. *Multiplicity* of beliefs refers to the extent to which the total pool of propositions available to a population includes, in any given context, alternative or contradictory possibilities. In general, the more extensive the pool of propositions people can draw from, the more problematic group beliefs become. In small, culturally-isolated groups, the distinction between individual and group beliefs may be minimal, whereas in large, culturally complex groups, the distinction can be so great that identifying any "group beliefs" at all may be difficult. In the process of transition from isolated small-scale society to heterogeneous cosmopolitanism, the locus of belief shifts from the group to the individual.[13] Thus, whereas in former circumstances Rotuman statements about spirits could reasonably be considered reflections of a cultural worldview, today they are more appropriately seen as indicators of an individual's personal beliefs.

It is one thing for people to share beliefs as a result of common experience, but quite another for a group to make shared belief an index of membership. Even in culturally complex settings, certain beliefs may come to be regarded as indicative of a particular group's character (e.g., ethnicity, sophistication, political commitments, solidarity). This, however, necessitates an *objectification* of belief (Bar-Tal 1989). The fact that Rotumans had no lexeme for belief is strong evidence they did not objectify it prior to European intrusion. The contrary teachings of Methodists and Catholics, however, firmly introduced awareness of shared beliefs as a powerful basis for defining group membership and allegiance.

CONCLUSION

The necessity of recognizing the complexities behind our commonsense notion of belief is especially important if we are to account for the type of change I have described for Rotuma. At issue are the ways in which worldviews are constructed, how knowledge systems (which are composed of beliefs) function in various cultural contexts, and the interrelationships between beliefs, emotions, thinking, and social action. I do not intend to provide a singular theoretical explanation for what I have observed on Rotuma, but rather wish to mirror the complexity of the phenomena by reflecting on a variety of possibilities, all or none of which may have contributed to change.

Let me begin by dismissing one possibility—that Rotumans have shifted *en masse* from a firm belief in spirits to disbelief (i.e., from acceptance to rejection of the proposition that spirits exist).[14] Merely refraining from talk about spirits does not in itself signify disbelief, and no other evidence at my disposal suggests outright rejection. More to the point is that Rotuman beliefs in spirits were primarily prescriptive/proscriptive rather than existential or evaluative. Rituals were the main channels for expressing belief; talk was secondary. One could therefore make a strong case for the continuance of spirit belief on the grounds that rituals persist, and that failure to conduct rituals properly is still a culturally appropriate explanation for misfortune. The decline in talk about 'atua may be little more than a minor concession camouflaging core beliefs.

It is also possible that Rotuman spirit beliefs were never central in the sense discussed above, and involved low levels of conviction and commitment. This would be consistent with a view of Rotuman beliefs as having a primarily social, as opposed to a psychological, function. Beliefs can perform social functions adequately without much conviction or commitment, especially in ritual contexts. If this were the case, the uncoupling of belief in 'atua from belief in immanent justice would not be surprising. Whereas 'atua provided a mechanism for justice, they are not necessary for it to occur (the Christian God or fate can be substituted, but even they are not necessary, since the mechanism need not be explicit).

Other processes may have been involved. Rotuman beliefs seem to be strongly context dependent. Perhaps the number of contexts for which spirits are relevant has been drastically reduced, thus removing beliefs concerning them to the peripheries of experience. This may have led to a diminished consciousness, and hence a reduction in talk about spirits. Sociolinguistic processes also might have contributed. Even if no significant changes in personal beliefs had occurred, conversational rules may have changed, inhibiting the mention of spirits. Maybe, for example, the social costs of mentioning spirits has increased, so that people are increasingly reluctant to express their personal viewpoints (in much the same way that American politicians are more reluctant to express bigotry, regardless of their beliefs, because of political costs). Whether this signals a temporary shift in talk patterns or a deeper change in Rotuman explanatory discourse remains to be seen.

Less talk about spirits also could have resulted from social changes that impugned others' credibility. A weakening of authority structures, with which beliefs in spirits were associated, may have been involved. Chiefs and elders had a strong stake in perpetuating spirit beliefs since spirits were said to punish disrespect and disobedience; a decline in the credibility of such authorities might have contributed to less attention being paid to reports of their experiences in favor of greater reliance on one's own. Or it may be that those with a Western education are now granted greater credibility, and that they are reluctant to talk about spirits because it suggests backwardness.

None of these possibilities implies finality. As conditions change, spirit beliefs could again regain centrality for at least a portion of the Rotuman population. Although contemporary Rotumans have not resorted to objectified beliefs to define their identity vis-à-vis others, they may find it expedient to do so in the future. If so, talk about spirits may again rise to prominence and play a significant role in defining what it means to be Rotuman.

NOTES

Acknowledgments. Elisapeti Inia, a retired Rotuman schoolteacher and Rotuman language expert, read over an earlier draft of this paper and made extensive comments, many of which I have incorporated. Her assistance has been invaluable. I would also like to thank Jack Bilmes and Jan Rensel for providing useful feedback. Portions of the research on which the chapter is based were supported by the National Institute of Mental Health, Wenner-Gren Foundation, and a Matsuda grant from the University of Hawai'i.

1   In this context *'atue* would be used rather than *'atua*. For example, *'eteu 'atue ta'a* means "I can conquer him (that person)" in wrestling or fighting. The "e" form (*'eteu 'atue* rather than *'otou 'atua*) is used in reference to eating; hence what is implied is "He will be my food" (Elisapeti Inia, personal communication).

2   Elisapeti Inia says Churchward was mistaken, and that the proper Rotuman gloss for "to pray" should be *rau 'aitu*; the word *rau* means "to recite."

3   *Tag(a)roa* is a generic term for high god in many Polynesian languages. According to Churchward, the modifier *sir'ia* [sir(i) + 'ia, which denotes the ingressive tense] means "to go past; to go further, go beyond; to surpass, excel, be more than." It therefore suggests preeminence. But *sir'ia* also means "to transgress, do wrong" (Churchward 1940:311). This nicely suggests the godlike power to go beyond the bounds of human civility. Elisapeti Inia suggests alternatively that the reference should be to *Tagroa siria*, *siria* being the name of a star used by seafaring ancestors to find Rotuma.

4   This may well be a consequence of Biblical translation, since *ape'aitu* was used by the missionaries to specify prophets in the Old Testament.

5   MacGregor wrote in his notes that *ape'aitu* seems to mean the mat of the god, associating the first segment of the term (*ape*) with the word for fine white mat (*apei*). This may well be the case, and would lend further credence to Hereniko's notion of *apei* as woven gods. Presumably the medium sits on an *apei*, facilitating the "capture" of the spirit, but the medium may also be like an *apei* insofar as he or she is a vessel for the spirit.

6   Elisapeti Inia says that free-roaming spirits live among rocks because they have no home. They are "bad" spirits intent on doing harm. This association is interesting because it suggests, quite plausibly in Rotuman cultural logic, that to be without a defining place is to be beyond the pale of culture.

7   The visit in 1987 was my first in twenty-seven years, and lasted only two weeks. I returned in 1988 for three months, in 1989 for six months, and in 1990 for two months to do field work. This was followed by an additional one-week visit in 1991 and a two-week visit in 1994.

8   They told me that when your hair stands on end you know there is an *'atua* nearby, and they instructed me to swear (*'a finak* = "eat shit") and spit behind me.

9   Elisapeti Inia reports that after the fourth death, somebody dreamt that "the four posts of the maternity ward are now completed," and that since then, everything has been all right.

10   Needham presents a strong case for dropping the concept of belief entirely from anthropological inquiry, but I agree with Saler (1974:865), who argues that it provides a useful heuristic for distinguishing three human capacities that transcend specific cultures: a capacity to generate statements about the world, a capacity to remember such statements, and a capacity to deem them true (or false).

11 Here we get into issues associated with reasoning processes, which are beyond the scope of this paper. For a recent discussion of such issues see Rips 1990.

12 According to Elisapeti Inia only a certain class of spirits (*sur ne 'aitu kat huar'ák ra*), those who had not had sex during their lifetimes, are agents of immanent justice. They are the spirits of people who were not devoured by *'atua* at the times of their death; their dwelling place was said to be in the *hanua favi* "anchored land," visible at times on the horizon (see above, p. 126).

13 Pruyser's observation about belief in contemporary society is relevant here. He notes that:

> In the bewildering pluralism of our time . . . the task of identifying oneself is not limited to espousing certain beliefs and rejecting everything else in unbelief. It is, rather, an anguished process of coming to terms with all the major beliefs, unbeliefs, and disbeliefs to which one is exposed, as well as the vehement strife between man and man and within every solitary breast. Most of us are most of our lives between all kinds of belief and all kinds of unbelief, in shifting patterns . . . We have an awareness of being "between the times," in an interim period between eras, and between the many beliefs and unbeliefs of yesterday and tomorrow. (1974:97)

It may well be that Rotumans are being drawn into such an experiential milieu vis-à-vis belief as they are increasingly exposed to cosmopolitan influences.

14 Disbelief can be distinguished from "unbelief," which can have as wide a range of forms and nuances as belief (see Goodenough 1965, Pruyser 1974).

7 Local and Foreign Spirits in Kwaio, Solomon Islands

David Akin

Nearly 10,000 Kwaio speakers make up one of ten ethnolinguistic groups on Malaita, an island about 100 miles long and thirty miles wide in the southeastern Solomon Islands. Today most Kwaio are Christians (Seventh-Day Adventist, The South Sea Evangelical Church, or Marist Roman Catholic) living in large coastal villages. Another 2,000 to 3,000 Kwaio remain in the mountainous interior, living in tiny hamlets, practicing swidden horticulture, and following their ancestral religion. These non-Christian Kwaio, whose beliefs are the focus of this paper, are in many ways isolated from the rest of the Solomons, and they occupy the lowest rung of their country's social and economic ladder. Most Solomon Islanders have, in recent decades, found new ways to participate in the cash economy through increased education and local development. But this has not been the case for Kwaio in the mountains, where there are no government schools, development projects, or medical services. Very few mountain Kwaio hold other than menial positions in government or businesses. This development gap is steadily widening, and the area is becoming increasingly marginalized. This is despite the fact that for the past 120 years Kwaio men have worked extensively as laborers abroad.

Kwaio attitudes toward outsiders' ways tend to be ambivalent and sometimes contradictory. Their devotion to ancestors and tradition often clashes with desires for foreign things and for social change. Much effort is expended in keeping unwanted alien influences out of the mountains by barring entry to Christians, refusing cash (Kwaio prefer their own shell money), and openly resisting government control. At the same time a steady stream of imported items and practices continues to find its way into the area. In public discussions, foreign infiltration is unanimously condemned but, in practice, most people are willing to compromise in order to accommodate desired changes. This contradiction is at the heart of modern Kwaio society and is also central to understanding local beliefs about ancestral and foreign spirits.

In Chapter 1 of this volume the authors describe how, in many Pacific Christian cultures, indigenous spirits have not disappeared, but rather have been transformed to fill new roles. The spirits now "bring into the public domain widely shared if poorly understood . . . problems that are generated by social change, and that threaten or overload traditional values and structures" (p. 21). In Pacific island societies generally, the social order has always been reflected in the numinous realm, and now social problems are finding expression there also. Even where indigenous spirits were once revered as ancestral pillars of community morality, they may now epitomize antisociality, a defect commonly attributed to many aspects of modern life. But what of Pacific societies that have not turned to Christianity, where local spirits have retained the moral high ground? How are spirit beliefs in these cultures being transformed by pressures of social change?

In what follows, I address this question for one such society, that of the Kwaio in the mountains of Malaita. For those Kwaio who have not converted, indigenous Kwaio spirits remain at the moral center of community life, and men and women interact with them on a regular, sometimes daily, basis. However, indigenous spirits have been joined by many new kinds of numinals that Kwaio men have imported for their special powers, while others have immigrated to Kwaio on their own. Some of these are dangerous, occupying a role in Kwaio similar to that of indigenous spirits in some Christian communities, as symbols and agents of antisocial forces. In this chapter, I examine beliefs about these foreign spirits and how they embody Kwaio perspectives on alien ways and on changes taking place in Kwaio and elsewhere in the Solomons.

Kwaio men and women fear that foreign ways are encroaching on and overwhelming their way of life. They perceive alien social, political, and economic forces as steadily undermining their culture. Kwaio ideas about foreign supernatural forces can only be understood against this background of what one might call a siege mentality. I argue here that these concerns are not merely reflected in beliefs about foreign spirits; rather they are, in an important sense, what foreign spirits are all about (cf. Clark 1993; Shipton 1989; Taussig 1980). Public discourse surrounding these spirits constitutes a critique of more general importation of foreign ways, and provides testimony to their inappropriateness for Kwaio people.

People often implicate foreign spirits in modern social problems in Kwaio, but their significance varies considerably within two different levels of explanation. First, people sometimes blame these spirits for specific community problems, especially illnesses and spirit possessions that are unresponsive to normal treatments. Such spirits are believed beyond control, and provide explanation for the inability of ancestral spirits and their priests to remedy difficult situations.

Second, a distinct discourse has developed about the impact of foreign spirits on the Kwaio community. When evoked in this more general sense, foreign spirits serve as a potent metaphor for alien ways and their negative impact on

Kwaio society. Tragic accounts of their importation speak to the moral and practical perils of carelessly adopting foreign things.

It is useful to analyze Kwaio talk about foreign spirit importation in terms of a "key scenario" (Ortner 1973). These scenarios, found in all cultures, are a type of analytic "elaborating symbol" that arranges complex events and experiences so they "both formulate appropriate goals and suggest effective action for achieving them" (Ortner 1973:1341). Accounts of alien spirit importation are but one expression of a broader scenario that Kwaio use to frame and conceptualize the process of cultural borrowing. In this scenario, individuals are seduced or pressured into careless cultural borrowing and thereby undermine ancestral culture and Kwaio society. This same scenario is central to Kwaio discussions of political, economic, and religious issues, but nowhere is it so vividly and elegantly expressed as in talk about foreign spirits.

The scenario builds upon several moral themes concerning the inappropriateness of cultural importation and the necessity of maintaining Kwaio traditions. It speaks to the responsibility individuals have to their community, the futility of reliance on non-Kwaio sources of power, and the importance of stability and continuity for living a meaningful life. Long fundamental to Kwaio ethos and worldview, these themes have taken on new significance and urgency in the modern Solomons. The preeminent symbols of these moral qualities are the spirits of Kwaio ancestors and the rituals and rules surrounding them. Alien spirits are viewed by Kwaio as antithetical to the ancestors. They are foreign, transient, and asocial or antisocial; they lack the very qualities most valued in and exemplified by ancestral spirits. These are the same shortcomings Kwaio traditionalists perceive in the expanding cash economy, in modern urban lifestyles and, especially, in Christian culture.

One type of female alien spirit called *buru* personifies this ethos. Since the 1930s *buru* have been purchased abroad by individuals seeking access to new supernatural powers. Once back in Kwaio, the buyers have lost control of the spirits, with dreadful results. Multiple suicides, dwindling support from ancestral spirits, and the disintegration of mountain communities have all been attributed to uncontained wild *buru*. In recent years these spirits have become more active and have been blamed for a growing number of social ills.

Another type of numinous power borrowed by Kwaio, called *parana*, can be used to temporarily sever connections with ancestral spirits while living abroad. Beliefs about *parana* accentuate themes implicit in those about *buru*, particularly the idea that foreign sources of power and wealth are ineffectual for Kwaio people.

THE MOUNTAIN KWAIO IN THE CONTEMPORARY SOLOMONS

The meanings foreign spirits have for Kwaio are, in significant ways, a product of how they perceive other Solomon Islanders and the rapid transformations taking place in their country. Most Kwaio view the world beyond their mountains with ambivalence and uncertainty, and often find themselves struggling to balance their allegiance to ancestral ways with strong desires for foreign things and social change. As we shall see, beliefs about spirits reflect this contradiction.

The social position of mountain Kwaio in the greater Solomons is in many respects unenviable. As followers of their ancestral religion, they are a dwindling religious minority in an enthusiastically Christian country. Kwaio in the mountains see their ancestors and their religion as under Christian attack, a view substantiated by the rhetoric and policies of the largest local churches (Adventist and Evangelical). This religious battle has been waged in Kwaio since the first decade of the century, and Christian and mountain communities remain sharply divided. Although for simplicity I use "Kwaio" without qualifiers in reference to non-Christian mountain people, the majority of Kwaio are now Christians living on the coast. The cultural themes and political attitudes I describe for the mountain Kwaio are expressed in very different and interesting ways in Christian communities, but these are beyond the scope of this chapter.[1]

The mountain Kwaio have received neither educational or medical services, nor economic development, and other Solomon Islanders stereotype Kwaio as backward, violent, and dangerous. Fear deters visits by development and medical workers, perpetuating the pattern of Kwaio social and economic isolation. Even the police are loath to enter their mountains, and fugitives from government law live normal lives there.

Kwaio maintain their own negative stereotypes about non-Kwaio people and ways, particularly when discussing them in the abstract. Kwaio philosophers— and there are many—maintain that a good life emerges, above all, from stability, continuity, and permanence. Foreign things are said to lack all of these qualities. Kwaio depict the cash economy, for example, as asocial or even antisocial, offering at best only fleeting rewards. Towns and plantations are portrayed as impersonal and alienating, profoundly lacking the deep sense of community found at home; urban dwellers live a transient and groundless existence.[2] However, Kwaio usually characterize the foreign world not as innately wicked, but as inappropriate for Kwaio and antithetical to the Kwaio way of life. Attempts to harness foreign sources of wealth or power are said to be doomed to failure. Those who import foreign things to Kwaio only undermine their community and weaken their kin.

These negative views of life abroad and cultural importation are powerfully expressed in Kwaio representations of foreign spirits, the most perilous imports of all. Stories describing the dangers of spirit importation iterate a ubiquitous theme in Kwaio religious, educational and political affairs: the most serious threat to Kwaio culture and "custom" is not foreign incursions, but the voluntary adoption of alien ways by Kwaio people themselves.

These ideas have long been reflected in a practice that Keesing aptly described as the "compartmentalization" of foreign culture apart from life in Kwaio (1992:199–206). Kwaio traditionalists guard against alien infiltration by excluding foreign cash wealth from the prestige economy and barring Christians from living in the mountains. Behaviors acceptable for men while living on plantations or in town are strictly forbidden at home, and men forbid women from leaving the area. Yet these barriers are only part of a very complicated picture. Compartmentalization has been selective, contextual, and only partly successful. Most of the men who voice grim assessments of foreign ways enthusiastically adopted them when abroad and have brought foreign things back to Kwaio. Both men and women selectively want foreign things, and many bitterly complain they are neglected while the rest of the country receives aid and "defelopmen."

These seemingly contradictory views of the external world reveal a tension that permeates Kwaio society at almost every level. On one hand, everyone professes devotion to Kwaio ancestors and their ways; all proclaim an unwavering commitment to political autonomy and self-reliance. Yet most express a desire for change, for greater Kwaio participation in the larger world community, and for foreign goods, education, and medical care for their mountain communities and their children. Kwaio are well aware that these stances conflict, and they reflect on the contradiction. Their situation is not unique. Throughout the Solomons and elsewhere, communities are attempting to balance devotion to indigenous ways and identities with aspirations for new lifestyles and opportunities. What sets Kwaio apart is the tenacity of their commitment to older ways and their lack of foreign wealth and options for change.

As individuals, Kwaio are given to seeking foreign wealth and knowledge, experimenting with new ways, and bending ancestral rules. But in public discussion, in rhetoric and community political action, the ideology of conservatism and isolationism holds sway. It is as part of this more public and conservative discourse that foreign spirits acquire their most powerful meanings.

KWAIO ANCESTRAL SPIRITS

At the heart of mountain Kwaio culture are the spirits of ancestors.[3] These spirits epitomize the social and moral order; they founded Kwaio traditions and continue to enforce rules of proper living among their descendants. Ancestral spirits are a central and immediate presence in nearly all aspects of Kwaio life. To use Geertz' terminology, ancestors for the Kwaio have tremendous "force" and "scope" (1971:111–12). Foreign spirits, including the Christian God, acquire important aspects of their meaning for mountain Kwaio as the antithesis of ancestral spirits.

The most important ancestors died many generations ago (usually eight or more), though people also interact with lesser spirits, especially those of parents and others whom they knew in life. Individuals maintain relations with distinct constellations of ancestors, reflecting both genealogical variation and the fact that people can, to some degree, select the spirits to whom they sacrifice. The most important ancestors receive pigs from hundreds of descendants in shrines all across Kwaio. Community sacrifices and other rituals generally are performed or officiated by male priests.

Most Kwaio religious activity centers around maintaining good relations with ancestors and thus assuring their support. This entails raising and sacrificing pigs for them and obeying their many prescriptive and proscriptive rules. As with relationships between living people, those between ancestors and descendants are built upon and expressed through exchange. In return for obedience and pigs, ancestors empower descendants for daily living and specific undertakings, and protect them from malevolent forces such as sorcery and dangerous spirits. However, it is important to underscore the fact that relationships between ancestors and descendants also are emotionally charged and morally valued.

When ancestors are unhappy with descendants' behavior they may punish them directly with illness, social or economic failure, or other hardships. Alternatively, ancestors may passively demonstrate displeasure by withdrawing protection, a potentially disastrous state of affairs. Almost any significant success or adversity is at least partly due to spirit influence, and a person's or group's quality of life is a general indicator of their relations with ancestors.

If serious misfortune occurs, those affected must determine what is displeasing the spirits. It might be that someone has violated a rule, or a particular spirit may require a pig or specific ritual performance. The most common means of finding the answer is divination, one of several channels through which people maintain an ongoing dialogue with their ancestors. Among the innumerable rules that ancestors enforce are prohibitions against eating certain foods, uttering taboo words, and killing one's codescendants. They also prescribe behaviors such as carrying out community rituals, gardening properly, and raising sacrificial pigs. When rule violations are discovered, or if spirits are angry for any reason, purificatory pigs must be given. Some rules are specific to local ancestors for whom hamlet residents sacrifice pigs, although many rules apply to all Kwaio.

All ancestors insist on certain kinds of gender separation within hamlets. They are particularly concerned that female bodily wastes and childbirth be contained within demarcated toilet, menstrual, and birth areas located downhill from family clearings. No man, or any object from elsewhere in the hamlet, may enter these areas. Above them, in the middle level of the hamlet, are secular houses where families socialize and most people sleep. Further above are the men's areas, containing one or more men's houses, gardens of sacred plants, and perhaps a small shrine. No women may ascend to these men's areas for any reason. The most commonly determined cause of ancestral anger in Kwaio is a woman's accidental urination or menstruation within the middle level of the hamlet. When discovered, whether by the woman alerting her kin or through divination, the ancestors require public confession and compensatory pigs (see Akin 1993:801–22).

Ancestral spirits *want* descendants to make use of their powers, and expect their relationship to be dynamic and ongoing. These spirits are best thought of as active members of the social groups that sacrifice to them. When alive, they gardened the same land (sometimes as the original cultivators), lived in the same clearings, followed the same religious rules and, in the case of more recent spirits, even sacrificed pigs to the same older ancestors in the same shrines. As spirits, they are intensely concerned that their descendants continue to carry out these activities properly. It is easy to see why a kin group's ancestors are the preeminent symbol of their identity, history, continuity, and place. In a more general sense, ancestors symbolize what it means to be Kwaio.

Like living people, ancestors have personalities, moods, egos, and jealousies. They are emotionally attached to their descendants, as are their descendants to them. Living Kwaio fear the wrath of angry ancestors, but they also express great "love" for them (*kwaimanadaiga*). Any given interaction with an ancestor is one episode in a lifelong (and beyond) social relationship between spirit and descendant. Though frequently depicted as cold and heartless toward descendants who break rules, at other times ancestors—especially recently deceased parents or other close relatives, referred to as "small ancestors"—are lovingly nurturant. Laeniamae, a priest and devoted father, described to me how he will protect his children after he dies:

> I'll guide my children. I'll tell them, "Do such-and-such [i.e., a sacrifice, a ritual], and your living will be good. If you don't do it for me, then your children will be sick." After I die, I'll protect them from the bigger ancestors. If there is something deadly approaching, I'll tell my eldest son, Diake, "Put together such-and-such, and you and your children will be all right, but if you don't do it they may get hurt.". . . An ancestral spirit cares for its people. Our living descendants can't see us, but wherever they go, we are standing there with them. No matter what may threaten them, I'll ward it off. Any bad thing that might menace them along the trail, I'll be there.

Even "bigger" ancestors of many generations ago sometimes express concern and affection for their descendants when speaking through someone they have possessed.

Finally, ancestral powers are harnessed by performing varieties of magic consisting of spells, rituals, and charms that work mechanically and automatically. Many of these harness the power of spirits, while others rely on unknown mechanisms. Magical knowledge is the incorporeal property of individuals or groups; some types may be purchased, or stolen by overhearing spells. Those who control efficacious curative and divinatory magic can earn significant amounts of shell money by performing it on behalf of others. For this reason, people are reluctant to sell magical knowledge to potential competitors. However, such knowledge is widely exchanged between individuals from different areas, particularly when they meet as laborers on plantations and in towns. Many magic varieties in Kwaio, including some used to manipulate Kwaio ancestors, are believed to operate through foreign spirits obtained abroad.

BURU SPIRITS

Buru spirits are an active and growing force in Kwaio. The Kwaio include them within a broader category of spirits that are "wild," over which living people have little influence. Important features of *buru* are illuminated by comparing them with another type of "wild" spirit in Kwaio, ancestors who have no living descendants. These spirits, known as *kwasi*, have either lost all of their descendants to death or Christianity, or they were themselves the last living member of their lineage.[4] *Kwasi* and *buru* are similar in that both are socially unconnected: *kwasi* have had their ties to society severed because they lack descendants, *buru* are foreigners. Kwaio rarely distinguish individual *buru* or *kwasi* with personal names (Coppet 1981:177), underscoring their asociality. Neither receive regular sacrifices, so are not subject to effective control by living people. As a result, both can be extremely dangerous.

There is an important difference between *kwasi* and *buru* as well: true ancestral spirits can easily control the weaker *kwasi* (weaker because they are socially isolated). Ancestors may abandon a hamlet to *kwasi* attacks, but only if they are angry with descendants who live there (Coppet 1981:178). This can also occur with *buru*, but unlike *kwasi*, *buru* may aggressively chase away a hamlet's ancestors by desecrating sacred men's houses or shrines. The foreign *buru*, therefore, are a serious invasive threat to the Kwaio social system in a way that *kwasi*, an integral part of that system, are not.

The most notorious and frequently recounted instance of spirit importation illustrates many facets of *buru* beliefs. The *buru* involved is probably the oldest in Kwaio and the likely prototype of generic *buru* narratives commonly heard today:

> Sometime in the mid-1930s, a man from the Uru mountains (whom I'll call "Defete") purchased the knowledge to control a *buru* from Langalanga for her reputed powers for pig raising and for attracting wealth. The spirit required offerings of pineapples instead of pigs and came with her own set of rules concerning certain foods and other behaviors. Defete brought the spirit home and, sure enough, before long his hamlet was fairly overrun with large pigs, and he accumulated a small fortune in shell money valuables. Word of the spirit's power spread, and soon men from other places came and paid Defete for knowledge to control the spirit.
>
> Events took an alarming turn when Defete's true ancestral spirits became jealous and angry at the intrusive presence of the *buru* and deserted him and his kin. Once the ancestors had departed, the now unbridled *buru* began afflicting people of Defete's group. Eventually, after several deaths, most of Defete's kin group had dispersed, many fleeing to the protection of Christian missions. But the *buru* did not stop there. She now also resided in the home territories of the other men who had purchased her. She began troubling people in those places as well, particularly through possession states that were difficult or impossible to exorcise and that sometimes ended in suicide. To make matters worse, she started afflicting people

in groups from which no one had purchased her, preying particularly upon women. The common explanation is that those who purchased the *buru* had not taken her rules seriously, or had not fully understood them, and that the angry spirit roamed in search of others to whom she might attach herself. This same *buru* is blamed for suicides and other problems in East Kwaio today.

The roving *buru* attaching herself to different people, and the offended ancestors abandoning their descendants, reflect an important feature of Malaitan spirits. If people do not maintain proper reciprocal relationships with them by following their rules or providing ample sacrifice, they withdraw and sometimes attach themselves to others. Many believe that some spirits entered Kwaio in search of human relationships after their descendants elsewhere abandoned them for Christianity. *Buru* resemble other active Malaitan spirits in wanting their powers used and may forcefully initiate relationships with living people.

Defete's *buru* was not the last one brought to Kwaio (and probably not the first).[5] Others have been purchased on plantations by men who believed they were buying benevolent spirits. Most were obtained for their powers for fighting, theft, or curing; for luck in fishing or gambling; or as love magic. In the late 1920s or early 1930s the devastation of two neighborhoods by epidemic disease was blamed on a foreign entity purchased by two Kwaio men in 'Are'are to the south. Some people say the sellers lied and claimed the spirit would bring shell money and other wealth, when in truth it was a deadly sorcery spirit.

Variations in beliefs about *buru* are too numerous to detail here, but several important themes emerge. First of all, *buru* spirits are female, a fact with numerous connotations for Kwaio. While some of the strongest ancestral spirits are female, and behave much as male spirits do, *buru* are quite different. Most Kwaio believe that, unlike Kwaio ancestresses, *buru* cannot enter shrines or sacred men's houses because of their gender. Inverting the behavior of ancestral spirits, a *buru* in a hamlet often establishes her "headquarters" in the women's menstrual or toilet areas, and may inflict sickness upon the hamlet's women by eating their feces and drinking their urine. A *buru* may haunt a hamlet for weeks but restrict her activities to these areas, frightening and sometimes possessing women there. Ancestral possession of women is not uncommon in Kwaio and is sometimes even viewed positively. Yet given the negative connotations and uncontrollable nature of *buru* possession, these spirits do little to directly empower women (although see Akin 1985).

A second important trait of *buru* is that they may attempt to chase a hamlet's ancestral spirits away through desecration. Even if they cannot enter sacred areas, *buru* can attack them by throwing feces or other material from toilet and menstrual areas into them, or even at the ancestors themselves. Once the ancestors have fled in disgust, a hamlet's unprotected residents are helpless to fend off the unhampered *buru*. In such situations *buru* want and expect people to use their full powers, and when they do not know how, the *buru* may punish them.

Buru also have a propensity and talent for impersonating genuine ancestors, especially those they have driven away. Their trickery can be difficult to detect because *buru* appropriate the usual channels for ancestral communication, such as divination and possession. Consequently, people may not even realize that their ancestors have fled. Usually they suspect that a *buru* is at work only when the spirits' promises are broken, when possessions persist despite extensive exorcisms, or when priests have repeatedly sacrificed to no effect. Thus *buru* are ineffectual almost by definition; they tend to surface as explanations for the failures of ancestral spirits and priests.

I must emphasize that those who purchased *buru* are said to have been ignorant of the danger the spirits posed. Believing they could control the *buru* with knowledge they had procured, Kwaio buyers did not realize the spirits' true nature. Here again, *buru* appear to be something they are not. Most men buy them for some relatively simple, singular purpose, and they purchase only the knowledge to manage the spirits at this restricted level. It is when the ancestors depart, leaving the *buru* unconstrained, that they can no longer be controlled.

The importation of *buru* into Kwaio is thus not a deliberate challenge to ancestors. *Buru* and other imported spirits do not compete with ancestors for pigs, a common source of jealousy among Kwaio ancestral spirits. Instead, purchased spirits demand offerings of unusual things such as coconut crabs or pineapples. Moreover, the acquisition of these spirits rarely represents an attempt to secure foreign goods, nor reflects aspirations for alien goals. Rather, purchasing spirits is a means of obtaining success within the established Kwaio economic, political, and social system. Buyers hope the new spirits will deliver the same kinds of rewards granted by ancestors: pigs, shell money, and productive or destructive powers.

POSSESSION

Both *buru* and indigenous Kwaio spirits sometimes possess men and women. Symptoms range from mild dissociation to extreme depression and sleeplessness to trancelike states during which spirits may speak through the person. People can become violent and may injure themselves or others if not restrained. In some contexts, possession by ancestors is seen as positive and is even sought after, while at other times it may indicate a spirit's anger with descendants. Unwanted ancestral possessions usually end soon after the sacrifice of pigs. But *buru* possessions (which more often afflict women) can be an entirely different matter. They are frequently manifest as serious and chronic mental illness, unresponsive to treatment. The expected, and occasionally realized, outcome of such possessions is attempted suicide.

When Kwaio discuss the negative consequences of *buru* importation in the abstract, talk often turns to suicide. Elsewhere (Akin 1985), I have described how Kwaio stereotypes about suicide are contradicted by case data. While suicides are blamed principally on *buru* in general discussions, only twenty percent of the specific cases I recorded were blamed on spirits of any sort.[6] Nevertheless, older Kwaio people uniformly assert that rates of incurable possession and suicide have soared since they were young, and most Kwaio blame this primarily on the arrival of *buru*.

Buru do not usually afflict the men who have purchased them, but rather their relatives or other innocents. The *buru* avoids attacking the one who sacrifices to her, and he is, therefore, often the last to suffer. Some have drawn an analogy with professional killers of the past who were seldom killed, while relatives were often murdered to avenge their deeds.

Possessions and suicides are not the only modern problems Kwaio blame on *buru*. Most interesting are Kwaio assertions that they are responsible for a modern-day increase in the breaking of menstrual and toilet rules by women. *Buru* are said to induce such violations as part of their desecration campaigns to chase away ancestral spirits. More than one informant explained a perceived decline in the Kwaio population as a result of ancestors' punishments of their descendants for *buru*-caused rule violations. Yet while *buru* sometimes are cited as a general explanation for increasing women's violations, only rarely are they implicated in actual cases of rule breaking.

Buru sometimes afflict a group whose ancestors have abandoned them for reasons unrelated to the *buru* itself, as illustrated by the following case:

In the 1970s a man began to suffer from semimonthly possessions that sometimes lasted for a week or more. An ancestral spirit was demanding that he use its powers to kill someone. Because the man's family had told the ancestor he could no longer kill because of the government, the spirit was punishing him with possessions. During these states the man would leap to his feet shouting "Let's go now and kill!" This was particularly striking given the man's normally mild disposition.[7] From 1979 to 1983, I was told by various relatives that he was being possessed by a recent ancestor, a famous warrior who desired that he use the power of an older fighting ancestor. They were worried because the spirit was continuing to demand a killing despite their performance of rituals that had pacified warrior spirits in the past. Some outside the group suspected that it was actually a *buru* possessing him, but close family members rejected this explanation (though a *buru* had afflicted others of their group).

When I returned in 1987 and 1992, the man had relocated to the coast and had become Christian in an attempt to escape the spirit. But his mental problems continued. Several relatives had now modified their diagnosis of his illness: he had indeed been possessed by a *buru* impersonating the ancestor, and that was why he had been incurable. The *buru* had been allowed to afflict him by their fighting ancestors who were angry that people had refused to use their powers. It was believed that this *buru* was the same one imported before the war by Defete.

Despite apparent longstanding and nearly unanimous agreement as to the undesirability of *buru*, they continue to make their way into Kwaio via individuals who think they are importing benevolent spirits. To prevent such blunders, the

Kwaio council of leaders enacted a 1987 bylaw forbidding the importation of foreign spirits of any kind. Orators advocating the ban reminded their audience of Defete's *buru* and of the many suicides she had caused.

OTHER IMPORTS

Buru are only one of many numinal varieties brought to Kwaio. Despite sweeping condemnations of such imports, many have proved useful and unproblematic. Many important Kwaio ancestors, especially those bestowing power for fighting and theft, are the spirits of émigrés from elsewhere on Malaita. These people brought their own ancestral spirits with them, along with associated rituals still performed by their Kwaio descendants. Such ritual complexes continue to be identified with their places of origin, despite generations of Kwaio priests who have carried out the rites and the unmistakable Kwaio stamp they have acquired.

More pertinent are the hundreds of spirits and magic varieties that individuals have imported to supplement ancestral power. Cross-cultural exchange of such things is not new to Kwaio or their neighbors; as in most of Melanesia, it is a long-standing tradition. The Kwaio have several myths describing numinous importations in the precolonial past. During the late nineteenth century, thousands of Malaitans were recruited as laborers for plantations in Fiji and Queensland. This provided unprecedented opportunities to acquire foreign religious ideas, spirits and magical powers through purchase or exchange (Mercer and Moore 1976; Moore 1986). Corris reports that Malaitans in Fiji had "found some of the Fijian cults and rituals meaningful and acceptable," and wrote of "the existence of at least one religious cult in [Malaita's Lau Lagoon] which has Fijian and Lau elements intertwined" (1973:97). In the 1930s Hogbin described returned Malaitan laborers doing "a brisk trade amongst themselves" in magic acquired from outsiders (1970:174). On Malaita, a purchased spirit or magic is not alienated from the seller or its home territory; what is sold is the knowledge to access its power.

Kwaio today continue to borrow and assimilate foreign spirits and magic, most notably powers for divination, curing, and pig raising. Ancestral spirits do not always react badly to foreign arrivals, and Kwaio say new spirits can even become "friends" with ancestors. These benevolent spirits, unlike *buru* and some other foreign entities, pose no threat to ancestors. Imported divination familiars enable them to better communicate with descendants, and pigs raised with foreign magic are given to them in sacrifice.

Kwaio contend that the importation of foreign sorcery is increasing. Beliefs about sorcery cannot be detailed here, but they share significant similarities with Kwaio ideas about *buru*. Local Kwaio sorceries are often depicted as morally neutral or even positive, since they can be used justifiably on behalf of entire communities and harness the power of ancestral spirits. Imported sorceries, by contrast, are portrayed as foreign commodities, purchased by individuals for selfish and antisocial purposes. Often they are motivated by jealousy of legitimately successful individuals within the Kwaio socioeconomic system. Many indigenous Kwaio sorceries have the same antisocial aspects attributed to newer alien ones, but Kwaio starkly contrast the two in the abstract, accentuating the positive aspects of indigenous sorceries and the negative aspects of foreign ones.

DISCONNECTING ANCESTRAL SPIRITS

When discussing societal decadence, Kwaio often portray their culture as under attack on two fronts: encroachment by alien ways, and a weakening of local sources of protective and effective power. This is sometimes brought about in a frighteningly direct way when *buru* chase away ancestral spirits, leaving descendants vulnerable. A more widespread and far more serious problem is that many Kwaio are voluntarily diluting their most important sources of power: they are abandoning community cooperation and solidarity, and along with it, their ancestors.

In discussing this, Kwaio often point to the increasing deployment of foreign magic and spirits that allow users to violate religious rules with impunity. These are used not to tap into foreign sources of power, but rather to neutralize Kwaio power, particularly the power of ancestral spirits. One from the island of Choiseul called *parana* is of particular interest. Beliefs about *parana* accentuate and extrapolate several themes also apparent in *buru* beliefs, especially the idea that dependence upon foreign sources of power is futile and will have deleterious effects.

Parana are usually acquired by men working on plantations in the western Solomons. They are small powdery stones that are scraped into one's food to allow it to be eaten without worry about ancestral culinary rules. Some types of *parana* allow users to violate other religious rules and offer protection from sorcery. *Parana* often are referred to as *adalo*, the Kwaio generic term for spirits, although people, when pressed, say they are unsure the stones actually work through spirits. *Parana* are foreign things, they say, of which they are ignorant.

What people do know is that *parana* can be a welcome resource abroad. To appreciate the value placed on the stones one must be aware of the difficulties faced by Kwaio men attempting to follow the rules of ancestral spirits while living outside Kwaio. Food rules are particularly onerous, especially for men who have eaten sacred pork. In Kwaio, such men may not eat or drink with women, and their food must be prepared in containers never before used for women's food. These restrictions are extremely difficult to observe in foreign settings where most people are non-Kwaio Christians, unaware of or unwilling to follow ancestral rules. As one man described the associated dangers of being abroad, "We always walk about with our eyes open and our minds sharp; we have to look out for ourselves." *Parana* can do much to alleviate such concerns.

Men have used *parana* for years at a time while working overseas with no adverse effects. As the following account illustrates, it is when stones are brought back to Kwaio that trouble ensues:

When Willie [a pseudonym] spent five years out in Western Province he ate using one of those stones from Choiseul. He ate women's food, and things like that. Then after five years he was ready to come back, and he thought, "This is a good thing I have going. I've used this stone for five years, and nothing bad has happened to me, and my ancestors have not afflicted me. I'm going to take it home." He brought the stone back with him, and he stuck it in a bag in his house. Eventually the ancestors made him sick, because of it. He got sick, and then got sick again, and he kept on getting sick, and it was terrible. They performed divination: "What kind of rule did he break to warrant *this*? Willie, what have you got?" But Willie didn't say anything. He didn't tell. They finally did *rioriota* divination [in which diviners actually *see* complex answers in a pool of water, rather than the simple yes or no answers of common divination]. "Hey! You've done something! You've hidden something away." Then Willie said, "Maybe it's that stone I stuck away." So they sacrificed pigs, and Willie threw that stone into the Kwaiba'ita River. He didn't get sick anymore.

Willie had received the stone from a Choiseulese friend as a gift. His sickness resulted from his having been forsaken by his ancestors, much as ancestors abandon those who import *buru*. According to the narrator, and later corroborated by Willie himself and others, when ancestral spirits see one of the stones in Kwaio, "They think it has been brought so that people won't need to give them any more purificatory pigs. So they abandon us."

Another man told of gathering *parana* stones himself in a Choiseul stream bed. They allowed him to violate ancestral rules abroad and protected him from foreign sorceries. But he found, as have other Kwaio, that the protection had a price: while one is using *parana*, one can't amass any wealth. As this man put it, "Money comes your way, but it just keeps on going."

Why can't one accumulate wealth while using *parana*? The answer is simple, yet it reveals a basic tenet underlying how Kwaio see the world: success in life requires support from others, and securing worthwhile support is necessarily difficult and burdensome. To maintain allies among living people one must contribute generously to their feasts and other endeavors. Retaining the support of one's ancestors requires sacrifice (both figuratively and literally) and the hard work of following their demanding rules. Ancestral rules are at the heart of people's reciprocal relationships with ancestral spirits. When a man evades these rules by using *parana*, he may suffer no ill effects, but, although his life becomes easier, he actually dilutes or severs his ancestral relationships. This separation usually is described as ancestors' abandoning their descendant, but from the ancestors' point of view, the descendant has deserted *them* by discarding their rules (cf. Frankel 1986:150). They merely respond in kind. Without ancestral help, a man (and in local Kwaio contexts, a woman) will enjoy no economic or social success. Such a person, at best, lives in a power vacuum without supernatural support and thus with no hope of a truly fulfilling life. *Parana* and similar spirits and magic do not confer power; they merely nullify it.

The fact that *parana* can be used safely outside of Kwaio accentuates the general lack of rules and sacrifice that, from the Kwaio perspective, typifies the moral emptiness of existence abroad. That one cannot accumulate wealth while using the stones reflects the unfulfilling quality of life outside and how little the foreign cash economy offers Malaitans. Unlike indigenous shell money accumulated in the prestige economy at home, cash earned within the market economy brings minimal social rewards. Cash is earned by individuals who work alone and flows not into the earner's own community, but into the stores and pockets of outsiders. Cash wealth is thus seen as a temporary phenomenon; when earned, cash always "just keeps on going"; it lacks the durable quality of shell money wealth, which embodies long-term commitments and lifelong social networks. When a man abroad mutes his relationships with ancestral spirits through magic like *parana*, he withdraws from a crucial—some would say defining—aspect of being Kwaio. He abandons himself to the pursuit of an empty lifestyle and fleeting wealth, and temporarily surrenders any hope of enduring success (see Clark 1993; Shipton 1989; Taussig 1980). Mountain Kwaio sometimes portray Christian Solomon Islanders as having permanently adopted just such an empty existence by having abandoned their ancestors.

Parana exemplify the more general abandonment of ancestral ways forced upon Kwaio men abroad, and so it is little wonder that ancestral spirits feel threatened when descendants bring the stones back to Kwaio. Like their ancestors, many living Kwaio also fear that liberal adoption of shallow foreign lifestyles is progressively infiltrating Kwaio and will result in their powerlessness and ruination. Where *buru* elucidate the potential dangers of foreign things, *parana* exemplify the emptiness and impotence that befall those who embrace them.[8]

VAGUENESS AND UNCERTAINTY IN FOREIGN SPIRIT BELIEFS

While it is tempting to offer formal analyses purporting to describe uniform systems of religious thought, such accounts always must be viewed with skepticism. Many anthropologists, including several Melanesianists, have warned against imposing on religious beliefs systematicity and granting what Brunton (1980) referred to as a "misconstrued order" (e.g., Barth 1987; Evans-Pritchard 1985:221; Frankel 1986:189; Keesing 1982:243–246; Schieffelin 1976:-103–104; Worsley 1968:xxiv–xxvi). This can be particularly distorting when describing a highly acephalous religious structure like that in Kwaio where (a) no central religious authority produces standardized doctrine, and (b) spirits enforce unique rules and behaviors among their own descendants. Special caution is required regarding Kwaio beliefs about foreign or wild spirits like *buru* and *kwasi*. Conceptions of them are notably more opaque, and inconsistencies are less subtle. Various categories of foreign spirits are lumped together by some, but adamantly differentiated by others. Kwaio descriptions of the nature, origins, motivations and powers of foreign spirits are far more varied than are their ideas about Kwaio ancestors.[9]

Why should this be? The answer lies partly in the politics of religious interpretation and control. Kwaio relations with ancestors are a matter of ongoing
negotiation and experimentation. Details of religious practice are the subject of
continual discussion, divination, and regulation in daily life. If relationships with
ancestors are properly conducted, the ritual community can enjoy happiness
and prosperity, but otherwise even the hardest work and the best behavior will
lead only to poverty and social calamity. Those with religious authority owe
much of their power to others' confidence in their knowledge of the ancestors
and their rules, and their resulting ability to ensure good relations with the spirits. Nevertheless these men have little influence over *buru* and other wild or alien
spirits. On the contrary, such forces usually enter the picture precisely as explanations for events obviously beyond the control of a community's ritual experts.
The presence of a *buru* typically is uncovered during investigations of why a
group's ancestral spirits have been unresponsive to prayer and sacrifice. People
discover they have been driven away by a *buru*. Within other religions, sorcery,
witchcraft, or evil spirits are similarly evoked to explain religious failures, but
buru are exceptionally suited for scapegoating because of their propensity for
impersonating legitimate spirits. Their detection provides the perfect explanation for an ancestor's inaction or nonfulfillment of promises.

A crucial attribute of *buru* and other wild spirits, then, is their unknowable
nature and consequent uncontrollability. Most are anonymous beings with no
personal names, and many are not identified with a known importer. Unlike true
ancestral spirits, there is little imperative for standardized beliefs about these
spirits, only for agreement as to their undesirability and ability to evade religious
control. Their mysterious character also increases their metaphorical fit with
foreign ways in general. The impenetrability of European and other alien cultures is seen to be central to the danger they pose for Kwaio society.

CONCEPTUAL UNDERPINNINGS

So far I have described Kwaio ideas about imported spirits and magic as they
appear on the surface. We have seen the dangers these forces present to individuals and their communities, and how they are invoked to explain misfortunes in
daily life. Now I turn to some less obvious meanings these alien forces have, and
attempt to contextualize beliefs about them vis-à-vis internal tensions in modern
Kwaio society. This section summarizes several themes manifest in spirit beliefs
that are fundamental to Kwaio conceptions of cultural difference and exchange.
I will conclude with a discussion of how these themes are linked together within a scenario of tragic spirit importation, and how this communicates a more
general scenario of foreign importation at the center of Kwaio discourse about
foreign ways.

While beliefs about spirits clearly reflect contemporary Kwaio concerns, they
also embody deeper cultural themes that likely predate contact with Europeans.
These themes have gained new force and meanings within the contemporary

social scene, particularly with the expansion of Christianity. At their core, conceptions of foreign spirits evince a marked sense of cultural relativism that is characteristic of Kwaio worldviews. Many people do not portray *buru* or most other imported spirits (excepting sorcery familiars) as inherently wicked. They suppose that some of these spirits are natural for the people from their place of origin, for whom they may even be conventional ancestors. The people of their native region, it is said, must possess (or must have possessed at one time) the knowledge to control such spirits properly, just as Kwaio know how to control their own local spirits. It is only when these foreign spirits enter Kwaio, where they do not belong, that they become a menace.[10]

A similar relativism underlies Kwaio views of most foreign ways. Only rarely are cultural traits depicted as "evil" in the sense of intrinsically bad or destructive.[11] More often they are represented as merely unsuitable for Kwaio; they belong to the customs of different people. Such relativism would necessarily have been part of Kwaio culture long before the arrival of Europeans because of the diverse, atomistic structure of Kwaio society.

This is particularly true regarding religious beings and practices. Kwaio regularly interact with people from other language groups, and Kwaio territory incorporates several recognized cultural zones and dialects. Moreover, each Kwaio neighborhood is subject to localized rules enforced by spirits to whom residents sacrifice. Even close neighbors likely follow rules that differ in some respects. Individuals also maintain secondary consanguineal or affinal memberships in several different groups that venerate different ancestors. A consequence of this diversity is that a xenophobic perspective in Kwaio is virtually impossible. Moreover, tolerance and flexibility are to some extent obligatory since Kwaio principles of liability require compensation payments if one violates others' rules or otherwise offends their spirits. The structure of Kwaio society ingrains in its members an acceptance of cultural diversity as natural, inevitable, and proper.

The same structure generates strong concepts of appropriateness and inappropriateness in cultural practice and borrowing. The ways of others, and particularly their spirits, are often impossible to adopt regardless of their appeal. One cannot take up an alien practice that is restricted to the descendants of a particular ancestor. The rightful descendants would object, and one's own ancestral spirits might disapprove as well. Many cultural practices also are markers of exclusive secular identities, and trespass is unthinkable (see Knauft 1985a; Schwartz 1975). Those who have imported problematic foreign spirits such as *buru* are seen to have violated cultural boundaries.

Kwaio beliefs about foreign spirits incorporate a corollary to these ideas of cultural relativism and appropriateness: efforts that overtly *mix* practices from different cultures will likely fail. This belief is commonly stressed when explaining disharmony between imported and ancestral spirits; emanating from different traditions, "how could they possibly coexist?" The problem of mixing also comes to the fore in other interactions with European culture, most notably within contexts involving curing and knowledge. Western medicine is thought ineffectual for treating "Kwaio sicknesses," ancestrally caused illnesses resulting from social or antisocial acts. Neither are Kwaio cures useful for treating foreign illnesses, for which Western medicines may be eagerly sought. A sickness resulting from a foreign spirit or sorcery usually will respond only to cures from the same foreign source (see Frankel 1986:182). Nor should therapies be combined. Patients receiving Kwaio treatments are often instructed not to take Western medicine as the combination will negate both cures. Kwaio have no detailed exegesis for such incompatibilities; the nullifying effect of cultural mixing is considered sufficient explanation.

Similar ideas have developed with regard to Western and Kwaio knowledge, and many feel one cannot effectively master both. This has some basis in Kwaio experience, as mission and government teachers have long taught students to scorn their own cultures. Since 1979, schools of a local cultural center have challenged presumptions of educational incongruity by incorporating indigenous knowledge into curricula (Akin 1995). One father, a neighbor and strong supporter of the center, nevertheless chose to teach his elder son "his custom" and bar him from school, while sending his youngest to classes and *not* teaching him ancestral knowledge. The father steadfastly maintained that no boy could possibly learn both. Other families have practiced a similar "division of knowledge" between children (see also Bennett 1987:341; Godelier 1986:205). A variation on the cultural segregation theme is also popular among Kwaio Christians. It dovetails with missionary insistence that converts must discard all aspects of ancestral culture, whether sacred or secular, in order to become true Christians.

When Kwaio discuss the failure of *buru* and other alien entities to deliver prosperity, they accentuate another Kwaio maxim: alien things are relatively powerless for Kwaio. This also is expressed in critiques of Christianity, in the way shell money is contrasted with cash, and in Kwaio beliefs about *parana* stones and the empty lifestyle they sustain. The similarity between traditionalists' perceptions of Christianity and *parana* is particularly salient in this regard. Like *parana*, God negates the power of ancestral spirits and allows Christians to violate their rules, but provides only negligible substitute power. In addition to God's alien nature, other reasons are cited for this lack of power, traits that Christianity is said to share not only with *parana*, but also with *buru* and European society in general. Most fundamentally, Christian society is represented as lacking the social quality of community. Mountain Kwaio perceive large Christian villages as having relatively weak common identities, few answerable leaders, and an abundance of socially delinquent "backsliders." Their criteria for measuring these qualities are their own closely knit groups of kin, living in tiny hamlets with strong leaders. Such standards of community integration are incompatible with heterogeneous Christian villages where populations sometimes number in the hundreds.

Christian communities are viewed as further weakened by church bans on bride price and mortuary and compensation payments, all of which are central to binding together mountain communities. Mountain people see no substitute for these in Christian life. As with *parana*, Christianity is perceived as requiring minimal sacrifice and yielding little of real social value. God, they believe, is "easy," whereas following the ways of ancestral spirits is "hard" but fulfilling. They note that, relative to other Solomons church communities, Christian villages in Kwaio lack Western affluence, and they cite this as evidence of the weakness of God's power for them. Kwaio Christians are portrayed as having forsaken their true heritage for a foreign way of life that, despite their allegiance to God, has treated them shabbily. Furthermore, they have endangered their relatives in the mountains, since ancestors are now less supportive even of loyal descendants because so many others have left them for God. To non-Christians, God is the most threatening foreign spirit of all.

Most basic to Kwaio conceptions of community strength and quality of life are the overlapping virtues of stability and continuity. As described earlier, Kwaio ancestral spirits are the ultimate symbols of these, and it is not surprising that foreign spirits exemplify their antithesis. Real power and security are said to come to those who maintain these qualities in their lives. This is made most explicit in the gardens of sacred plants that are tended above every Kwaio men's house. Most of these plants are magical and consecrated to ancestral spirits to ward off illness, accusation, wild spirits, and sorcery. Much of this magic has been passed down from the founding ancestors of the land where they are now grown. The gardens' primary function is to divert those things that would disrupt the community and perhaps force the hamlet to move. For a community to be stable, or *fuu*, is indicative of its strength and a confirmation that its people properly follow the ways of their ancient ancestors. These ancestors are themselves known as *adalo fuu*, stable and permanent spirits who have resided in Kwaio for generations. It is in juxtaposition to *adalo fuu* that new foreign spirits, asocial in nature, transient and unstable, acquire much of their negative symbolic significance.

BURU AND THE FOREIGN THREAT

Beliefs about problematic foreign spirits are well-grounded in the deep-seated principles just described, but they have been shaped by modern conditions. Most obvious are widespread fears among mountain Kwaio that their way of life is being undermined and overrun by alien forces. But Kwaio also see a more insidious threat: Kwaio is being weakened from within by individuals seduced by foreign ways.

Talk about dangerous foreign spirits, particularly *buru* spirits, is part of a well-developed public discourse condemning cultural importation, and it cannot be properly understood in isolation. Such condemnation is a prominent theme in modern Kwaio political rhetoric; it is also explicit or implicit in many other kinds of talk. The remainder of this paper is concerned with the meanings that foreign spirits have within this broader set of ideas.

First we must understand Kwaio talk about cultural importation on a more general level. I use a model similar to the "key scenario" model developed by Ortner. By this Ortner means a scenario that symbolically "formulates [a] culture's basic means-ends relationships in actable forms," and "implies clear-cut modes of action appropriate to correct and successful living in the culture" (1973:1341). One of Ortner's examples is the scenario of the Horatio Alger myth, in which a poor boy makes good through hard work and faith in the American system. Another, from Sherpa culture, is "the hospitality scenario, in which any individual in the role of host feeds a guest and thereby renders him voluntarily cooperative vis-à-vis oneself" (1973:1341; see also 1989). Schieffelin has applied a similar, "cultural scenario," model to his study of the Kaluli in New Guinea, showing how a "reciprocity scenario" orders and propels events ranging from gift exchange to ceremonial performances and even conversion to Christianity (1976; 1981). The Kwaio scenario presented here has similarities and differences with those analyzed by Ortner and Schieffelin.

What I refer to as the "importation scenario" includes the following elements: A Kwaio person or group adopts something foreign. Once the foreign introduction becomes established it begins to undermine and erode indigenous Kwaio culture (or *kastom*). Eventually, borrowers and their communities find themselves facing the world equipped only with alien ways. But because these are foreign, they are barren or even dangerous for Kwaio people. If the process is allowed to fully unfold, the community will be destroyed or left living a powerless and meaningless existence.

Variations on this scenario are articulated in such diverse settings as formal speeches at feasts, in priests' monologues to ancestors in shrines, and in elders' lectures to young people on proper behavior. Sometimes it is presented in the abstract as a generic depiction of debilitating importation, but more commonly it appears in reconfigured and elaborated forms in conjunction with specific topics, such as the rejection of Western cash, the condemnation of Christianity, or the boycotting of government courts. Linkage between different expressions of the scenario is occasionally made explicit.

This importation scenario is most evident within *kastom* politics, which have dominated Kwaio since World War II (see Jolly and Thomas 1992; Keesing and Tonkinson 1982; Lindstrom and White 1993). Indeed, *kastom* ideologies in Kwaio have long embraced a version of the scenario as their dominant theme: European ways have undermined indigenous culture and identity; rejection of the former and revitalization of the latter must take place before Malaitans can prosper and reverse progressive social anomie. Nori, leader of the Maasina Rule political movement that dominated Malaita in the years following World War II, is widely remembered as proclaiming the folly of adopting European ways. Typical is one man's recollection of what Nori, from neighboring 'Are'are, told a large crowd during his first visit to Kwaio in June of 1945:

> We have held meetings with the white men, and you've seen all of those laws they've brought. They don't belong to us Solomon Islanders. They are *their* laws from *their* country. They came and gave us their laws, and we didn't understand them, and we just followed them. But now, under this Maasina Rule we are organizing, you will no longer follow another man's laws. You will follow your own *kastom*. You must select a leader for yourselves and for all of your affairs. Your leader must be a man whose body is like yours. If he is like you, then, when he tells you something, you can believe him. But if you follow some other man whose body is different, eventually you yourself will be different too. You'll be different from your own place. He will turn you in a different direction with his talk, and eventually you will be led astray. No. You must follow a man whose body is black like yours, and who speaks your language. Then you'll be following something true. (Sale Kakalade, 1982)

Kwaio leaders make very similar speeches today, sometimes ending with demands that foreign ways be excluded not just from the political realm, but from all aspects of Kwaio life.[12] Comparable pronouncements are heard in less formal contexts as well. The importation scenario dominates Kwaio discourse about their position relative to the non-Kwaio world.

Crucial aspects of Kwaio beliefs about foreign spirits can only be understood as part of this more general perspective. Nowhere is the scenario of destructive importation more powerfully or thoroughly depicted than in idealized accounts of *buru* importation. Consider a few parallels. In many versions of the importation scenario, foreign things are, like the alien spirits, depicted as initially attractive and seductive. Thus individuals are lured by European wealth, exotic forms of knowledge, or Christian freedom from ancestral rules. But in the end these things prove barren. Unlike their Kwaio equivalents, they are obtained from outsiders, or even strangers. Like *buru*, these foreign enticements are socially unattached and require little in the way of commitment or sacrifice.

Just as the imported *buru* provoke ancestral abandonment, the individuals who embrace other foreign things are portrayed as alienating themselves from Kwaio culture. More importantly, they are undermining Kwaio society as a whole and weakening the social ties that bind it together. All Kwaio have a moral obligation to consider the greater community welfare when importing foreign things, be they spirits or corrupting social practices. As a *buru* importer's innocent relatives are afflicted by the spirit, so is the entire community undermined by other alien ways that individuals bring into Kwaio.

An aspect of the *buru* scenario that resonates most strongly for non-Christian Kwaio is that the spirits desecrate Kwaio ancestors. Desecration of ancestors is considered the most destructive facet of foreign infiltrations into Kwaio. Particularly glaring are intentional desecrations by Christians who demand that newly converted women sleep on ancestral symbols, or who openly consume sacred foods in a secular manner. More subtly, men inevitably are exposed to defilements while visiting Christian villages or towns. Even within the Kwaio mountains, religious rules are not followed as strictly as before, and many once-elaborate rituals have been distilled to bare essentials. These changes, all blamed on decadent foreign penetration, not only have debilitated the living Kwaio community, they have defiled and weakened the ancestral spirits themselves.

We have seen how *buru* importers lack the knowledge to manage these spirits without ancestral help. So too, as traditions are abandoned for inappropriate foreign ways, Kwaio find themselves increasingly dependent on an alien culture over which they have little control. At some point, many Kwaio predict, Kwaio ways will no longer be able to coexist with foreign ones and will be overwhelmed by them; "Kwaio *kastom* will be finished" and they will be left dependent on a cultural system they cannot comprehend. Kwaio are acutely aware of their ignorance of European ways and commonly refer to it to explain their loyalty to their own ancestral spirits and traditions, which they "know."

The Kwaio importation scenario exhibits both similarities and differences with the "key" and "cultural" scenarios analyzed by Ortner and Schieffelin. Like them, the Kwaio scenario is a symbol that sorts out aspects of experience and orders them in processual form. Also like them, the structure and meanings of the importation scenario are readily transposable to a wide range of social realms (e.g., political, economic, or religious affairs), linking them metaphorically. Like other metaphorically linked cultural domains analyzed by Kelly (1976), each expression of the Kwaio scenario enhances the cultural meanings of its other expressions. The meaning of the *buru* scenario is inextricably tied to the broader importation scenario, as well as to its own counterparts in other realms.

The Kwaio importation scenario differs from those described by Ortner and Schieffelin in important ways. Unlike Sherpa hospitality and Kaluli reciprocity scenarios, the Kwaio importation scenario seems to be a relatively recent construction. More study is needed, but it appears to have emerged in tandem with Kwaio consciousness of threats to their cultural system. The area for which we have the best evidence of this is spirit importation. Older Kwaio insist that *buru* and other foreign spirits were not a serious problem until the late 1920s and 1930s. This was the period just after the imposition of British military control (1927), when Christian churches first began making significant inroads in the area. As difficulties stemming from government and church incursions have intensified in the decades since, and as the barriers insulating Kwaio from foreign ways have weakened, concerns about invading spirits have increased as well.

A more important difference in the importation scenario is found in its relationship to Kwaio practice. Ortner's and Schieffelin's scenarios actually are *enacted* by people. Not only do they order how people perceive or portray events, they also energize people's actions; they organize and "drive forward social process" (Schieffelin 1981:152; see also Ortner 1989:126–29). These scenarios lay out proper sequences of action for people to follow (e.g., as a host, to reciprocate a gift or a hurt). The importation scenario, by contrast, proscribes behavior that is inappropriate, fruitless, and dangerous. While it influences how Kwaio comprehend events and how they react to particular situations (and thus contributes to the production and structuring of behavior), the relationship is less direct. Like Sherpa and Kaluli scenarios, the Kwaio importation scenario clearly prescribes the proper course of action for correct and successful living— to follow only Kwaio ancestors and Kwaio traditions. But it does this in a more general way, by vividly portraying consequences of contrary behavior.

On another level, the Kwaio importation scenario, and particularly its *buru* variant, is less evident in the practical events of day-to-day living. Although sometimes important to the interpretive structuring of actual events, it more often surfaces as an idealized depiction of general social processes, particularly in public discussion. There is a distinct difference between how Kwaio portray foreign things as abstractions and how they approach them in practice. In abstract discussion, Kwaio emphasize the radical asociality of urban life, or they starkly contrast the social qualities of indigenous and introduced sorceries. In practice, however, Kwaio men live, work, and socialize with relatives in towns, and, in fact, some indigenous sorceries are as objectionable and antisocial as any foreign ones. We have seen that Kwaio make sweeping condemnations of imported numinals, but in practice many foreign spirits and magic varieties have proved beneficial, and have long coexisted in harmony with the ancestors.

Nowhere is this pattern more evident than in Kwaio talk about *buru*. *Buru* are indeed sometimes implicated in cases of suicide, religious transgression, and other difficulties. But their significance is greatly overstated. They are much more important within general discussions and explanations of social problems than they are in accounting for actual occurrences of those problems in daily life.

This point is crucial to understanding the significance of the *buru* and other versions of the importation scenario in Kwaio life, and also a final way in which they resemble the scenarios described by Ortner. In her more recent work, Ortner notes that key scenarios (in the form of historically expressed "cultural schemas") appear to have tremendous durability through time, and she hypothesizes that this is because they speak to and resolve central contradictions in their cultures (1989:60-61, passim). I believe that the Kwaio importation scenario plays a similar role, albeit in a quite different way.

As noted previously, a deep tension runs through Kwaio society. Though most Kwaio insist on the essential truth of idealized notions of cultural appropriateness and borrowing, they often appear to disregard them. Public advocacy of cultural conservatism is frequently contradicted by private social practice. No one today is content to follow only the ways of their ancestors, and, indeed, this would be impossible in the modern Solomons. People adopt many foreign things, including new spirits. Particular importations are only rarely portrayed as problematic, and other moral imperatives may be cited to emphasize their propriety.

For instance, a man labors abroad for cash to open a store selling Western goods for shell money. But he will use the shell money for mortuary feasting, bride price payments, or some other morally righteous endeavor that strengthens his social group. Again, some foreign spirits and magics actually enhance communication with ancestors or produce more and better pigs for them. Exotic cures are purchased to prevent human suffering and to thwart immoral attacks by those using foreign sorceries. In other words, everyone condemns the general phenomenon of individualistic or careless intercultural borrowing, but people rarely view their own importations this way.

The difficulties associated with all foreign importations can, for traditionalist Kwaio, be reduced to one central problem. Their effect, whether foreign spirits, Christianity, or capitalist amorality, is to undermine Kwaio sociality and the Kwaio community. The importation scenario clearly speaks to the contradiction between devotion to ancestral ways and pursuit of foreign ones, but it does not mediate or resolve it. On the contrary, it stands defiantly on one side of it, a critique of the foreign in favor of the traditional.

But in another sense it does address the problem. The *buru* and other importation scenarios constitute the framework of a highly social discourse, the discourse of political discussion and formal meetings of *kastom* politics. Beginning with government tax collections in the early 1930s, political gatherings have been Kwaio social occasions par excellence. Indeed, these were the first Kwaio-wide social gatherings; today, *kastom* meetings remain the principal events that draw together participants from throughout the area (Akin 1993:207). It is here that the contradiction is resolved, or at least diffused. These highly social meetings themselves have a group performative quality in that, by their regular occurrence, they deny the dissolution of Kwaio society and confront the threat of foreign-induced anomie. The principal activity of the meetings is talk, and that talk is a discourse built around importation scenarios and their constituent themes. Within this discourse, the *buru* scenario and other portrayals of foreign spirits convey their most powerful meanings, emerging as shared statements of resistance to antisocial foreign penetration. While the acquisition and activities of foreign spirits exemplify the centrifugal forces pulling Kwaio society apart, talk about them pulls the community together in unanimous condemnation of the destructive importation of foreign ways.

Notes

Acknowledgments. Field research was carried out during 1979–1983, 1987, and 1992, and was partly funded by the East-West Center and the University of Hawai'i Program on Conflict Resolution. Special thanks are due to Laeniamae, Ma'aanamae, John Laete'esafi, and the late Jonathan Fifi'i. Helpful comments were made on earlier incarnations of this paper by Wallace and Peggy Akin, Jack Bilmes, Ben Burt, David Gegeo, Dan Jorgensen, Nancy Lutkehaus, Jeannette Mageo, Mimi Mayer, Eugene Ogan, Jan Rensel, Michael Scott, Geoffrey White, and especially Terre Fisher and Alan Howard.

1   For a historical and ethnographic examination of Kwaio Christian culture, and an analysis of why Kwaio do and do not become Christians, see Akin 1993. The Christian communities that I discuss here are those in eastern Kwaio. The situation across the mountains in western Kwaio is quite different. Most notably, the Catholic Church is strong in the west but is by far the smallest denomination represented in the east. There has also been much more development along the western Malaitan coast.

2   This is an exaggeration, as even Kwaio social networks are extended abroad to some degree; see Frazer 1985.

3   Detailed analyses of Kwaio religion can be found in Akin 1993 and Keesing 1982. For brevity, I use "ancestors" in a gender-neutral sense to refer to both male and female ancestral spirits as a group. However, some very important spirits are ancestresses.

4   At a higher taxonomic level, all wild spirits are known as *kwasi*, but I use only the term's more specific sense. Some people do not differentiate between *buru* and *kwasi* at any level. For simplicity, only the more common perspective is described here; alternative views are not significantly incongruent with the model presented. This is a prime example of the variation within Kwaio beliefs about wild spirits that is discussed later.

5   A history of *buru* on Malaita is beyond the scope of this paper, but can be found in Akin 1993:239–47, 636–40; see also Burt 1994:135–39, 144–47.

6   Spirit possession *is* commonly blamed for *unsuccessful* suicide attempts.

7   This man visited the author in 1982 desperately seeking a treatment for his illness and describing his symptoms in some detail. These included intense hallucinations of geometric shapes and letters "bright like stars." Relatives said he knew when possession was imminent and would cry, saying he did not want it.

8   There are also indigenous Kwaio magics with similar functions as *parana*, but limits on space preclude my addressing them here (see Akin 1993:658–61).

9   Fox and Drew long ago noted similar discrepancies between beliefs about malevolent non-ancestral spirits on the neighboring island of Makira, which they attributed to uncertainty and confusion (1915:178–79, 200–202). Malinowski wrote that the inconsistencies in Trobriand beliefs about *Yovova* witchcraft "can never be sufficiently emphasized..." (1961:238–39).

10 Less relativistic notions of *buru* are held by those who lump them together with *kwasi* spirits (see note 4). Some of them describe *buru* as grotesque, burly beings dripping from head to toe with human feces. Coppet (1981:177) describes how people of the 'Are'are area of southern Malaita greatly fear foreign spirits that originate in Kwaio.

11 The most notable exceptions are behaviors Kwaio consider purely secular. For example, they condemn the relatively loose sexual mores sometimes found in towns. Kwaio are also quick to condemn specific acts of foreigners as immoral, particularly offenses against Kwaio people. For a discussion of Kwaio cultural relativism, see Akin 1993, Chapter 7.

12 Since Maasina Rule, Malaitan politics have become more atomized, increasingly concerned with more localized concepts of *kastom* rather than the *kastom* of Malaita as a whole. Consequently, there are sometimes calls not only for purging of European ways, but also for avoiding inappropriate *kastom* of other Malaitans. In Kwaio, at least, this was probably true to some degree even during Maasina Rule.

8 Apparitions, Orations, and Rings

Experience of Spirits in Dadul

Harvey Whitehouse

The Mali Baining live on the island of New Britain in Papua New Guinea. In the late nineteenth century, German colonists settled the northeastern coast of New Britain, which rapidly became a center of colonial government. It continues to be one of the wealthiest and most cosmopolitan regions of the country. Mali Baining communities, however, remain dispersed in the comparatively untouched rain forest of the island's interior, and along less accessible parts of the coastline. Nevertheless, because of their geographical proximity to the economic and administrative center, the Mali Baining have been subject to missionary influence since the early part of this century. In the inland village of Dadul, traditional religious practices were largely eliminated in the 1930s as conversion to Christianity intensified. In the late 1960s, a new religion spread to Dadul: a Christian-syncretic cargo cult with strong millenarian and nationalist elements. This new religion, which continues to encompass several language groups, stands firmly opposed to the Christian missions, despite its appropriation of Christian doctrines. In Dadul, certain aspects of pre-Christian ideas about spirits persist alongside Christian-syncretic conceptions of ancestors, ghosts, and devils.

This chapter concerns the people of Dadul, a Mali Baining village of about seventy persons in East New Britain. Like many other New Guinea peoples, the Mali Baining believe that they share the surrounding rain forest with capricious, nonhuman spirits. Nevertheless, these spirits, known as *sega*, do not figure highly in moral discourse. For the past twenty years, the people of Dadul have been ardent supporters of a large-scale millenarian movement, known as the Pomio Kivung, which focuses moral and religious concerns on local *ancestors*. This has led to three basic types of experience with spirits in Dadul, each with a distinctive set of psychological and political ramifications.

First is the experience of *sega*, a striking feature of which is an absence of religious salience and a sense of entropy with respect to the pre-Christian cosmological system in which *sega* used to figure. *Sega* are nowadays perceived in Dadul to be amoral supernatural agencies that have no direct bearing on religious thought, and are somewhat vaguely associated with forgotten initiation rituals, dances, and magic largely eliminated in the early phases of missionization. In the modern context, the psychological experience of *sega* is impoverished, not merely by the loss of indigenous cosmology, but because the metaphors involved in ritualized interactions with *sega* lack the poignant and revelatory character of contemporary religious ritual in Dadul. The sterility of this mode of interaction with the supernatural realm, and its neutrality in religious terms, means that it constitutes an innocuous, "neutral" field of discourse and ritual action among members of opposed religious sects.

The most heated sectarian antagonism obtains between Christians and supporters of the Pomio Kivung. The latter maintain that a great number of Christian teachings are valid, although they argue that missionaries also peddle deceits that are designed to obstruct the laity from attaining salvation. Meanwhile, Christians are highly critical of what they call the "cargo cult" element of Pomio Kivung religion, and its preoccupation with ancestors. Nevertheless, both Christian and Pomio Kivung moral systems demand harmonious relations between rival groups, and this is expressed in regular cooperation at major celebrations and funerals. The religious aspects of these occasions cannot stimulate goodwill, and what tends to be emphasized instead is a set of common "Baining customs," converging on so-called "fire dances" and divinations. These occasions, focused on relations with *sega*, provide the main contexts in which Christians and Pomio Kivung supporters cooperate.

Second is the experience of spirits (primarily ancestors) in the doctrine and ritual of the mainstream Pomio Kivung. This movement has an elaborate, coherent, and logically integrated body of doctrine that is codified in the repetitive sermons of local orators. As we shall see, the way ancestors are apperceived is to be understood in terms of specific connections between cognition and codification, which in turn affect patterns of leadership and spread within the movement.

A third mode of experiencing spirits prevails in the context of temporary splinter groups in Dadul, which break away from the mainstream Pomio

Kivung movement at regular (but infrequent) intervals. Splinter-group activities are concerned with the cultivation of sensually and emotionally arousing experiences of ancestors through collective rituals, some of which are markedly traumatic. The nonverbal modes in which ideas about the ancestors are transmitted are linked with the small scale and sporadic nature of splinter-group activity within the Pomio Kivung.

These modes of interaction with the spirit world show significant contrasts. Experience of *sega* is marginalized in the religious discourse of Dadul. Its political significance resides in the fact that this experience is shared among doctrinally opposed religious camps: the profound antagonism between Christians and Pomio Kivung supporters is temporarily put aside on occasions when rituals concerning nonhuman spirits are jointly performed.

Religion in Dadul focuses on ancestor worship, enacted in contrasting modes: that of the mainstream movement, in which there is a complex interplay between verbalization, routinization, hierarchy, centralization, and universalism; and that of the splinter group, which entails iconicity, revelation, emotionality, infrequent transmission, and particularism

At the core of my analysis is the claim that the experience of spirits, and its articulation with politics and cosmology, is a matter not so much of "what people believe," but of the way these "beliefs" are codified and transmitted.

SEGA

A broad distinction can be made between individual experiences of *sega* in magic, dreams, and various types of misfortune, and collective experiences in divinations, funerals, and "fire dances." Both types of experience of *sega* lack cosmological salience and coherence, in contrast with people's experiences of ancestors which, as we see below, constitute the focal representations of religious life in the Pomio Kivung.

Sega are thought to look like humans, although few people have actually seen any, except in dreams. People cannot readily explain how they recognized what they had seen as a supernatural being, rather than as a mortal stranger. Those who claim to have encountered *sega* describe the experience as very frightening, which is the main evidence that they saw something unworldly. They sometimes add that the apparition disappeared when they averted their eyes, or that it had not been heard approaching. Ordinarily, however, *sega* are invisible to human eyes; many *sega* are in the forest, and they are particularly active after dark. A special kind of "sight," available to anybody while dreaming, is required to perceive them, and indeed most people have encountered *sega* when asleep. Stories are told of gifted individuals who are able to visit the *sega* at will in their dreams and thereby sustain regular relations with them. Such people are called *agungaraga*, and their abilities are held in high esteem; they sometimes learn from the *sega* reasons for human problems, such as illness or crop failure. A typical cause of such misfortunes might be that a person inadvertently damaged the home of a *sega* in the forest, or walked through its "garden," mistaking it for undergrowth. *Sega* are not offended by moral transgressions injurious to humans, and only punish unwanted interference in their own affairs. The problem is that, unlike dangers in the forest that can be seen (e.g., pythons, nettles, sharp objects), *sega* cannot usually be identified and avoided, and the fact that they have been disturbed or provoked only becomes apparent later, when misfortune strikes. This is when people in Dadul are heard talking about *sega* and speculating about how they may have been offended.

Sega, however, can be useful to humans, especially to men. Villagers think that hunting successfully is virtually impossible without the *sega's* assistance, which is solicited through the performance of magical rites. Some of the most powerful spells contain the names of specific *sega*; it is assumed they were revealed in dreams and passed down through the generations. Hunting magic and other spells are ordinarily transmitted by older men to younger men, most commonly from father to son. A youth may ask any senior man known to possess magical knowledge to teach him spells, in return for which the young man may be called on to assist in the older man's gardens, or to help with other manual tasks. The following example illustrates how spells are used to intervene in the world of *sega*.

Our house in Dadul was guarded by a dog named Kaukau, who always slept at the door and repelled unfamiliar visitors. In the daytime he was often used as a hunting dog. One day, a hunter returned to the village at dusk, and said that Kaukau had come with him in the morning but had soon disappeared in the dense undergrowth of the forest. That night, another man in the village had a dream in which he visited a "house" (*abuga*) built in the base of a large tree. This was the house of a *sega*, and around it had been planted flowers. Among these flowers, hens were digging the earth in search of food. Then Kaukau appeared, chasing a black rooster and causing the hens to scatter. Kaukau was so absorbed in the chase that two *sega* were able to grab him as he ran past, and they took him into their "house." Kaukau was unable to escape from the base of the tree.

News of this dream rapidly spread around the village, and finally a man said that he would perform a magical rite to retrieve Kaukau. He obtained some lime powder and went to a secluded place at the edge of the village. There he clasped the lime powder in his hand, close to his mouth, and murmured the following words (my translation):

Go to fetch him.
Go to fetch the named one.
Go to fetch the named one, Kaukau.
Look here, he will come wherever I am.
All will look, and will talk, ["express amazement"]
Look here, my two helpers, Basir and Sordem [names of *sega*].

All will look at me sending you with my lime-powder.
You two, go to seek him.
You must not avoid searching a mountain, or a hill, or a water source, or a
    tree; you both seek him wherever he is and fetch him here.

Then he opened his hand and blew off the lime powder. If it had stuck to his
hand, the lime powder would have been "cold," indicating that Kaukau was
dead. In this case, however, the powder dispersed on the wind. He then held up
his hand. If the wrist bone made a "cracking" sound, then Kaukau would be
very distant; if his elbow cracked, then Kaukau would be quite near; if his shoulder cracked, Kaukau would be very close at hand. His elbow cracked. Word
would now spread among the *sega* that Kaukau must be released and shown
the way home. Sure enough, that evening, Kaukau returned to the village, none
the worse for his adventure.

A number of common features of spells, and ideas about *sega*, are illustrated
by this example of the use of retrieval magic. The physical actions of the magician utilized the principle of bodily iconicity whereby, in this case, relative distances between the torso and points along the arm corresponded to distances
between the village and the dog being retrieved. This is a typical feature of Mali
Baining magical rites, wherein the body and movements of the magician mirror
effects or states that are desired in some other part of the physical world (e.g.,
suddenness and force are required of the ropes in pig traps and are replicated in
the ritualized body movements entailed in hunting magic). This may seem familiar in terms of a Frazerian conception of contagious and homeopathic magic; I
will, however, examine these kinds of metaphoric processes in a very different
context below. Three important points to bear in mind at present are: (a) that
the rite to retrieve Kaukau was performed by a single magician; (b) that it was
construed as a conventional action, rather than an innovative or "authored"
one; and (c) that the efficacy of this rite depended on the correct observance of
a technical sequence that anyone can learn, and that did not require a sense of
the aptness or poignancy of the metaphors involved.

The story about Kaukau reveals something of the way *sega* impinge on everyday life. A misfortune occurred, namely, the disappearance of Kaukau, for
which there was no obvious secular explanation. Dogs are taken hunting all the
time, and it is very rare for one to be lost, unless it is killed by a wild boar or
beaten severely by a hunter. In such cases, the reasons for a dog's absence are
plain to see, but Kaukau's disappearance was mysterious. Inevitably, suspicions
were aroused that *sega* were somehow involved. These suspicions were confirmed by a dream, which is the usual method of learning about the activities of
sega. In this dream, a man was able to "see" the door and windows of a house
in the base of a tree. If he had visited the site while conscious, it would have
looked like any other tree. The dreamer could also see flowers and hens which,
in his wakened state, would have looked like undergrowth and leaves. The

dream showed that *sega* are like people, not only because they live in houses and keep livestock, but because they wanted a hunting dog. They stole Kaukau because he was muscular and ferocious, in other words for precisely the same reasons that he was valued by the people of Dadul. The Mali Baining know that *sega* are unlike them, in that they operate in another dimension and are normally invisible. But nobody knows much else about *sega*. Village life and the spirit world operate in parallel dimensions, which (most of the time) are kept separate.

Nevertheless, men's activities in the bush necessarily bring them into contact with *sega*. If hunting is to succeed, *sega* must be induced to assist; if walking through the bush disturbs the *sega*, they must be dissuaded from punishing. *Sega* can be manipulated in this way only through magical rites. Since men are the ones who travel and hunt in the bush, they are regarded as the natural custodians of this magic (although there is nothing in principle to prevent women from learning it). Yet, knowledge of the *sega* is largely confined to knowing how to recognize their effects and to manipulate their behavior. There is no moral interest in the spirit world and no corpus of cosmological knowledge relating to it.

Two irregular contexts in Dadul in which *sega* directly impinge on village life, namely funerals and "fire dances," involve a mixture of Christians (mostly Catholics or members of the United Church) and Pomio Kivung supporters. It is important to bear in mind that an underlying tension or mutual antipathy always exists between Christians and Pomio Kivung supporters, in spite of their basically shared apperceptions of the *sega*.

Funerals in Dadul begin at dusk at the house of the deceased, where the corpse is laid out. Relatives and friends, often arriving from distant locations, cram into the house and, depending on their closeness to the deceased (construed primarily in terms of emotional and material dependency), either sit soberly to one side or wail inconsolably over the body. At the door of the house, a fire is kept burning to keep out the *sega*. Whether or not the death was caused by *sega*, these nonhuman spirits are thought to revel in its occurrence, indicating their fundamental enmity to humans. Mourners are reluctant to venture out of the house alone during the night for fear of encountering triumphant and malevolent *sega*. At dawn, the body is carried to the cemetery and given a Christian burial.

The evening after a funeral is sometimes devoted to the performance of a divination. In divinations, a large section of bamboo is carried by a team of boys and young men, and, in response to questions from an older man, the bamboo moves so as to indicate "yes" or "no" answers. The aim is to elicit from the deceased the reason(s) for his or her death. It usually takes some time for the dead person's spirit to gain control of the bamboo, for the earth is believed to weigh heavily on him or her. During the first part of the divination, therefore, it is *sega* who cause the bamboo to move. The boys holding on are not considered responsible for the lurching of the bamboo, but seem to be pulled along with it.

This activity is described as "playing with *sega*." It produces high excitement, laughter and enjoyment, in stark contrast to the fearfulness of the night before. The reason generally given for this change of mood is that *sega* are no longer feeling vindictive, and that the villagers are together (i.e., *sega* only attack people when they are alone, isolated from their fellows).

Sega are also abroad at "fire dances." The Baining are best known to anthropologists and visitors to East New Britain for their daytime/nighttime dance cycles, which involve extraordinarily large and intricate dance masks. The English gloss "fire dance" is used everywhere by Baining peoples as a catchall term for a variety of night dances, each of which has a separate local name. As a result of missionary influence, the Mali Baining night dance, part of a cycle known as *Mendas*, has not been performed in Dadul for a long time. Other forms of the night dance survive, however, and are mounted in Dadul to celebrate Christian holidays or the completion of community projects. Such fire dances have a celebratory character and, in keeping with Christian and Pomio Kivung thinking, are no longer considered by the participants to have a religious dimension. They do, however, involve ideas about supernatural agencies, notably *sega*. *Sega* are believed to follow the nocturnal dancers as they parade in the masks around a huge bonfire or run into the flames. It is even possible for *sega* to possess one or more of the dancers, so that the man inside the mask loses his control over bodily movements and (like the boys at a divination) feels himself to be pulled this way and that on the dancing ground. Like divination, this is an occasion when contact with *sega* is welcomed, when those congregated, in common with the *sega*, are supposed to share a festive and joyful spirit.

SPIRITS IN THE MAINSTREAM POMIO KIVUNG

The experience of spirits in the Pomio Kivung is filtered through language in an elaborate and logically integrated body of doctrines. This style of codification affects not only the way people in Dadul think about spirits, but the way the movement is spread, reproduced, and hierarchically structured. In the Pomio Kivung movement as a whole, spirits are divided into three broad classes: morally pure and omniscient ancestors, ghosts tainted by sin, and diabolical forces.

Morally pure ancestors are usually invisible to the living, but they appear to one another in the form of Europeans (i.e., white men, women, and children). Their white skins are soft and cool, unblemished by sores and other afflictions. They do not toil in gardens, enjoying free access to all the foods they desire. They experience no sexual feelings and do not produce children. They possess all the technological knowledge of the West, and can produce any kind of cargo, from radios to airplanes, by a mere wish. The home of these ancestors is often referred to as Paradise, located underground and connected to the earth's surface by invisible holes, described as "eyes." The ancestors travel widely, and every living person is under continuous surveillance by one or more of them. They constantly scrutinize not only people's behavior, but their thoughts, and are gratified by morality and offended by sinfulness. The omniscience of the ancestors and the morality they uphold renders them close to the local conception of the Christian God. Indeed, they are often described as manifestations of God, fulfilling His will at all times and sharing the incalculable powers available to Him. God is conceptualized as a distinct being and is said to "rule" the spirit world.

Since the Pomio Kivung encompasses many language groups, it was spread in the common medium of Pidgin. A group of ancestors together forms a hierarchical body known as the Village Government *(Vilij Gavman)*—a ghostly assembly of those ancestors who have achieved expiation for their earthly sins. A special building, known as the Cemetery Temple *(Haus Matmat)* is to be found in every Kivung village. These temples are the meeting places of the Village Government. Offerings of food, drink, and money are laid out for the Village Government during its daily meetings. A particular village official (whose title I translate as "witness") keeps vigil within the temple at these times. His task is to look for signs of ancestral visitation (e.g., knocking sounds, interference with the offerings by unseen hands). If, as occasionally happens, signs of visitation are lacking, the community is assumed to have offended the ancestors, and the offerings are thought to have been rejected. Relations with the spirits of the dead have to be repaired immediately if the Village Government is to reconvene in the Cemetery Temple. This is accomplished through monetary donations.

The purpose of presenting offerings in the Cemetery Temple is to cultivate close bonds between the living and the dead. The basic idea is that the living offer food as an embodiment of their spiritual devotion. It is the moral rather than the material substance of the food that is consumed by the Village Government. For this reason, various taboos apply to the preparation of temple offerings. Ultimately, it is hoped that the continuous demonstration of goodwill and obedience to Kivung doctrine will persuade the Village Government to "break the fence" *(brukim banis)* separating the living and the dead, so that the ancestors will assume a fully corporeal form in this world. The ancestors will then establish a great industrial complex, generating enough wealth for Kivung members to "pay" for their sins, and achieve the state of moral perfection and omniscience attributed to God. This is referred to as the Period of the Companies *(Taim Bilong Kampani)*. It will culminate in a Day of Judgment, after which all remaining sinners will be cast into hell *(kalibus)* and the remainder will experience an indefinite period of supernatural bliss, ruled by the Village Government. This is referred to as the Period of the Government *(Taim Bilong Gavman)*.

There are many Kivung rituals besides those connected with temples, which are intended to expedite the miracle of returning ancestors. In addition to ritual acts performed in sacred gardens, and those associated with monetary donations and meetings, are a variety of taboos and "laws" that have to be observed, including a modified version of the Ten Commandments, around which Kivung morality pivots. This should be sufficient, however, to provide an impression of the way ancestors in the Village Government are conceptualized, and the broad range of techniques for cultivating bonds with them.

In addition to perfect and omniscient ancestors are "ghosts," mostly of the recently deceased, who are tainted by sin and have not yet been granted entry into the Village Government. These spirits wander invisibly around Kivung villages and in the surrounding bush, often lingering outside temples (which they are not permitted to enter). Such ghosts are usually harmless and excite considerable pity among the living, who mount regular donations of money to "pay" for their sins. As a result, a continuous flow of ghosts into the Village Government are delivered from limbo through the altruism of their living kinsmen.

Diabolical forces, meanwhile, take a wide variety of forms. The main obstacle to the occurrence of the Period of the Companies is Satan. Until such time as Kivung members are impervious to the temptations of Satan, the miracle cannot occur. Satan is always close at hand, and people who succumb to his influence are temporarily unprotected by the ancestors. Once a sinner has been purified through the donation of money, he or she is once again secure. Until this occurs, however, Satan takes every opportunity to kill the sinner and propel his or her soul into a wilderness of loneliness and torment. Upon their death, the souls of unpurified murderers go directly to hell. Most other sinners enter limbo, and the speed with which they are admitted to the Village Government depends on the severity of their crimes. Those who remain sullied at the Day of Judgment will be damned.

Nonhuman spirits can act as agents of Satan to lure Kivung members into sin and to strike them down. The precise nature of these spirits varies according to the cultural area to which Kivung members belong. In keeping with the teachings of missionaries, Kivung ideology maintains that all indigenous classes of nonhuman spirits dwelling in the bush are potential agents of Satan. They are classified together under the catchall Pidgin term *masalai*. In Dadul, *sega*, which are everywhere construed as amoral and capricious, are seen as potentially satanic forces. In general, unintended contact with *masalai* (e.g., *sega*) is assumed to have a diabolical character; the only desirable context for interactions with such spirits is through the correct performance of benign magic. Pomio Kivung teachings endorse the use of spells intended to induce nonhuman spirits to assist the living in morally acceptable ways. This applies particularly to the manipulation of such spirits for the purposes of hunting and healing magic.

The precise meanings of Kivung rituals and taboos, and the logical connections uniting them, are far more elaborate and complex than this brief summary is able to convey. Nevertheless, the efficacy of ritual acts and observances requires a thorough understanding of the extensive ideology surrounding them. Temple rituals, for example, would be ineffective if those preparing offerings were not aware of the nature and significance of taboos applying to their work.

Likewise, a witness could not discern the signs of ancestral visitation if he did not fully appreciate the structure and purposes of the Village Government, or lacked faith in the eschatological themes of the Pomio Kivung. Monetary donations, too, are effective only if donors understand the complex nature and causes of sin and the process whereby ancestors dispense absolution and catharsis.

In these respects, the way in which Kivung members experience relations with the spirit world parallels their experience of Christian ceremonial. The meanings of mission liturgy, which were established prior to the spread of the Pomio Kivung, were accessible only because priests, catechists, and other sermonizers provided an elaborate ideological framework for Christian worship. Similarly, the Pomio Kivung provided a complex array of rituals, the meanings of which were unintelligible in the absence of extensive exegesis. A critical difference, however, was that Christian preachers derived authoritative dogma from sacred texts, whereas the ideology of the Pomio Kivung was sustained through oral transmission. Reliance on memory rather than on the written word inevitably introduced a risk of innovation. (This simple observation in other contexts has stimulated a substantial body of theory concerning the relationship between literacy and religious transformations.) But the Pomio Kivung presents a strikingly effective solution to the problem in the form of community meetings or *kivung*.

The approximate equivalent of the European priest in the Pomio Kivung is the *komiti*, "orator," who preaches to his flock (the local community) on two afternoons every week, in the formal surroundings of a special building known as the Meeting House (*Haus Kivung*). Typically, three orators in every community take turns speaking at meetings. Over time, their speeches cover every aspect of Kivung ideology, with the result that these ideas are kept alive in people's thoughts. But, unlike church sermons, which are intended to complement and clarify rather than to reproduce sacred texts, the speeches of orators *are* the authoritative ideology or "text." Since speeches are presented with great frequency, the risk of innovation is minimized. If an orator modifies what has been said at previous meetings, his audience will point this out, and he is required to seek forgiveness from the ancestors. In this way, Kivung ideology is deposited and constantly reviewed in collective memory. Everybody in the community knows as much as the orator and, as a group, they occasionally show that they know slightly more and have to correct him. This even distribution of knowledge in the community is readily acknowledged by the orators—what sets them apart is the personal confidence and skill to speak engagingly in public.

Like the mission, the Pomio Kivung provides an experience of interaction with the other world based on a verbally codified cosmology and extensive exegesis. In both cases, religious materials are sustained through regular transmission, in the form of sermons. But the transmission of Christian dogma to the local community has been incomplete. The purveyor of Christianity might at any time introduce some surprising or unexpected revelation, legitimated by texts that the indigenous laity could not read.

Frustration with this situation led to cults that preceded the Pomio Kivung in the Baining region, for example Melki's Movement, which provided the "true" framework in which to understand the sermons of Methodist ministers. In contrast, Kivung orators are unable to disorient their audiences with new or confusing pronouncements. They serve to reproduce what is already known. But to sustain a community of religious experts in a nonliterate society requires even more frequent and comprehensive repetition of ideology than that provided by the missions. With this consideration in mind, leaders of the mainstream movement insisted that their teachings be continually transmitted according to a fixed schedule. The Ten Laws were transmitted in five-week cycles, one law being covered at each of the twice-weekly community meetings by orators who took turns in fixed rotation.

This system is still in operation, nearly thirty years after the foundation of the movement. All the crucial ideas about spirits, especially the Village Government, are likewise covered on a regular basis at these meetings. In common with Christian ceremonial, Pomio Kivung rituals are highly routinized, but Kivung members stress that their ritual program is better adapted than Christianity to the maintenance of complex ideology. Church services, they point out, are brief and are held only weekly—too infrequently to sustain elaborate ideas. Christian doctrine is likened to the white shirts worn at Sunday worship, and put aside ("forgotten") for the rest of the week. In contrast, the Pomio Kivung supplies an array of daily, twice-weekly, and weekly rituals that render meaningful the sermons they accompany.

In the temples and gardens, or when preparing for the rituals performed there, Kivung members experience the "other world" in terms of cognitively elaborate models, codified and sustained in language. Day in and day out, week in and week out, their conceptions of ancestors are reproduced in routinized performances and speeches. Interactions with the Village Government have assumed a highly repetitive character. But, aside from the intellectual persuasiveness of the ideology, there is little to excite enthusiasm within this unremitting regimen. In the next section I examine some of the ways in which flagging commitment to mainstream Kivung rituals is rejuvenated through temporary attempts to restore "traditional" religious models, founded on an altogether more intense and moving experience of the spirit world.

SPIRITS AND SPLINTER GROUPS

In 1988, the people of Dadul combined with a Mali village to the south, known as Maranagi, to form a splinter group bent on breaking away from the mainstream Pomio Kivung. This splinter group cultivated a deeply moving, even traumatic experience of the "other world," but failed to achieve its millenarian objectives. Its supporters were finally obliged to disperse and return to a more routinized existence, under the aegis of the mainstream movement. In the light of similar outbursts of climactic ritual in the past, I argue that the splinter group of 1988 contributed another dimension to relations between humans and spirits, and was most likely in the long term to reinforce rather than to undermine commitment to the institutions of the Pomio Kivung.

I worked in both Dadul and Maranagi between 1987 and 1989 and directly observed the events outlined below. The splinter group was founded by two "brothers" (matrilateral parallel cousins) called Baninge and Tanotka, who were believed to be acting as vehicles for the will of the Village Government and were eventually designated members of it. Their apotheosis was acknowledged only within the two villages concerned, however, and they never came close to assuming leadership positions within the mainstream Pomio Kivung movement. One reason for this was that the revelations they introduced were most effectively conveyed by collective ritual performances, rather than by words.

The initial emergence of the splinter-group leaders occurred within the constraints of mainstream institutions, since innovation could be tolerated only if it carried the demonstrable backing of the Village Government. The process by which this occurred initially owed a great deal to the use of persuasive speech, and the "voices" were many and varied.

The earliest advocate of the splinter group was an ancestor called Wutka, who spoke "through" Tanotka in a state of possession. The possession itself was somewhat ambiguous and was initially interpreted by many as a mere sickness rather than a genuine possession. Baninge, however, cultivated support for the idea that his brother had been used as a vehicle for three important messages: that a "post" (i.e., leader) would emerge; that Dadul and Maranagi had nearly satisfied the conditions for the occurrence of the Period of the Companies; and that an obscure myth relating the adventures of an ancestor called Aringawuk provided a key to understanding and expediting the imminent miracle. Each message was extended and elaborated by further messages from the Village Government, flowing though a variety of channels.

Firstly, there was Tanotka himself, who rapidly became a regular medium for ancestors, then a kind of prophetic interpreter in his own right, and finally a divinity, on a par with the leaders of the mainstream movement (see Whitehouse 1995, In Press). He was described as "the post," and his inauguration was marked by a formal installation ceremony (subsequently performed also for his brother, Baninge).

Secondly, verbal messages were received from the ancestors in the course of temple rituals, through an extension of the role of witnesses. Witnesses began to "hear" statements or "reports" from the Village Government during their vigils, endorsing the arguments of Baninge and Tanotka, persuading the orators to support them publicly.

Thirdly, some people, especially Baninge, had dreams that were likewise thought to originate with the ancestors, and the dreams were disseminated by the orators. Thus, the initial cultivation of support for the splinter group drew heavily on words, through which compelling logical arguments were expressed, demonstrating the legitimacy of innovations and persuading doubters that they were consistent with the ideological framework of the Pomio Kivung.

Yet enthusiasm for the splinter group, and its most impressive revelations, was not cultivated in verbalized arguments, but through the iconicity of new collective rituals. These were founded substantially around the restoration of traditional religious practices, many of which had been eradicated by early missionaries who regarded them as evil. The precontact religious system had taken the form of a fertility cult, concerned primarily with the health and promulgation of the population and the staple crop (taro). Its most elaborate rituals were associated with initiations, which took up to eight months to prepare and culminated in a daytime/nighttime dance cycle known as the *Mendas*. Initiation into the male cult required a period of seclusion at sacred sites in the bush, and the transmission of knowledge concerning the construction of dance masks. This entailed laceration of the tongues of novices and painful incisions at the base of the spine. A strict taboo was imposed on contact between novices and women during this period, and violations were punishable by death. During the years separating such activities, religious life focused primarily around a sacred building or temple, ministered by initiated men and dedicated to a single deity, Kanunga (in other areas, his "sister," Morki, was worshiped). Prior to World War II, the mission effectively eradicated many of these practices. Stories are still told of the extreme hostility that European priests expressed toward indigenous rituals, and it is widely believed that Kanunga was destroyed because his relics (which are thought to have been shipped to Germany) were confiscated. Some older men also recall acts of violence on the part of one particular priest, who is said, for example, to have beaten costumed dancers with a staff.

The splinter group of 1988 determined to restore many of the practices the missions had attempted to eradicate. The old religion was described as a "fire" that the priests had attempted to extinguish ("scatter in the dust"), while Tanotka and his brother were described as a "wind" that would rekindle the flames. Favorable reports from the Village Government (i.e., those supporting the ascension of splinter-group leaders) were celebrated in large dances and feasts, attended by traditional costumed figures known as *awanga*. In this endeavor adherents relied heavily on the memories of elders. Memory gaps were filled by the Village Government, who supplied authoritative guidance through reports, dreams, and the pronouncements of Baninge and Tanotka. The rituals were planned and orchestrated in secret meetings of knowledgeable men, who assumed many of the functions of initiators in establishing the details of *awanga* construction and performance.

In addition to these traditional practices, explicitly new kinds of rituals were devised, of which the most prominent were "ring ceremonies." The inspiration for ring ceremonies was provided by a dream by Baninge in which he and Tanotka were enclosed by a circular wall divided across the center by a fence. Baninge and Tanotka stood in one semicircle, and the Village Government was congregated on the other side of the fence. Tanotka called out to the boss of the Cemetery Temple, asking him whether the other members of the splinter group would be permitted to enter the ring. The ring represented the spiritual elect, and the idea was that when all splinter group members had entered the ring alongside Baninge and Tanotka, the fence would be broken (i.e., the Period of the Companies would commence). Following the telling of this dream, the community redoubled its efforts to achieve purification. This eventually resulted in the performance of the first "ring ceremony," at which the whole community gathered to form a wall of human bodies encompassing Tanotka, who stood at the center. One by one, people came forward to shake Tanotka's hand, indicating allegiance to him. The ring ceremony was subsequently adapted for other purposes connected with protection against evil.

The new collective rituals of the splinter group were deeply impressive. Unlike the rituals of the mainstream Pomio Kivung, they provoked a diversity of emotions and sensations. The haunting and stirring melodies and rhythms accompanying the dances, the splendor of *awanga* costumes, the athleticism and aggression of the participants, the synchrony and eloquence of collective movements, all contributed to intense feelings of solidarity and ethnic pride, consolidated by the fact that the people of Dadul and Maranagi were the main surviving descendants of Kanunga's "people." The heat, smells, sounds, and visual impact of dances created a dramatic sensual experience quite unlike that of mainstream rituals. The first ring ceremony was likewise profoundly evocative. It was performed in a state of virtual nakedness, which (in the mists of dawn, when it was performed) caused people to shiver with cold and, above all, confronted them with erotic areas of the body. People were obliged to repress sexual excitement, or "shame" connected with their own exposure, and to focus instead on images of Paradise, which their nakedness was intended to connote.

The emphasis in these new rituals was not on the codification of religious ideas in language, but on the cultivation of concrete metaphors through collective rituals acts. The dances of the *awanga* dramatically enacted the return of the ancestors who emerged from the sacred garden known as Paradise and converged on the center of the village (thus enacting the occurrence of the Period of the Companies). Female dancers (symbolizing the processes of sexual reproduction) then occupied the dancing ground but were displaced by the returning *awanga*, expressing the ancestral victory over menstruation and childbirth (and so establishing the Period of the Government). A similar pattern of iconic codification was evident in the first ring ceremony.

Beyond the obvious fact that the ring of bodies corresponded to the spiritual elect depicted in Baninge's dream, the bodies also represented the wall posts of traditional round houses (the last of these seen in the region was a temple dedicated to Kanunga). The rafters of such houses were supported by a central post, represented in the ring ceremony by Tanotka, and the obvious (though largely unstated) implication was that Tanotka would support the community (the surrounding posts) in its pursuit of salvation. The fact that Tanotka was already referred to as a "post" encouraged such an interpretation. But the image of the post had numerous levels of meaning within the splinter group, some of which were cautiously stated to me and some of which were only obliquely suggested. For example, Tanotka was clearly associated with the post erected at the entrance to every Kivung village on which the Roman numerals I to X are inscribed (representing the Ten Laws). Part of the post is hidden (buried) underground, suggesting that only part of the "truth" was visible (like our "tip of the iceberg" metaphor). Being the post, Tanotka had access to the whole entity (or "knowledge"), including its hidden regions. Other interpretations of the post metaphor abounded. They were not given an authoritative form in language, but were creatively inferred by the participants in rituals.

Another example of the metaphorical character of the first ring ceremony is connected with the fact that it was scheduled to occur at dawn, its performance coinciding with the transition from darkness (representing ignorance and suffering) to daylight (representing enlightenment and warmth). The alleviation of coldness under the first rays of the morning sun provided an experiential taste of salvation (the removal of discomfort) and omniscience (the ability to see clearly). Thus, the conception or idea was constructed nonverbally through a collective act that was simultaneously a statement, experience, and expression of feelings about salvation and solidarity. No words, nor even the most impassioned speeches, could have cultivated as satisfactory an appreciation of these ideas.

Undoubtedly the most powerful and enduring images to come out of the splinter group were generated toward the end of its life, through a program of climactic rituals intended to usher in the Period of the Companies. What distinguished these rituals was the scale and traumatic character of their performance. The most effective of all were the nocturnal vigils held in a specially constructed round house at Maranagi. The house closely resembled the design of Kanunga's last remaining temple (insofar as elders could remember it). Night after night, the combined populations of Dadul and Maranagi, along with a few kinsmen of core members from other villages, gathered in the round house to await the Period of the Companies. These vigils frequently involved singing, and the repeated possession of a young woman by her dead father (the boss of Bernard's Temple in Dadul).

The root metaphor transmitted in the vigils obviously reverberated with ideas about the "ring" and the "post," since the layout of the house precisely corresponded to the layout of the ring. These images, however, were charged with even more intense emotional and sensory experiences than those cultivated in ring ceremonies. In part, this had to do with the scale of vigils, encompassing some two hundred persons tightly crowded into the roundhouse. The sight of such large gatherings caused many of the participants to weep, especially the elders who recalled the serious depletion of the population that resulted from bombing, executions, food shortages, and the spread of disease during World War II. But this feeling of numerical strength also had a strong impression on everybody, young and old, because it demonstrated the intensity and scale of collective support for the splinter group program, and lent it a kind of credibility or legitimacy that reasoned arguments alone could not sustain. The gathering was rare and momentous, particularly since it comprised a bounded social universe incorporating participants' closest relatives and friends.

The power of the vigils also inhered in the suffering that they inflicted on everyone involved. Severe overcrowding, overheating, and poor ventilation in the round house was compounded by the fact that people were prevented from leaving the house to visit latrines and were obliged to urinate where they sat. Key officials in the splinter group were responsible for barring the door, and ensuring that none of the participants fell asleep in the course of the night. These restrictions had to do in part with the maintenance of unity, for it was feared that the miracle could not occur if some people were physically or mentally absent.

The suffering of participants also served to emphasize the sacredness of the post, around which people congregated, and the price exacted by its revelation. Above all, this confinement and discomfort cultivated a powerful desire for release, which was readily transformed into a longing for deliverance from all the miseries of this world. Participants were encouraged to think about all the most deplorable forms of suffering in worldly life, of pain, sickness, and bereavement, and to reflect on the implications of transcending them. In the traumatic conditions of the round house, such thoughts produced tears, moans, and an intensified yearning for salvation.

During the month of vigils at Maranagi, verbal transmission of ideology was markedly reduced. The two leaders, Baninge and Tanotka, made very few public statements at this time, and their special significance in the community was conveyed more prominently by the imagery of the central post in the round house than by their pronouncements. This initiated a shift away from dynamic, innovative leadership and toward the symbolic representation of figureheads, emerging out of the community's actions. The crucial act of transmission was tied to the context of ritual performance and imposed definite limits on the scale and longevity of the religious organization. Before the end of the month, Maranagi's gardens had been depleted as a result of the influx of people, and the community had to hunt and gather food to sustain itself. Hunger was one of the crucial factors causing the splinter group to break up. The organization was not built to endure or expand, and its real power lay in the fact that it cultivated enduring memories, which were capable of exerting an influence, in the long term, on the political and religious lives of participants.

After the splinter group was disbanded, the nonoccurrence of the miracle was accounted for by the presumed intervention of Satan. Baninge and Tanotka put aside their sacred task for the time being, but they (and many others) said it would be resumed at a later date, probably within a few years. Some activities of the splinter group resulted in threats of legal prosecution from critics of the Pomio Kivung and, along with food shortages, effectively prevented further performances of vigils in the short term. Meanwhile, the people of Dadul and Maranagi restored the ritual cycles of the mainstream movement.

People's attitudes had clearly been transformed, however. The intense solidarity cultivated most forcefully in the vigils had left a deep impression on people's minds, and this was manifested in the way they talked about their collective identity and relations with external agencies (see Whitehouse 1995). Moreover, the performance of temple rituals and other routinized activities was haunted by the dramatic revelations of the post, the ring, and the round house. The simplicity of iconic codification, and the impressive conditions in which concrete metaphors were transmitted, rendered them highly memorable, and quite different in quality from the extensive strings of ideology conveyed in mainstream community meetings, which required continual repetition to be preserved intact. In this way, religious experience in the routinized regimen was enriched and deepened by the memory of much closer and more intense interactions with spirits experienced in the splinter group—through possession, dreams and reports, and above all, through the highly charged revelations of collective ritual.

The splintering of 1988 was but one episode in a series of similar outbursts in Dadul and Maranagi. Oral histories and patrol reports indicate that similar activities occurred in the brief years preceding independence—in 1975, again in the late 1970s, and possibly around 1982. This suggests that events of this kind occur with slightly greater frequency than the precontact initiation rituals upon which they are modeled. It is not clear that all such activities incorporated *awanga* performances; what they had in common with initiation rituals was a distinctive emphasis on iconic codification and emotional/sensory stimulation. In this respect, they contrast starkly with the language-dependent regimen of cultural transmission that characterizes the routinized movement. The fact that such climactic rituals recur every few years demonstrates the efficacy that people attach to them. The memories they inculcate, far from being productive of disillusionment or cynicism, have an enduring religious value.

POLITICS AND THE EXPERIENCE OF SPIRITS

The three types of spirit experience described above—individual and collective encounters with *sega*; experiences with ancestors, ghosts, and *sega* through the lens of verbalized doctrine in the mainstream Pomio Kivung; and experiences with ancestors through the performance of traumatic splinter-group rituals— each has a complex set of political ramifications.

In the context of daily life, *sega* are avoided, blamed, and manipulated through individual action. Neither avoidance nor blaming necessitates a vivid impression of *sega*. They are dimly construed as being "at large" in the forest, and probably each person, when taking a wide berth around a tree or explaining an illness, has in mind a different and rather fuzzy image of the spirit responsible, and its motives. All people know is that *sega* are humanoid, incorporeal beings with no apparent moral inclinations of their own. When *sega*, uninvited, become involved in human affairs, it is usually in an undesirable way. Either they are retaliating, much as a cornered animal might do to an invasion of their space, or else they are stirring up disharmony or misery as agents of Satan, in keeping with Christian and Kivung understandings of diabolical forces.

Being morally neutral, *sega* can also be manipulated by human agents in a positive way, through the performance of magical rites. These rites, however, do not conjure up particularly compelling or vivid experiences of the spirit world. They are treated as technical procedures rather than as instruments of revelation. This is strongly reminiscent of J. F. Weiner's conception of the use of metaphor in Foi magical rites, which he describes as "cutting off" signification rather than "revealing" or "explicating" (1992:27). Magical rites, handed down through the generations, portray spirits as fixed in time and space, like the spells themselves—objects that can be stored, shared, or utilized.

These spells are not evocative of fresh imaginings, or what Weiner calls a "resynthesis of lived experience" (1992:28). Much the same could be said of the way *sega* are represented in dreams. For example, the *sega* who "stole" Kaukau were just like any other *sega* in any other dream. The images of their house, flowers, and livestock merely signaled that they were *sega* but afforded no novel insights into their nature or their significance for human affairs. Likewise, the iconicity used in the ritual to retrieve Kaukau operated at a purely technical level, rather like a map drawn in the dust.

On the face of it, divinations and nocturnal dances would seem capable of providing a more poignant or evocative experience of spirits. In practice, however, this is not the case. The image of the bamboo pole seems to evoke no cosmological understandings; nor do the activities surrounding the "fire dance" resonate with a coherent religious tradition. The discourse surrounding both activities is consistent with a process of cultural atrophy, in which the moving and mysterious rituals of the past have degenerated into mere entertainment. Divination is described as a "game" and the fire dance as a "party." Yet this fits entirely with the fact that the performers do not hold the same religious views. The people of Dadul disdain the prayers, confessions, and liturgies of their Catholic neighbors, and the choirs and Sunday schools of the United Church. Likewise, Christians who join with the people of Dadul in performing a divination or fire dance repudiate their ideas about "feeding the dead" and "waiting for cargo and ancestors." Since the Pomio Kivung is steeped in Christian thinking, many ideas are inevitably shared by these groups. The differences, however, loom large and prevent both sides from recognizing any common ground with the other. At funerals, for example, Kivung supporters are inclined to view their participation in mourning as a sham, for they expect to be reunited with the deceased before long. This difference in outlook is part of the hidden agenda on such occasions, and what is openly shared among mourners (name-ly the "entertainment," including material gifts as well as the divination) is sep-arated from the sphere of religious action, where real ideological conflict resides.

In short, the separation of ideas about *sega* from religion is consistent with a diminution of the cosmological importance of the former. The fact that atti-tudes toward nonhuman spirits are shared among Christians and Kivung sup-porters reduces rather than enhances their religious significance, but it provides a rare ceremonial form in which opposing groups can cultivate a harmonious exterior amid the vestiges of a once common culture.

Ideas about the spirits of dead people (i.e., ancestors) in Dadul are far more elaborate and coherent. Discourse concerning ancestors is dominated by Pomio Kivung cosmology and morality. It is considered blasphemous to refer to the dead directly, and the Mali word for "ancestor" (*wayiaikana*) is rarely heard. The euphemism commonly deployed is *amorka*, "man," or the Pidgin phrase *Vilij Gavman* (see above). Paradoxically, the term *sega* is quite frequently heard, even though ancestors rather than *sega* are the main focus of religious action in Dadul.

I have pointed out that there is a close relationship between doctrinal com-plexity and coherence, the codification of ideas in language, and frequent repe-tition or "routinization." The interdependency of these features is explicitly recognized by the Pomio Kivung leadership. Indeed, it is plain to see that elab-orate, logically integrated doctrine requires language, and that such a corpus of verbalized knowledge can be sustained (in the absence of inscribing practices such as literacy) only in a regimen of frequent transmission, based around ser-monizing. This type of codification has political implications I have explored elsewhere (e.g., Whitehouse 1992, 1994, 1995).

Where religious ideas are readily verbalized, they can be spread over great distances by just a few proselytizing orators (see also Barth 1990). Moreover, this is consistent with the emergence of centralized leadership, envisaged as the source of authoritative dogma. Ideological uniformity can then be sustained through the designation of a middle tier of officials, who patrol strongholds of the expanding movement, leading to the kind of hierarchical structure that is found in the Pomio Kivung, Yali's movement, and Paliau's movement.

A drawback with regimes of this type, as Steinbauer observed in relation to Paliau's movement, is that life becomes "austere and regulated almost like a military establishment" (1979:69), and ritual activities "lack spontaneity" (1979:71). However intellectually persuasive the daily sermons may be, the ten-dency in such movements is for the doctrines to become platitudinous and the rituals to become mechanical, humdrum routines. It is against this background that innovators sporadically succeed in whipping up support for more climactic and emotionally arousing religious action.

Sporadic breakaway cults in the Pomio Kivung are fundamentally rooted in mainstream ideas, but they introduce a distinctive way of experiencing these ideas. In the verbalized discourse of the mainstream movement, ancestors are depicted as a corporate group (the Village Government) which exists on the other side of a cosmic fence. Orations dwell on this scenario and on the hope that the fence will one day be broken. Splinter-group ritual, by contrast, physically enacts the process of breaking the fence. In the examples given here, the *awanga* left Paradise to re-enter the village, and the people entered a ring in which they were united with the Village Government. On the face of it, this seemed to entail the same symbolic process that I described in the context of retrieval magic. In such cases, bodily movements mimic some external process or relationship. Yet the common element of bodily iconicity in magical rites and splinter group ritual belies a fundamental divergence.

Unlike the concrete metaphors of Mali Baining spells, images of the ring were collectively triggered, emotionally charged, and revelatory. What they revealed could not be reduced to a verbal statement. Revelation lay in the emotional experience of suffering and the prospect of deliverance, the visible reality of darkness transformed into light, the tactile experience of unity in the cramped round house, the voices of choir members harmonizing as one, and the feet of dancers that moved in synchrony. An important aspect of the way in which such experiences are handled cognitively is highlighted by theories of autobiographical or "episodic" memory (Tulving 1972). Splinter group rituals were extraordinary events, a major departure from the routines of everyday life. As such, they were encoded as distinctive events in the life history of each participant. Moreover, their iconicity struck resonances from rings of human bodies, from posts that formed the round house, from dancers in the *Haus Kivung*, and from *awanga* charging in a circle.

These and other representations of the ring were poignant because they were at once novel, unexpected, revealing, sensually and emotionally arousing, and expressive. The fact that such images were collectively and nonverbally triggered, rather than emanating from the mouths of experienced orators, placed constraints on the scale and structure of the political unit involved. Religious experience in the splinter group could only be spread by admitting outsiders into the ritual community or by displacing the community itself, unlike verbalized doctrine that could be transported by one or a few leaders. Moreover, the fact that revelations were eventually generated through a process of personal inference or "inspiration," rather than being transmitted by a prophet or messiah, meant that the splinter group could not (at least during its climactic phase) sustain dynamic leadership. The group itself became the source and focus of religious insight.

CONCLUSION

Sega are peripheral to religious life in Dadul, in the sense that they are not concerned with the soteriological quest for a solution to worldly suffering. This quest is construed in Dadul in terms of a Christian-syncretic cosmology that originated among non-Baining groups to the south and was disseminated through the medium of Pidgin. Christian and Pomio Kivung thinking has fundamentally displaced a religious tradition founded around initiations and dances. The place of *sega* in this preexisting scheme has been substantially forgotten; what remains are pieces of a jigsaw puzzle that do not effectively cohere. Both Christian and Pomio Kivung doctrines have appropriated ideas about *sega* to the extent that they portray them as potential agents of Satan. Yet the *sega* are themselves construed as amoral—objects, more or less, over which control may be exerted for good or evil. The idea of *sega* as "objects" is also apposite in the sense that they are represented in magic, dreams, and general discourse as fixed entities; they are and always have been around in the bush, like sharp rocks or stinging nettles, a threat to the careless explorer, but a potential resource in magico-technical procedures. As invisible, amoral objects, peripheral to the concerns of local cosmology, *sega* are not clearly or elaborately cognized, and they are not a focus of debate and ideological conflict. This is consistent with the fact that the communal activities in which *sega* figure provide a forum for cooperation between otherwise divided religious communities. When Christians and Pomio Kivung supporters gather together around the bamboo pole at a divination, or the arena of a "fire dance," a sort of uneasy harmony is established which publicly ignores the doctrinal gulf between them. This is possible only because *sega* are part of a distant but common history, so firmly displaced to the periphery of contemporary religious thinking that it disguises more recent sectarianism.

In contrast, the people of Dadul sustain a rich and complex discourse about ancestors. If the marginality of ideas about *sega* in cosmology makes them suited to the negotiation of relations on the political boundaries, i.e., between religious communities, then the ideological centrality of ancestor worship coincides with its importance for internal political structure. I have suggested that ancestor worship is enacted in contrasting modes: the routinized, language-based, evangelical mode of the mainstream movement, and the sporadic, nonverbal, localized mode of the splinter group. My point is that the experience of spirits in Dadul is related to styles of codification, cultural transmission, and political association and cannot be reduced to a set of statements about local "beliefs" concerning spirits.

ACKNOWLEDGMENTS
This chapter is based on field research carried out in Papua New Guinea between 1987 and 1989. I am grateful to the ESRC for funding this research and to Trinity Hall, Cambridge, for funding my visit to the ASAO conference in New Orleans, which led to this volume. I should like to thank Alan Howard, Jeannette Mageo, Roy Rappaport, and Dan Jorgensen for their incisive comments on earlier drafts. My greatest debt of thanks goes to the people of Dadul, Maranagi, Sunam, Riet, and Mamal for their generosity and tolerance.

9   Spirit Possession in Chuuk

Francis X. Hezel
Jay D. Dobbin

Chuuk (formerly known as Truk) is an island group with a population of about 50,000 that lies in the geographical center of
the Federated States of Micronesia (FSM), one of the newest
Pacific nations. The island group took its name from the mountainous basaltic islands in the lagoon constituting the nucleus
of the island group. The name belies the reality, however, for
the culture that developed in Chuuk is more distinctive of coral
atolls than of high islands. Chuuk has always lacked the more
complex social organization and the powerful chieftainships of
many of its island neighbors. Authority was fragmented; the
largest unit of government in traditional times was the "district," normally comprising a village or two and ruled by the
clan with the earliest land rights.

Generally shunned by European and American ship cap-
tains in the last century because of its reputation for hostility,
Chuuk was one of the last island groups in Micronesia exposed
to intensive foreign contact. Merchants and missionaries
arrived simultaneously in the 1880s; within a few years most of
the population accepted Christianity, and trade emporia were
established on every island. When the German government,
which had purchased the Carolines and Marianas from Spain
in 1899, sent a warship to Chuuk demanding that the people
turn in their weapons and cease the interisland warfare that
had been an ongoing feature of life there, the Chuukese people
willingly complied. For nearly the entire century they submitted
to colonial rule, Japanese and American following the short
period of German rule, until Chuuk won its independence in
1986 as part of the FSM.

The rapid modernization program inaugurated in the 1960s
radically increased wage employment and set in motion a
process of sociocultural change. The traditional formal lineage
organization remains, but the lineage has surrendered many of
its functions to the household and the nuclear family.

Supervision of young males has become problematic in recent years, and drinking among the young and the violent behavior associated with it have become serious concerns. Suicide rates have also risen in Chuuk, as in the rest of Micronesia, since the late 1960s. Within this same period, involuntary spirit possession among females, the theme of this chapter, appears to have become a relatively common phenomenon.

Chuukese today, like most other Micronesians, assume the existence of spirits and their intervention in human affairs. Their belief in spirits persists despite the conversion of Chuuk to Christianity late in the last century.[1] Although many people disavow a belief in spirits when asked directly, especially by a church minister, their behavior indicates otherwise. They are uncomfortable walking alone in the woods in the evening and avoid places associated with the more notorious nature spirits. Women, especially, take precautions when venturing into the vicinity of "sea spirits," which are believed to cause miscarriage and problems in childbirth. People continue to use traditional "medicine" to ward off malevolent spirits, even as they still believe in the efficacy of love potions (ómwmwung) to win the affections of those whom they find sexually attractive.

In this chapter, we explore the changing role of spirits in Chuukese culture. We begin by introducing relevant features of Chuukese religion during the period of early contact, then go on to describe their transformations and the nature of spirit–human relations in the contemporary society.

GODS AND SPIRITS IN PRE-CHRISTIAN CHUUK

Chuukese numinals (énú) resist easy classification, as anthropologists have frequently noted (see for example Lessa 1987:498; Alkire 1989). Certain beings were sky dwellers: regarded as the oldest and most powerful were the trinity—Anulap, "Great Spirit," the uncreated being who lives remote from mortals and their affairs; Lukeilang, "Middle of Heaven," son of Anulap and lord of all in the realms of spirits and mortals; and Olofat, the eldest son of Lukeilang, a trickster god and the subject of a cycle of popular tales (Frazer 1968 III:124–25). A number of other figures might be called gods—figures like Semenkoror, "Father of Wisdom," Sinenap, "Skilled One"; and Aremei, "Achiever" (Bollig 1927:6–7). One of the most popular and most often supplicated is Inemes, the goddess of love or the "Venus of Chuuk," as Bollig (1927:6) called her. She is implicated in the love magic that has survived to the present day.

An abundance of nature spirits were thought to occupy the atolls, reefs and adjacent waters. Their origins are lost in the mists of the past, although some Chuukese knowledgeable in traditional lore maintain they were human spirits that in time became associated with a particular locality. Some were sea spirits (oos) who lived in the open ocean but were believed to come ashore to sleep at night (Mahoney 1969:140). One of the best known, and most feared, was Anumwaresi, the spirit of the rainbow, who is still thought to afflict pregnant women (Anonymous nd:4). Spirits known as *chénúkken* resided on the reefs and shallows inside the lagoon. Mostly female, they were often named— Inepeitan and Inepauoch were identified with shoals near Toloas, while Inaun was believed to live off a section of Uman (Anonymous nd:4). Two separate spirits sharing the name Niipecheefóch, "One-Legged Spirit," were thought to live just off the islands of Fono and Pis (Mahoney 1969:140).

On the land, especially in crevices and fissures, lived the spirits of the soil, each with its own name (Mahoney 1969:140). In addition were spirits of bread-fruit trees (*anumumai*), among them Seningeruu, who was known to sow discord among people (Bollig 1927:12). The Chuukese also recognized spirits associated with particular mountains, bushes, rocks, and other landmarks (Bollig 1927:4-5). Nature spirits could be classified only in the most general way, but they shared as a common trait their fearsomeness to people (Bollig 1927:12).

Formerly Chuukese believed that two spirits inhabited each individual: a good spirit and a bad spirit. At death, the bad spirit would hover around the grave of the deceased, sometimes taking the form of a fruit bat or other animal and terrorizing those who lived nearby. The bad spirit could attack people and "bite" them, the effect of which might be to darken the victim's mind or cause temporary insanity (Mahoney 1969:134–35). But any harm the bad spirit could do was limited, for it was confined to the immediate vicinity of the grave, stalked only at night, and could be frightened off by light. If the spirit became too annoying, a sorcerer was called to drive it into the earth to rejoin the body of the deceased (Bollig 1927:20–22). The good spirit, which had the power to roam more freely before it eventually drifted up to its abode in the sky, was a source of blessings for its former family. If well disposed to the family, it could reveal a wealth of valuable information on new kinds of medicine, ideas for dances, and the location of good fishing grounds. However, good spirits could become a scourge if not treated with proper respect and placated with gift offerings (Mahoney 1969:137). When angry, good spirits could cause serious illness and might be more of a threat than bad spirits. It was through good spirits that Chuukese families attempted, in years past, to establish communication with deceased members.

MEDIUMSHIP

Early accounts agree on the essentials of mediumship in Chuuk. It normally occurred in a lineage meeting house in which was hung a model double-hulled canoe (*náán*), 30 to 50 centimeters long, that served as a vehicle for the spirit. A spirit medium (termed variously *souawarawar*, *wáátawa*, or *wáá-naanú*) was seated in the midst of the family, smeared with fragrant perfume. As the family chanted the name of the dead relative with whom they wished to speak, the medium "mumbles to himself, begins to moan, breathes several times with his mouth wide open, and then lapses into convulsive trembling" (Anonymous nd:8). As the trembling became more violent, the family, recognizing that the medium was now in a state of possession, began asking questions of the spirit. The medium's voice did not usually change, although he spoke in a special "spirit language" that had to be interpreted by someone knowledgeable in this form of speech. Girschner fills in additional details about the medium:

> The art is learned, but a certain talent is required; fathers teach their sons, older brothers teach the younger. Before performing his duties, the *Waitaua* partakes of magic ingredients, mashed coconut leaves, which have been consecrated, and the fruit of the seir tree, which it is believed carries the spirits, which they like to eat. If there are not enough magic ingredients eaten beforehand, the *Waitaua* can not enunciate clearly the words of the spirits, and mumbles. If one wishes to get advice from the spirits, one goes to the *Waitaua*, tells him what is desired, and gives him gifts for his services. The sorcerer sits on the ground and calls the spirits. They come and set themselves down on him ... ; he is possessed by them, and becomes an *auwarawar*, a possessed one ... This is manifested in his quiverings, cramped hand motions, nodding head, and such. He enters a state called *merik*; the spirits open his mouth ... and speak through him. First one, then another spirit speaks, for anyone can, if he wants to, receive an answer through the seer, but in a special language, different from the ordinary, the spirit language. The *merik* state does not last long, about 15 minutes, and after awakening the *Waitaua* tells the others what he has heard. (1911:n.p.)

Later accounts from the German period (1899–1914), provide additional details. Whether this represents an evolution of spirit belief under the influence of Christianity or the result of more acute observation is unclear. Certainly by the time of Bollig's account, in 1927, missionization had changed some beliefs, as he acknowledges. But like Girschner, Bollig found spirit mediums still active. On the island of Fefan he identified ninety in a population of 2,000 (Bollig 1927:63).

Bollig associates the vocation of spirit medium with sickness and death (1927:31,80). He reported that on the second, fourth, sixth, or eighth day after death, kin of the deceased make a ritual fire of the deceased's movable property. The spirit was said to fly up with the smoke (1927:22) and take residence in a *náán*, "miniature double-hulled canoe" (1927:31).

According to Bollig (1927:60–61), a person acting as medium would tremble, perhaps foam at the mouth, and feel the heaviness of the spirit sitting on his shoulder. Often his head jerked back and forth, his neck was bent "under the weight of the spirit," and his hands began to quiver. Then the spirit began to speak. After the episode the spirit retreated to its miniature canoe and its human host returned to normal. The chosen host, interestingly, now became *wáánaanú*, "canoe of the spirit." Henceforth the *wáánaanú* called the spirit from the canoe when people had questions or were sick.

Episodes did not always produce the desired result, however. The possessed person might become violent and say nothing, or the spoken revelation might turn out so unconvincing as to be considered a fake. *Wáánaanú* called on spirits to reveal new cures (*sáfei*), allowing them to practice as healers (*sousáfei*). Curing practices included placing necklaces of stripped palm fronds on the patient, massaging, and reciting incantations (Girschner 1911).

Mahoney (1969:46, 137) speculated that Christian missionaries were responsible for the disappearance of the *wáánaanú* before World War II, although a brief resurgence of the practice occurred during the war years. Nevertheless, he found Chuukese healers still quite active in the 1960s, and reported hearing speculations concerning which *roong*, "spirit powers," were at work in particular instances. For example, crying, red-spotted skin, boils, itching, diarrhea, and fever were associated with certain sea spirits (Mahoney 1969:50). Mahoney found healers possessing varying degrees of expertise, and classified them as amateurs (*chonsáfei*), experts (*sousáfei*), and specialists (*souroong*) (Mahoney 1969:11).

CONTEMPORARY ENCOUNTERS WITH SPIRITS

While Chuukese beliefs concerning spirits persist, they are limited and reactive (rather than initiating) when compared with the past. Contemporary Chuukese use every means possible to avoid the harm they believe spirits can do, but they no longer make offerings or pray to propitiate spirits. Insofar as this is the case, most Chuukese have satisfactorily integrated their belief in spirits with their Christian faith. Christian teaching, after all, recognizes the reality of a spirit world of its own, populated by demons and angels. The panoply of Chuukese spirits are regarded as a potent but lower order of beings subordinate to the Christian God. Hence, the spirit world of Chuuk might be seen not as an alternative to Christian beliefs, but as a substratum of professed Christianity, even when devoutly embraced. Indeed, the Christian God is often called upon to counter the destructive influence of Chuukese spirits.

Chuukese today attribute many kinds of misfortunes to the influence of spirits, ranging from injuries that Westerners would simply label accidents to suicide attempts. Beyond this, they sometimes report direct encounters with spirits. People frequently speak of seeing ghosts and occasionally of being "bitten" by ghosts (*ochei énú*). Since Chuukese do not trouble themselves with fine distinctions in the typology of spirit encounters, it is often difficult to know whether they consider the individual "possessed"—that is, whether the spirit in question has, in their judgment, actually occupied the body of the victim—or whether the spirit has acted as an external force on the person. The Chuukese term *awarawar énú*, "the coming of the spirit," suggests a simple encounter, while the word *wáánaanú*, "the vehicle of the spirit," implies what Westerners would think of as possession. Yet, Chuukese often use the terms interchangeably, and few seem concerned with making a rigorous distinction.

Reported Encounters

Not many years ago, a woman in her early 30s was net fishing with a group of other women in the shallow water just offshore. As she was hauling in her section of the long fishing net, she became entangled in it. While struggling to free herself, she saw a big, naked black man in the deep water advancing toward her. Upon freeing herself from the net, she ran toward the house screaming in panic. An adult male relative intercepted her on the way, but she threw him to the ground with apparent ease. She cowered in the house over the next several days, and an expert in medicine (*sousáfei*) was summoned from another island to treat her. After applying his remedies and relieving the woman's distress, he explained that she had been afflicted by Soumwerikes, the ghost that troubles women who have recently given birth. The woman had delivered her sixth child a few weeks prior to the incident.

Another story is told of a girl, 16 years old, from a different island in Chuuk, who was pregnant and due to deliver. One night as she was preparing to go to sleep, she saw a stout man clad entirely in yellow who lasciviously clutched at her dress. She fought off the "man" with remarkable strength while the household looked on in astonishment at her wild thrashing. Members of her family saw no assailant, but they said that the girl seemed to be pulled toward the door and resisted violently, screaming all the while. She calmed down later that evening, but further episodes took place during the next few weeks. The family called the Catholic priest to assist them, and the incidents stopped when the girl delivered. It should be noted that this girl, like the woman in the previous case, was unmarried when she became pregnant.

In both cases the women were said to be agitated by an encounter with a spirit, but neither is a clear-cut instance of what might be called possession. Although Chuukese informants were quick to attribute the abnormal behavior of the women to spirits, they could not say whether the spirit was actually "on" them. The informant for the second instance suggested that the young woman in question was not really possessed because there was no change in her voice. Although both women suffered intermittent episodes for a week or two, the duration of symptoms was not considered a telling sign of possession. Whatever designation we use for these cases, they share important features with the majority of documented spirit possession cases, as we shall see.

POSSESSION

One cannot live for any length of time in Chuuk without hearing tales of spirit possession. As Catholic priests residing in Chuuk, Hezel and his colleagues have been summoned dozens of times to bless persons who were said to be possessed.

In 1989, Cathy Hung, then a Peace Corps volunteer in Chuuk, generously offered to assist Hezel in the collection of case reports on spirit possession. Within two months she had collected from Chuukese women accounts of fifty-seven spirit encounters, more than forty of which could be considered spirit possession. The case reports are admittedly thin, since there was normally only one informant for each incident and she or he was asked to provide information on an event that sometimes occurred years before. Nonetheless, what the case files lack in depth they compensate for in quantity, since the number and variety of cases gathered for the study is exceptional.

Illustrative Cases of Possession

A young woman, whom we shall call Loretta, complained of a severe headache one night just before retiring. She awoke some hours later when she began hearing voices. Soon after she was babbling to herself and carrying on conversations with spirits of dead relatives. Adopting the speech patterns and voice characteristics of the deceased family members, Loretta harangued her family about a quarrel that had taken place a few days before. The spirits demanded an apology from errant members of the family for their misbehavior. Loretta contiued this behavior off and on for several days until she recovered. Subsequently, however, Loretta experienced two or three recurrences of possession.

Another incident involved Fermina, the fifteen-year-old daughter of devout Christian parents. One evening a few years ago she went to bed complaining of a pain in her stomach. By the next morning her body was twitching uncontrollably, and she was seized with convulsions. As the family gathered around her mat to comfort her, they heard her suddenly reprimand a much older male relative, angrily telling him to "Leave the house, because I don't like what you are doing." The words came from Fermina's mouth, but the voice was that of her mother, who had died a year or two earlier. Fermina recovered within two or three days of the incident, but she has had similar experiences a few times since this one.

Michko, a woman in her late thirties, fell into a seizure one evening and began speaking in the voice of her deceased grandfather. Her grandfather was summoning her to join him outside the house. Michko shouted in her own voice, "Wait for me, I'm coming." Her family gathered at the door of the house to prevent her from leaving, but with what seemed preternatural strength she thrust her brother and another man aside. Only the combined efforts of several men in the family sufficed to restrain her. A few hours later Michko was back to normal, although she had similar experiences once or twice after this.

In each of these cases the victim was thought to be possessed by the spirit of a dead relative, for whom she served as a vehicle for the transmission of messages from beyond the grave. The change in voice—in Michko's case to the husky timbre of an elderly male—was taken as a sign of the women's status as "possessed." This is not to say that everyone in their families accepted the episodes as genuine; the father of one of the victims, at the onset of her episode, slapped her and accused her of faking possession. Whether everyone accepted the authenticity of the possessions or not, however, they immediately recognized the role the women were assuming. They were defined as a "possessed person," for which there is a clear niche in Chuukese society.

More extensive information is available for Mariana:

> A few days before Mariana's possession began, her brother started coming home drunk every night, although he did not normally drink alcohol before this. The family took his unusual behavior as an indication that he had an unspoken grievance against someone in the family.
>
> The night Mariana became possessed, the spirit of her dead mother came upon her. Mariana's voice changed to that of her deceased mother, who asked her son (Mariana's brother) to hold her hand because it hurt (their mother apparently died from an affliction which pained her right arm). The spirit said she loved and pitied her son. Mariana's sisters were enjoined to show their love for their brother by washing his clothes, as good sisters should, and take pains to prepare tasty food for him. Mariana herself did not escape "her mother's" reproach, for she, too, was scolded for neglecting her poor brother. Implicitly understood in this admonition was that if the brother were treated properly by his family he would have no reason to continue his drinking, and peace would again be restored to the family.
>
> Mariana's family wanted her to go to the hospital, but she refused, and moved with her husband to Moen soon after. On Moen she was possessed every night for a week. During the day she was like her normal self, but each night awoke from sleep shouting and crying. When possessed she would talk and act like her mother. On one occasion, Mariana's husband reported that she threatened to pluck out and eat their son's eyeballs. She started physically hurting the boy, and family members had to pull him away from her. In subsequent episodes, the spirit seemed to be choking her, clutching at her throat.
>
> Local Chuukese healers (*sousáfei*) were called in and asked to help. They told Mariana not to change residences, but to stay in one house since it was bad to be so public. (The family compound has four houses; after being possessed in one house Mariana wanted to move to another the following night.) They tried various kinds of holy water, but the treatment proved ineffective. They took her to bathe in a stream and she improved temporarily, but the healers were not optimistic about the outcome.

At the time Mariana's case material was collected, her family expected her to die a painful death. At one point they authorized a radio announcement calling family members from her island to pay their last respects and prepare for her death.

The individual who provided the case material asserted the authenticity of Mariana's possession. He implied that the family's troubles began when Mariana consented to have sex with her second cousin via a liaison arranged by her sister's husband. After that, Mariana's husband and brother started getting drunk and causing problems. The informant reported that Mariana and her husband did not talk with one another about their feelings. Nevertheless, he inferred from the fact that her husband tried hard to find effective healers that he genuinely cared for her.

Patterns of Possession Experience

The cumulative case materials reveal spirit possessions, as distinguished from mere encounters with spirits, to be strongly patterned in Chuuk. Characteristically the episode begins with a severe pain, often a persistent headache or abdominal pain, or with a bout of illness. One woman's possession was preceded by a sore throat and laryngitis; another started with a pain in the chest that endured despite all the remedies she used. The victim then takes to her sleeping mat as the rest of the family gathers around to look after her.

Next, the afflicted person typically experiences a violent bodily upheaval. She begins yelling and screaming, or possibly sobbing uncontrollably. She may begin flailing her arms at those around her, or her body might start convulsing or shaking, resembling a seizure. This phase often includes an assault on people present—one young girl suddenly grabbed her grandmother and began to throttle her; another victim picked up a broom and struck an older relative standing nearby. Sometimes possessed individuals chase people around the house, throwing things and grappling with them, occasionally even wrestling them to the ground. Again and again informants comment on the remarkable strength of afflicted women, who are often capable of besting a grown man much heavier than themselves. Yet, it is also noteworthy that the violence exhibited by the possessed person is controlled, much as a young man on a drunken rampage in Chuuk will carefully moderate his violence despite appearances to the contrary (Marshall 1979:112–18). The relatives of the possessed woman may be scratched and bruised from restraining her, but there are no instances in our data of anyone receiving a serious injury from a possessed person.

Possessed individuals demonstrate other sorts of unusual behavior, some of it flagrant transgressions of the code of propriety in Chuukese society. Much of the time, afflicted persons simply moan unintelligibly or babble nonsense, but at times their speech has a sharp edge. They may wantonly insult those around them, even using vulgarity that Chuukese women, under ordinary circumstances, would never dream of uttering in the presence of their brothers and other male relatives. At times their remarks take on a sexual tenor, as when they describe sexual fantasies they have experienced. One woman hitched up her skirt and scratched her pubic area while her family tried to modestly cover her and pull her hand away. Another young woman, after telling some of her older relatives how ugly they were, made sexual overtures to pre-teenage boys standing nearby. The actions of possessed Chuukese women have parallels in the behavior of female jesters in neighboring Polynesian societies, for example Rotuma, Samoa, and Tokelau (Hereniko 1992, Sinavaiana 1992a, Huntsman and Hooper 1975), and likewise express a counterpoint to proper behavior for women.

In roughly one-third of the cases, informants recalled that the possessed person demonstrated prescience. They seemed to know who was about to come in the room, often announcing the person's arrival before they appeared. Possessed women are often described as able to point out exactly where lost or hidden objects are to be found. One young girl gave detailed instructions on where a pistol belonging to a recently deceased relative might be found. Before his death, the man had concealed the pistol in a house in a distant village; it reportedly was found in the exact spot that the girl indicated. Many years ago a woman in a possessed state predicted that a group of men who had gone off to a distant island to work on a plantation would be back very soon. They did in fact return a week later. The same evening that the woman had made her prediction, as her kinfolk later learned, the men were boarding the ship that would bring them back to Chuuk. Another woman allegedly correctly told her family that a boy who had been missing for a few days had hanged himself in the bush, and she told her family where they might find his body. At times clairvoyance takes ominous forms. Possessed women have been known to predict the deaths of relatives. They also have publicly revealed intimate details of family members' personal lives, including clandestine sexual relationships. For these reasons, the families of a possessed person do everything possible to avoid provoking an angry outburst.

For Chuukese, one of the most dramatic and telling signs of possession is the change in voice that occurs when the spirit begins speaking. Indeed, this transformation involves more than a change in voice; the possessed person usually takes on the very persona of the spirit that is upon her. The timbre and tone of her voice and her speech patterns become those of the dead person; these are accompanied by corresponding changes in gestures, facial expressions, and other mannerisms. When one stooped old woman began speaking in the voice of her brother, she walked around the house ramrod straight—the first time anyone could remember her doing so—and began smoking, just as her brother had done when he was alive. In another instance, a possessed woman stroked her throat while speaking, just as her mother did during her lifetime, and conversed in the same soft, strained voice that her mother used.

At times a possessed person may adopt the personae of two or three spirits in an evening. In one recent case a young girl, in a virtuoso performance of characterization, took on the speech and mannerisms of four different spirits during a single episode.

Although changes in persona are usually brief, lasting only a few minutes at a time, seizure episodes have a much longer duration. Individual episodes may range from a day or two to a couple of weeks, with some apparently dragging on for as long as two or three months. One old woman was said to have been possessed from the time of her paralysis through the last year of her life. Sometimes it is difficult to tell precisely when one episode ends and another begins, for some of the afflicted women have such long and continuous histories of such experiences that they can almost be called chronically possessed. For example, two younger women had a series of incidents that began in the early 1980s and continued intermittently until 1990. One informant, whose sister-in-law was first possessed in 1980 at the age of fifteen, said that in recent years the afflicted woman has exhibited possession symptoms every three months.

Possession As Illness

Within the framework of Chuukese Christianity today, possession is associated with Satan and the forces of evil at work in the world. On another level, spirit possession is seen as dangerous because it represents a violent upheaval of the established social order. Possessed women defy the canons that govern social conduct in Chuuk: women flaunt their sexuality in the presence of male relatives; they voice publicly what ought to go unspoken; they flail, verbally and often physically, at those to whom they are expected to show respectful restraint. Possession, which brings people into proximity with the dark spirit realm, also introduces an element of chaos that threatens to unravel the social fabric of their community lives.

In the face of such a threat, Chuukese sometimes turn to local healers for traditional remedies. More commonly, however, they seek treatment from within Christianity, from the God who they have been taught is superior to all the powers and principalities, the lower order of spirits that roam the world. Frequently the family of a possessed person will pray over the afflicted family member or sprinkle holy water on her. If the episode continues for more than a day or two, many will summon a Catholic priest to minister to the possessed person, even if the family is Protestant. Part of the attraction of Catholic services no doubt lies in the church's ritual, often conducted with litanies, candles, religious medals or relics, and abundant ablutions with holy water. In some cases, though, Catholic families have turned to Protestant faith healers for treatment, especially when the latter are known to use chants and more theatrical techniques.

For all their reliance on religious cures, however, Chuukese are well aware of another, more mundane dimension to spirit possession. When informed of a possession, they almost invariably ask what brought it on, suspecting a family problem. Most often this is correct.

To understand the importance of family tensions in bringing on possession episodes we need only look at messages delivered in the name (and voice) of the dead relative. One woman, whose older sister had a longstanding dispute with her brother over disposal of family land, warned her family, through the persona of her dead mother, that the sister would be taken from them (presumably through death) unless the bickering ended. Soon after the episode brother and sister were reconciled. A young girl, in the voice of her recently deceased aunt, chastised her family for not properly caring for the dead woman's children. The aunt's husband had remarried shortly after his wife's death and the children were being neglected, to the dismay of the young possessed girl. Some women, in their possessed state, have chided their sons or daughters for failing to do family chores or for seeking to marry someone of whom the family disapproved. A possessed man (one of the few male cases in our data), in his mother's voice, urged all his brothers and sisters to show a proper sense of family solidarity by taking good care of one another and their older kinfolk. He then picked up a broom and started buffeting a niece who had been negligent in visiting his mother the months before she died.

Although squabbles over land or fractiousness over family responsibilities are the most common antecedents to possession, other kinds of stress may also trigger incidents. Frequently possession occurs shortly after the death of a family member, sometimes during the weeklong mourning period for the deceased. A family death occurring under unusual circumstances, as in the case of suicide, may pose a particular threat. Five women exhibited first signs of possession shortly after the suicide of a close family member, and one possessed girl had lost two young men in her family to suicide within a month. Pregnancy, especially in the case of unmarried girls who sense their family's disapproval, has also been known to occasion possession episodes. Overall, family disruption is likely a major factor contributing to possession episodes.

Questions still remain, however: Why is it that women become victims and mouthpieces for problems generic to entire families? What is it about women's roles in modern Chuuk, and particularly young women's roles, that befits them for possession? Why do they require this outlet?

The Historical Transformation of Possession

A comparison of early descriptions and contemporary cases of possession reveal both continuities and changes in form. In pre-Christian Chuuk, an incantor (*awarawar*) contacted spirits during ecstatic behavior (Kubary 1969:22), with a lineage chief acting as middleman between caller and spirit, asking questions and interpreting the incantor's mumblings. Success in contacting invasive spirits leads to a second phase, in which the spirits speak. Early reports emphasized that the *wáánaanú*'s mumblings or unintelligible words needed interpretation. Girschner listed over forty-five expressions in the special spirit language, and reported seeing one medium mumble unintelligibly for twelve minutes.

Parallels are recognizable in recent episodes. Observers may ask of the spirit, "Who are you?" while the host acts in much the same way as the *wáánaanú* of old (see Bollig 1927:61,63). If the host is particularly inarticulate and only mumbles, someone knowledgeable in Chuukese medicine is called in to coax the spirit into speaking. Considering that calling chants of the *wáánaanú* were classified as medicine, contemporary healers may well be considered the functional equivalents of spirit mediums.

As in prior times, contemporary episodes are often marked by a shift from erratic or violent behavior to a calm state, wherein the spirits speak. Calmness and a quiet, soft voice are significant cultural symbols for the Chuukese; they signify reason and responsiveness to cultural norms. A calm host therefore suggests a spirit open to negotiation, one who may be receptive to human pleas. In general, therefore, the old and the new are similar in that possession involves an articulation process aimed at inducing the spirit to speak in a reasoned manner.

The kinship focus of contemporary possession also represents continuity. Earlier writers agree that possession was in the service of the clan, lineage, or family. The medium in traditional spirit possession was, ideally at least, someone from within the inner family group who showed sensitivity to the spirit's movements. Anyone—man, woman or child—might be chosen as a medium. Bollig records that those upon whom the family looked as its leading candidates were placed on mats and told to relax until one of them suddenly jumped up with a shout, signifying to all that he was selected by the spirit as its medium (Bollig 1927:61). Judging from Bollig's estimate of ninety mediums on Fefan Island, just about every lineage had its own medium, with many apparently having more than one. Spirit powers (*roong*) and medicines were jealously guarded and passed on to someone within the kin network. Just as the *wáánaanú* articulated the lines of communication between spirit and observer, so also did they mediate between generations.

Contemporary episodes are likewise linked to Chuukese kinship obligations, although recent cases appear more restricted to the host's personal problems. If the old *wáánaanú* had self-interest at heart, Bollig noted, it was in offering services to kin for a price or gift (1927:62).

While spirit possession occurring today is similar in form to the type of possession described in the early literature, however, it shows some significant differences. For one, traditional possession was purposeful; it resulted from a deliberate attempt to communicate with spirits of the dead (nature spirits and gods could not be summoned). When serious illness befell someone, the family would often gather to summon the spirit of one of their deceased members in hope that the spirit would reveal the nature of the illness. At other times of family crisis—during a famine or confrontation with another family, for instance—the lineage might call on a spirit to provide crucial information needed to survive unharmed. Spirits were also consulted on the whereabouts of missing valuables or about what would happen in the future. Shortly after the death of someone in the family, relatives would frequently initiate communication with the spirit in the hope of gaining access to knowledge hidden from the living that might have value for them.

Spirit possession in Chuuk, then, appears to have undergone a substantial transformation in this century. Whereas possession incidents described in the early literature were intentional, aimed at obtaining important information from ancestors, and mediated by either males or females, those recorded today are involuntary, occur mostly at times of family stress, and involve mostly women as hosts. It is difficult to date this change with precision, but our data strongly suggest the newer form became increasingly common after World War II. The fact that all four cases of unambiguously intentional possession in our records occurred in the 1930s or 1940s supports this supposition. The model double-hulled canoe (*náán*) that once hung from Chuukese meeting houses to facilitate spirit communication could no longer be found after World War II, although it was remembered by older informants (LeBar 1964: 181–3).

One of the major reasons for the disappearance of voluntary spirit possession was the growing influence of Christianity in Chuuk. What might be called "possession on demand" was discountenanced by a society that had enthusiastically embraced Christianity. Anything that might be interpreted as spirit worship, including offerings to the spirits or supplication for assistance, was judged by missionaries and early local pastors as incompatible with Christian practice. Chuukese, of course, continued to believe in the ghostly powers of sprites, goblins, sea creatures and spirits of the dead much as before. It was one thing to acknowledge the power of the spirit world, however, and quite another to actively seek help from this realm. Chuukese Christians might retain a fearful respect for the traditional spirit world and attempt to counter the ever-present threat of these beings—normally by an appeal to the higher powers that Christianity put at their disposal—but they would not initiate contact with the spirits to secure their assistance. Christianity, therefore, did not eradicate belief in spirits among Chuukese any more than it did among First Century converts in Asia Minor; it simply eliminated, over a period of time, their propitiation.

Today in Chuuk, spirits and God (who has replaced "the gods") do different kinds of work. Spirits adjudicate family conflicts by allowing individuals to express themselves in ways that would normally be considered impolite and improper. They also provoke a temporary inversion of status relationships in Chuukese families. A woman, usually a young woman, takes an authoritative and even preemptory role vis-à-vis others in the family and demands they desist from inappropriate or troubling behavior. God plays a more important role in the community at large, and may be called upon to control spirit activities, or evoked to drive out possessing spirits.

The difference between God and spirits in modern Chuuk is symbolized in their different relations to magical waters. God is associated with holy water, which is often used as a palliative or antidote for possession. Spirits, amorous and shady, are associated with charmed perfume. Several instances in the case materials illustrate these associations: (1) A possessed woman struck a boy she claimed was using charmed perfume, presumably to seduce her; (2) the family of a woman healer used charmed perfume to induce her possession, then used holy water to "calm her down"; (3) two young women were said to have been possessed because some boys were trying to put a spell on them, "trying to get the women to like them." The women used charmed perfume to counteract the spell, and "it turned back on them." A Catholic priest sprinkled holy water on the women as an antidote, and "witnesses say that the water made a hissing sound"; (4) a woman was said to become possessed when exposed to "any kind of perfume"; (5) a woman's possession was attributed to the victim's deceased mother spraying her with perfume; (6) a man afflicted by possession would lose consciousness, after which his family would spray him with perfume, and he would awake, crying and shouting.

Thus, whereas charmed perfumes, associated with love magic and premissionary spirit beliefs, bring on involuntary states like uncontrollable passion and spirit possession, holy water is associated with the Christian God and is used to bring people back to a socially controlled existence.

A FEMALE THING

As the brother of one afflicted girl said, possession is "a female thing." Possession in Chuuk today has indeed become almost a monopoly of females, in marked contrast to the gender distribution earlier in the century. Kubary and Girschner used only male pronouns for the *wáánaanú*, which may reflect the sexist bias of the day, although Girschner recorded *wáánaanú* lore being passed from father to son, older brother to younger brother. Bollig observed that the role of *wáánaanú* was open to both sexes and all ages, depending on the choice made by the spirit (1927:60,63). Bollig's insistence that he knew of two female *wáánaanú* suggests that possession was more common among men than women at this time.

Of the forty-four clear-cut cases of possession from among the fifty-seven reported spirit encounters collected in 1989, all but four of the possessed individuals were women. The victims were mostly in their teens or twenties, although our information on ages is often uncertain. The age profile shows eight victims in their thirties and forties, and at least two much older women: one about sixty and another in her mid-seventies.

This strong linkage of contemporary spirit possession with females has parallels in other parts of the world (Lewis 1971). Mageo (Chapter 2) and Gordon (Chapter 3) report similar observations in Samoa and Tonga respectively, and initial inquiries into possession cases in other island groups in Micronesia suggest a preponderance of female victims there as well. The same linkage with females is reported for Trinidad (Ward 1980), Malaysia (Teoh and Tan 1976), the Philippines (Bulatao 1982) and in the Zar cult found in Ethiopia and Liberia (Torrey 1967), among other places.

The strong gender link that modern possession has acquired, together with our analysis of the context in which it typically occurs, suggests that spirit possession has become a cultural vehicle that women utilize under stress to express grievances and resolve family tensions. In present day Chuuk, as in other island societies undergoing rapid modernization, levels of social stress have heightened even as old strategies for alleviating conflict and tension have disappeared or become attenuated. To take but one example, monetization of the traditional land-based economy has seriously weakened the Chuukese lineage, once the basic family unit, as Hezel (1989; 1990) has pointed out. With the contraction of the extended family, some important female roles in familial affairs have been lost, opportunities for women to share in corporate decision-making within the family unit have diminished, and the network of collateral relatives that once provided support to young people in times of tension is much abbreviated.

What is said here of stress for females is all the more true of Chuukese males, especially young males. For years, signs of distress have been unmistakable among young men in every part of Micronesia: a high suicide rate, serious alcohol abuse, and abnormally high rates of mental illness, as recorded in a recent epidemiological survey (Hezel & Wylie 1992). Indeed, our initial interest in spirit possession stemmed, in large part, from the fact that it appeared to be a female "problem." It seemed to provide one answer to the recurrent question: How do women manage their stress, particularly in view of the several mechanisms that men have available?

Previous studies of suicide and drunkenness in Micronesia have shown the high degree of patterning in these acts (Marshall 1979; Hezel 1981). Both are culturally sanctioned means of venting negative feelings in a society that curtails their expression. Whatever other attractions drinking may have for males, it is commonly used as a way of defining oneself as "drunk" and placing oneself outside usual cultural restrictions, enabling the expression of exasperation or irritation. If a young man is angry at someone in the family, he can get drunk and have his say with a freedom not ordinarily permitted. The drunken youth also draws attention to himself, another enticement for someone who may feel he has been thrust into the shadows of home and community. Suicide serves similar functions for the young victim. In most cases, it is a rebuke to the victim's family for not providing the love and material care expected. At the same time, it is an obvious ploy to draw attention to his plight, not with the intention of remedying this in his short lifetime, but in the hope of winning an eternal place in the affections of the family (Hezel 1987:286–87).

Spirit possession may serve a similar function for women. Possession draws attention to the plight of the afflicted woman inasmuch as a seizure is sure to bring the family together at her bedside. It wins her the family's sympathy, for the victim is treated as a special kind of sick person, obvious to anyone who has watched families show their concern for a possessed individual. Possession also gives her a platform from which to speak. The messages communicated by a possessed person to her family are almost always a plea—sometimes even a command—to mend quarrels, care for neglected members of the family, and resolve the tensions pulling the family apart. It allows a woman—more rarely, a man—to say what would otherwise be forbidden, without incurring disapproval from relatives.

Spirit possession, unlike the largely male phenomena of drunkenness and suicide, is not merely a strategy for coping with stress by expressing grievances and dramatizing personal dissatisfaction; it is a means of resolving domestic conflicts.

This significant difference is related to traditional gender-role differences in Chuuk. Women have always played an important role as peacemakers, whether by initiating truces between warring parties in an earlier age or by conciliating angry family members when strife breaks out within the lineage circle. Where men often threaten the security of their kin group by their rash and aggressive behavior, women are expected to intervene so as to restore harmony and protect their family from harm. Even today, the kinswomen of an obnoxious drunk will stand poised to drag him off to the safety of his household if someone should threaten to respond to his taunts and curses (Marshall 1979:93–94). Hence women, who have always played a vital role in conflict resolution, continue to do so through spirit possession, which is as much a means of redressing grievances as expressing them.

CONCLUSION

By their very nature, possession episodes create ambiguity that requires interpretation. One source of ambiguity concerns the actions of the spirits. They may descend on a host, producing convulsions and outlandish behavior and do no more; attempts at elicitation may or may not get spirits to speak; or a spirit's voice may not be readily recognized. If a spirit does speak, it is often in cryptic form, including unintelligible words, and mumbled.

Another source of ambiguity is the activities of observers and healers. Although specialists in Chuukese medicine may be called in, such experts are no more predictable than frightened kinfolk; their explanations vary, contradict each other, stumble along. The nature of the possession and the name of the spirit may not be immediately apparent, inviting considerable speculation. If there are several episodes, ensuing discussions may multiply possible interpretations. Thus, although there is a general cultural script for possession, each episode is open-ended and generates its own meanings (see Lambek 1989:57).

Because they draw on Chuukese symbols of order, possession episodes are useful vehicles by which to initiate reparative discourse. Initial stages of an episode may involve actions that appear, at first glance, to be wild and unpatterned, but the behavior is incorporated into a well-organized communication process. Lambek sees this as the essential paradox of possession: it has the power to impose order while in apparent disorder (1981:183).

The critical stage in Chuukese possession is therefore not the erratic behavior that marks its onset, but when the spirits speak. Until they speak, there is a distinct possibility that the encounter is with malevolent spirits who bite and devour and cannot be drawn into the cultural order. This central concern with the spirits' speaking suggests that the Chuukese were not, and are not, focusing on what a Westerner might call "the phenomenon." Even the most neutral of Western classifications focuses on the trance state and perhaps classifies such episodes as "altered states of consciousness." But trance is only one part of one phase of the total phenomenon for the Chuukese. The most important "phenomenon" is the speaking. In earlier West Indian fieldwork with trance dancing, Dobbin's informants were very much interested in the phenomenon of trance, much as a Westerner would be. His idiom was "trance" or "altered state"; theirs was "turning" or "do'en dee dance" (Dobbin 1986). Only if the trance/turning were "hot," that is, genuine, would they consider listening to the words of the spirits (the *jombees*). The Chuukese, in contrast, surround the trance itself with an interaction and communication pattern that includes calling the spirits, discerning the spirit. Speech, talk, and discourse are central; trance is but a prelude. If speech does emerge in the articulating process, then the content is about proper Chuukese behavior. In this sense, Catherine Lutz's metaphor for Ifaluk possession applies well to Chuuk: it is moral discourse.

When spirits do speak they initiate a conversation that includes their host, her kin, and perhaps a major segment of the community. The conversation is usually emotionally charged; it is about life, pain, suffering, and/or death. It is a conversation in which the spirits have the final say. Not surprisingly, then, the Chuukese express both fear of and attraction to the spirits, a mystery not unlike Rudolf Otto's (1950) description of the sacred as a *mysterium tremendum et fascinosum,* a realm of experience that excites both fear and fascination.

NOTE
1   The population is now divided almost equally into Catholics and Protestants.

10   Cultural and Experiential Aspects of Spirit Beliefs Among the Toraja

Douglas Hollan

The Toraja, an Austronesian-speaking people, number approximately 350,000 and live in the interior, mountainous regions of South Sulawesi, Indonesia. They are primarily wet-rice farmers who also cultivate small gardens of sweet potatoes, cassava, and assorted vegetables. Although long in contact with the lowland Islamic Bugis and Makassar, the Toraja were relatively free of outside influence until 1906, when the Dutch entered the highlands and began to establish missions and schools. Kinship is traced bilaterally, and Toraja society is stratifed into three primary groups: those of noble or aristocratic descent (*to makaka*); commoners (*to biasa*); and dependents (formerly referred to as *kaunan*). While one's position in this hierarchy theoretically is ascribed at birth, status and prestige also can be achieved by slaughtering animals at community feasts.

The traditional religion of the Toraja, *Alukta,* is based on the veneration and propitiation of gods/spirits (*deata*) and deceased ancestors (*nene'*). Although the majority of the population is now Christian, some middle-age and older villagers remain adherents of *Alukta.* Much of this religious movement can be attributed to political and economic motives, as the Toraja have attempted to acquire educational and employment opportunities that first the Dutch and then the Indonesian national government have preferentially awarded to Christians.

The Toraja embrace of education has been especially important in undermining the traditional social structure and way of life, since it is by learning to read, write, and speak the national language, *Bahasa Indonesia,* that commoners and dependents have gained employment in industry and commerce outside the highlands. The income that is earned in such pursuits is frequently used to buy and slaughter animals at community feasts, prestige-generating actions that formerly only the landed aristocracy could afford.

Much of the data presented in this chapter derive from fieldwork conducted in a relatively isolated village in northwestern Tana Toraja. Christianity did not enter this village until the 1940s, and many of its inhabitants remain *Alukta* adherents.

In this chapter I discuss Toraja understandings about the spirit world, including how and why spirits are thought to interact with humans. I describe ritual performances involving spirits and discuss ways in which beliefs about and experiences with the spiritual world have been affected by the introduction of Christianity.

Throughout, I attempt to assess the emotional and cognitive "saliency" (Spiro 1984) or "directive force" (D'Andrade 1984) of Toraja spirit beliefs. As Hallowell has noted:

> The traditional approach of cultural anthropology, having as one of its primary goals a reliable account of differential modes of life found among the peoples of the world, has not been directly concerned with the behavior of individuals. It has been culture-centered, rather than behavior-centered. . . . No matter how reliable such data are, or whatever their value for comparative and analytic studies of *culture*, of necessity the material is presented from the standpoint of the outside observer. Presented to us in this form, these cultural data do not easily permit us to apprehend, in an integral fashion, the most significant and meaningful aspects of the world of the individual as experienced by him and in terms of which he thinks, is motivated to act, and satisfies his needs. (1955:88)

The notion that we must investigate "saliency" and "dimensions" of spirit beliefs (Howard, Chapter 6) as well as their more formal cultural aspects is an important one. The extent to which spirit beliefs and practices actually structure and motivate behavior should be actively investigated, rather than merely assumed. Some aspects of spirit belief and practice may be more important in shaping thought, emotion, and behavior than others, and individuals may differ in the extent to which they are motivated by spiritual beliefs.

I explore issues related to personal saliency by examining data gathered through participant observation and loosely structured life-history interviews.[1] The interview materials are examined for the ways that individual Toraja respondents use cultural beliefs and symbols to represent and interpret life experiences. This approach is important for the person-centered perspective (LeVine 1982) it provides. In a review of three recent works[2] based on in-depth interviews, Marcus and Fischer note that the mark of such approaches is "the display of discourse—self reflective commentaries on experience, emotion, and self; on dreams, remembrances, associations, metaphors, distortions, and displacements; and on transferences and compulsive behavior repetitions—all of which reveal a behaviorally and conceptually significant level of reality reflecting, contrasting with, or obscured by public cultural forms"[3] (1986:54).

After describing traditional religious ideas and spirit beliefs, I examine the ways and extent such ideas and beliefs have been integrated with village Christianity. In the latter part of the chapter I examine in greater detail beliefs about, and experiences of, two of the most important and personally salient types of Toraja spirit beings—ancestral souls (*nene'*) and gods/spirits (*deata*).[4]

In some respects *nene'* and *deata* correspond precisely to the categories of "gods" and "spirits" outlined in Chapter 1 of this volume. *Nene'* for example, are clearly defined, personlike beings who are thought to take a direct interest in the affairs of humans, while the *deata* are more amorphous beings whose actions and intentions are less predictable and less humanlike. Yet in other respects *nene'* and *deata* defy categorization. For example, some *deata* are godlike to the extent they are bound by elaborate ritual and attended to by high status functionaries, and *nene'* are spiritlike in the way they directly manifest themselves in dreams.

I suggest that the integration and complementarity between these two groups of Toraja spiritual beings, and the cultural and psychological work they perform, is consonant with a local social order that combines hierarchical and egalitarian characteristics (see Chapter 1) and with a broader pan-Indonesian culture that places a high value on balance and the integration of order with disorder in everyday life (Wellenkamp 1988a, Heider 1991). With regard to the latter point, Bateson, commenting on the form and composition of a traditional Balinese painting, has noted that:

> The crux of the picture is in the interwoven contrast between the serene and the turbulent . . . the picture can be seen as an affirmation that to choose either turbulence or serenity as a human purpose would be a vulgar error. . . . The unity and integration of the picture assert that neither of these contrasting poles can be chosen to the exclusion of the other, because the poles are mutually dependent. (Bateson 1972:151–152)

TRADITIONAL CULTURE AND RELIGION

According to van der Veen's published version of a Toraja ritual invocation that narrates the origin of the world, the world was created when the initially undifferentiated universe was separated into the heavens, the earth, and the underworld. The earth was divided into rice fields, mountains, rivers, and other geological features characteristic of the present-day landscape, and Puang Matua, the "Old Lord," used his bellows to create the ancestors of humans and of certain plants and animals, who later descended from the Upperworld to the Earth (Van der Veen 1965).

The first humans purportedly lived in close contact with the gods and enjoyed direct access to the upper world via a ladder or staircase. Later, however, after an important taboo was violated—in one account, a prohibition against brother-sister incest; in another, a prohibition against theft—the ladder to the Upperworld was destroyed (Nooy-Palm 1979:145). The gods then became "inaccessible," "unapproachable," and "not to be beheld." They became "enclosed behind a curtain" and "enfolded within a wall"; they were "sleeping ones" and "slumbering ones" who had to be aroused and awakened by prayers (van der Veen 1965:31–35).

The gods later established another, more comprehensive set of ritual prescriptions (*aluk*) and prohibitions (*pemali*) that continues to guide traditional *Alukta*[5] practice today. In return for compliance with these ritual and behavioral regulations—including periodic offerings of water buffaloes, pigs, chickens, *pangngan* (areca nut, betel, and lime), and other valuable substances—the gods (*deata*) and deceased ancestor figures (*nene'*) are thought to be obligated to provide humans with bountiful crops, thriving livestock, and numerous, healthy children. Should these prescriptions and prohibitions be ignored, humans can expect illness, misfortune, and death. The observation of these rites and prohibitions forms the core of traditional religious practice.

A number of these themes resonate with the concerns and interests of contemporary villagers, notably, an awareness of the tension that exists between order and disorder (Wellenkamp 1988a); the nostalgic sense that times were once better, either in one's own life or in the past; and the importance of rules for the orderly conduct of life. Also noteworthy is that relations between humans and spiritual beings are conceptualized in reciprocal and pragmatic terms: one can expect blessings (*tua'*) of fortune and prosperity, but only if giving of oneself or one's property in return. Thus Nene'na ("Grandfather of") Limbong,[6] an expert on traditional beliefs and practices, says that sacrifices and offerings are the tools by which blessings from the gods and ancestors are secured. Conversely, omissions or transgressions of *aluk* are viewed as "debts" that must be repaid.

VILLAGE CHRISTIANITY

Christianity, as it is practiced by village adherents—particularly those living in areas some distance from the market towns of Makale and Rantepao—is infused with elements of the traditional religious system. Many of the fundamental beliefs of *Alukta* have been retained by directly substituting Christian terms for concepts found in the traditional religion. This has occurred both because early missionaries made a self-conscious attempt to graft Christian doctrine and beliefs onto preexisting indigenous concepts, in keeping with their view that primitive religions had devolved from belief in an authentic Christian-like God to a corrupted state of spirit worship and polytheism (Bigalke 1981), and because villagers themselves readily make these substitutions. Nene'na Tandi, for example, a prominent member of the Protestant Church, says, "Christians say that their bridge to God is Jesus Christ. The *Aluk* people also have a bridge to their creator, [namely] the *deata*. There is no difference. They [Jesus Christ and the *deata*] are both the same." He also directly equates the *pemali*, "prohibitions," of *Alukta* to the Ten Commandments of Christianity.

A few major differences between *Alukta* and Christian beliefs cannot be so easily reconciled. Whereas *Alukta* adherents worship the gods and ancestors by maintaining prohibitions and performing rites and rituals involving costly offerings and sacrifices, Christians worship God by praying, by contributing to the church, and by upholding Christian tenets of conduct. The Christian belief that God will provide prosperity and well-being in return for such seemingly simple acts of worship strikes village Christians as both welcome, and, at times, puzzling and disconcerting (see Hollan 1988b). Still, for adherents of both religions, the relationship with spiritual beings is essentially the same: just like the traditional gods and ancestors, God is entreated to provide protection and blessings in the form of large rice harvests, plentiful livestock, healthy children, and a long life in exchange for specific acts of worship.

Another major difference is that Christians are officially barred from performing a number of rituals directed toward the *deata*. These restrictions stem from the 1920s when the Dutch mission in Tana Toraja established a commission to devise guidelines for distinguishing between religious practice, *aluk*, participation in which would be prohibited for Christians; and customary practices, *ada'*, which Christians could continue to follow (Bigalke 1981:221). Although discussion continues regarding lines of separation between "religion" and "custom," these early guidelines are still officially endorsed today (Wellenkamp 1988a).

THE INFLUENCE OF SPIRITS ON FATE AND FORTUNE

One of the implications of believing prosperity is linked to compliance with the *aluk* and *pemali* or to the Ten Commandments is that wealth becomes symbolic of moral and spiritual standing. If individuals prosper, it is generally assumed they have fulfilled their obligations to spiritual beings; if they do not prosper, they are suspected of having failed in their obligations to these beings. Lack of prosperity reflects negatively on one's own or one's family's moral and social worth, and is one of the most common reasons villagers initiate offerings to spiritual beings or convert from one religion to another.

Few villagers would assert, however, that compliance with religious rules and practices guarantees wealth and prosperity. Many also contend that good fortune is at least paritally dependent on one's practical efforts and labor. It is more accurate to say that villagers believe that spiritual beings offer opportunities for wealth and prosperity but that realization requires an expenditure of personal energy. Thus, while spiritual beings might ensure rice seed will germinate and fields will eventually fill with water, villagers must plant and care for the rice seedlings to bring them to fruition. This notion—that one must actively seize the good fortune offered by spiritual beings—is a recurrent motif in both folk tales and in respondents' accounts of their life experiences. In one common scenario, a person begins with a single chicken. Through careful husbandry and the beneficence of spiritual beings, the chicken reproduces and is eventually sold to buy a piglet. The piglet is then raised and sold to buy a buffalo, which in turn is sold to buy rice land.

Although lack of prosperity reflects negatively on moral and spiritual standing, villagers also believe there are limits to human agency and responsibility. Both Christians and *Alukta* adherents say that ultimately one's fate lies in the hands of spiritual beings. One can long for good fortune and work hard to attain it, yet all prosperity is actually a "gift." Nene'na Tandi comments, for example:

> Indeed, it is true when elders say that your fate/fortune can't be changed by humans, only by God. So we can't buy it, and we can't take it with force. . . . It [good fate/fortune] is all a gift from God. There is not a human alive who can command, "Today I will be wealthy." "Tomorrow I will be wealthy." "The day after tomorrow I will be wealthy." No, that is not true. Good fortune is only from God. . . . If, for example, we deliberately try to take it [fate/fortune] . . . after awhile we'll get tuberculosis, or after awhile we'll go crazy.

In addition to spiritual beings associated with the Upperworld, the Lowerworld, and the Afterlife, Toraja villagers also recognize several types of earthly spirits (see Hollan and Wellenkamp 1994:34–38). Although many of these beings are thought potentially dangerous, they usually are not propitiated; rather, villagers, knowing these spirits' usual abodes and habits, generally try to avoid them. Their overall significance varies considerably from individual to individual.

TORAJA RITUALS AND THE SPIRIT WORLD

Traditional Toraja religion is organized around two separate and distinct ritual spheres: "smoke-descending" (*rambu solo'*) rites, addressed to the souls of the newly dead (*bombo*) and ancestor figures (*nene'*), focusing on funerals; and "smoke-ascending" (*rambu tuka'*) rites, addressed to the gods and spirits (*deata*), focusing on fertility, prosperity, purification, healing, and thanksgiving. While the relationship between the two ritual spheres is thought of as complementary in nature, much as that between husband and wife or between the verbs "to leave" and "to return," "the objects and activities associated with one ritual sphere should be kept strictly separate from the other sphere" (Wellenkamp 1988a:313). As Wellenkamp notes:

> Each sphere has its own set of directions, time of day, plants, food, vocabulary, and so forth with which it is associated. Prominent in smoke-ascending rituals, commonly referred to as good (*melo*) rituals, are rice and poultry; the colors

white, pink, green, turquois, and especially yellow; and the directions north, east, right, and up. Prominent in smoke-descending rituals, commonly referred to as bad (*kadake*) rituals, are water buffalo meat, corn, and sweet potato; the color black; and the directions south, west, left, and down. . . . It is prohibited (*pemali*), for instance, to wear black clothing to a smoke-ascending ritual, to harvest rice or remove rice from one's ricebarn after having eaten meat from a funeral, and to cook any meat received at one type of ritual with meat received from the other. If such prohibitions are violated, misfortune in some form such as illness, famine, infertility, or death is believed to inevitably follow. (1988a:313)

The orderliness of Toraja ritual is both model of and model for the order and constraint of everyday life. Linguistic forms mark social and geographical space; the physical layout of villages, houses, rice barns, and certain trees and plants are carefully coordinated with the cardinal directions; certain rituals and games may only be performed, and certain foods only eaten, at designated times of the year; differences in social status are carefully marked by type and quality of meat received at community feasts and the order in which it is received, by seating position, architectural decoration, the location of burial vaults, and so on; and art and architectural designs are dominated by geometric patterns and motifs.

This concern with order and constraint is found at the personal, psychological level as well. Villagers place a high value on emotional equanimity and on the maintenance of smooth, nonconflictual interpersonal relationships (Hollan 1988a, 1992; Wellenkamp 1988a). Conversely, they attempt to avoid those emotional states—for example, extreme anger, grief, or anxiety—thought to result in severe mental or physical illness, or to induce persons to act in offensive or shameful ways (and so cause others to become emotionally upset or vengeful). The close interconnections and feedback that the Toraja conceptualize between social/moral and emotional order, on the one hand, and social/moral and emotional disorder, on the other, are clearly evident in the metaphors used to describe both types of phenomena (Hollan and Wellenkamp 1994:45–46).

ENCOUNTERS WITH BOMBO AND NENE'

Alukta adherents (and some Christians) refer to the souls of the recent dead or those near death as *bombo*. According to traditional belief, *bombo* are thought to linger among the living until funeral ceremonies are held for them, after which they begin their journey to the Afterworld.[7] Although some villagers downplay beliefs about *bombo*, Indo'na Tiku claims that her fear of such beings led her to quickly entomb her foster mother following her death, and To Minaa[8] Sattu claims that he has, more than once, actually seen a bombo:

(Have you ever seen a *bombo*?) When I was [still] herding buffalo, I saw one. [The *bombo*] of a person who had not yet died. (Not yet dead?) Yes. Not yet dead. There was a funeral going on—this was before I was married—and I had gone there to *ma'badong* [sing a funeral chant]. [After it was over], all the people went home. [But] I stayed at the rice barn and sat for a while. [Then] I decided to go home, and I started down the trail. Just as I started, I met someone in the middle of the trail. I asked, "Who is it? Who is it?," but she didn't answer. I looked [and thought], "Oh, this is a *bombo*." She had a string of coins around her waist and a piece of cloth on her head. And she had a plate on her head [picking up a plate to demonstrate]. [The appearance of the apparition is identical to that of a female *tatau*—an effigy of the dead constructed during traditional funeral rites.] I looked [and thought], "This is a woman from X who has come to Paku Asu. She heard the *badong*, and her *bombo* has come." I met her in the middle of the trail and asked, "Who is it?" But she didn't answer! I looked [and thought], "This is a *bombo*."

[Then] I ran straight to the dead person's house. I entered the house and there she [the *bombo*] was! She was sitting behind the dead person. She ate the betel and sweet potato that the dead person had been given [as an offering]. And she drank the palm wine [that the dead person had been given]. And after she had eaten meat and sweet potato and corn, she took some *pangngan* [betel, lime, and areca]. Her name was Ne' Bua. (Did you know her?) Yes, I knew her because she was a relative of mine. When I went home, I told people that I had seen Ne' Bua and that she would soon die [in accordance with the belief that a person's *bombo* is only visible if he or she is near death]. And sure enough, about one week later, she died.

At some point *bombo* become ancestral spirits, *nene'*, a term also used to refer to living grandparents. It is difficult to overemphasize the cultural and psychological significance of *nene'* for the Toraja, both Christians and *Alukta*. Like God and the *deata*, *nene'* are thought to watch over the affairs of humans, directly affecting their fates and fortunes. Generally, however, *nene'* are viewed as having a more protective, parental role in their relationships with humans than *deata*, who are more feared.

Nene' are most directly acknowledged during smoke-descending rituals (funerals and secondary burials) when they are implored to bring blessings of health and prosperity. Such solicitations of compassion and generosity, embedded in an interpersonal style of "appeal" (Schieffelin 1976), are widespread among the Toraja and are related to a hierarchical social structure and to cultural values emphasing interdependence (see Wellenkamp 1992; Hollan and Wellenkamp 1994).

Some *nene'*—those for whom the highest level of funeral is performed and for whom sacrifices are made at subsequent rituals (the *ma'nene'* and *ma'maro* in the Paku Asu area)—are said to become *deata* eventually. In general, long-dead ancestral spirits are considered more powerful than the recent dead, although the recent dead, especially parental and grandparental figures, are more prominent in villagers' lives.

While ancestral spirits are generally thought to remain immaterial, they are sometimes seen in dreams. Such dreams, like spirit-attack nightmares, are thought to be "real" experiences in which the dreamer's mind or soul directly communicates with *nene‘*. Dreams of ancestral spirits are one of the most common types reported by respondents, and are usually thought to be prophetic. Ambe‘na Patu, when asked if he has had dreams of deceased relatives, replied:

> Yes, I have. I've seen my grandmother and my mother and other people who have died . . . (Did you speak to them?) Some I spoke to and some I didn't, I just saw them . . . (What does your grandmother say [in dreams]?) She talks. Sometimes she talks, sometimes she doesn't. But [in the dream] I think that she's still alive. When I awake, [I think], "Wah, what did I see in my dream?"

In many dreams, deceased relatives bring gifts (e.g., vegetables, cloth, medicine) or convey special talents or powers (such as the ability to heal or knowledge of amulets). Such dreams are considered auspicious in nature. Indo‘na Rante says:

> When we dream like that [of one's deceased parent], often they are true . . . If we dream he/she comes carrying vegetables for the pigs, [that means] our pigs will thrive . . . Also usually if we're sick, and then we dream that the dead person comes bringing us water, we quickly recover! Or for example, if he/she comes, bringing us a letter, we will receive money . . . Yes, several times I have had dreams like those examples.[9]

In other dreams, deceased relatives may offer the dreamer advice, of either a general nature (e.g., "Take good care of your children") or containing specific instructions. Indo‘na Rante and her family changed residences, for instance, after she dreamed that her husband's deceased mother told her to move next to the mother-in-law's former house. Nene‘na Tandi converted to Christianity (for the second time) when he was very ill and his wife's aunt dreamed that he would die if he were to remain *Alukta*:

> The night before she had a dream, and early in the morning she came to tell me [about it]. She herself sent [someone] to go find the minister . . . I didn't know anything about it. Not until the minister arrived did she tell me, "It's like this. I called for the minister and the church elders . . . so that you would be returned to being a Christian." I said, "Why, Mama?" She said, "Last night I dreamed a person wearing white clothes came, a very old person. He/she told me, 'If Nene‘na Tandi remains *Aluk To Dolo*, we will have to take his spirit'. . .Then I said [to her], 'Thank you [for telling him] . . . People prayed and right after they said, 'Amen,' I asked for rice porridge!" . . . After a week, I could walk [and then] I went to the church.

Before Nene‘na Tandi converted, however, he had to convince his *Alukta* parents to agree to it. He eventually persuaded them by asking if they would be happy were he to die as the dream predicted, and because they thought if they "forced" him to remain *Alukta*, he might become insane.

Ambe'na Patu once had a dream of his deceased mother, who told him that he should go ahead with his plans to build a house, even though he thought he still did not have the necessary resources.

> My mother came [in the dream] [and said], "Gather together the bamboo." [I said], "Ah, there isn't enough rice yet [to feed the villagers who would assist him with the labor]." . . . She said, "The point is, just do it." Wah, I woke up and I thought and thought about it. [I thought], "Where am I going to get this rice?"

Ambe'na Patu said that he was able to obtain the rice from a variety of sources and build his house, and thus the dream was "indeed true."

What is noteworthy about such dream experiences is not only the importance that villagers attach to them, but also the psychological support they provide, and the desire for continued ancestral attachment that they illustrate. This is especially clear in the following dream, in which To Minaa Sattu's dream spirit attempts to visit his deceased parents in the Afterlife, even though such a journey is generally thought to be life threatening:

> (Have you thought about your death, about going to *Puya*?) Me? (Yes.) Yes, I've already [been there], when I was sick, I went to *Puya*. (You've already been there?) Yes, when I was dreaming, you know? . . . I went up a mountain first, and then descended [the other side]. I came to a forest . . . and after that there was some barren ground. A desert. And then I arrived in *Puya* . . . There was a person who came to meet me, but I didn't know his/her name. He/she said, "Why did you come here?" I said, "I want to see my father and mother, because they have been at *Puya* for a long time." The person grabbed me [saying], "If you meet with your father and mother, you will die!" My reply was, "I don't care if I die." The person pointed out my father's house . . . It was in the mountains . . . I wanted to go to his house, but the person forbid me! . . . He/she said, "Go back!" . . . I said, "If I can't meet with my father and mother, then show me their water buffalo." The person said, "Your father and mother's buffalo are there on the mountains, being herded." Then I left *Puya* . . . Then I arrived at my house. So that's how it was. I've already been there [to *Puya*]. . . .

Inauspicious dreams, in which deceased relatives request or openly confiscate valued persons or property, also are common, though among my respondents they appear less frequently than dreams of receiving gifts or advice. Indo'na Rante reports one such dream:

> One time I dreamed that my mother came and asked for a chicken, which I gave her. Suddenly, one of my children died. Yes, she/he died [and] I called the *to minaa* [who explained], "that's the way it is. If a dead person comes [in a dream] and [takes] a chicken, pig, or buffalo, that represents our children. Or it may even represent ourselves!"

Nene'na Limbong once dreamed that he himself was attacked by an ancestral spirit, in this case, his own father:

> One time I dreamed that my [dead] father came and tried to take me away with him! He came to me and said that he wanted to take me because my time in the village was up, and I had to go. I said, "I don't want to go!" But he grabbed my arms and tried to take me. He said, "I must take you." But I said that I didn't want to go! [I said], "It's not time for me to follow you!" But he grabbed my arms again and tried to take me. I struggled with him, and he tried to grab me. I was sitting at the front of the rice barn, but he dragged me away from the barn. But I continued to struggle. As he dragged me by the front of the house [which was directly opposite the rice barn], I wrapped my legs around a stone and held on. Then I was able to pull my arms away, and I ran! After that, my father left, and I didn't see him again.

Nene'na Limbong says that he had this dream years before our interviews, sometime after the death of his father in 1948. Although he was still relatively young at the time, he was already familiar with conventional dream interpretations (see Hollan 1989; Hollan and Wellenkamp 1994) and knew immediately that the dream was prophetic, foretelling his own death. Frightened by this prospect, he went to a dream expert, who reinterpreted the dream and gave it a new meaning. The assault on Nene'na Limbong was not a sign of his impending death; rather, it was a reminder to Nene'na Limbong to feed and nurture a hungry father. Later, in accordance with the directions of the *to minaa*, Nene'na Limbong sacrificed a pig to his father.

Toraja beliefs about the survival of the human soul after death and about the direct involvement of *nene'* in human affairs are further illustrated by Nene'na Tandi as he explains why he need not fear that villagers will steal his daughter's inheritance after his death:

> If I were to know that on this day, at this moment I was going to die, like I said earlier, there is a kind of poison . . . it's a kind of oath. I have one child [and I might say to people], "Whoever bothers or takes any of my possessions [before my daughter can claim them], . . . I will come [as an ancestral spirit] and take you [i.e., kill you], not you yourself . . . but all of your children and your wife, I will take them all." It is also said [by dying persons] . . . "I'm above watching you." . . . Those words are heavy ones. It's said to be an oath of a dead person . . . So here . . . [a dying person] sends for . . . elders and rich people [and says], "Sit here and listen to these words." . . . So I don't feel hesitant/worried [thinking] that if tomorrow or the day after I die, all of my things might disappear because my child isn't here [in the village]. No![10]

ENCOUNTERS WITH DEATA

While order, constraint, and "coolness" are emphasized in everyday life, sometimes lack of constraint is expected and even encouraged (Wellenkamp 1988a: 315). This usually occurs in the context of smoke-ascending rituals when the *deata*, with their life-giving powers of fertility, prosperity, purification, and heal-ing—which are thought to involve elements of "heat" and disorder—are asked for their blessings. Like some other highland groups of insular Southeast Asia (Wellenkamp 1988a; McKinley 1979), the Toraja believe that powerful, unruly cosmic and supernatural forces normally residing outside the village must occa-sionally (and briefly) be brought inside, to ensure continued prosperity and to rid the community of disease and misfortune.

The Ma'maro

The *ma'maro* ceremony is one of those occasions when the *deata* are asked for blessings and the only one in which they physically manifest themselves by pos-sessing villagers.[11] While *ma'maro* ceremonies may be organized for a number of reasons, including as a prelude or denouement to other types of rituals (Hol-lan 1984:244; Nooy-Palm 1986:121–51), they, like all the smoke-ascending rit-uals, are primarily concerned with furthering the prospects of wealth and prosperity and with avoiding illness and misfortune. Previously, *ma'maro* cere-monies were held regularly, perhaps annually; this has changed, however, with the introduction of Christianity. Now, Christians are strongly discouraged from holding smoke-ascending rituals, including the *ma'maro*, since they involve sac-rifices to "pagan" gods and spirits. This decline in community participation has meant that smoke-ascending rituals of all kinds have become much less frequent and, according to many *Alukta* adherents, less efficacious, since the presence of nonbelievers at such ceremonies may offend the *deata* and lead them to ignore human pleas for health and prosperity.

Ma'maro ceremonies are usually held in the dry months between last harvest and new planting, and after the recently dead have been buried.[12] The cere-monies may last several days or longer depending on type and complexity, and involve the sacrifice of scores of chickens and usually some pigs. As Wellenkamp notes:

> Images of heat and fire are prominent in the *ma'maro*, as are images of dissolu-tion, disorder, and transformation. Some of the feats reportedly performed by rit-ual specialists involve crushing eggs and crabs that then become whole again, and chickens that are killed and eaten but from the pile of bones are brought back to life. . . .
> The importance of disorder and lack of constraint is further reflected in the prominence of the chicken as the main sacrificial animal at the *ma'maro*. As Crys-tal and Yamashita (1987:64–65) point out in their discussion of *ma'bugi* (a ritual very similar to the *ma'maro*), the chicken is associated with, among other things, aggression, dynamism, and possibly illicit sexual behavior. According to ritual verses, the ancestor of chickens, *Puang Maro* (Lord of *Maro* or Madness), con-stantly pecked, a reference perhaps to incestuous behavior. (Crystal and Yamashita 1987:65) (Wellenkamp 1988a:315–316)

Like most Toraja rituals, the *ma'maro* ceremony consists of a number of stages and activities spread out over hours and days. In the following account I discuss only those activities directly related to human interactions with the spirit world.[13]

A central activity of the *ma'maro* ceremony in the Paku Asu area is the construction of a tall trident-shaped banner called a *bate*. Made of bamboo poles and decorated with the red leaves of the *tabang* plant (*Cordyline terminalis*) and with heirlooms such as swords and cloths thought to possess magical powers, the *bate* is used like a lightning rod to attract and hold the attention of the spirit world throughout the ceremony. The *bate* is first erected in the hosts' courtyard and later moved to an open ritual field. In both places participants become possessed, in conjunction with the rhythmic chanting of paired verses called *gelong*.

When *gelong* are performed as a prelude to the arrival of the spirits,[14] they are accompanied by the driving beat of a drum. They are performed while a group of participants hold hands and dance, initially circling slowly, then increasing the tempo of their movements as the tempo of the singing increases.[15] The *gelong* call upon the *deata* of the Upperworld, Earth, and Lowerworld to gather together at the site of the ceremony, promising submission if they do:

Spirits here in this village
Lord (*puang*) here in this village
Ruler (*datu*) at the edge of the house
Come here, let us be together jumping,
Spirits surround/cover my body
Lord at the edge of my outside
Do not go far from the jumpers
I follow the custom of the ancestors
Exemplar guarding the earth
Does not want to be left behind
Returns to be remembered.

Whatever you desire
Whatever you wish in your heart
Go there and take me
Even if only for one night
Make visible your world
Whatever you desire from my heart
Go there and take me
Go and take it from me
Even if only for one night. (Zerner 1981:106–107).

You must possess me,
Press on as I feel faint,
Awareness is ending,
You drive me quivering to earth.
(Crystal and Yamashita 1987:54).

Other verses describe the ritual ground as "truly red, surely on fire" (Zerner 1981:106) and speak of monumental changes in the earth's surface: mountains are pressed down and valleys are lifted up (Zerner 1981:106) while rivers reverse direction (Nooy-Palm 1979:182). Zerner observes: "The cataclysmic geophysical imagery . . . is both a sign of the powers of the arriving spirits and the turmoil, movement, and agitation which follow as people invite and are taken by the spirits" (1981:106).

EXPERIENTIAL ASPECTS OF SPIRIT POSSESSION

As the *deata* draw near and "close to the skin" (Zerner 1981:107), certain participants, including relatively younger men and older women, enter a state of possession called *ma'deata* in which they may beat others and themselves with sticks and branches, cut or poke the skin with knives and swords, walk on fire or burning embers, and behave or move in sexually provocative ways.[16] Such behaviors are viewed as extraordinary and as evidence of the presence and power of the spirits.

Following Lambek's suggestion (1989:56) that possession be viewed as a system of communication that "establishes channels, senders, receivers, and information," the following sections examine Toraja possession behavior and experience from both the possessed's and observers' points of view. My data come from Jane Wellenkamp's and my own observations of two quite lengthy *ma'maro* ceremonies as well as from extensive, open-ended interviews with several ritual participants.

The Possessed's Point of View

Once participants are "with" (*sisola*) or "taken by" (*diala*) the *deata*, the *deata* are said to order them to perform specific behaviors. Should a possessed person refuse to obey a *deata*'s request, people say that he or she will become seriously ill, crazy, or die. According to To Minaa Sattu:

> (Once) our stomach starts going like this [he breathes very shallowly and rapidly to force his stomach to expand and contract slightly] . . . and our breath becomes rapid . . . If we were not to obey . . . after we had already started doing that [rapid breathing and expansion and contraction of the stomach], we would become crazy if we didn't obey. And become sick. That's why those who don't obey have thin bodies . . . Yes, they have thin bodies, those who don't obey. And they become permanently sick inside . . . Inside their bodies. And that is the worst sickness of all! So those who don't obey age very quickly.

Others agreed that one has no choice but to obey the *deata* once a request has been made. One wealthy, high-status man said that for some time he has tried to persuade his wife not to participate in the *ma'maro*, fearing that she would eventually be hurt while beating herself with branches. He said, however, his wife fears it would be far more dangerous to disobey the *deata*'s commands than to continue to participate. Another person reported that the *deata* who possessed her once said they would kill anyone who tried to interrupt or prevent her participation.

Notably only a small minority of people present at a *ma'maro* become possessed,[17] often those who have both a personal and family history of such involvement.

While the feats and behaviors performed by the possessed (*to kandeatan*) during a *ma'maro* ceremony may vary, many involve aggressive acts directed against self or others. During one of the ceremonies we witnessed, for example, the first person possessed was an older woman who ran through the audience kicking people. In other instances, *to kandeatan* chased after people with branches and sticks. One person says that he often tries to engage others in kick fights when he is possessed, and another man reported that he puts on a pair of buffalo horns and charges at people.

Acts of autoaggression are especially prominent, however. Many participants beat themselves on the forearms or the back of the legs with sticks and branches, or press the blades of machetes or ancient swords into the flesh of their forearms, their stomachs, or calves. Others lean over and press their stomachs into the blade of a sword held horizontally at waist height, either in front of the possessed person or behind him or her. Still others use small knives to prick wounds in their foreheads or slash cuts in their tongues. (The blood that flows from head and tongue cutting is then smeared on the leaves of the *tabang* plant and used to heal sick villagers.) One woman we observed walked repeatedly over a small fire, eventually putting it out by stamping on it.

Based on observations and interviews, *ma'maro* participants generally appear to experience a temporary state of psychological dissociation "in which ongoing behavior is not subject to recall when the actor emerges from that state" and in which "the actor behaves, but his behavior is closed to his conscious level of awareness" (Spiro 1978:159). According to To Minaa Sattu, for example:

> [We] feel our bodies go like this [jump of their own accord] . . . If we are possessed, we are just like a crazy person! We don't recognize anyone. [We think], "Who is this?" [when looking at others]. . .Only after the *gelong* is recited [the sacred verses which end the *ma'maro* ritual] do we begin to remember a little.

While most people claim to have amnesia for the period that they are possessed, in a few instances participants report visualizing the *deata*. To Minaa Sattu says, for example, that during some *ma'maro* celebrations he has seen the *deata*:

> (So when the *deata* came, could you see them?) Yes, I could see them! They looked like humans. But they had very small bodies. And their hair was blue . . . [They] were like shadows . . . (Male or female?) A mixture, just like humans. Many came. . . . (So there were more than one?) Yes, lots!

A similar vision was reported by another man who claimed that he, too, had seen tiny humanlike figures (no larger that the end joint of his smallest finger), though in his case the *deata* appeared to have blond hair.

Though people say the possessed have no choice over acts the *deata* ask them to perform,[18] individuals tend to "specialize" in certain kinds of feats, performing them consistently over the years, and some individuals are renown for performing particular behaviors. There also is considerable individual variation in the intensity with which *to kandeatan* attack themselves. Some people hit themselves hard enough to raise welts, while others handle the blades or branches delicately, leaving no physical marks. The following excerpt from my field notes describes several feats performed by a young man who exhibited especially intense and violent behavior:

> He cracks himself repeatedly over the head with bamboo stalks—hitting himself hard enough to crack and splinter the bamboo. Then he uses a bunch of small branches (which are used to sweep the house or yard) to whip himself on the forearms and the backs of the legs. Next he uses a long knife or sword to press into his forearms, his legs, the back of his neck, and his stomach. He then places the knife, blade up, in a small slit in the earth and stands on it in his bare feet. Then he repeatedly rolls over the blade on his back. Next, several men brace a sword against the ground with the tip of the blade pointed up, and he leans over the sword and places his entire body weight on its tip, drawing his feet completely off the ground. Finally, he lies under a mat on the ground while men pile large stones at least two feet deep on top of him. After he is completely buried, he attempts to explode out of the rubble, but the weight of the rocks causes him to stumble, and he struggles to his feet. He then repeats the burial and resurrection routine three times.

Aside from those who intentionally drew blood from their foreheads or tongues to use for healing purposes, we witnessed only one person hurt in a *ma'maro* ritual—a man who stumbled and hit his shin. Though his injury was minor, he appeared alarmed by the sight of his blood, and some people commented the *deata* probably were angry at his failure to follow their orders, or for his lack of faith in their powers.

From the *Alukta* point of view, the lack of injuries at most *ma'maro* ceremonies is explained by the fact that although the *deata* order villagers to perform these apparently punishing acts, they also use their power to protect *to kandeatan* from serious injury—contingent upon the possessed person's faith and obedience. In addition, people say that wounds incurred during a possession ceremony are immediately cured through the healing powers of the sacred *tabang* plant, the leaves of which are rubbed and massaged on the *to kandeatan*'s body during and after a performance. The highly theatrical nature of many punishing acts also minimizes injuries; blades are held to the skin, but only rarely are they pressed into the flesh with significant pressure, and many of the swords and knives used to cut and poke at the skin appear to be quite old and blunt.

Interestingly, despite the fact that the possessed are not held formally accountable for their behavior during a *ma'maro* ceremony, since ostensibly they act only in accordance with the wishes and demands of the *deata*, several *to kandeatan* we spoke with are somewhat embarrassed or ashamed by their ritual behavior (which is described to them by their relatives and neighbors). This illustrates how deeply internalized is the general cultural disvaluation of losses or lapses of self-awareness and self-control. Thus, when To Minaa Sattu is asked to describe what it feels like to be possessed, he replies:

> Our bodies start going like this [jumping and twitching of their own accord] . . . And when we are in front of all the people [acting out the *deata*'s wishes], we aren't ashamed. Because we have been seized by the *deata*. But after we have recovered for a while, we feel ashamed a little bit. (Really?) Yes, really [laughing and smiling with embarrassment]. (Why do you feel ashamed?) Because we [pause] . . . Because we begin to remember, "Oh, this is what the *deata* had me do." But most people aren't seized [by the *deata*]. That's why we feel a bit ashamed. Because everyone has been watching us. That's why feelings of shame begin to arise a little bit . . . All possessed people feel a little bit ashamed after they have begun to recover! But what can one do? It is not we [the *to kandeatan*] who are in control. Indeed, it is not we who are in control. It is the *deata* who are in control. [It is they] who seize us and bring us in front of all the people. What is one to do?

While To Minaa Sattu reiterates the cultural doctrine that people who become possessed are not responsible for their actions, he himself became so discomforted by his ritual behavior over the years that he began to drink magical water which, he claims, prevents him from becoming possessed. At the time of the interviews, ten years had passed since To Minaa Sattu had last become possessed.[19]

THE OBSERVERS' POINT OF VIEW

How do observers view possession behavior? Most people, Christian and *Alukta* alike, appear to accept the authenticity of spirit possession. Some Christians say that possession behavior is foolish or silly, and they sometimes compare the *deata*'s powers unfavorably to those of God. Others criticize *Alukta* adherents for becoming involved with "satanic" forces. But Christians do not, for the most part, doubt that possessed people are under the influence of spiritual forces or that their ritual behavior is beyond their personal control. Many villagers are impressed by the apparently miraculous feats performed during the course of a *ma'maro* ceremony. Ambe'na Kondo remarks, for example: "If we who do not *ma'deata* [become possessed] tried to [do what those who are possessed do] . . . we would surely die!"

Many villagers also are frightened by the sight of those possessed. Indo'na Tiku, who enjoys watching kick fights, feels differently about watching people who are possessed: "I [only] go for a while to watch, and then I return home. Because in my view those *maro* people are like . . . crazy people . . . They jump up and down. Have you seen them?" (Yes) "They are . . . exactly like crazy people."

Asked what she feels when she watches someone who is possessed, she says, "I am afraid to watch. Especially if they use knives or a machete [to apparently cut themselves], eeh, I am very frightened to see that!"

Indo'na Sapan, asked the same question, replies, "We feel frightened, because they don't feel anything." And Ambe'na Kondo remarks, "People who are possessed, they aren't conscious anymore. . . . They don't feel anything. If we look at them, we are frightened."

The fear of watching possession behavior seems connected to the realization that the possessed are no longer in "conscious" control of their behavior. Such losses of consciousness are often directly associated with states of anger, madness, and drunkenness (Hollan and Wellenkamp 1994:461–505). Ambe'na Kondo, says, "[People who become possessed] don't remember anything. They are like [he pauses to think] an angry person!"

Similarly, Nene'na Tandi comments, "Possessed people are like drunk people . . . They are like mad people or drunken people. They don't feel anything."

Insane people are often referred to as *to maro-maro*, literally "*maro* people," and the behavior of the possessed is often compared to that of the insane. Recall that To Minaa Sattu says quite explicitly, "If we are possessed, we are just like a crazy person!"

The audience's association between possession behavior and culturally disvalued states of anger, madness, and drunkenness also helps to explain why *to kandeatan* may feel ashamed of their possession behavior.

INTERPRETATION AND ANALYSIS

1) Possession behavior among the Toraja is striking in its inversion of order and constraint in everyday life, both culturally and psychologically. This seems to fit Levy's observation that some form of dissociative-like behavior is to be expected in cultural systems that:

> (a) encourage the development throughout the life cycle of organized systems of meaning; (b) select among them in a limited way for acceptable everyday adult "selves"; and (c) support the culturally prevalent dissociated systems by giving them expression and interpretation in special, bounded contexts. (1973:492)

Among the Toraja, overtly aggressive, and perhaps sexual, aspects of the self seem organized outside of conscious awareness. However, the ongoing erosion of possession belief and practice indicates that agreement about what constitutes "acceptable everyday adult selves" is diminishing. It also may indicate a gradual shift from an associative (situation-centered) to an integral (person-centered) model of selfhood, consistent with the growing influence of Christianity (see Levy et al., Chapter 1).

2) While Toraja possession behavior is highly organized and integrated in the way that Levy suggests, it is important to remember that only a handful of individuals present at a *ma'maro* experience dissociation and that those who do often act in very different ways. Because the use of spirit beliefs and symbols involves a degree of choice, either conscious or unconscious, possession behavior may be thought of as a type of "personal symbol" (Obeyesekere 1981) having simultaneous cultural and personal significance.

3) Why are the possessed often ashamed of their possession behavior, and why is the audience often frightened by it?

For about fifty years now, Christian Toraja have been discouraged from participating in smoke-ascending rituals, especially the *ma'maro*. While this has not prevented these rituals from being performed, even the most dedicated *Alukta* adherents expect the traditional religion to disappear. Many of their beliefs and practices are ignored, if not ridiculed, by non-*Alukta* villagers. Such historical and cultural changes make the remaining *to kandeatan* self-conscious about their ritual behavior.

But there is more to this shame reaction than the growing presence of non-believers. As mentioned above, the shame also illustrates a deep internalization of public disdain for lapses in self-awareness and self-control. In comparison to other insular Southeast Asia groups, the Toraja seem positioned between two rather different ways of generating and maintaining health and prosperity. Like simpler, more egalitarian highlands groups (e.g., the Wana [Atkinson 1989]), they have a notion that cosmic, supernatural sources of power must occasionally be brought into the community, even if this means temporary periods of chaos and disorder and complete human submission, including losses of memory, identity, and consciousness.

However, like lowland groups influenced by Indic notions of potency concentrated at a divine, immobile center *within* the human community, and of askesis as a means of acquiring and/or maintaining such potency (e.g., the Javanese [Geertz 1960, Keeler 1987] and the Bugis [Errington 1989]), the Toraja place a high value on emotional equanimity and self-control (Hollan 1988a, 1992; Wellenkamp 1988b) and are discomforted by the loss or diminution of such control (Hollan and Wellenkamp 1994). Toraja possession behavior can be viewed, then, as a compromise formation: one submits to the *deata* in order to avoid punishment and to ensure health and prosperity, but the submission is embarrassing. The Javanese display a similar ambivalence toward spirit mediums who, on the one hand, are sought out and respected for their gifts of prophecy and healing, but on the other hand, are disparaged because they do not consciously channel potency through askesis and meditation, as do the more respected *wong tuwa*, "individuals who are thought to be particularly potent." Instead, they gain power by surrendering their conscious selves to the spirits (Keeler 1987:119–24, Wellenkamp 1988a:320).

This concern with self-awareness and self-control helps to explain the audience's reaction to possession behavior as well. Villagers are frightened of possession behavior not only because it very likely suggests that they, too, have parts of the self organized outside their awareness, but also because it clearly illustrates to spectators what people are capable of if they lose their self-control. As Levy et al. note (Chapter 1), possession by spirits may thus serve as a source of gnosis, communicating knowledge about a community and its inhabitants that is otherwise unknowable and unspoken.[20]

Bourguignon (1979:233–69) suggests that possession trance is most likely to occur in hierarchically organized agricultural societies that place a high value on reliability, nurturance, and especially compliance. (Compliance, after all, is one of the hallmarks of possession behavior, whereby a person surrenders his or her identity, even if involuntarily, to a supernatural being.) She further argues that since it is women in these societies who are most likely to be marginalized and oppressed, they are most likely to use the possessed role to vent their frustrations, to act out forbidden desires and impulses, and to empower themselves. Except for the last point, almost all of this is true of the Toraja. My data suggest that Toraja men are just as likely to become possessed as Toraja women; in fact, the role of the possessed healer in a *ma'maro* ceremony is often filled by a man. Why this variation from the typical pattern observed by Bourguignon?

Like many other groups who speak an Austronesian language in insular Southeast Asia and the Pacific, the status and economic power of women among the Toraja is relatively high. Though women may not compete actively for prestige at public or governmental events, they are allowed to own and inherit land and property, their opinions on both public and private matters are sought and valued, and they usually control and manage the household's finances. Also, they infrequently experience the stress and strain of being displaced from their natal villages, since there is a strong tendency toward uxorilocal residence.

What social factors, if any, distinguish those who become possessed from other villagers? My limited observations suggest that older women and relatively younger or poorer men, of all social ranks, are most likely to become possessed. I propose that this is related to the fact that older women no longer give birth to and raise children, one of the most valued and respected tasks in Toraja society, and that younger and poorer men do not have the resources to actively compete for status at community feasts. It is not that these groups are actively oppressed, then, but rather that relative to other groups they have fewer means of maintaining and enhancing a valued identity, and so must rely on less culturally esteemed ways of gaining recognition.

SUMMARY AND CONCLUSION

The Toraja behavioral environment is densely populated with spiritual beings of traditional, Christian, and even Islamic origin. For most villagers the question is not, Which of these spiritual beings actually exist and which do not?, but rather, Which of these beings—at any given moment in one's life—has the power to influence the course of one's fate and fortune, and so should be acknowledged and perhaps propitiated? (cf. Howard, Chapter 6). For many middle-aged and older villagers—those who were raised as *Alukta* adherents and were exposed to Christian beliefs only later in life—this has not always been an easy question to answer. Some, like Ambe'na Toding, have converted from *Alukta* to Christianity (and from one Christian sect to another) and back again repeatedly, depending upon whether a particular religious affiliation has seemed to promote fortune or misfortune. Others, like Nene'na Tandi, have developed relatively stable Christian identities, yet still ponder the extent to which God may enforce traditional proscriptions and prohibitions (see Hollan 1988b:282–83); they still look for ways to demonstrate to themselves and others God's spiritual ascendency. In the following passage, for example, Nene'na Tandi imagines pitting the power and authority of God against that of the *deata* during the course of a *ma'maro* ceremony. If God were really more powerful than the *deata*, so he reasons, then one could imagine that the possessed would become insane:

> For example, if I, a Christian, were to [challenge] a possessed person [during a *ma'maro* ceremony] and he/she did not suffer, if he/she were not defeated, then indeed, the *deata* are powerful. But if he/she is defeated [i.e., if God were to prevail], then certainly he/she would become insane. Like that. So that would be a way of comparing religions.

On the other hand, many younger villagers—those raised as Christians or those exposed to Christian beliefs early in life—now have little doubt that it is God they must "fear." Ambe'na Patu says:

> When [I became a Christian], I was in school. And I read the Bible. I read that this world and everything in it was made by God, not the *deata*. So I became afraid of God. It was God who made humans. It was God who made the world. So I thought, "Wah, it would be better if I, ah … [pause] prayed to God. It would be better if I became a Christian because God might ask, 'Why do you not believe in me?'"

The significance of *deata* for these younger villagers varies from individual to individual. Some dismiss *deata* as relatively powerless, marginal spiritual beings. Others view them as potentially dangerous "satanic" forces. Yet few of them directly propitiate *deata* the way their *Alukta* elders once did. However, some remnants of *deata* belief and practice can be seen in the contemporary practice of possession by the Holy Spirit among Toraja Pentecostals (see Hollan and Wellenkamp 1994).

In contrast to the declining significance of *deata*, *nene'* remain of central importance in the lives of Toraja individuals, Christian and *Alukta* alike. This is in part because church officials, in contrast to their stance on smoke-ascending rituals, have accepted such beliefs as part of traditional "custom" (*ada'*) rather than challenge them as a remnant of traditional "religion" (*aluk*). But it is also because *nene'* beliefs and smoke-descending practices continue to serve important social and psychological functions, including the maintenance of collective and personal conscience and the gratification of desires for continued parental and grandparental support and advice. Also, unlike *deata* beliefs, which are experientially validated largely through the execution of costly and relatively infrequent rituals, *nene'* beliefs are reinforced each time a villager dreams about a deceased relative.

Thus while Christianity has tended to undermine the personal saliency of some traditional spirit beliefs, it has accommodated, if not reinforced, that of others. It is also noteworthy that the ways villagers interact with Christian spiritual beings, and ascertain their relative power and authority, still closely resemble *Alukta* patterns (Hollan 1988b).

NOTES

Acknowledgment. I am grateful to Jane Wellenkamp for her comments and suggestions.

1   Jane Wellenkamp and I tape-recorded in-depth, open-ended interviews with a total of eleven Toraja of varying social and economic backgrounds. Wellenkamp interviewed the women, and I interviewed the men. All direct quotations presented in this paper are taken from these life history interviews. For a social profile of the respondents and a discussion of interviewing procedures and techniques, see Hollan and Wellenkamp 1994.
2   These are Levy 1973, Kracke 1978, and Obeyesekere 1981. Levy interviewed rural and urban Tahitians, Kracke interviewed Kagwahiv political leaders and their followers, and Obeyesekere interviewed religious specialists in Sri Lanka.
3   For a more detailed discussion of the uses of the open interview in anthropological fieldwork see Levy and Wellenkamp (1989:223–25).
4   Because I find it difficult to categorize *nene'* and *deata* as either "spirits" or "gods" as defined by Levy et al. (Chapter 1), I use indigenous terms to refer to them throughout the chapter.
5   The traditional religion is also referred to as *Aluk To Dolo*, "The Way of the People of Before," and *Aluk Nene'*, "The Way of the Ancestors."
6   This is a pseudonym, as are all proper names in this chapter.
7   However, some people claim the *bombo* leaves soon after death.
8   The "*to minaa*" designates this man's position as a traditional religious specialist.
9   He/she is a literal translation of the Indonesian word *dia*, a personal pronoun that does not specify gender. I translate *dia* as "he/she" throughout the paper unless the gender of the person referred to is clear and unambiguous.
10   A fear of theft and trickery is not uncommon among the Toraja. See Hollan and Wellenkamp 1994.
11   Possession, as far as I know, does not occur outside a ritual context.

12 As mentioned above, funeral and smoke-ascending rituals may not be held concurrently.

13 For a more complete description of the *ma'maro* and *ma'bugi*, see Nooy-Palm 1986:121–42, Crystal and Yamashita 1987, Coville 1988, and Zerner 1981.

14 *To minaa* begin recitation of *gelong* before the main celebration.

15 In the *ma'maro* rituals I witnessed, the pace of the singing and dancing increased as soon as one of the members of the dance circle—often an older woman—appeared to be possessed.

16 Women, for example, may loosen their hair and allow it to flow over their shoulders in a way that is usually done only in private, intimate contexts. Broch (1985:276) notes that sexually provocative behavior occurs in Bonerate (South Sulawesi) possession ritual as well, though there, apparently, it is only women who become possessed.

17 At least one informant claims that more people became possessed at *ma'maro* rituals when he was young than now. Bourguignon (1979:261) suggests that possession trance typically is experienced by a minority of people in a community.

18 Some people say that participants may request permission from the *deata* to perform certain behaviors.

19 To Minaa Sattu began to be possessed while he was a youth and for over twenty years he regularly attended *ma'maro* rituals.

20 Spectators are of course also frightened by the seemingly miraculous power of the *deata*.

11 Afterword

Spirits and Their Histories

Michael Lambek

The papers in this volume speak about the shadows, the unfocused, the uncanny—things that are hard to grasp by analytic reason or that appear to be marginal to the central concerns of the societies in which they are found. Yet in their scrupulous attention to documenting changing statements and practices surrounding spirits, the authors take us right to the heart of the anthropology of religion. One cannot read them without thinking about the debate among intellectualists and social symbolists to explain the presence and patterns of gods and spirits. Likewise, one is drawn to Weber's questions regarding the progressive disenchantment of the world.

Such a return to fundamentals is healthy, even though we have long been skeptical about the need to choose between such theoretical positions or commit to one of them. Not only have the natives' beliefs changed since our first encounter with them, but so have our beliefs about theirs. Wisps of disembodied functionalist and intellectualist theories linger and occasionally confront us, but for the most part, like many of the Pacific spirits we encounter in this book, they are now fragments, observed more in our individual imaginations than granted value in our collective discourse. Through our own transformation, best marked in the field of religion by the publications of Lévi-Strauss' proto-deconstructionist *Totemism* (1963) and Evans-Pritchard's skeptical *Theories of Primitive Religion* (1956), we have lost the naive certainties that (supposedly) inspired our intellectual ancestors.

I do not wish to place a value judgment on the decline of

enchantment, nor indicate an irreversible direction to the process. After all, as the term suggests, it is only our *dis*enchantment that we can notice. But perhaps our shifts, as anthropologists and natives, share more than we might suppose; our respective experiences may be mutually informing. Hence I have no intention to re-enchant you with certainty. Rather than exerting closure, mistaking the privilege of the afterword for the authority of the last word, I offer instead a series of takes on things that have come into greater focus for me in the course of reading these papers. Like any reading, mine is partial, and, while I emphasize spirit possession, I recognize that one of the achievements of this rich set of papers is to place possession in a wider context.

Stated succinctly, *Spirits in Culture, History, and Mind* makes three major contributions. First, it historicizes spirits, documenting changes in practice through time. Second, it shows the diversity of statements about spirits and variety of practices that may be found simultaneously within a single locale, and does not attempt to conceal the resulting ambiguity beneath a false theoretical front. The "essential contestability" (to borrow Gallie's term) of local concepts and practices is made explicit. Third, and following from the previous achievements, it demonstrates the permeability of spirit possession and related phenomena. Shifts from talk about spirits, to sightings, to outright possession, to parodies of possession, and thence to transvestite theatrical performances or cheering at cricket matches (documented by Mageo), profound as they may be for participants, are easily made. The accounts presented here should dissuade us from the urge either to reify discrete institutions or to reach premature conclusions on the directionality of change.

Spirit Possession: General Remarks

Spirit possession forms a complex and exciting subject for anthropological analysis for two main reasons. First, it combines spirits as a semiotic system and an order of collective practice whereby hosts are initiated, particular voices are legitimated, and spirits are provided with spaces in which to perform. Possession thus provides a context in which contemporary experience is actively mediated by past myth models, and vice versa. Second, it provides an instance in which the collective and personal clearly interpenetrate. Collective forms are internalized by individuals and become self-transforming. Likewise, individual intentions are externalized and given form through the voices and acts of the spirits and the careers of their hosts (Obeyesekere 1981). Performances of possession therefore have a degree of unpredictability that many other kinds of rituals lack. Possession raises fascinating questions of agency and accountability for participants and anthropologists alike.

Spirits are products of imagination, partial world constructions that are fictional but not simply fictitious. If we take seriously the idea of spirits as imaginative constructions—local takes on experience and the world—then what we, as relative outsiders, have to offer is first, a series of appreciative, critical readings of the products and second, a consideration of the historically situated acts and conditions of production. Our readings, like critical readings of works of art or literature, can never be definitive. They are informed by our language, our context, our interests. They are the points of fusion between horizons, discursive spaces in which ideas from two imaginative worlds meet and form something new, or they are the product of longstanding conversations between parties holding incommensurable views. Readings are open for contestation or further elaboration by other readers, other interlocutors. We can aspire to virtuoso readings, but ultimately the hermeneutic situation prevails. We too can be "read" by possession.

As mimetic forms and practices that are skewed, altered, distorted forms of their original objects (Taussig 1993), spirits are often taken to represent Difference itself, an "other" world against which the quotidian is set off. Nukulaelae spirit talk, as recounted by Besnier, is about a Samoan spirit, but one used to adjudicate local issues. Spirits often specifically represent a difference that has invaded the self and that has become personally problematic. Akin's Kwaio spirits are foreign but troubling because locals have bought into them, often literally. Fritz Kramer has argued that possession provides a means of differentiating identity and that it does so by imitating the cultural other. Representations of collective difference are internalized so that one finds "a fusion of the other within the subject" (1993:38). For Kramer the external other is of interest insofar as it provides a vehicle for expressing internal difference, the other within oneself.

To argue that spirits are imagined is not to hypostatize them but to locate the work of imagination in its social context, in history. Since the object of mimesis is almost always conceived to be very powerful, an interpretation of possession must address questions of hegemony and resistance, as Mageo does (cf. Comaroff 1985). Moreover, since power is not merely represented, but addressed, possession is almost certain to be at least implicitly a discourse on morality, as Besnier makes clear (cf. Boddy 1989, Lambek 1981, 1993a). As a mimesis of power and a discourse on morality, possession is attuned to contemporary circumstances. Frequently bringing the authority of the past to bear on the present, it is also highly flexible and ready to change.

If spirits are imagined, they may become like works of art that, in turn, seize our imaginations, then seduce and overwhelm us with their power, their interest, their beauty, their sublimity. They may, indeed, "possess" us. Kramer (1993) speaks of this as passion. Yet possession is significantly different from such captivating modern aesthetic forms as film. Spirits demand to be taken literally, in the here and now. Possession is an embodied phenomenon. It manifests itself in physical pain, spiritual trauma, convulsive behavior, temporary dissociation, and sometimes, as among the Toraja, with explicit auto-aggression. It demands a response, often in the form of a treatment that requires addressing the spirit as a distinct entity from the sufferer, from the one impassioned.

Possession and spirits are "real" only to the degree that they are able to continuously naturalize themselves. Acts of imagination must be disclaimed, their products understood not as text but as context. As is evident from these papers, one of the primary means for maintaining the viability of possession develops from the fact that negotiation between the host and spirit is a public, social event. Possession is not simply a matter of uneasy dreams, glimpses in the forest, or an internal dialogue. It takes place in public with the presence of third parties—among families and healers in Chuuk, Samoa, and Tonga, and before clients and spectators in Nukulaelae. The advent of the spirit is corroborated through public witnessing of the embodied transformation of the host, legitimated through collaboration in dialogue with the spirit, and by the actions and statements of the host who must exhibit competence at shifting frames. The performative constitution of spirits as distinct persons is mystified to the participants so that they come to understand themselves as simply "meeting" entities whose existence is independent of such acknowledgment.[1]

The difference between disembodied and embodied spirits is precisely the degree to which their presence is concretely realized. Bodies provide the vehicle by means of which spirits can be held in focus, as it were, through which they can be sustained in steady communication, and from which they can be expected to speak. Thus, as Whitehouse puts it, "the experience of spirits, and its articulation with politics and cosmology, is a matter not so much of 'what people believe,' but of the way these 'beliefs' are codified and transmitted." These are not necessarily the effects of radically different belief systems, but of weaker and stronger forms of collective legitimation and spaces for performance. The stronger the legitimation and the more the spirit is realized as an external, autonomous entity, the less need will exist for resorting to a psychological discourse.

Spirits are often associated with trauma and healing. Sometimes the possessed are independently ill, and a diagnosis of possession provides an entree into therapy or a rationalization for its inadequacy. At other times, illness may be an idiom of possession, as it appears in Samoa, Tonga and Chuuk. Illness sustains possession's embodied qualities, naturalizing the arrival of spirits in human bodies, independent of the hosts' wills. Illness is contextualized by means of accountability narratives; spirit talk is full of moral references.

To speak of embodiment is also to speak of performance. Performances are comic or dramatic, suspenseful or gay. They may make use of music, dance, costume (although these props do not appear to be critical to most of the contemporary cases described in this volume), and, of course, distinctive speech patterns and comportment. Performance traditions differ, but always striking is the evident discrepancy between the features of the host as a recognized member of the community and the transformation that overlays them as she is possessed by the spirit. Possession performances may be linked to broader ritual cycles or political processes, as in Dadul. Spirits may be displayed before a crowd, restricted to privileged audiences, or, as in Chuuk and Tonga, embedded in kinship relations. Some of the most significant episodes of possession may take place in private settings among intimates.[2]

To the degree that spirits are embodied, they impinge on the selfhood of their hosts. Embodiment may be constituted by processes of dissociation, raising the question of how the dissociated parts of the self are linked in some larger whole.[3] Possession implies weakly bounded conceptions of self, but not necessarily weak selves per se. Moreover, although not documented in this collection, possession can provide a means for the growth of insight or maturity. Here Kramer's emphasis on passion needs to be complemented by one that notes the agency of spirits and hosts, especially their moral agency, as well as the dialogical quality of possession.

Possession establishes a system of communication, providing alternate voices, authority, and critical distance (Lambek 1993b), but also anti-language and ambiguity (Boddy 1989) and the possibility for the simultaneous transmission of opposed messages. The communicational properties of possession bear similarities to other forms of psychotherapeutic discourse.

To return to our starting point, it may be fair to say that our appreciation of spirits as intrinsically imaginative entities has been delayed by their frequently embodied qualities and association with trauma—either personal or historical, and often at the intersection of both. Rather than approaching spirits from primarily psychological, social structural, or aesthetic angles, this collection contributes importantly to a comparative reassessment of the link between history and the religious imagination.

BOUNDARIES

In training our own sights on spirits we have to ensure that our apparatus is not too powerful, overexposing its subjects. The double merit of these papers is both to examine the margins, the fuzzier of collective representations, and to do so in a way that preserves the fuzzy quality of their subjects. The contributions here recognize and preserve the significance of the margins in human experience (cf. Corin 1995).

These margins of the cultural world are not just beliefs in unruly forces, but unruly beliefs in such forces. Anthropology has tended to focus on that which is most systematic or most elaborated, hence to provide the most elegant analysis or fullest reading. But the unsystematized is not necessarily unimportant, either for the locals or for refining our own theoretical understanding of religion and culture. Indeed, this *absence* of system may be part of what Weber meant by enchantment.[4]

There is paradox in shedding light on moving shadows. The very words that belong in a semantic domain of "spirits" often do not form part of a systematic vocabulary, whether organized as a taxonomy or a paradigmatic set. Feinberg makes this explicit when he writes that Anutans "emphasize categories that shade into one another, avoiding terms or concepts that imply absolutes." This should not be surprising, for several reasons. First, we are dealing with the realm of the imagination, the fictional; there are no obviously autonomous signifieds against which the validity of particular signifiers can be independently measured. We err if we expect spirits to follow a Linnaean model of distinct "species," notable for the discreteness of their identities. The biological species is a particular semantic form, inappropriate in most religious matters (though, to be sure, it forms the basis of totemic logic). It does not underlie Christianity, which is noted for the (in some quarters, scandalous) fact that its God is simultaneously single and tripartite. In Evans-Pritchard's (1956) account of Nuer religion the various spirits are seen as so many refractions of a larger whole. Nuer spirits (like Nuer descent groups) are distinguished individually only in appropriate contexts; one cannot produce a list or taxonomy of spirits in the abstract.

Second, not only may the numinous beings and key conceptual categories of a given "religion" depart from a model of fixed, clearly demarcated entities, but no rigidly formulated boundary exists between one religious system and another. Hollan illustrates how problematic distinguishing among them may be. A Toraja man learned he should "reconvert" to Christianity—a revelation delivered by a highly traditional dream interpretation on the part of a relative. This raises fascinating questions about the heteroglossic nature of communication, and challenges dominant models of conversion. The issue is phrased explicitly by Besnier, who argues that Nukulaelae "spirits are embedded in a *fundamentally* heteroglossic conceptual domain" (my emphasis). Not only do multiple voices emerge through possession, but the very talk *about* spirits is fraught with conflicting messages of affirmation and skepticism, interest and disinterest, pleasure and denial.

The Kwaio appear to challenge this picture; they make distinctions between belief systems and attempt to preserve their borders. And yet it is precisely the complexity of these boundary problems that makes Akin's account so fascinating. Foreign spirits move in under false pretenses and even succeed in imitating ancestral ones, so that the Kwaio are uncertain as to who is who. The identity of a spirit is resolved only after the fact, when prosperity is gained or havoc ensues. The Kwaio recognize that foreign religious practices infiltrate local ones—that is precisely the reason for their attempt (reminiscent of the gendered spatial segregation of their "traditional" hamlets) to keep everything in its place. But at the same time, cross-border traffic is active.

Third, central religious concepts need not be commensurable with one another. Should we not, outside exceptional cases of rationalizing priesthoods and highly elaborated theologies, expect this? Incommensurability in the domain of religious affairs is particularly noticeable in matters of translation. Howard provides us with a lovely example: Methodists and Catholics each chose the reverse member of a pair of Rotuman terms to indicate "god" and "devils" respectively! But I want to go further and suggest that the central

terms of any given ethnographic case (itself the cumulative product of historical layering and borrowing) may not be commensurable with each other. It is
this incommensurability of fundamental concepts that requires a local
hermeneutics, the ongoing production of interpretative talk and activity that
constitutes culture.[5] Moreover, the incommensurability of specifically religious
concepts contributes to rendering them profound and mysterious.

Another important dimension is raised by Feinberg when he speaks of the
permeable boundaries between human and spirit as well as self and other. This
is evident also in Mageo's descriptions of Samoan practice, for example that the
deeper people walk in the woods, the more spiritlike they become, or the transformation of persons in the final phases of the *pōula* entertainments. It is apparent as well in Gordon's account of Tongans possessed by deceased kin. The
departure from naturalized Western models of highly bounded individuals and
species ("humans" versus "spirits") in favor of a more open conception of selfhood has been admirably conceptualized by Leenhardt in his depictions of a
"cosmomorphic" world and "relational personhood."[6] At the same time, as the
discussion in Chapter 1 makes clear, comparisons of selfhood themselves should
not be delineated in simplistic binary terms ("ours" versus "theirs"), but need to
be illuminated through contextual explorations of the signifying practices of real
persons.

VOICE AND AGENCY

If the local categories do not necessarily refer to discrete "natural" entities, neither should our analytical categories. Bound and unbound spirits are not discrete, fixed entities. Nor are possession and mediumship. Rather, they are
alternate yet overlapping modes of conceptualization and practice, or degrees of
emphasis, that can easily shift into one another as spirits (and their vehicles) gain
voice and voices gain authority. The choice of whether to exorcise a demon or
assimilate a spirit generally represents less a distinction of kind than a local politics of religion, as well as an informed reading of the immediate social context
and personal circumstances of the particular host.

As Hollan and Howard, among others, argue, context is critical. Spirits are
intrinsically connected to the contexts in which they appear. These contexts are
multiple, not just the obvious ones of public versus private, female versus male,
or insider versus outsider (all of which we see here), nor simply the Foucaultian
discourses that construct the objects of which they speak. The contexts of phenomenological distance or loci of attention on the part of individual actors are
primary. Indeed, the more the external, political, "objective" contexts were
attacked and destroyed by Christianity, colonialism, and capitalism, the more
obvious the significance of the subjective (though not, thereby, autonomous)
contexts becomes.

In Samoa, we see the decline of oracular authority and the displacement of
spirits from highly ranked individuals onto the ill, as well as the shift from an

apparently equitable gender distribution to a preponderance of female hosts. Mageo interprets this as a transformation that enables young women to express resistance to Christian expectations of respect, albeit in encapsulated form. She also shows how episodes of possession condense elements of both the pre-Christian and Christian moral orders.

In Chuuk, as well, the spirits withdraw from the public sphere. Hezel and Dobbin highlight the contemporary significance of switching voices in order to negotiate family issues, primarily by taking on the voice (i.e., persona) of a deceased senior kinsperson. The means of legitimacy also changes. They note that as possession has been decoupled from the political arena and become relocated in a "therapeutic realm," so too is the possession of an individual medium legitimated more by its supposedly "involuntary" quality. As legitimacy is withdrawn under the challenge from Christianity or the collapse of the political order, so now a woman cannot help being possessed; she is "attacked" by the spirit.

These shifts illustrate that possession cannot be defined or explained in terms of any single specific cause or function. Rather, it works as a system of communication that can be applied to changing circumstances, a system that bends to contemporary constraints. Hezel and Dobbin emphasize that the critical aspect is not the "trance" but the "speaking." While they point to possession as an index of women's stress, it is noteworthy that in many of the cases women in trance speak not directly to their own problems but to those faced by members of their families; women act as moral agents.[7]

The issue here—as Besnier, interlaced with the benevolent voice of Bakhtin, emphasizes throughout his marvelous essay—is one of heteroglossia. Possession entails the construction, elaboration, and deployment of alternative and multiple voices that join and transform larger conversations. Such additional voices provide a measure of critical distance and often speak with more authority, more freedom, or more levity, than other voices. This is surely one of the reasons for the frequent gender imbalance among hosts. Mageo describes an episode in which an adolescent girl becomes her own grandmother when criticizing her mother as "validat[ing] the power relations it temporarily preempts."[8] How new voices are established (or old ones suppressed) and how they are kept in play (or excluded from it), what new conversations they enable or what new arguments or points of view they contribute to ongoing conversations, how truth is established, are central questions. And in their explicitly heteroglossic qualities spirits highlight a feature that is always central to social life.

In Tonga, likewise, formal mediumship conducted by priests is gone. But as religion, in Gordon's apt phrase, has been "democratized," so now possession by deceased kin is ubiquitous. Possession speaks to recurrent themes of status, rank, and gender; most importantly, it helps negotiate the competing pull of patrilateral and matrilateral kin and the emotional conflict to which this gives rise. Here, however, possession is restricted to embodying rather than speaking explicitly about the conflict. The voices are not directly those of the host or spirit, but of healers and family members commenting on the event. Especially through the subsequent narratives of possession events, after the fact, are the issues worked through. Similarly among the Toraja, Hollan emphasizes the embodied performances, often highly specialized, of the spirits rather than their speech.

In all of these cases, as the respective authors make clear, the invocation of spirits raises questions of agency and serves as a discourse on morality. A question that the authors do not fully address, however, is the effects of possession on the subjectivity of the hosts, especially from a longitudinal biographical perspective.

ENCHANTMENT AND HISTORY

The essays emphasize how closely religious expression is linked to power, politics, and social change. Akin, for example, describes how Kwaio understanding of the dilemmas caused by the seductiveness of foreign ways is articulated through talk of new forms of spirit practice. Well-meaning attempts to enhance local ends by importing foreign spirits prompt abandonment by the very ancestors who underpin a successful life. Mageo demonstrates that the contemporary form of possession, held to exemplify Samoan "tradition," is actually a product of the colonial period.

What we learn from the various contributions is that over time, spirits are brought into greater or lesser focus. They may be sharply defined, their voices clear and their presence highly framed, or they may retreat to the fuzzy margins of fleeting glimpses, ephemeral presence, inarticulate speech. The questions the volume raises have to do with the myriad ways in which such movement, in and out of the light, as it were (though the aural may be as important as the visual), is accomplished. At the same time, this suggests that the distance may not be great between a context in which spirits are glimpsed on occasion, or merely spoken of, and one in which they are forcibly encountered in the bodies of living hosts.

The papers encompass what Taussig, a magical realist writing on the magically real, phrases as the opposition between "enlightenment" and "enchantment," an opposition which, in the Polynesian cases, we learn here, may be taken quite literally. Taussig speaks also of enlightenment as a progressive disembodiment (1993:18). Spirits withdraw from bodies and shrink from sight, retreating to the shadows where some of their brethren have always remained. As their substance evaporates, it becomes ever more difficult to yield to them, to give oneself over to that active passion or passive action that constitutes spirit possession or the shaman's magic. One might wish to see a causal or logical connection between the increasing fetishization of commodities and the depersonalization of spirits, yet the present volume demonstrates that this would be too neat; Pacific spirits sometimes seem to prosper in modernity.

These essays remind us of the mistake in assuming that Weber's state of enchantment is any more than an ideal type. Imaginatively constituted worlds are never fully realized. The spell is never so tightly woven; "belief" is never complete or uncompromised by skepticism. Likewise, Taussig's "active yielding" is never absolute; space abounds for ambivalence and ambiguity. Both enchantment and enlightenment have their seductive qualities; we know from our own experience that they are not mutually exclusive.[9]

If circumstances change, then spirits change along with them, but not as a passive reflection of more fundamental "facts." Spirits emerge or recede as products of discourse and loci of power, authority, or resistance. Collectively authorized and celebrated, or restricted to the realm of individual dysphoria, spirits provide an idiom with which to get a handle on experience, a means to step beyond the quotidian, the better to understand it. And yet for participants the stance is not that of the distant, detached observer, but its very opposite—not "outside," but intensely, immediately, and deeply "within." Spirits provide a vehicle with which to experience a loss of control, to speak from and about it, but also to recapture control.

The description by Whitehouse of the complex situation in Dadul illuminates these points. Whitehouse explores how multiple and sometimes competing constructions of spirits can coexist in the same society. Moreover, he distinguishes conventional and technical metaphorical acts from those that are innovative and evoke poignant responses. The former, he even says, are "consistent with a process of cultural atrophy, in which the moving and mysterious rituals of the past have degenerated into mere 'entertainment.'" Whitehouse writes, "There is no moral interest in the spirit world, and no corpus of cosmological knowledge relating to it." This is contrasted to the active mediumship of leaders of a splinter group during its charismatic phase. It is here where the Melanesian community seems to offer us a kind of public religious experience largely missing from the descriptions of other societies. This experience, argues Whitehouse, is generated by iconic images viscerally experienced, not by language in which beliefs may be codified and routinized. But this in turn cannot be spread widely beyond the community; hence it cannot develop into a political movement of the kind that would grant possession the sort of central place it had in the chiefly societies of precolonial Polynesia, where official mediums bore the spirits. In other words, it is the community as a political entity that both enables and ultimately limits the scope of religious experience. In turn, the polity is shaped and limited by the form of religious expression.

DEGREE OF FOCUS
Are numinal creatures named, individual characters whose exploits are widely recognized, or are they largely anonymous beings? Is their existence manifest in general statements and collective tales, or does their identity come into focus only as they intervene concretely in particular human affairs? In what manner,

as Howard asks, are they objectified? This axis of focus might be relevant in addressing the distinctions between "gods" and "spirits" raised in Chapter 1 as well as questions of social change.

Perhaps, to follow Howard's highly suggestive discussion, "beliefs" themselves ought not to be viewed as discrete, clearly focused objects that can be placed in binary categories of "sincere" and "insincere" and that are consistent over time. Consistency might be expected only when beliefs are rationalized as part of an orthodoxy—and even here the requirements of the creed might depart from the actual experience of the adherents. When "beliefs" are not objectified, elaborated in a meta-discourse or linked to various disciplinary measures or ritual cycles, when they are located in the realms of imagination or commonsense, then why should they not remain inchoate, ephemeral, inconsistent? Here, as Leenhardt (1979) saw, they are not *things*, on the order of species, or even acts, on the order of claims or commitments, but qualities, attitudes, or forces, on the order of interests or emotions. (This is not to say they should be reduced to interests and emotions.) As Howard argues, beliefs can vary according to their precision, their intensity, and their elaboration.

Without wishing to deny the importance of the semantic content of beliefs, the pragmatic dimension is always relevant. As Hollan (and Evans-Pritchard before him) notes, the typical question is not, Which of these spirits exist? but Which of them has power to influence my life now? In other words, we need a phenomenological approach that avoids propositional assertions ("spirits exist") in favor of various kinds of attitudes or degrees of focus. We need to distinguish Schutzian experts and well-informed citizens, who may be interested in rationalizing and theorizing, from the man or woman on the street who simply wants a problem solved (Schutz 1964). Christianity in Oceania appears to have delegitimated the attitudes and practices of experts with regard to local spirits, but less so the lay person's stance, for which legitimacy is not in any case the issue. If it takes more than a change in doctrine to make spirits disappear, this is precisely because the spirits are not themselves merely fixed in doctrine, and hence not exclusively in direct competition with imported creeds.

As the authors of Chapter 1 remark, "Beliefs based on doctrinal authority and faith have different vulnerabilities than beliefs based on personal experience; hence gods and spirits are differentially affected by historical change." As long as the authority-building institutions are in place, one would expect the former to be more durable and more consistent than the latter. But a point can come at which authority is sufficiently undermined, and collective practices suppressed, so that public faith collapses and the personal or, let us say, the less highly focused, is left the more durable. This is not simply the durability of spirits over gods, but of the vague experiences of spirits over more sharply defined forms of possession. As the public functions of spirits decline, so too go the contexts of witnessing in which the reality of spirits are established. The privatization of possession is a step in its devaluation, leaving it vulnerable to skepticism, shame (as among the Toraja), or scorn. This may stabilize in the kind of possession found in Tonga or Chuuk, but in the absence of embodied forms, talk of spirits may become increasingly ambivalent, as in Nukulaelae, or lose all interest, as in Rotuma.

Why has possession gone out of focus in some Pacific societies whereas in much of urban Africa (e.g., Giles 1987, Sharp 1993) and many other parts of the well-lighted world, such as Brazil, it is thriving? Perhaps it has to do in part with the fact that the numinals who possessed people in the Pacific were gods and ancestors more often than outsiders. Hence possession holds fewer of the "anthropological" functions of processing the meanings of history, modernity, and diversity and of patrolling and transgressing cultural boundaries than it does, for example, among the northern Sudanese (Boddy 1989). Here Akin's discussion of the Kwaio is closest to the African situation. Some of the chapters do indicate ways in which the objectification of the spirit world may serve new discourses of emerging national identity, but the issue of outsiders does not appear to be (to this outsider) particularly salient in the cultural imagination.

To understand the differences among the various cases, it might be helpful to look more closely at the imposition of Christianity and the diverse ways in which it has incorporated or suppressed local spirits. Mageo provides a lovely illustration of the susceptibility of missionaries in Samoa to local spirits, remembering that spirits were a significant feature of the Victorian milieu. Mageo argues that Christian attempts to suppress sexual entertainments may actually have opened the way for increased possession. Colonial attitudes to spirits were surely not unconnected to their function in legitimating traditional forms of political power and may have unwittingly contributed to possession's democratization. However, in assessing Western influence we cannot stop here. Perhaps the missing factor in explaining the decline of spirits is the penetration of new forms of subjectification—discourses of psychology, of sexuality, and of morality that turn the locus of truth away from external numinals and toward the newly constituted, interiorized modern "self" (cf. Foucault 1978, Taylor 1989).

Drawing on Godfrey Lienhardt (1961), Kramer (1993) makes a strong case for treating possession as *passiones*. To be possessed is to be "carried away," much as we might be "carried away" by a project we are working on. In a move that to Oceanists must evoke the path-breaking work of Maurice Leenhardt, Kramer suggests that modernity ultimately locates agency within the self, replacing cosmology with psychology, passion with action. In this way, devotion to the other is lost, and our links to the external, but intrinsically interconnected world, are reconstituted as internal qualities of mind. This broad discursive transformation may be partially responsible for the withdrawal to the shadows of the spirits on some of the Pacific Islands we have just encountered.

In the end, the essays in this volume suggest that we need to reflect on the evidence provided by social change in order to understand what "religion" is—that its fundamental nature cannot be grasped by a structural synchronic analysis alone. The qualities and force of beliefs or practices can only be revealed in their shifting deployment. This is a more profound statement than merely saying we cannot understand why a given religion is the way it is now without understanding how it got that way. The point is that religion is something always undergoing change; hence its objects perhaps are not "things" at all but the relatively transitory effects of continuous focusing mechanisms. And the spirits left on the margins are a reminder that there is always a residue, something left out of focus when we attempt to classify and objectify the world.

NOTES

Acknowledgments. This paper was written with the support of the Social Sciences and Humanities Research Council of Canada. Brief portions have been drawn from my article "Possession," to appear in the *Encyclopedic Dictionary of Social and Cultural Anthropology*, edited by Alan Barnard and Jonathan Spencer (Routledge). Alan Howard, Jeannette Mageo, Jacqueline Solway, and two reviewers have provided supportive criticism.

1   This argument is developed by means of case material in Lambek 1981.
2   On performance see especially Leiris 1980, Kapferer 1991, and also Lambek 1988. Lambek 1981 illustrates the importance of intimate settings.
3   The question of subjectivity is especially well handled in Boddy 1989. Kapferer 1991 examines the reconstitution of the self during the conduct of specific rituals, while Crapanzano and Garrison 1977 and Obeyesekere 1981, drawing on psychoanalysis, view it from a biographical perspective.
4   The notion of "enchantment" is ambiguous, calling up at once both the totalizing conceptual systems and mythological worlds elaborated by structuralists and symbolic anthropologists and the sort of amorphousness that is the antithesis of rationalization. Leenhardt's depiction of the mythological world of southern Melanesians nicely transcends the difference (Leenhardt 1979, cf. Clifford 1992).
5   Alas, I do not have the space here to develop the argument, which is heavily indebted to Bernstein (1983:79ff; see Lambek 1993a, especially Chapter 12). Incommensurability is distinguished from both incompatibility (logical contradiction) and incomparability. The incommensurability argument claims neither that there is an overarching framework in terms of which the key terms could be measured against each other point by point, nor that each is encased in a radically different framework such that comparison between them is impossible. Rather than rule out comparison, it implies that the forms of comparison and interpretation will be multiple. The incommensurability of key concepts is analogous to that of distinct art styles.
6   Leenhardt, op. cit. A psychoanalytic parallel to relational personhood is found in object relations theory (Chodorow 1989, Mitchell 1988; see Lambek 1995).
7   It would be interesting to know whether possession is used to enable those who died by suicide to speak.
8   Possession enables the presence of mutually incompatible ideologies, often concerning gender (see Lambek 1981, Chapter 5).
9   Compare Bourdieu's dialectic of embodiment and objectification (1990).

References

Abu-Lughod, Lila. 1990. Shifting Politics in Bedouin Love Poetry. In *Language and the Politics of Emotion*, edited by Catherine Lutz and Lila Abu-Lughod. Cambridge: Cambridge University Press.

———. 1991. Writing Against Culture. In *Recapturing Anthropology: Working in the Present*, edited by Richard G. Fox. School of American Research Advanced Seminar Series. Santa Fe, NM: School of American Research Press.

Akin, David. 1985. Suicide and Women in East Kwaio, Malaita. In *Culture, Youth and Suicide in the Pacific*, edited by Francis Hezel, Don Rubenstein, and Geoffrey M. White. Honolulu: Pacific Islands Studies.

———. 1993. Negotiating Culture in East Kwaio, Malaita, Solomon Islands. PhD dissertation, University of Hawaii.

———. 1995. Cultural Education at the Kwaio Cultural Centre. In *Cultural Policy in Melanesia*, edited by Geoffrey M. White. Suva: Institute of Pacific Studies, and Papua New Guinea National Research Institute.

Alkire, William H. 1989. Land, Sea, Gender, and Ghosts on Woleai-Lamotrek. In *Culture, Kin, and Cognition in Oceania: Essays in Honor of Ward H. Goodenough*, edited by Mac Marshall and John L. Caughey. Washington, D.C.: American Anthropological Association.

Atkinson, Jane. 1989. *The Art and Politics of Wana Shamanship*. Berkeley: University of California Press.

Babcock, Barbara A., editor. 1978. *The Reversible World: Symbolic Inversion in Art and Society*. Ithaca: Cornell University Press.

Bakhtin, Mikhail. 1981. *The Dialogic Imagination: Four Essays*, edited by Michael Holquist, translated by Caryl Emerson and Michael Holquist. Austin, TX: University of Texas Press.

———. 1986. *Speech Genres and Other Essays*, edited by Caryl Emerson and Michael Holquist, translated by Vern McGee. Austin: University of Texas Press.

Bar-Tal, Daniel. 1989. *Group Beliefs: A Conception for Analyzing Group Structure, Processes, and Behavior*. New York: Springer-Verlag.

Barth, Fredrik. 1987. *Cosmologies in the Making: A Generative Approach to Cultural Variation in Inner New Guinea*. New York: Cambridge University Press.

———. 1990. The Guru and the Conjurer: Transactions in Knowledge and the Shaping of Culture in Southeast Asia and Melanesia. *Man* 25:640–53.

Bateson, Gregory. 1958. *Naven*. Stanford: Stanford University Press.

———. 1972. Style, Grace and Information in Primitive Art. In *Steps to an Ecology of Mind*. New York: Ballantine Books.

Bateson, Gregory, and Margaret Mead. 1942. *Balinese Character: A Photographic Analysis*. New York: Special Publication of New York Academy of Sciences, Vol. II.

Bem, Daryl J. 1970. *Beliefs, Attitudes and Human Affairs*. Belmont, CA: Brooks/Cole.

Bennett, George. 1831. A Recent Visit to Several of the Polynesian Islands. *United Service Journal* 33:198–202, 473–82.

Bennett, Judith. 1987. *Wealth of the Solomons: A History of a Pacific Archipelago, 1800–1978*. Honolulu: University of Hawaii Press.

Bernstein, Richard. 1983. *Beyond Objectivism and Relativism: Science, Hermeneutics, and Praxis*. Philadelphia: University of Pennsylvania Press.

Besnier, Niko. 1989. Information Withholding as a Manipulative and Collusive Strategy in Nukulaelae Gossip. *Language in Society* 18:315–341.

———. 1990a. Conflict Management, Gossip, and Affective Meaning on Nukulaelae. In *Disentangling: Conflict Discourse in Pacific Societies*, edited by Karen A. Watson-Gegeo and Geoffrey M. White. Stanford, CA: Stanford University Press.

———. 1990b. Language and Affect. *Annual Review of Anthropology* 19:419–51.

———. 1993a. Reported Speech and Affect in Nukulaelae Gossip. In *Responsibility and Evidence in Oral Discourse*, edited by Jane H. Hill and Judith T. Irvine. Cambridge: Cambridge University Press.

———. 1993b. The Demise of the Man Who Would Be King: Sorcery and Ambition on Nukulaelae Atoll. *Journal of Anthropological Research* 49:185–215.

———. 1994. Polynesian Gender Liminality through Time and Space. In *Third Sex/Third Gender: Beyond Sexual Dimorphism in Culture and History*, edited by Gilbert Herdt. New York: Zone Books.

———. In Press. Authority and Egalitarianism: Discourses of Leadership on Nukulaelae Atoll. In *Leadership and Change in the Western Pacific: Essays Presented to Sir Raymond Firth*, edited by Richard Feinberg and Karen Ann-Watson Gegeo. London School of Economics Monographs on Social Anthropology. London: Athlone.

Bettelheim, Bruno. 1975. *The Uses of Enchantment: The Meaning and Importance of Fairy Tales*. New York: Random House.

Bigalke, Terrance. 1981. A Social History of "Tana Toraja" 1870–1965. PhD dissertation, University of Wisconsin, Madison.

Black, Mary. 1973. Belief Systems. In *Handbook of Social and Cultural Anthropology*, edited by John Honigmann. Chicago: Rand McNally.

Bocock, Robert. 1986. *Hegemony*. London: Tavistock.

Boddy, Janice. 1989. *Wombs and Alien Spirits*. Madison: University of Wisconsin Press.

Bollig, P. Laurentius. 1927. *Die Bewohner der Truk-Inseln. Religion, Leben und Kurze Grammatik eines Mikronesiervolkes*. Anthropos Bibliothek, No. 8. Münster: Anthropos.

Bourdieu, Pierre. 1990 [1980]. *The Logic of Practice*. Stanford: Stanford University Press.

———. 1991. *Language and Symbolic Power*. Cambridge, MA: Harvard University Press.

Bourguignon, Erika. 1973. *Religion, Altered States of Consciousness, and Social Change*. Columbus: Ohio State University Press.

———. 1979. *Psychological Anthropology: An Introduction to Human Nature and Cultural Differences*. New York: Holt, Rinehart, and Winston.

Bowles, John R. 1985. Suicide and Attempted Suicide in Contemporary Western Samoa. In *Culture, Youth and Suicide in the Pacific: Papers from an East-West Center Conference*, edited by Francis X. Hezel, Don H. Rubinstein, and Geoffrey M. White. Honolulu: Center for Asian and Pacific Studies, University of Hawaii.

Broch, Harald Beyer. 1985. "Crazy Women are Performing in Sombali": A Possession Trance Ritual on Bonerate, Indonesia. *Ethos* 13:262–82.

Brunton, Ron. 1980. Misconstrued Order in Melanesian Religion. *Man* 15:112–28.

Bulatao, Jaime. 1982. Local Cases of Possession and Their Cure. *Philippine Studies* 30:415–425.

Burt, Benjamin. 1994. *Tradition and Christianity: The Colonial Transformation of a Solomon Islands Society*. New York: Harwood Academic Publishers.

Butler, Gary R. 1990. *Saying Isn't Believing: Conversational Narratives and the Discourse of Tradition in a French-Newfoundland Community*. Social and Economic Studies, 42. St. John's, NF: Institute of Social and Economic Research, Memorial University of Newfoundland.

Cain, Horst. 1971. The Sacred Child and the Origins of Spirits in Samoa. *Anthropos* 66:173–81.

———. 1979. *Aitu*. Wiesbaden: Franz Steiner Verlag GMBH.

Chambers, Anne, and Keith S. Chambers. 1985. Illness and Healing in Nanumea, Tuvalu. In *Healing Practices in the South Pacific*, edited by Claire Parsons. Laie, HI: Institute for Polynesian Studies.

Chodorow, Nancy J. 1989. *Feminism and Psychoanalytic Theory*. New Haven: Yale University Press.

Churchward, C. Maxwell. 1940. *Rotuman Grammar and Dictionary*. Sydney: Australasian Medical Publishing Co.

———. 1959. *Tongan Dictionary*. Nukuʻalofa, Tonga: Tongan Government Printing Press.

Churchward, William B. 1887. *My Consulate in Samoa*. London: Richard Bentley and Son.

Clark, Jeffrey. 1993. Gold, Sex, and Pollution: Male Illness and Myth at Mt. Kare, Papua New Guinea. *American Ethnologist* 20:742–57.

Clement, Dorothy. 1974. Samoan Concepts of Mental Illness and Treatment. PhD dissertation, University of California at Irvine, University Microfilms # DCJ74–27849. Cambridge, MA.

Clifford, James. 1988. *The Predicament of Culture: Twentieth-Century Ethnography, Literature, and Art*. Cambridge, MA: Harvard University Press.

———. 1992. *Person and Myth: Maurice Leenhardt in the Melanesian World*. Durham: Duke University Press.

Collocott, Ernest E. V. 1923. Sickness, Ghosts and Medicine in Tonga. *Journal of the Polynesian Society* 32:136–42.

Colvocoresses, George M. 1852. *Four Years in a Government Exploring Expedition*. New York: Cornish & Lampost.

Comaroff, Jean. 1985. *Body of Power, Spirit of Resistance*. Chicago: University of Chicago Press.

Comaroff, John, and Jean Comaroff. 1992. *Ethnography and the Historical Imagination*. Boulder: Westview.

Coppet, Daniel de. 1981. The Life-giving Death. In *Mortality and Immortality: The*

Anthropology and Archaeology of Death, edited by S. C. Humphries and H. King. London: Academic Press.

Corin, Ellen. 1995. Meaning Games at the Margins: The Cultural Centrality of Subordinated Structures. In *Beyond Textuality: Asceticism and Violence in Anthropological Interpretations*, edited by Gilles Bibeau and Ellen Corin. Berlin: Mouton de Gruyter.

Corris, Peter. 1973. *Passage, Port and Plantation: A History of Solomon Islands Labour Migration 1870–1914*. Melbourne: University of Melbourne Press.

Coville, Elizabeth. 1988. "A Single Word Brings to Life": The Maro Ritual in Tana Toraja. PhD dissertation, The University of Chicago.

Cowling, Wendy. 1987. Eclectic Elements in Tongan Folk Belief and Healing Practice. In *Tongan Culture and History*, edited by Phyllis Herda, John Terrell, and Neil Gunson. Canberra: Australian National University.

Crapanzano, Vincent, and Vivian Garrison, editors. 1977. *Case Studies in Spirit Possession*. New York: Wiley.

Crick, Malcom. 1979. Anthropologists' Witchcraft: Symbolically Defined or Analytically Undone? *Journal of the Anthropological Society of Oxford* 10:139–46.

Crystal, Eric, and S. Yamashita. 1987. Power of Gods: Ma'bugi Ritual of the Sa'dan Toraja. In *Indonesian Religions in Transition*, edited by Rita S. Kipp and Susan Rodgers. Tucson: University of Arizona Press.

D'Andrade, Roy G. 1984. Cultural Meaning Systems. In *Culture Theory: Essays on Mind, Self, and Emotion*, edited by Richard A. Shweder and Robert A. LeVine. Cambridge: Cambridge University Press.

Davis, Natalie Zemon. 1978. Women on Top: Symbolic Sexual Inversion and Political Disorder in Early Modern Europe. In *The Reversible World: Symbolic Inversion in Art and Society*, edited by Barbara A. Babcock. Ithaca: Cornell University Press.

Dobbin, Jay D. 1986. *The Jombee Dance of Montserrat*. Columbus: Ohio State University Press.

Durkheim, Émile. 1965 [1915]. *The Elementary Forms of the Religious Life*. New York: Free Press.

Eagleston, John Henry. 1832. Log of the ship Emerald, Vol. 3. Peabody Museum, Salem, MA.

Errington, Shelly. 1989. *Meaning and Power in a Southeast Asian Realm*. Princeton: Princeton University Press.

Evans-Pritchard, E. E. 1956. *Nuer Religion*. Oxford: Clarendon.

——— . 1965. *Theories of Primitive Religion*. Oxford: Clarendon.

——— . 1985 [1937]. *Witchcraft, Oracles, and Magic among the Azande*. Oxford: University Press.

Favret-Saada, Jeanne. 1980. *Deadly Words: Witchcraft in the Bocage*, translated by Catherine Cullen. Cambridge: Cambridge University Press.

Feinberg, Richard. 1979. *Anutan Concepts of Disease: A Polynesian Study*, with foreword by D. Carleton Gajdusek, M.D. Laie, HI: Institute for Polynesian Studies.

——— . 1980. History and Structure: a Case of Polynesian Dualism. *Journal of Anthropological Research* 36:361–78.

——— . 1981. *Anuta: Social Structure of a Polynesian Island*, with foreword by Sir Raymond Firth. Laie and Copenhagen: Institute for Polynesian Studies in cooperation with the National Museum of Denmark.

——— . 1982a. Structural Dimensions of Sociopolitical Change on Anuta. *Proceedings of Conference on Evolving Political Cultures in the Pacific Islands*, edited by Gloria Cronin. Laie: Institute for Polynesian Studies.

——— . 1982b. Some Observations on a Polynesian Naming System: Personal Names and Naming on Anuta. *Journal of the Polynesian Society* 91:581–88.

——— . 1983. What's in a Name? Personal Identity and Naming on Anuta. *Central Issues in Anthropology* 5:27–42.

——— . 1986. The "Anuta Problem": Local Sovereignty and National Integration in the Solomon Islands. *Man* 21:438–52.

——— . 1988a. *Polynesian Seafaring and Navigation: Ocean Travel in Anutan Culture and Society*, with foreword by Ben R. Finney. Kent, OH: Kent State University Press.

——— . 1988b. Socio-spatial Symbolism and the Logic of Rank on Two Polynesian Outliers. *Ethnology* 27:291–310.

——— . In Press a. Sanctity and Power on Anuta: Polynesian Chieftainship Revisited. In *Leadership and Change in the Western Pacific: Essays Presented to Sir Raymond Firth*, edited by Richard Feinberg and Karen Ann Watson-Gegeo. London School of Economics Monographs on Social Anthropology. London: Athlone.

——— . In Press b. Christian Polynesians and Pagan Spirits. *Journal of the Polynesian Society*.

Firth, Raymond. 1936. *We, the Tikopia*. London: George Allen and Unwin.

——— . 1939. *The Work of the Gods in Tikopia*. London School of Economics Monographs on Social Anthropology, Numbers 1 and 2. London: Athlone.

——— . 1940. *The Work of the Gods in Tikopia*. London: Lund, Humphries.

——— . 1964. Problem and Assumption in an Anthropological Study of Religion. In *Essays on Social Organization and Values*. London School of Economics Monographs on Social Anthropology, 28. London: Athlone.

——— . 1967. *Tikopia Ritual and Belief*. London: Allen & Unwin.

——— . 1970. *Rank and Religion: A Study of Polynesian Paganism and Conversion to Christianity*. Boston: Beacon Press.

Fisiy, Cyprian F., and Peter Geschiere. 1991. Sorcery, Witchcraft and Accumulation: Regional Variations in South and West Cameroon. *Critique of Anthropology* 11:251–78.

Forge, Anthony. 1970. Prestige, Influence, and Sorcery: A New Guinea Example. In *Witchcraft Confessions and Accusation*, edited by Mary Douglas. London: Tavistock.

Foucault, Michel. 1978. *The History of Sexuality*. Volume I: an Introduction, translated by Robert Hurley. New York: Random House.

Fox, Charles E. 1985. *My Solomon Islands*. Honiara: Church of Melanesia.

Fox, Charles E., and F. H. Drew. 1915. Beliefs and Tales of San Cristoval. *Journal of the Royal Anthropological Institute* 45:131–85, 187–228.

Franco, Robert W. 1989. Samoan Representations of World War II and Military Work: The Emergence of International Movement Networks. In *The Pacific Theater: Island Representations of World War II*, edited by Geoffrey M. White and Lamont Lindstrom. Honolulu: University of Hawaii Press.

Frankel, Stephen. 1986. *The Huli Response to Illness*. New York: Cambridge University Press.

Frazer, Ian. 1985. Walkabout and Urban Movement: A Melanesian Case Study. In *Mobility and Identity in the Island Pacific*, edited by Murray Chapman. *Pacific Viewpoint* (Special Issue) 26:185–205.

Frazer, James George. 1968. *The Belief in Immortality and the Worship of the Dead.* Vol. 3: The Belief Among the Micronesians. London: Dawson's.

Freeman, Derek. 1983. *Margaret Mead and Samoa: The Making and Unmaking of an Anthropological Myth.* Cambridge: Harvard University Press.

Freud, Sigmund. 1942. Obsessive Acts and Religious Practices. In *Collected Papers of Sigmund Freud,* translated by Joan Riviere. Vol. II:25–35. London: Hogarth and the Institute for Psychoanalysis.

———. 1953. *The Interpretation of Dreams: And On Dreams,* translated by James Strachey. London: Hogarth and the Institute for Psychoanalysis.

Gailey, Christine W. 1987. *From Kinship to Kingship.* Austin: University of Texas Press.

Gardiner, J. Stanley. 1898. Natives of Rotuma. *Journal of the Royal Anthropological Institute* 27:396–435, 457–524.

Garrett, John. 1982. *To Live Among the Stars: Christian Origins in Oceania.* Geneva: World Council of Churches in association with the Institute of Pacific Studies, University of the South Pacific.

Geertz, Clifford. 1960. *The Religion of Java.* Chicago: University of Chicago Press.

———. 1971. *Islam Observed: Religious Development in Morocco and Indonesia.* Chicago: University of Chicago Press.

———. 1976. From the Native's Point of View: on the Nature of Anthropological Understanding. In *Meaning in Anthropology*, edited by Keith H. Basso and Henry A. Selby. Albuquerque: University of New Mexico Press.

Gegeo, David, and Karen Watson-Gegeo. In Press. Priest and Prince: Integrating *Kastom,* Christianity, and Modernization in Kwara'ae Leadership. In *Leadership and Change in the Western Pacific: Essays Presented to Sir Raymond Firth*, edited by Richard Feinberg and Karen Watson-Gegeo. London School of Economics Monographs on Social Anthropology. London: Athlone.

Gerber, Eleanor. 1985. Rage and Obligation: Samoan Emotion in Conflict. In *Person, Self, and Experience*, edited by Geoffrey White and John Kirkpatrick. Berkeley: University of California Press.

Gifford, Edward W. 1929. *Tongan Society.* Honolulu: Bernice P. Bishop Museum Bulletin No. 61.

Giles, Linda. 1987. Possession Cults on the Swahili Coast: A Re-Examination of Theories of Marginality. *Africa* 57:234–57.

Gilson, Richard P. 1970. *Samoa 1830 to 1900.* Melbourne: Oxford University Press.

Girschner, Max. 1911. *Die Karolineninsel Namoluk und Ihre Bewohner.* Bässler-Archiv, Band II, 123–215. English translation of section on mythology on file at Micronesian Seminar, Chuuk. No date; no pagination.

Glick, Leonard. 1967. Medicine as an Ethnographic Category: the Gimi of the New Guinea Highlands. *Ethnology* 6:31–56.

Gluckman, Max. 1956. *Custom and Conflict in Africa.* New York: Barnes & Noble.

Godelier, Maurice. 1986. *The Making of Great Men: Male Domination and Power Among the New Guinea Baruya.* New York: Cambridge University Press.

Goffman, Erving. 1979. Footing. *Semiotica* 25:1–29.

Goldman, Irving. 1970. *Ancient Polynesian Society.* Chicago: University of Chicago Press.

Goldsmith, Michael. 1989. Church and Society in Tuvalu. PhD dissertation, University of Illinois at Urbana-Champaign.

Goodenough, Erwin R. 1965. *The Psychology of Religious Experiences*. New York: Basic Books.

Goodenough, Ward. 1963. *Cooperation in Change*. New York: Russell Sage Foundation.

Goodman, Richard A. 1971. Some Aitu Beliefs of Modern Samoans. *Journal of the Polynesian Society* 80:463–79.

Gordon, Tamar. 1990. Inventing the Mormon Tongan Family. In *Christianity in Oceania: Ethnographic Perspectives*, edited by John Barker. ASAO Monograph No. 12. Lanham: University Press of America.

Grimshaw, Beatrice E. 1907. *In the Strange South Seas*. London: Hutchinson.

Hahn, Robert. 1973. Understanding Beliefs: An Essay on the Methodology of the Statement and Analysis of Belief Systems. *Current Anthropology* 14:207–29.

Hallowell, A. Irving. 1955. *Culture and Experience*. Philadelphia: University of Pennsylvania Press.

——— . 1960. Ojibwa Ontology, Behavior, and World View. In *Culture in History: Essays in Honor of Paul Radin*, edited by Stanley Diamond. New York: Columbia University Press.

Hanson, F. Allan. 1987. Polynesian Religions: an Overview. In *The Encyclopedia of Religion*, edited by Mircea Eliade et al. Volume II:423–32. New York: Macmillan.

Heider, Karl. 1991. *Indonesia Cinema: National Culture on Screen*. Honolulu: University of Hawaii Press.

Helu, I. Futa. 1985. Thinking of a Psychotic: Tonga. Manuscript in Hamilton Library, University of Hawaii, Honolulu.

Henry, Brother Fred. 1983 [1979]. *History of Samoa*. Apia: Commercial Printers Limited.

Hereniko, Vilsoni. 1991. Polynesian Clowns and Satirical Comedies. PhD dissertation, University of the South Pacific, Suva, Fiji.

——— . 1992. When She Reigns Supreme: Carnival Clowning in Rotuman Weddings. In *Clowning as Critical Practice*, edited by William Mitchell. Pittsburgh: University of Pittsburgh.

——— . 1995. *Woven Gods: Female Clowns and Power in Rotuma*. Honolulu: University of Hawaii Press.

Hezel, Francis X. 1981. Youth Drinking in Micronesia. A Report on the Working Seminar on Alcohol Use and Abuse among Micronesian Youth Held in Kolonia, Pohnpei, 12–14 November.

——— . 1987. Truk Suicide Epidemic and Social Change. *Human Organization* 46:283–91.

——— . 1989. Suicide and the Micronesian Family. *The Contemporary Pacific* 1:43–74.

——— . 1990. Unmaking of the Micronesian Family. Unpublished paper.

Hezel, Francis X., and Michael Wylie. In Press. Schizophrenia and Chronic Mental Illness in Micronesia: An Epidemiological Survey. *Isla*.

Hobsbawm, Eric, and Terrence Ranger, editors. 1983. *The Invention of Tradition*. Cambridge: Cambridge University Press.

Hocart, Arthur M. 1915. On the Meaning of the Rotuman Word 'Atua'. *Man* 15:129–31.

Hogbin, Ian. 1970 [1939]. *Experiments in Civilization: The Effects of European Culture on a Native Community of the Solomon Islands*. New York: Schocken Books.

Hollan, Douglas. 1984. "Disruptive" Behavior in a Toraja Community. PhD dissertation, University of California, San Diego.

——— . 1988a. Staying "Cool" in Toraja: Informal Strategies for the Management of Anger and Hostility in a Nonviolent Society. *Ethos* 16:52–72.

——— . 1988b. Pockets Full of Mistakes: The Personal Consequences of Religious Change in a Toraja Village. *Oceania* 58:275–89.

——— . 1989. The Personal Use of Dream Beliefs in the Toraja Highlands. *Ethos* 17:166–86.

——— . 1992. Emotion Work and the Value of Emotional Equanimity Among the Toraja. *Ethnology* 31:45–56.

Hollan, Douglas, and Jane C. Wellenkamp. 1994. *Contentment and Suffering: Culture and Experience in Toraja.* New York: Columbia University Press.

Holmes, Lowell D. 1974. *Samoan Village.* Palo Alto: Stanford University Press.

Hovdhaugen, Even. 1987. *From the Land of Nafanua: Samoan Oral Texts in Transcription and Translation, Notes and Vocabulary.* Olso: Norwegian University Press.

Howard, Alan. 1960. Field Notes from Rotuma.

——— . 1979. The Power to Heal in Colonial Rotuma. *Journal of the Polynesian Society* 88:243–75.

——— . 1982. Interactional Psychology: Some Implications for Psychological Anthropology. *American Anthropologist* 84:37–57.

——— . 1985. History, Myth and Polynesian Chieftainship: The Case of Rotuman Kings. In *Transformations of Polynesian Culture*, edited by Antony Hooper and Judith Huntsman. Auckland: Polynesian Society.

——— . 1989. The Resurgence of Rivalry: Politics in Post-colonial Rotuma. *Dialectical Anthropology* 14:145–58.

——— . 1990. Dispute Management in Rotuma. *Journal of Anthropological Research* 46:263–92.

Huebner, Thom. 1986. Vernacular Literacy: English as a Language of Wider Communication and Language Shift in American Samoa. *Journal of Multi-Lingual and Multi-Cultural Development* 7:393–411.

Huntsman, Judith, and Antony Hooper. 1975. Male and Female in Tokelau. *Journal of the Polynesian Society* 84:415–30.

Hutton, James. 1874. *Missionary Life in the Southern Seas.* London: Henry S. King.

Irava, Ieli. 1977. History, Superstition and Religion. In *Rotuma: Hanua Pumue (Precious Land)*, Anselmo Fatiaki et al. Suva: Institute of Pacific Studies, University of the South Pacific.

James, Kerry. 1987. Gender Relations in Tonga: a Paradigm Shift. In *Tongan Culture and History*, edited by Phyllis Herda, John Terrell, and Neil Gunson. Canberra: Australian National University Press.

Jilek, Wolfgang G. 1988. Mental Health, Ethnopsychiatry and Traditional Medicine in the Kingdom of Tonga. *Curarae* 11:161–76.

Jolly, Margaret, and Nicholas Thomas, editors. 1992. The Politics of Tradition in the Pacific. *Oceania* (Special Issue) 62(4).

Kaeppler, Adrienne L. 1971. Rank in Tonga. *Ethnology* 10:174–93.

——— . 1987. Polynesian Religions: Mythic Themes. In *The Encyclopedia of Religion*, edited by Mircea Eliade et al. Volume 11: 432–35. New York: Macmillan.

Kapferer, Bruce. 1991. *A Celebration of Demons: Exorcism and Healing in Sri Lanka.* Washington, D.C.: Smithsonian Press. Second edition.

Karp, Ivan. 1989. Power and Capacity in Rituals of Possession. In *Creativity of Power: Cosmology and Action in African Societies,* edited by W. Arens and Ivan Karp. Washington, D.C.: Smithsonian Institution Press.

Keeler, Ward. 1987. *Javanese Shadow Plays, Javanese Selves.* Princeton: Princeton University Press.

Keesing, Felix M. 1934. *Modern Samoa: Its Government and Changing Life.* London: Allen & Unwin.

Keesing, Roger. 1982. *Kwaio Religion: The Living and the Dead in a Solomon Islands Society.* New York: Columbia University Press.

———. 1992. *Custom and Confrontation: The Kwaio Struggle for Cultural Autonomy.* Chicago: Chicago University Press.

Keesing, Roger, and Robert Tonkinson, editors. 1982. Reinventing Traditional Culture: the Politics of Kastom in Island Melanesia. *Mankind* (Special Issue) 13(4).

Kelly, Raymond. 1976. Witchcraft and Sexual Relations: An Exploration in the Social and Semantic Implications of the Structure of Belief. In *Man and Woman in the New Guinea Highlands,* edited by Paula Brown and Georgeda Buchbinder. Washington, D.C.: American Anthropological Association.

Knauft, Bruce. 1985a. Ritual Form and Permutation in New Guinea: Implications of Symbolic Process for Socio-Political Evolution. *American Ethnologist* 12:321–40.

———. 1985b. *Good Company and Violence: Sorcery and Social Action in a Lowland New Guinea Society.* Berkeley: University of California Press.

Kneubuhl, John. 1993. Comic Theater of Samoa: An Interview with John Kneubuhl. *Manoa* 5:99–105.

Kneubuhl, Victoria. 1987. Traditional Performances in Samoan Culture: Two Forms. *Asian Theater Journal* 4:166–76.

Kracke, Waud H. 1978. *Force and Persuasion: Leadership in an Amazonian Society.* Chicago: University of Chicago Press.

Kraemer, Augustin. 1949 [1923]. *Salamasina: Scenes from Ancient Samoan Culture and History,* anonymous translator. Unpublished manuscript. American Samoa Community College Pacific Collection.

———. 1978 [1902]. *Die Samoa Inseln.* Stuttgart: E. Schweizebartische Verlagsbuchandlung (E. Naegele). Theodore Verhaaren, unpublished translation. American Samoa: Department of Education, Vol. 1(2).

Kramer, Fritz. 1993. *The Red Fez: Art and Spirit Possession in Africa.* Translated by Malcolm R. Green. London: Verso.

Kubary, Johann S. 1969 [1888]. The Religion of the Palauans. English translation of Die Religion der Palauer. In *Allerlei aus Volks und Menschenkunde,* edited by Adolf Bastian. Berlin: E. S. Mittler, Vol. 1.

Lambek, Michael. 1981. *Human Spirits: A Cultural Account of Trance in Mayotte.* Cambridge: Cambridge University Press.

———. 1988. Graceful Exits: Spirit Possession as Personal Performance in Mayotte. *Culture* 8:59–70.

———. 1989. From Disease to Discourse: Remarks on the Conceptualization of Trance and Spirit Possession. In *Altered States of Consciousness and Mental Health: A Cross-Cultural Perspective,* edited by Colleen A. Ward. Newbury Park: Sage Publications.

———. 1993a. *Knowledge and Practice in Mayotte: Local Discourses of Islam, Sorcery, and Spirit Possession*. Toronto: University of Toronto Press.

———. 1993b. Cultivating Critical Distance: Oracles and the Politics of Voice. *Political and Legal Anthropology Review* 16:9–18.

———. 1995. Choking on the Quran and Other Consuming Parables from the Western Indian Ocean Front. In *Religious and Cultural Certainties*, edited by Wendy James. ASA Monographs. London: Routledge.

Leach, Edmund. 1954. *Political Systems of Highland Burma: A Study of Kachin Social Structure*. London: Bell.

———. 1967. Virgin Birth. *Proceedings of the Royal Anthropological Institute* 1966:39–50.

LeBar, Frank M. 1964. *The Material Culture of Truk*. Yale University Publications in Anthropology, No. 68. New Haven: Yale University.

Leenhardt, Maurice. 1979 [1947]. *Do Kamo: Person and Myth in the Melanesian World*. Translated by Basia Miller Gulati. Chicago: University of Chicago Press.

Leiris, Michel. 1980. *La Possession et ses Aspects Théatraux Chez les Ethiopiens de Gondar*. Paris: Le Sycomore.

Lessa, William. 1987. Micronesian Religions: An Overview. In *The Encyclopedia of Religion*, edited by Mircea Eliade et al. Volume 9:498–505. New York: Macmillan.

Lesson, René. 1838–39. *Voyage Autour du Monde . . . sur . . . "La Coquille"*. Paris: Pourrat Fréres.

LeVine, Robert A. 1982. *Culture, Behavior, and Personality: An Introduction to the Comparative Study of Psychosocial Adaptation*. New York: Aldine Publishing.

Lévi-Strauss, Claude. 1963. *Totemism*. Boston: Beacon.

Levy, Robert I. 1971. The Community Function of Tahitian Male Transvestism: A Hypothesis. *Anthropological Quarterly* 44:12–21.

———. 1973. *Tahitians: Mind and Experience in the Society Islands*. Chicago: University of Chicago Press.

———. 1984. Electrification Solaire de L'Atoll de Napuka; Impact Socio–Cultural. Paris: L'agence Francaise pour le Maitrise de l'energie.

———. 1985. Horror and Tragedy, the Wings and Center of the Moral Stage. *Ethos* 13:175–87.

———. 1989. Notes on the Quest for Mind in Different Times and Different Places. In *Issues in Social History and Consciousness*, edited by Andrew E. Barnes and Peter N. Stearns. New York: New York University Press.

———. 1990. *Mesocosm: The Organization of a Hindu Newar City in Nepal*. Berkeley: University of California Press.

Levy, Robert I., and Jane C. Wellenkamp. 1989. Methodology in the Anthropological Study of Emotion. In *Emotion: Theory, Research, and Experience* (Volume 4: The Measurement of Emotion), edited by Robert Plutchik and Henry Kellerman. New York: Academic Press.

Lévy-Bruhl, Lucien. 1931. *The Supernatural and Nature in Primitive Mentality*. Paris: F. Alcan.

Lewis, Ian M. 1971. *Ecstatic Religion: An Anthropological Study of Spirit Possession and Shamanism*. Harmondsworth: Penguin.

Lienhardt, Godfrey. 1961. *Divinity and Experience: The Religion of the Dinka*. Oxford: Clarendon Press.

Lindstrom, Lamont, and Geoffrey White, editors. 1993. Custom Today. *Anthropological Forum* (Special Issue) 6(4).

Linnekin, Jocelyn. 1991. Structural History and Political Economy: The Contact Encounter in Hawaii and Samoa. *History and Anthropology* 5:203–32.

Lowie, Robert H. 1970 [1924]. *Primitive Religion*. New York: Liveright.

Lyons, John. 1977. *Semantics*. Vol. 2. Cambridge: Cambridge University Press.

MacGregor, Gordon. 1932. Rotuma Field Notes. Bishop Museum Archives, Honolulu, HI: SC MacGregor.

Macpherson, Cluny, and La'avasa Macpherson. 1985. Suicide in Western Samoa, a Sociological Perspective. In *Culture, Youth and Suicide in the Pacific: Papers from an East-West Center Conference*, edited by Francis K. Hezel, Donald H. Rubinstein, and Geoffrey M. White. Honolulu: Center for Asian and Pacific Studies, University of Hawaii at Manoa.

———. 1987. Towards an Explanation of Recent Trends in Suicide in Western Samoa. *Man* 22:305–30.

———. 1990. *Samoan Medical Belief & Practice*. Auckland: Auckland University Press.

MacRae, Donald G. 1974. *Weber*. New York: Viking.

Mageo, Jeannette Marie 1989a. Amio/Aga and Loto: Perspectives on the Structure of the Self in Samoa. *Oceania* 59:181–199.

———. 1989b. Ferocious is the Centipede: A Study of the Significance of Eating and Speaking in Samoa. *Ethos* 17:387–427.

———. 1991a. Samoan Moral Discourse and the Loto. *American Anthropologist* 93:405–20.

———. 1991b. Ma'i Aitu: The Cultural Logic of Possession in Samoa. *Ethos* 19:352–83.

———. 1991c. Inhibitions and Compensations: A Study of the Effects of Negative Sanctions in Three Pacific Cultures. *Pacific Studies* 14:1–40.

———. 1991d. Red Hibiscus: Decoding Possession in Samoa. Paper circulated for the 1991 meetings of the Association for Social Anthropology in Oceania.

———. 1992. Male Transvestism and Cultural Change in Samoa. *American Ethnologist* 19:443–59.

———. 1994a. Samoa, On the Wilde Side: Oscar Wilde and the Relation between Art and Gender in Samoa. Paper delivered at the 1994 meetings of the Association for Social Anthropology in Oceania.

———. 1994b. Hair Dos and Don'ts: Hair Symbolism and Sexual Politics in Samoa. *Man* 29:407–32.

———. 1995. The Reconfiguring Self. *American Anthropologist* 97:1–15.

———. n.d. Possessed by History: Historicizing Possession and Historicized Ethnopsychiatry in Samoa.

Mahony, Frank Joseph. 1969. A Trukese Theory of Medicine. PhD dissertation, Stanford University, Stanford, CA.

Malinowski, Bronislaw. 1954 [1925]. Magic, Science, and Religion. In *Magic, Science, and Religion and Other Essays by Bronislaw Malinowski*. Garden City, NY: Doubleday Anchor Books.

———. 1961 [1922]. *Argonauts of the Western Pacific*. New York: E. P. Dutton.

Marcus, George, and Michael Fischer. 1986. *Anthropology as Cultural Critique: An*

Experimental Moment in the Human Sciences. Chicago: University of Chicago Press.

Marshall, Mac. 1979. *Weekend Warriors: Alcohol in a Micronesian Culture.* Palo Alto: Mayfield.

Martin, John. 1981 [1817]. *An Account of the Natives of the Tonga Islands [. . .]; Compiled and Arranged from Extensive Communications of Mr. William Mariner, Several Years Resident in Those Islands.* Neiafu: Vaaʻu Press.

McKinley, R. 1979. Zaman dan Masa, Eras and Periods: Religious Evolution and the Permanence of Epistemological Ages in Malay Culture. In *The Imagination of Reality: Essays in Southeast Asia Coherence Systems,* edited by Alton L. Becker and Aram A. Yengoyan. Norwood, NJ: Ablex.

Mead, Margaret. 1929. Americanization in Samoa. *The American Mercury,* No. 63, March 1929:264–70.

———. 1969 [1930]. *The Social Organization of Manuʻa.* Honolulu: Bishop Museum Press.

———. 1961 [1928]. *Coming of Age in Samoa.* New York: Morrow Quill.

Meleisea, Malama. 1987. *Lagaga: A Short History of Western Samoa.* Suva: Institute of Pacific Studies, University of the South Pacific.

Mercer, Patricia, and Clive Moore. 1976. Melanesians in North Queensland: The Retention of Indigenous Religious and Magical Practices. *Journal of Pacific History* 11:66–88.

Milner, G. B. 1979 [1966]. *Samoan Dictionary.* Pago Pago: American Samoa Government (reprint).

Mitchell, Stephen A. 1988. *Relational Concepts in Psychoanalysis.* Cambridge, MA: Harvard University Press.

Moore, Clive. 1986. *Kanaka: A History of Melanesian Mackay.* Boroko: Institute of Papua New Guinea Studies.

Morris, Brian. 1987. *Anthropological Studies of Religion.* Cambridge: Cambridge University Press.

Moyle, Richard. 1975. Sexuality in Samoan Art Forms. *The Archives of Sexual Behavior* 4:227–47.

———. 1988. *Traditional Samoan Music.* Auckland: Auckland University Press in association with the Institute for Polynesian Studies.

Needham, Rodney. 1972. *Belief, Language, and Experience.* Oxford: Basil Blackwell.

Nooy–Palm, Hetty. 1979. *The Saʻdan-Toraja: A Study of Their Social Life and Religion.* Volume I, Organization, Symbols, and Beliefs. The Hague: Martinus Nijhoff.

———. 1986. *The Saʻdan-Toraja. A Study of Their Social Life and Religion.* Volume II; Rituals of the East and West. Cinnaminson: Foris Publications.

O'Meara, Tim. 1990. *Samoan Planters: Tradition and Economic Development in Polynesia.* Fort Worth: Holt, Rinehart & Winston.

Obeyesekere, Gananath. 1981. *Medusa's Hair: An Essay on Personal Symbols and Religious Experience.* Chicago: University of Chicago Press.

Ochs, Elinor. 1988. *Culture and Language Development: Language Acquisition and Language Socialization in a Samoan Village.* New York: Cambridge University Press.

Ortner, Sherry. 1973. On Key Symbols. *American Anthropologist* 75:1388–1346.

———. 1981. Gender and Sexuality in Hierarchical Societies. In *Sexual Meanings,* edited by Sherry Ortner and Harriet Whitehead. Cambridge: Cambridge University Press.

———. 1989. *High Religion: A Cultural and Political History of Sherpa Buddhism.* Princeton: Princeton University Press.

Otto, Rudolf. 1923. *The Idea of the Holy.* Oxford: Oxford University Press.

———. 1950. *Belief, Language, and Experience.* Oxford: Basil Blackwell.

Parsons, Claire. 1981. Sickness Experience and Language: Aspects of Tongan and Western Accounting. PhD dissertation, University of Waikato, Hamilton, New Zealand.

———. 1983. Developments in the Role of the Tongan Healer. *Journal of the Polynesian Society* 92:31–50.

———. 1984. Idioms of Distress: Kinship and Sickness among the People of the Kingdom of Tonga. *Culture, Medicine and Psychiatry* 8:71–93.

———. 1985. Tongan Healing Practices. In *Healing Practices in the South Pacific,* edited by Claire Parsons. Honolulu: Institute for Polynesian Studies, University of Hawaii Press.

Parsons, Talcott. 1968 [1937]. *The Structure of Social Action.* New York: Free Press.

Price, H. H. 1969. *Belief.* London: Allen & Unwin.

Pritchard, William T. 1866. *Polynesian Reminiscences; or, Life in the South Pacific Islands.* London: Chapman and Hall.

Pruyser, Paul. 1974. *Between Belief and Disbelief.* New York: Harper & Row.

Rensel, Jan. 1991. Housing and Social Relationships on Rotuma. In *Rotuma: Hanua Pumue (Precious Land),* Anselmo Fatiaki et al. Suva: Institute of Pacific Studies, University of the South Pacific.

Rips, Lance J. 1990. Reasoning. *Annual Review of Psychology* 41:321–53.

Ritchie, Jane, and James Ritchie. 1989. Socialization and Character Development. In *Developments in Polynesian Ethnology,* edited by Alan Howard and Robert Borofsky. Honolulu: University of Hawaii Press.

Rivière, Peter. 1970. Factions and Exclusions in Two South American Village Systems. In *Witchcraft Confessions and Accusation,* edited by Mary Douglas. London: Tavistock.

Rogers, Garth. 1977. The Father's Sister is Black: a Consideration of Female Rank and Power in Tonga. *Journal of the Polynesian Society* 86:157–82.

Rokeach, Milton. 1960. *The Open and Closed Mind.* New York: Basic Books.

———. 1968. *Beliefs, Attitudes and Values.* San Francisco: Jossey Bass.

Romilly, Hugh. 1882. *A True Story of the Western Pacific in 1879–80.* London: Longmans, Green, and Co.

Russell, William E. 1942. Rotuma. *Journal of the Polynesian Society* 51:229–55.

Saler, Benson. 1967. Beliefs, Disbeliefs, and Unbeliefs. *Anthropological Quarterly* 41:29–33.

———. 1974. Review of *Belief, Language, and Experience,* by Rodney Needham. *American Anthropologist* 76:861–66.

———. 1977. Supernatural as a Western Category. *Ethos* 5:31–53.

Schieffelin, Edward. 1976. *The Sorrow of the Lonely and the Burning of the Dancers.* New York: St. Martin's Press.

———. 1981. Evangelical Rhetoric and the Transformation of Traditional Culture in Papua New Guinea. *Comparative Studies in Society and History* 23:150–165.

Schoeffel, Penelope. 1979a. Daughters of Sina. PhD dissertation, Australian National University.

——. 1979b. The Ladies Row of Thatch: Women and Rural Development in Western Samoa. *Pacific Perspective* 8:1–11.

——. 1983. Women's Associations and Rural Development in Western Samoa and East New Britain. *Pacific Perspective* 11:56–61.

Schultz, Erich. 1911. Samoan Laws Concerning the Family, Real Estate and Succession, translated by Rev. E. Bellward and R. C. Hisaioa. Housed in the University of Hawaii Pacific Collection.

——. 1985 [1949–1950]. Samoan Proverbial Expressions, translated by Brother Herman. Suva: Polynesian Press and the Institute for Pacific Studies. [Reprinted from the *Journal of the Polynesian Society*]

Schutz, Alfred. 1964. The Well-Informed Citizen. In *Alfred Schutz, Collected Papers*, edited by Arvid Brodersen. Vol. 2, Studies in Social Theory. The Hague: Martinus Nijhoff.

Schwartz, Theodore. 1975. Cultural Totemism: Ethnic Identity Primitive and Modern. In *Ethnic Identity: Cultural Continuities and Change*, edited by George DeVos and Lola Romanucci-Ross. Palo Alto: Mayfield.

Sharp, Lesley. 1993. *The Possessed and the Dispossessed: Spirits, Identity and Power in a Madagascar Migrant Town*. Berkeley: University of California Press.

Shipton, Parker. 1989. *Bitter Money: Cultural Economy and Some African Meanings of Forbidden Commodities*. Washington, D.C.: American Anthropological Association.

Shore, Bradd. 1977. A Samoan Theory of Action. PhD dissertation, University of Chicago.

——. 1978. Ghosts and Government. *Man* 13:175–99.

——. 1981. Sexuality and Gender in Samoa. In *Sexual Meanings*, edited by Sherry B. Ortner and Harriet Whitehead. New York: Cambridge University Press.

——. 1982. *Sala'ilua: A Samoan Mystery*. New York: Columbia University Press.

Sinavaiana, Caroline. 1992a. Traditional Comic Theater in Samoa: A Holographic View. PhD dissertation, University of Hawaii.

——. 1992b. Where the Spirits Laugh Last: Comic Theater in Samoa. In *Clowning as Critical Practice*, edited by William Mitchell. Pittsburgh: University of Pittsburgh.

Singh, Y. N., T. Ikahihifo, M. Panuve and C. Slatter. 1984. Folk Medicine in Tonga: A Study on the Use of Herbal Medicines for Obstetric and Gynecological Conditions and Disorders. *Journal of Ethnopharmacology* 12:305–29.

Sloan, Donald. 1940. *The Shadow Catcher*. New York: The Book League of America.

Some Remarks about the Religious Views of Our Islanders, translated by the Micronesian Seminar. Unpublished paper, n.d.

Spiro, Melford. 1952. Ghosts, Ifaluk and Teleological Functionalism. *American Anthropologist* 54:497–503.

——. 1978. *Burmese Supernaturalism*. Philadelphia: Institute for the Study of Human Issues.

——. 1984. Some Reflections on Cultural Determinism and Relativism with Special Reference to Emotion and Reason. In *Culture Theory: Essays on Mind, Self, and Emotion*, edited by Richard A. Shweder and Robert A. LeVine. Cambridge: Cambridge University Press.

Stair, Rev. John B. 1897. *Old Samoa*. London: The Religious Tract Society.

Stanner, W. E. H. 1953. *The South Seas in Transition: A Study of Post-War Rehabilitation and Reconstruction in Three British Pacific Dependencies*. Sydney: Australian Publishing Company.

Steinbauer, Friedrich. 1979. *Melanesian Cargo Cults: New Salvation Movements in the South Pacific*. London: George Prior.

Stuebel, C. 1976. *Myths and Legends of Samoa*, translated by Brother Herman. Wellington: A. H. & A. W. Reed.

Tambiah, Stanley J. 1990. *Magic, Science, Religion, and the Scope of Rationality*. The Lewis Henry Morgan Lecture Series. Cambridge: Cambridge University Press.

Taussig, Michael. 1980. *The Devil and Commodity Fetishism in South America*. Chapel Hill: University of North Carolina Press.

———. 1993. *Mimesis and Alterity: A Particular History of the Senses*. New York: Routledge, Chapman & Hall.

Taylor, Charles. 1989. *Sources of the Self*. Cambridge: Harvard University Press.

Teoh, Jin-inn, and Eng-seong Tan. 1976. An Outbreak of Epidemic Hysteria in West Malaysia. In *Culture-bound Syndromes, Ethnopsychiatry, and Alternate Therapies*, edited by William Lebra. Honolulu: University of Hawaii Press.

Thomas, Nicholas. 1992. The Invention of Tradition. *American Ethnologist* 19:213–32.

Titifanua, Mesulama. 1995 [1938–1939]. *Tales of a Lonely Island*. Suva: Institute of Pacific Studies. [Reprint of articles originally published in *Oceania*.]

Torrey, E. Fuller. 1967. The Zar Cult in Ethiopia. *International Journal of Social Psychiatry* 13:216–23.

Tuiteleleapaga, Napoleone A. 1980. *Samoa Yesterday, Today and Tomorrow*. New York: Todd and Honeywell.

Tulving, Endel. 1972. Episodic and Semantic Memory. In *Organization of Memory*, edited by Endel Tulving and Wayne Donaldson. New York: Academic Press.

Turner, George. 1984 [1884]. *Samoa: A Hundred Years Ago and Long Before*. London: Macmillian.

———. 1986 [1861]. *Nineteen Years in Polynesia: Missionary Life, Travel and Researches*. Apia: Western Samoa Historical and Cultural Trust.

Turner, Victor. 1967. *The Forest of Symbols*. Ithaca: Cornell University Press.

———. 1968. *The Drums of Affliction*. Oxford: Clarendon Press.

———. 1977 [1969]. *The Ritual Process: Structure and Anti-Structure*. Chicago: Adline.

Tyler, Stephen A. 1978. *The Said and the Unsaid: Mind, Meaning, and Culture*. New York: Academic Press.

Tylor, Edward B. 1871. *Primitive Culture*. London: J. Murray.

van Baal, J. 1985. *Symbols for Communication: An Introduction to the Anthropological Study of Religion*. Assen, The Netherlands: Van Gorcum & Co.

van der Veen, H. 1965. *The Merok Feast of the Sa'dan Toradja*. 's-Gravenhage: Martinus Nijhoff.

Ward, Colleen. 1980. The Psychodynamics of Demon Possession. *Journal of the Scientific Study of Religion* 19:201–207.

Watson-Gegeo, Karen, and Geoffrey White, editors. 1990. *Disentangling: Conflict Discourse in Pacific Societies*. Stanford: Stanford University Press.

Weiner, James. 1991. *The Empty Place: Poetry, Space, and Being among the Foi of Papua New Guinea.* Indianapolis: Indiana University Press.

Wellenkamp, Jane C. 1988a. Order and Disorder in Toraja Thought and Ritual. *Ethnology* 27:311–26.

——— . 1988b. Notions of Grief and Catharsis Among the Toraja. *American Ethnologist* 15:486–500.

——— . 1992. The Meaning of Crying and the Importance of Compassion in Toraja, Indonesia. In *Social Perspectives on Emotion*, Volume I, edited by David F. Franks and Viktor Gecas. Greenwich, CT: JAI Press.

White, Geoffrey M., and John Kirkpatrick, editors. 1985. *Person, Self, and Experience: Exploring Pacific Ethnopsychologies.* Berkeley: University of California Press.

Whitehouse, Harvey. 1992. Memorable Religions: Transmission, Codification, and Change in Divergent Melanesian Contexts. *Man* 27:777–97.

——— . 1994. Strong Words and Forceful Winds: Religious Experience and Political Process in Melanesia. *Oceania* 65: 40–58

——— . 1995. *Inside a Cult: a Study of Religious Innovation and Transmission in Papua New Guinea.* Oxford: Oxford University Press.

——— . In Press. From Possession to Apotheosis: Transformation and Disguise in the Leadership of a Cargo Movement. In *Leadership and Change in the Western Pacific: Essays Presented to Sir Raymond Firth*, edited by Richard Feinberg and Karen Watson-Gegeo. London School of Economics Monographs on Social Anthropology. London: Athlone.

Wilkes, Charles. 1845. *Narrative of the United States Exploring Expedition During the Years 1838, 1839, 1840, 1841, 1842.* Philadelphia: Lea and Blanchard.

Williams, John. 1984 [1830–1832]. *The Samoan Journals of John Williams*, edited by Richard M. Moyle. Canberra: Australian National University Press.

——— . 1842 [1838]. *A Narrative of Missionary Enterprises in the South Sea Islands.* London: John Snow.

Williams, Raymond. 1977. *Marxism and Literature.* London: Oxford University Press.

Williams, Walter L. 1986. *The Spirit and the Flesh: Sexual Diversity in American Indian Culture.* Boston: Beacon.

Willis, Laulii. 1889. *The Story of Laulii: A Daughter of Samoa*, edited by William H. Barnes. San Francisco: Jos. Winterburn.

Wilson, Peter. 1967. Status Ambiguity and Spirit Possession. *Man* 2:366–78.

Worsley, Peter. 1968. *The Trumpet Shall Sound: A Study of "Cargo" Cults in Melanesia.* New York: Schocken Books.

Zerner, Charles. 1981. Signs of the Spirits, Signature of the Smith: Iron Forging in Tana Toraja. *Indonesia* 31:89–112.

Contributors

DAVID AKIN, Kwaio Cultural Center, East Malaita, Solomon Islands

NIKO BESNIER, Department of Anthropology, Victoria University, Wellington, New Zealand

JAY D. DOBBIN, Asian Division, University of Maryland, Guam

RICHARD FEINBERG, Department of Sociology and Anthropology, Kent State University

TAMAR GORDON, Department of Language and Communication, Rensselaer Polytechnic Institute

FR. FRANCIS X. HEZEL, Micronesian Seminar, Pohnpei, Federated States of Micronesia

DOUGLAS HOLLAN, Department of Anthropology, University of California, Los Angeles

ALAN HOWARD, Department of Anthropology, University of Hawaii

MICHAEL LAMBEK, Department of Anthropology, University of Toronto

ROBERT I. LEVY, Department of Anthropology, Duke University

JEANNETTE MARIE MAGEO, Department of Anthropology, Washington State University

HARVEY WHITEHOUSE, Department of Social Anthropology, The Queen's University of Belfast

Author Index

Subject Index

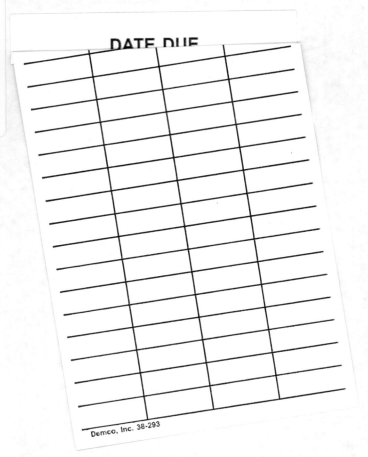